ROUTLEDGE LIBRAR
THE ENGLISH LA

Volume 27

WORD MAPS

WORD MAPS

A Dialect Atlas of England

CLIVE UPTON, STEWART SANDERSON AND
JOHN WIDDOWSON

LONDON AND NEW YORK

First published in 1987

This edition first published in 2015
by Routledge
2 Park Square, Milton Park, Abingdon, Oxon OX14 4RN

and by Routledge
711 Third Avenue, New York, NY 10017

Routledge is an imprint of the Taylor & Francis Group, an informa business

British Library Cataloguing in Publication Data
A catalogue record for this book is available from the British Library

ISBN: 978-1-138-92111-5 (Set)
ISBN: 978-1-315-68654-7 (Set) (ebk)
ISBN: 978-1-138-91822-1 (Volume 27) (hbk)
ISBN: 978-1-138-91823-8 (Volume 27) (pbk)
ISBN: 978-1-315-68802-2 (Volume 27) (ebk)

Publisher's Note
The publisher has gone to great lengths to ensure the quality of this reprint but points out that some imperfections in the original copies may be apparent.

Disclaimer
The publisher has made every effort to trace copyright holders and would welcome correspondence from those they have been unable to trace.

Printed and bound in Great Britain by
TJ International Ltd, Padstow, Cornwall

WORD MAPS

A DIALECT ATLAS OF ENGLAND

CLIVE UPTON, STEWART SANDERSON and
JOHN WIDDOWSON

Cartography by
DAVID BROPHY

CROOM HELM
London • New York • Sydney

Croom Helm Ltd, Provident House, Burrell Row,
Beckenham, Kent BR3 1AT

Croom Helm Australia, 44-50 Waterloo Road,
North Ryde, 2113, New South Wales

Published in the USA by
Croom Helm
in association with Methuen, Inc.
29 West 35th Street,
New York, NY 10001

British Library Cataloguing in Publication Data

Upton, Clive
Word maps : a dialect atlas of England.
1. English language — Dialects — England
— Maps
I. Title II. Sanderson, Stewart
III. Widdowson, J.D.A.
912'.1427 PE1705

ISBN 0-7099-4410-1
ISBN 0-7099-5409-3 Pbk

Library of Congress Cataloging-in-Publication Data

Upton, Clive.
Word maps.

Includes index.
1. English language — Dialects — England — Maps.
I. Sanderson, Stewart. II. Widdowson, John. III. Title.
IV. Title: A dialect atlas of England.
G1816.E3U6 1987 912'.1427 87-675293
ISBN 0-7099-4410-1
ISBN 0-7099-5409-3 (pbk.)

Typeset by Leaper & Gard Ltd., Bristol, England
Printed and bound in Great Britain
by Billing & Sons Limited, Worcester.

Contents

Preface

The maps presented in this volume are based on the material of the *Survey of English Dialects* which was collected from over 300 localities between 1948 and 1961 and which is now deposited in the School of English at the University of Leeds. We are indebted to the University and to its Institute of Dialect and Folk Life Studies for permission to use these extensive and unique data.

We also acknowledge the support of the University of Sheffield and its Department of English Language in the furtherance of this work. Finally, we are grateful for the encouragement of our colleagues, and in particular to Professor William Kirwin of the Memorial University of Newfoundland who offered valuable advice on the Introduction, and to Mrs Beryl Moore for her assistance with the typing of the final draft.

Clive Upton
Stewart Sanderson
John Widdowson
Centre for English Cultural
Tradition and Language,
University of Sheffield.

Word Map Names and Numbers

(underlined letters are the subjects of pronunciation maps)

Terms Used

Middle English:	the second historical period of the language, approximately from 1100 to 1500 A.D.
Old English:	the first historical period of the language, approximately from 450 to 1100 A.D.
Old French:	the dialects spoken in the modern geographical area of France approximately from the mid-ninth to the fifteenth century.
Old Norse:	the language of the Viking invaders from Scandinavia who settled in northern England and East Anglia in the ninth and tenth centuries.
Received Pronunciation:	a standard of pronunciation which is generally considered correct and is also used as a model for the teaching of English to foreigners.
Standard English:	the generally accepted varieties of English which are comparatively free from the more localised differences in pronunciation, vocabulary, grammar and word order which typify regional dialects.

Key to Pronunciation

The system for indicating pronunciations on the pronunciation maps is simple. It is based as closely as possible on common sounds of the ordinary letters of the English alphabet. In almost all cases you will reproduce the sounds accurately if you read them aloud as they are written.

For guidance, notes are given below on the representation of vowel-sounds, and of consonants for which some special comment is necessary.

The vowel system

The basic building blocks are the five English vowels, **a**, **e**, **i**, **o**, and **u**. In the maps these are sometimes used alone, sometimes doubled, and sometimes combined with other vowels or with consonants to indicate more complex sounds. Looking at each vowel in turn, together with other sounds that can be grouped with them, there are five groups:

the **a** group

- **a** as in *man.*
- **aa** the sound in *man*, made longer.
- **ah** the sound in *far*, without sounding the *r.*
- **aw** as in *draw.*
- **ay** as in *day.*
- **a-i** the **a** in *man* plus the **i** in *pin* (the vowel-sound of *time* in southern British English).
- **ah-i** the **ah**-sound in *far* plus the **i** in *pin.*

the **e** group

- **e** as in *pen.*
- **ee** as in *been.*

the **i** group

- **i** as in *pin.*
- **i-uh** the **i** in *pin* plus the **uh**-sound in *fun.*

the **o** group

- **o** as in *hot.*
- **oo** short, the sound in *put.*
- **oo** long, as in *moon.*
- **oo-uh** the short **oo**-sound in *put* plus the **uh**-sound in *fun.*
- **oy** as in *boy.*

the **u** group

- **uh** the sound in *fun* in southern British English. When combined with a consonant, this sound is written **u**.
- **uh-i** the **uh**-sound in *fun* plus the **i** in *pin.*

The consonant system

Most letters need no explanation: simply say them in an everyday British English accent. The following need some comment:

- **dh** the 'hard' *th*-sound in *this* (**th** has been used exclusively for the 'soft' *th*-sound, as in *thin*).
- **ngg** the ordinary *ng*-sound as in *ring* plus an additional 'hard' *g*-sound.
- **zh** the sound of the second *g* in *garage,* using the 'softer', non-*j* pronunciation.

Introduction

A language of dialects

British English is a language of dialects. Wherever one goes in England, or elsewhere in Britain, there are very obvious differences between the ways in which people speak in different places. It is so with the words used, with the grammar or the way in which words are organised, and very noticeably with pronunciation or accent. Everyone in the country seems to be aware of this variety to some extent, and most of us take this diversity for granted much of the time. Paradoxically, variation in dialect, and especially in pronunciation, is a subject about which most people when pressed, and many people without requiring any invitation, are quite prepared to voice an opinion. Stop anyone in the street and ask what their word is, for example, for the soft shoe that is worn when playing sports, or what their opinion is of a Geordie or a Brummie or a Cockney accent, and you can almost guarantee an interesting and an interested response. Listen to radio or television, or read the newspapers, and you will not have to wait very long before a letter is broadcast or printed, probably signed 'Disgusted', about an accent or the pronunciation of a particular word.

The rich variety of dialects in England, of which we are all aware, can in large measure be attributed to the simple fact that English has been spoken in the country for upwards of fifteen hundred years. Even in North America, where the language has been in use for over three hundred years, there has been insufficient time for fragmentation of the language to occur on the scale to which it has occurred in England, although many regional varieties of English have transplanted to the New World. Yet it is not the time-scale alone that has resulted in such a wealth of dialect. Language, like culture, is always changing, and to understand the dialect situation in this country we must look not only at the *number* of years that the language has existed here but also at what has taken place with regard to the language *during* those years. Forces might have acted, and indeed have acted, to suppress the trend towards dialectal development. That these forces were weaker than the forces working for the growth of dialect is an important feature of the history of the language at various stages of its evolution.

English was brought to Britain by Germanic invaders usually called Anglo-Saxons. The language itself, as spoken by these people after they arrived in Britain, is sometimes called Anglo-Saxon but nowadays more usually Old English. It was a member of the West Germanic family of languages, and in the form in which it was brought to Britain it was spoken, doubtless with many local variations, over wide areas of northwest Europe at the close of the Roman period.

Attacks by Anglo-Saxon raiders were under way before the Romans left Britain in 410 A.D.: a late Roman military title for the commander whose task it was to guard the southeast coast was 'Count of the Saxon Shore'. When the Roman garrison was withdrawn from Britain, however, Anglo-Saxon raids and settlement inevitably increased. This was the age of Hengist and Horsa, reputedly recruited as mercenaries to fight the Picts from Scotland. Invited or not, the Germanic newcomers became increasingly assertive from around 450 A.D. onwards. The native Britons, called *wealhas*, 'foreigners' or 'Welsh' by the Anglo-Saxons, were eventually absorbed or driven to the west.

The encroachment of the Germanic invaders on Britain was not a rapid operation, nor were the invasions carried out on a particularly large scale. Small war bands, invited or uninvited, came to fight and passed the word back that the land was good. For several generations settlers spread out over the land from the south and east, in much the same way as American pioneers settled the United States centuries later. They suffered checks — several apparently at the hands of a Romano-British warlord called Arthur — but eventually they came to dominate that land we now call England, together with part of southern Scotland.

To picture an Anglo-Saxon community in England around 500 A.D. is to see a small group of armed farming families, perhaps separated from other similar settlements by miles of forest or fenland. All or most of the inhabitants of one community would be drawn from one small area of the northwest European seaboard. Linguistic and other social characteristics would be local, and there would be strong pressure to conform. Even when, in the course of time, powerful leaders established kingdoms, these were at first very small, and for much of the Anglo-Saxon period England was divided into a minimum of seven kingdoms. Anything approaching a truly national identity only emerged in the ninth century.

Furthermore, it appears that it was not only the history of the Anglo-Saxons after they had settled in England that encouraged the development of local idiosyncrasies. The Anglo-Saxon historian Bede claimed that the Germanic invaders were drawn from three distinct peoples, the Angles, Saxons, and Jutes. The Jutes, early settlers in Kent from where they colonised the Isle of Wight and part of Hampshire, may have come from Jutland, although there is little evidence to prove this. The Angles came from southern Denmark, from an area that became known as Angeln, and settled in the eastern parts of the country as far north as south-east Scotland and throughout the English Midlands. But whereas the Angles certainly and the Jutes probably had as their core a tribal unit, the Saxons were a much more loosely knit group. Taking, or being given, their name from the *seax*, the single-bladed long-knife that was one of their favourite weapons, they were raiders from anywhere along the coastal lands from what is now northern Germany to northern France. These raiders settled in the largest numbers in the south and southwest of Britain. Such a loose confederation of war bands would have brought with them a multiplicity of customs, traditions and dialects. Also, they might be expected to hold together only so long as unity was needed against a common enemy. And indeed, once they were established in 'England', the Saxons, and the Angles and Jutes too, proved to be as ready to fight each other as to fight the Britons.

A final important factor working against any tendency towards uniformity of language, at least for the first two centuries of Anglo-Saxon settlement, was that most people, from the king downwards, were illiterate. The Christian missionary Augustine arrived in southern England in 597 A.D., and Columba in the north a little later. With Christianity and 'education' some pressure for conformity to a standard language, at least within individual kingdoms, came to be felt by those who could write: it is the experience of most of us that we write in a much more conformist, conservative way than we speak. By the time this pressure developed, however, English was well established in the country in a wealth of spoken forms, and most people can have had little cause or opportunity to write it anyway.

The legacy bequeathed to English by those who brought the language into England was, therefore, one of variety. There was little need for the Anglo-Saxons to invent or conform to a widespread standard and, doubtless, for many people there was every inclination to promote their own local brand.

Then came the Vikings. Beginning in about 800 A.D., raids rapidly increased in size, intensity and duration, until by the 860s Viking armies were staying in England for several years at a time. By the late ninth century Scandinavian settlements were being established in the north and east, and the Vikings were transformed from raiders into conquerors controlling roughly half the land of England.

The Viking invasions created some pressure towards standardisation of English. Most of the northern kingdom of Northumbria was overrun, and so too was the eastern part of the Midland kingdom of Mercia. English resistance to the Vikings, and the survival of English tradition and language, came to be centred on Alfred's southern kingdom of Wessex. Then, with Alfred's victory over the Viking Guthrum in 878 A.D., the relationship between the two peoples was in large measure stabilised. The 'Danelaw' was established for the Vikings north and east of a line running roughly from London to Chester; Wessex, with west Mercia also under Alfred's control, was secure. The culture and language of Wessex became synonymous with English culture and language for those for whom learning was significant.

Yet although the permanent settlement of Vikings in England forced a measure of uniformity on the English language, it also introduced further variety. The language spoken by the Vikings, today variously called Old Norse and Old Icelandic, was, like Old English, a member of the West Germanic language family. Limited communication may have taken place between Anglo-Saxons and Vikings using their own languages, especially if the former used an Anglian form of English. At first pure Norse would have been spoken in the Scandinavian settlements in England, no doubt with Danish, Norwegian, Icelandic, and dialectal variations. In time, however, the 'English' Vikings adopted an English identity. Their language assumed an increasingly English character whilst retaining strong Norse features, elements of which can be clearly seen in the dialects and place-names of the old Danelaw today.

The upheavals of the Viking period in England had hardly subsided when a new invasion occurred. The Norman Conquest of 1066 was not quite the devastating event that it is sometimes made out to have been. Edward the Confessor was half Norman; the Normans were only four or five generations removed from Viking forbears. Cultures in Normandy and England were not entirely dissimilar, and at court level at least there was considerable contact. Nevertheless, because of the manner of their coming and the language which they brought, the Normans had a profound effect on English, not least in ensuring the continued existence and even the strengthening of dialectal forms.

The Normans, in spite of their Scandinavian ancestry, spoke French. Being a Romance rather than a Germanic language, French was 'foreign' to English in a way that Norse had never been. There could be little contact between English and Norman unless one learnt the other's language. However, the Normans came to England not as settlers, to mingle with the native population, but as a master race, to rule and to exploit. For some generations they had little interest in learning the native language, and only a few gifted or privileged English men and women acquired Norman French, usually as members of Norman households or in the service of the Norman administration. French was the language of a small elite. English was the language of the village and the workplace, used by the majority, the ordinary and usually unlettered people. As such it was a spoken language, used, as early Old English had been, within restricted geographical areas for everyday communication. It had little need to be anything other than homely and local. And if regional diversity helped to obscure it and to inhibit its mastery by aliens, one suspects that the popular opinion was 'so much the better!'.

Slowly, with the weakening of ties with Normandy and France, English came to be rehabilitated as the national language. In 1362 the king's speech at the opening of parliament was in English for the first time, and in the same year business in the law courts began to be carried out in English too. In the later part of the fourteenth century Chaucer in an East Midland dialect, Langland in a Southwest Midland dialect, and the 'Gawain Poet' in the Northwest Midlands were in the forefront of a flowering of vernacular literature, in which English was married to borrowed French vocabulary and artistic forms. English was clearly finding favour in high places.

Through such influences as those of Chaucer, the universities of Oxford and Cambridge, and London with its court and large population, an East Midland variety of English came to be regarded as the written standard. The establishment of this standard took a long time, and at first it only applied to English written for widespread consumption. At the heart of the court in the late sixteenth century, Sir Walter Raleigh is reputed to have retained his Devon speech, though his writing is not obviously dialectal. As evidence that pressure was on to standardise the written language whilst recognising that even upper class speech was dialectal we have only to cite the following, written in 1589 in a handbook on the art of the poet, *The Arte of English Poesie*:

> neither shall he take termes of Northernmen, such as they vse in dayly talke, whether they be noble men or gentlemen, or of their best clerkes all is a matter: nor in effect any speach vsed beyond the river of Trent, though no man can deny but that theirs is the purer English Saxon at this day, yet it is not so Courtly nor yet so currant as our Southerne English is, no more is the far Westerne mans speach: ye shall therfore take the vsuall speach of the Court, and that of London and the shires lying about London within xl myles, and not much above.

From this point onwards the way for dialectal English was downwards in the estimation of the arbiters of fashion. The Restoration squire was ridiculed for his local speech as for his provincial manners. Ridicule turned increasingly to distaste in the eighteenth century, as influential intellectuals such as Swift, Dryden, and Johnson argued for the imposition or 'fixing' of a standard language, and grammar writers strove to describe English according to the Latin model. Increasing democratisation of society in the nineteenth century, together with improved communications, began the slow process of exposing everyone to the rich variety of regional dialects existing in the country. On the other hand, the same developments spread the powerful influence of the standard form of the language, and progress in education, in the professions, and in society continued to depend on the possession of an acceptable accent and a grasp of the 'correct' grammar and vocabulary. In the course of time the BBC would come to select its announcers and newsreaders on considerations of accent which went far beyond the dictates of intelligibility. Yet with their roots firmly fixed in the history of the language, the dialects of England have persisted through the generations. Whatever was useful in each new age has been added to local speech as well as to the standard language: Scandinavian and French words through invasion; Classical and Romance words in the Renaissance; words from many other languages through colonisation and trade; continuous changes in pronunciation. Nevertheless, the diversity of accent, vocabulary, and grammar could not be levelled by forces which had little meaning for the vast majority of English people, as today's vigorous dialects show. Such levelling as there has been is most evident in standardisation of grammar and in erosion of obsolescent sections of vocabulary including, for example, many variants of older agricultural terms. This is, however, simply part of a continuing process of change which has left regional accents relatively unscathed.

Discovering dialects now

> There can be no doubt that pure dialect speech is rapidly disappearing even in country districts, owing to the spread of education, and to modern facilities of intercommunication. The writing of this grammar was begun none too soon, for had it been delayed another twenty years I believe it would by then be quite impossible to get together sufficient pure dialect material to enable any one to give even a mere outline of the phonology [pronunciation] of our dialects as they existed at the close of the nineteenth century.

This was written by Joseph Wright in the Preface to the *English Dialect Grammar*, which was part of the six-volume *English Dialect Dictionary* that he published between 1898 and 1905. There is an important sense in which Wright was quite correct: improved communications and increasing social mobility *were* causing an acceleration in the pace of dialectal change at the time in which he was writing. Many ancient speech forms, especially in pronunciation but also in vocabulary and grammar, were disappearing from even the most conservative, isolated rural areas. However, it should not be inferred from Wright's comment that he believed that the dialects which were changing in his day were, being 'pure', unaltered from those which had existed in former times. Wright was an eminent student of language and linguistic change and knew that this was not the case. The dialects of late nineteenth century England, like those of today, were the result of continuous evolution.

But there is also in Wright's comment a suggestion that English dialect study beyond the 1920s would be a less rewarding occupation than it had been for Wright himself. That this has not proved to be so is demonstrated by the many studies of language variety which have been and are being carried out by individuals and institutions. The subject which Wright did so much to make popular and academically 'respectable' now has followers studying, for example, 'traditional' regional dialects, the dialects of the cities, the dialects of ethnic minorities, occupational dialects, and the relationship between dialect and social class.

The Survey of English Dialects, from the findings of which the maps in this book have been produced, was the earliest of what may be thought of as the modern dialect enquiries. It provides a link between older and more modern types of investigation, since its subject matter is the traditional, essentially rural dialects examined by Wright but its research method was based on careful selection of informants and the use of a questionnaire, phonetic notation, and taperecorders. The Survey was the idea of the Englishman Harold Orton and the Swiss Eugen Dieth. Based at the University of Leeds, fieldworkers collected information in 313 mainly rural localities in England between 1948 and 1961. The dialect speakers sought were elderly, locally-born people with little formal education, the aim being to record speech that was not greatly influenced by outside social pressures or by radio and television and other developments in communication. This aim reflects the special interest of Orton and Dieth in the history of English, an interest which they shared with Wright. In creating the first, and to date the fullest, systematically-collected body of dialect material for all the English regions, however, they also provided data for further non-historical linguistic enquiry and laid foundations on which later scholars have been able to build.

Most of the books which have been published as a result of the work of the Survey of English Dialects have been 'academic' in their approach. That is, they require from their readers some special commitment to and knowledge of linguistics, such as an ability to read phonetic script. There have been two books of countrywide maps, the official atlas of the Survey, *The Linguistic Atlas of England*, and a further book of vocabulary maps, *A Word Geography of England*: both present information which requires large-scale, complex mapping to show the distribution of forms. *Word Maps* is produced with the intention of providing the reader with a set of maps that can be readily understood without the need for detailed instruction or prior knowledge of language studies.

The maps presented here have been chosen to provide as wide a spread of subject and interest as possible, consistent with the need to create small-scale maps that are not too complicated to be easily readable. It is hoped that for many users this atlas will prove to be a springboard to the publications of the Survey and to other aspects of dialect study.

How to use *Word Maps*

The base map on which the dialect information is presented has the new, post-1974 county boundaries marked on it to provide points of reference for readers to identify particular localities. (Although the metropolitan counties shown have now been abolished, the areas which they covered continue to bear the same names for postal or other purposes.) A map showing the names of all the counties is given on page 17. Also, since the records of the Survey of English Dialects refer to the old, pre-1974 counties, a map is provided on page 16 which shows the earlier boundaries and county names.

The two hundred maps are arranged alphabetically according to title. The title of each map is a word or group of words which speakers of standard English will readily understand. Most of the maps are concerned with variation in vocabulary, the actual words of the dialects: these are the maps whose titles do not have any letters underlined, and on which information is written in capital letters. The maps which have underlined letters in their titles, and on which information is written in small lettering, are concerned with variation in pronunciation: the underlined letters in the titles are those for which dialectal pronunciations are given. Phonetic script has not been used on pronunciation maps. Instead, the ordinary letters of the alphabet have been used, in what is technically known as a respelling system, to represent the sounds of the dialects. A key to this respelling system is provided on pages 5 and 6, and wherever special mention of some aspect of the system is felt to be needed, for example when **dh** is used to represent the *th-* sound as in the word *then*, reference is made to it below the map itself.

The different dialect areas on a map are delineated by lines called isoglosses. These are drawn to run midway between localities which were shown by the Survey of English Dialects to use the different words or pronunciations which are the subject of the map. Each map reveals areas in which particular words or pronunciations are concentrated, and it should be borne in mind that the labels in the different areas are those for the forms which were found to be *dominant* there. Sometimes a locality within an area was found to have a different usage, or one locality exhibited both the form used throughout the surrounding area and another, less usual, form. Such occurrences have not been included in *Word Maps*, although all the information is of course available in the various other publications based on the Survey. There have also been occasions when, in order to avoid creating a larger number of areas than can comfortably be included on a small-scale map, similar forms have been grouped together as one. A good example of this is in the AUTUMN map, where the minor variations *fall of the leaf* and *fall of the year* are regarded as examples of FALL. Where this has been done to any significant extent an explanatory note is given at the foot of the map. Again, full details of the forms recorded are available in the Survey's publications.

Dialects are, of course, essentially spoken, and the spelling of dialect words sometimes presents problems. It is good policy to spell spoken words as they sound wherever possible, and this policy has been followed here. However, there are some words in *Word Maps* which have been spelt in the *Oxford English Dictionary* or the *English Dialect Dictionary* in ways which reflect their history as written words. Since it is likely that readers may wish to look up words there, those dictionaries' spellings are used unless they are likely to be particularly misleading. So, although *nieve*, 'fist', could helpfully be written NEEV, the dictionary form NIEVE is used as it is unlikely to cause a reader great difficulty.

It will be seen that some maps, such as those for ASK and BRIDGE, are presented as vocabulary maps although in fact they deal with different ways of saying the same word. This has been done because the reader's attention is being drawn to some essential differences in the way in which the word is used around the country, and the other variations which would have to be shown in a full pronunciation map would introduce unnecessary distinctions and distractions. For example, in the BRIDGE map the essential distinction is between the Old English-derived BRIDGE and the Old Norse-derived BRIG: the various pronunciations of BRIDGE, although interesting in their own right, would, if shown, obscure this difference.

It should be remembered that the maps are concerned with England, including the Isle of Man and, for reasons still prevailing when the Survey was undertaken, Gwent (formerly Monmouthshire) in southeast Wales. The isoglosses indicating dialect boundaries on the maps therefore stop at the Scottish and Welsh (and Gwent-Glamorgan) borders. When, for reasons of space, a label has been written across a national boundary, it must only be taken to be relevant for that area of England and Gwent to which it is attached. The Isle of Man is usually given its own label detailing the forms recorded there, although since only two localities were studied on the island it is left unlabelled if those localities produced different forms.

The dialect areas shown on each map are, as we have said, based on generalisations, and the labels within them only refer to dominant dialectal forms. It should not be inferred from the maps that forms other than those labelled for a region are never used dialectally in that region. Also, isoglosses are never firm boundaries restricting the movement of dialectal forms from place to place. The boundary lines are always moving: some may even disappear completely and new ones may appear while collectors record their information and analyse it. Our language is changing all the time, and we hope that readers will wish to test this for themselves, using the maps in this book as a starting point for their own investigations.

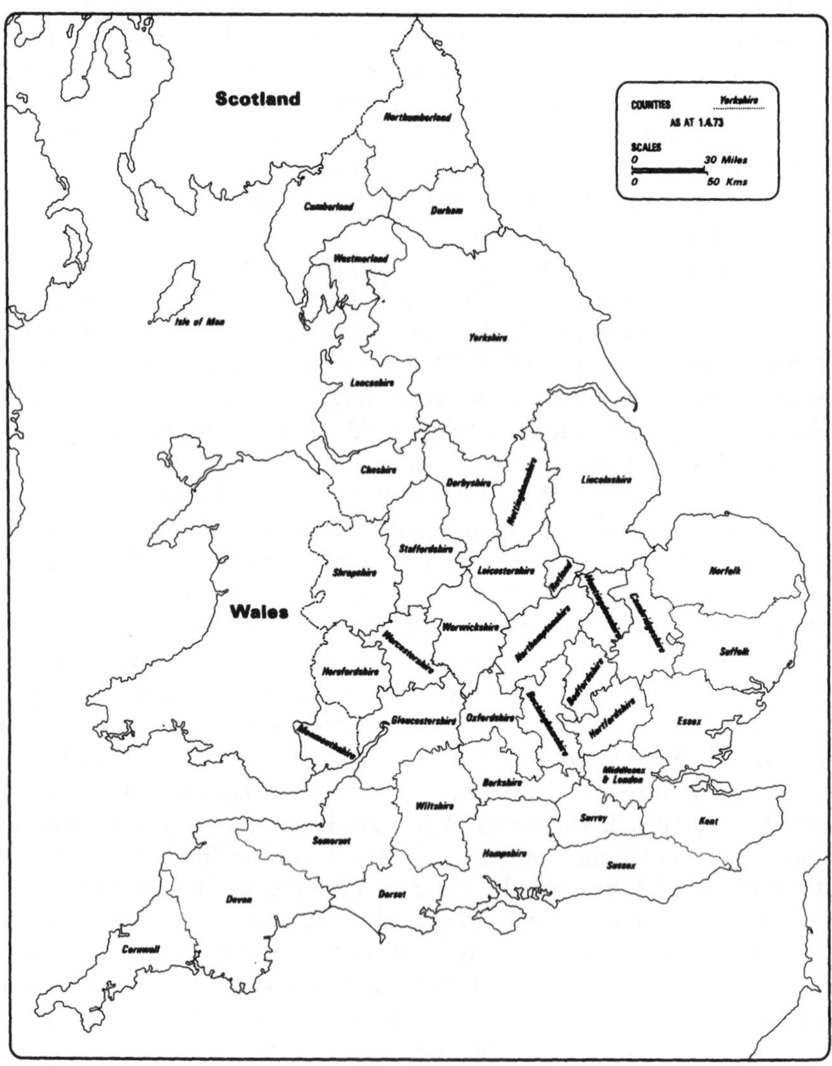

The county boundaries to 1974, as used in the Survey of English Dialects.

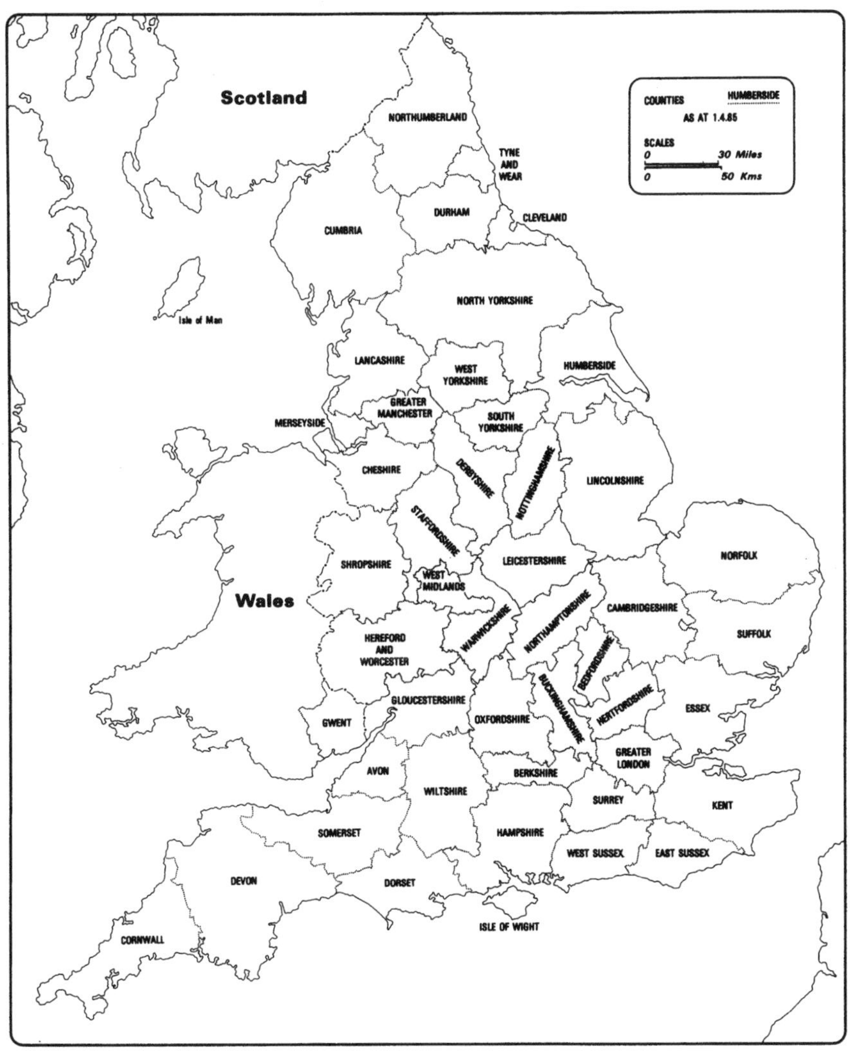

The county boundaries after 1974, as used in the Word Maps.

Word Maps

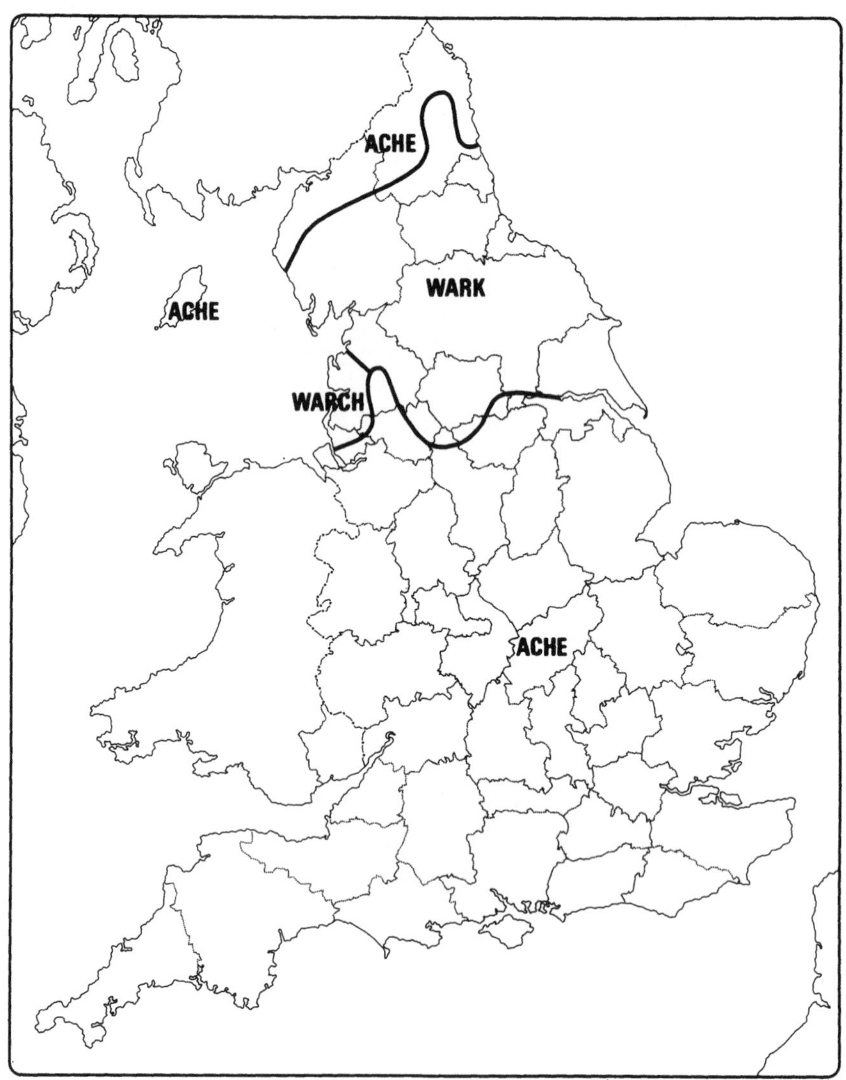

Map 1: ACHE (to ...)

WARK is derived from Old English and was no doubt reinforced in northern localities by a similar form from Old Norse.

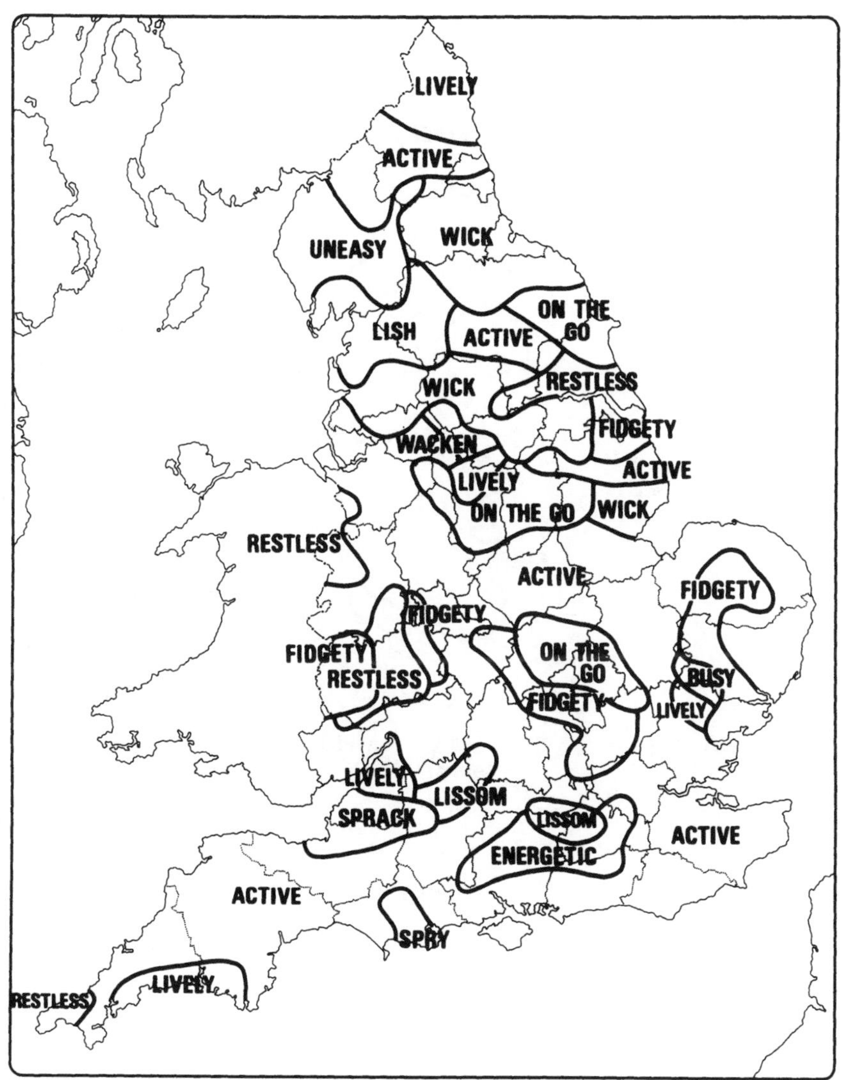

Map 2: ACTIVE (child)
Other terms recorded include *frim*, *brave*, *litty*, *pert*, *upstrigolous* and *wiggy-arsed*.

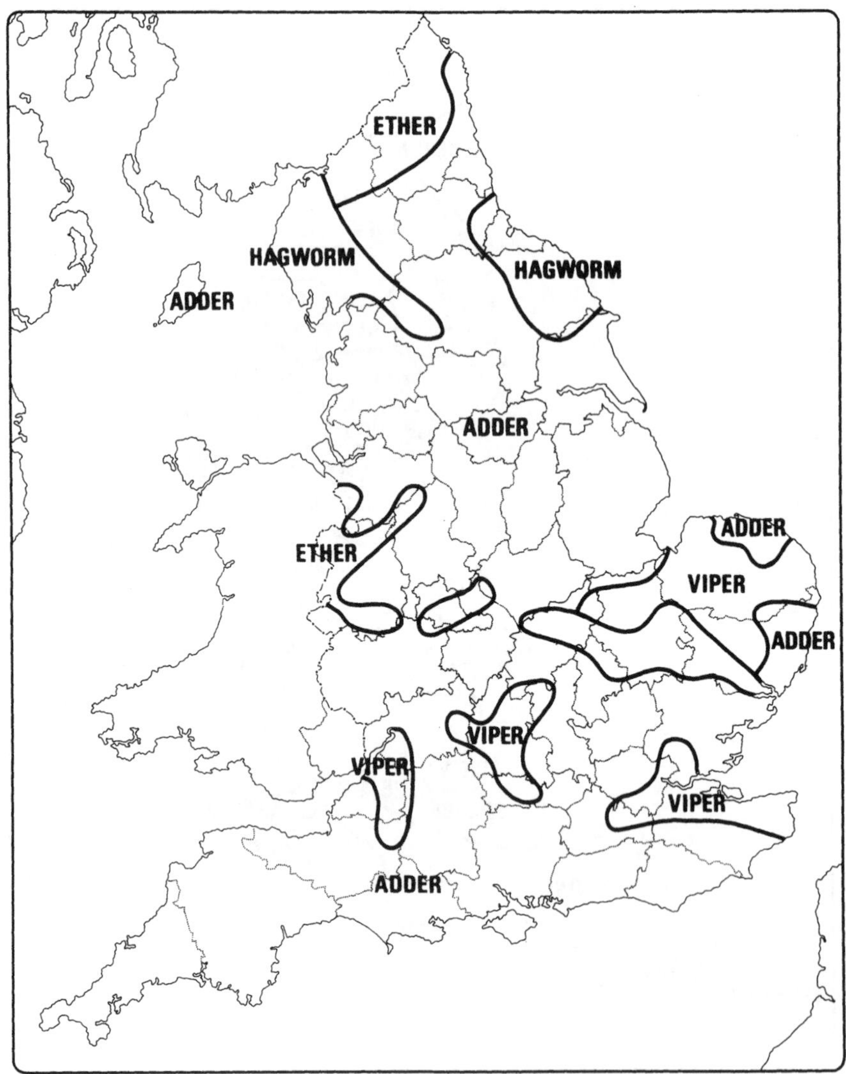

Map 3: ADDER

Note that there are places in the Midlands and East Anglia where no words for *adder* were recorded, probably because the adder is less commonly found there. **ADDER** is seen to be the most common term and is frequently found in areas where **VIPER** is the main form. **ETHER** rhymes with *heather*.

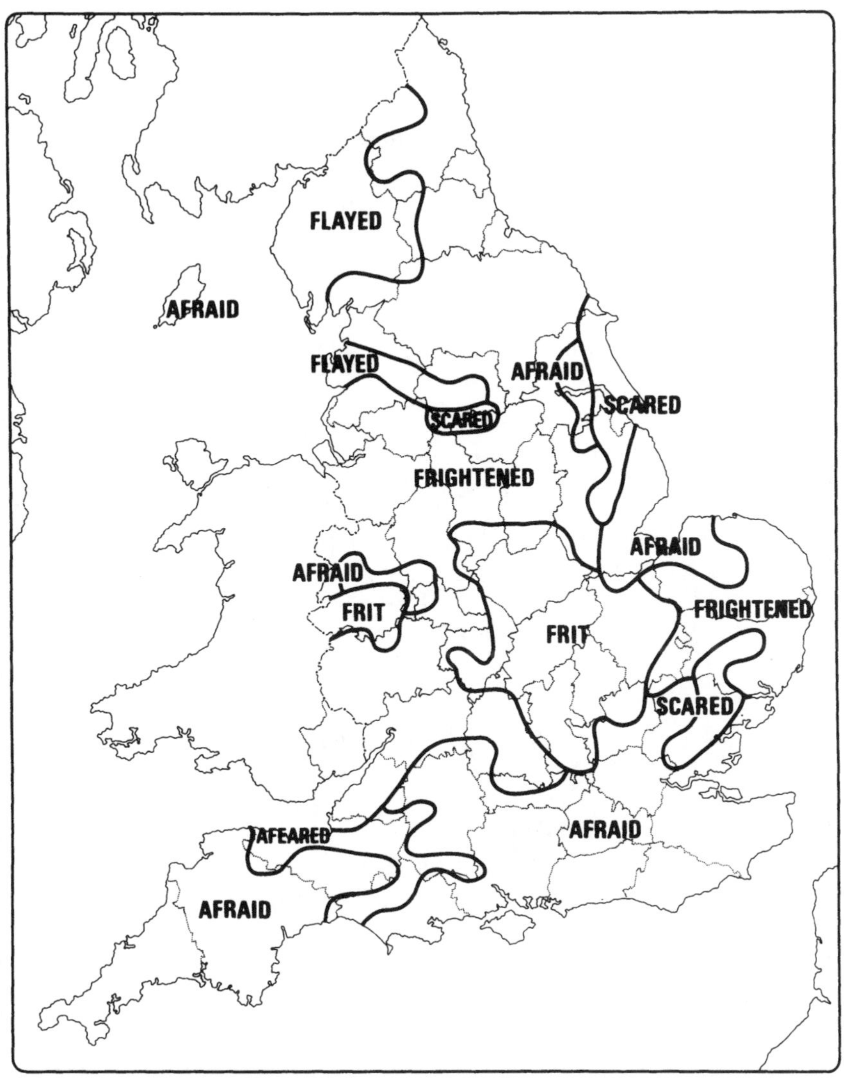

Map 4: AFRAID
FRIGHTENED is found widely in all areas.

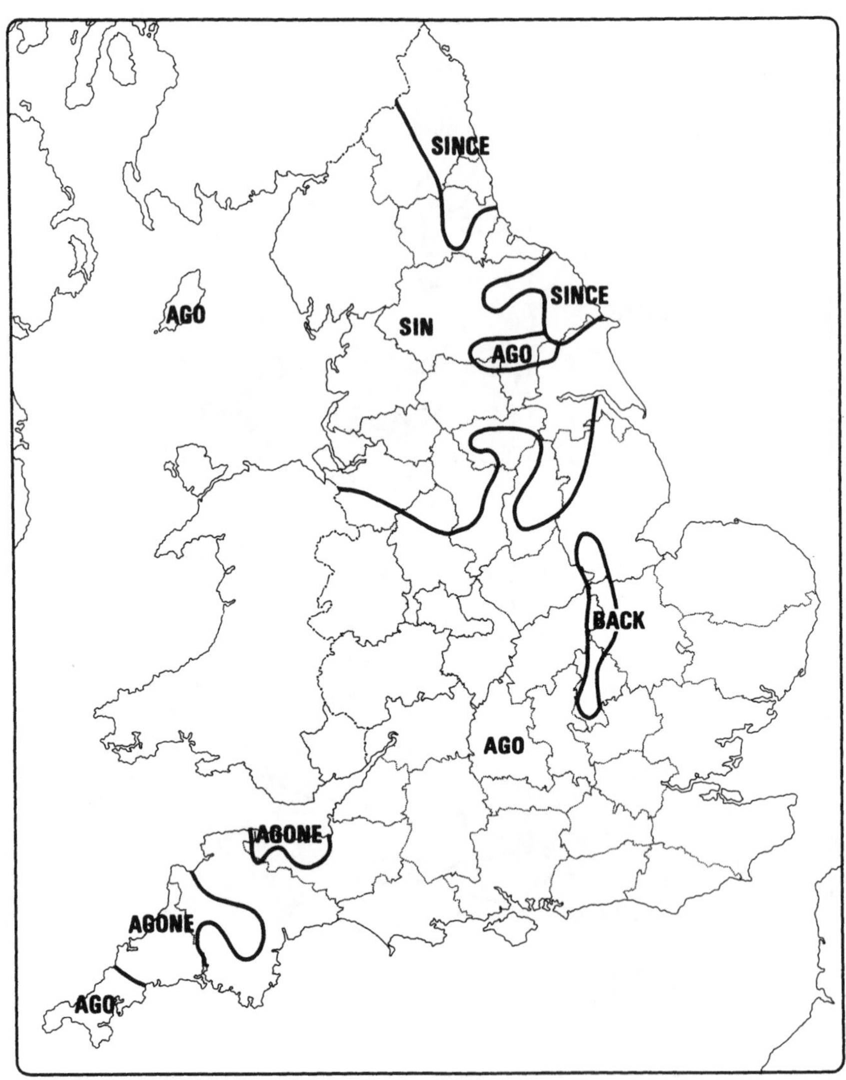

Map 5: AGO (a week . . .)

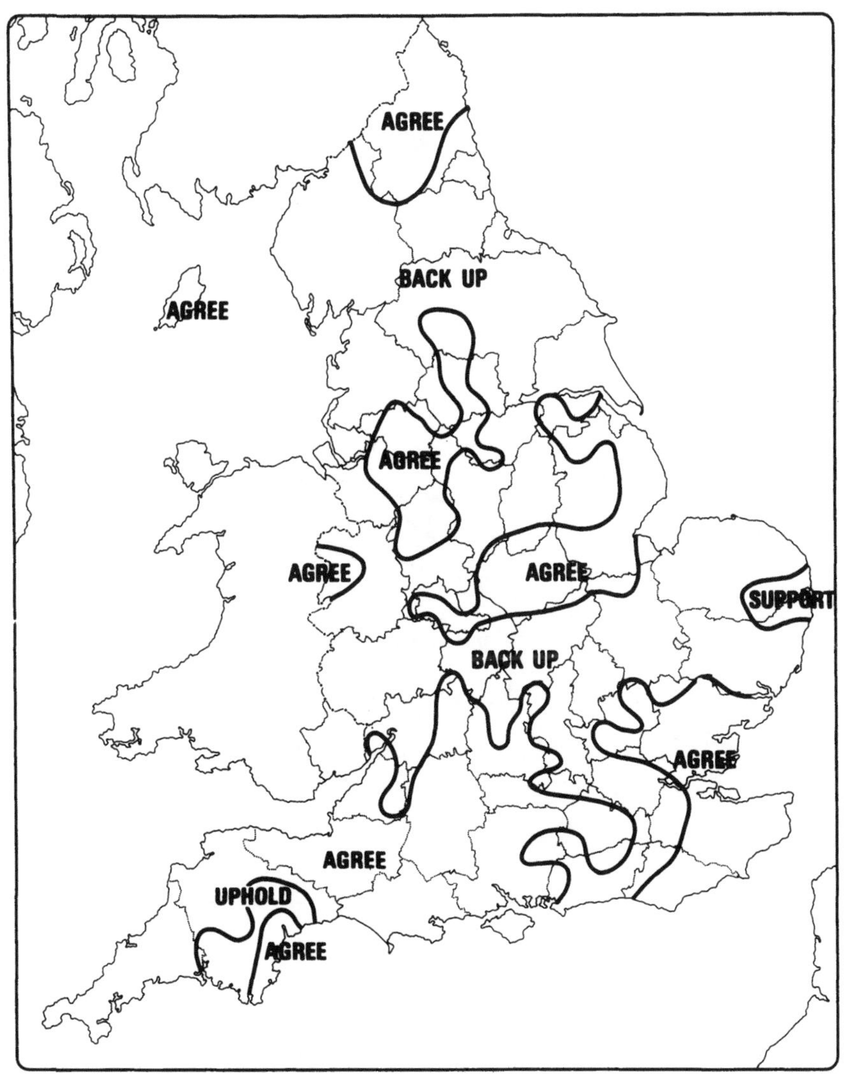

Map 6: AGREE (... with someone)

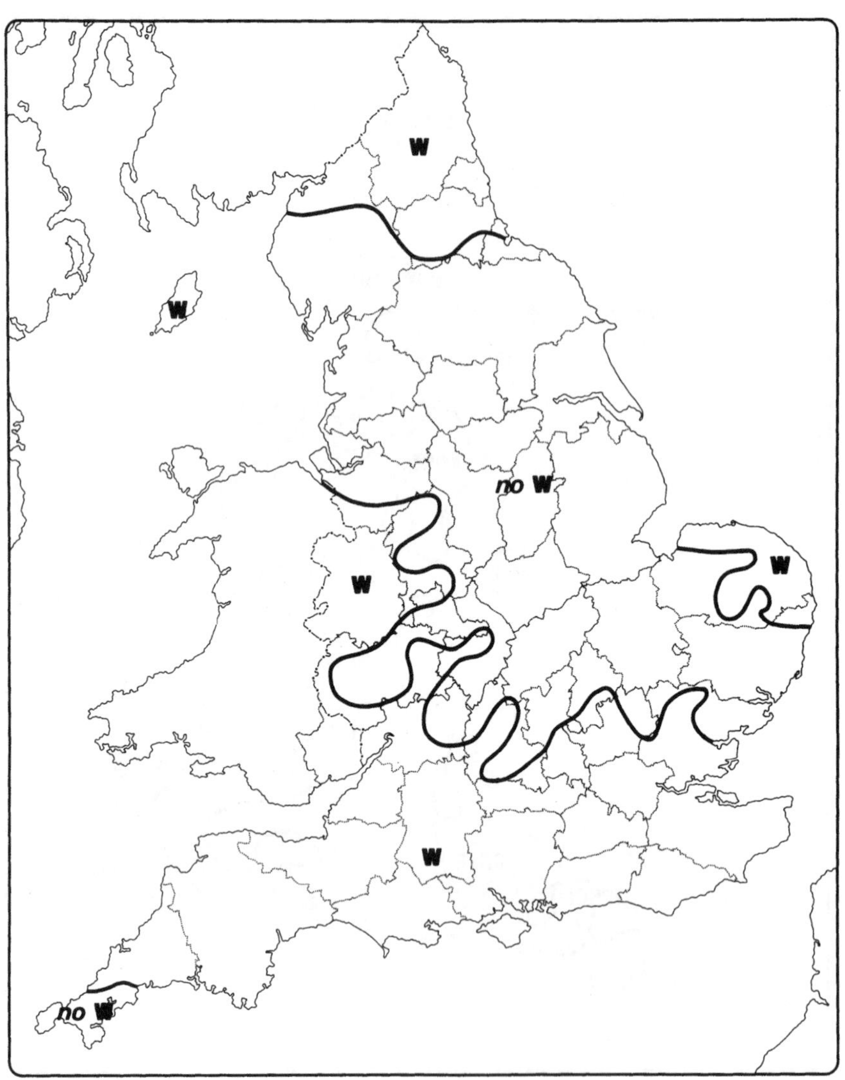

Map 7: AL_W_AYS

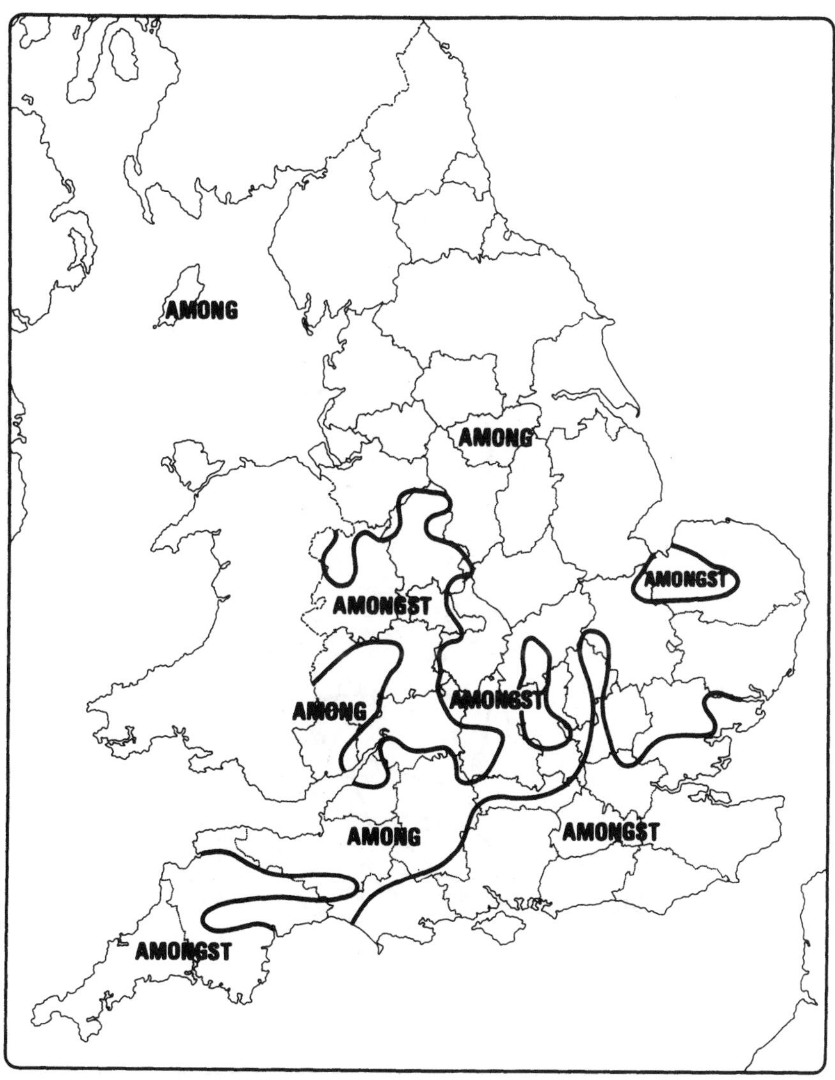
AMONG
AMONG
AMONGST
AMONGST
AMONG
AMONGST
AMONG
AMONGST
AMONGST

Map 8: AMONG

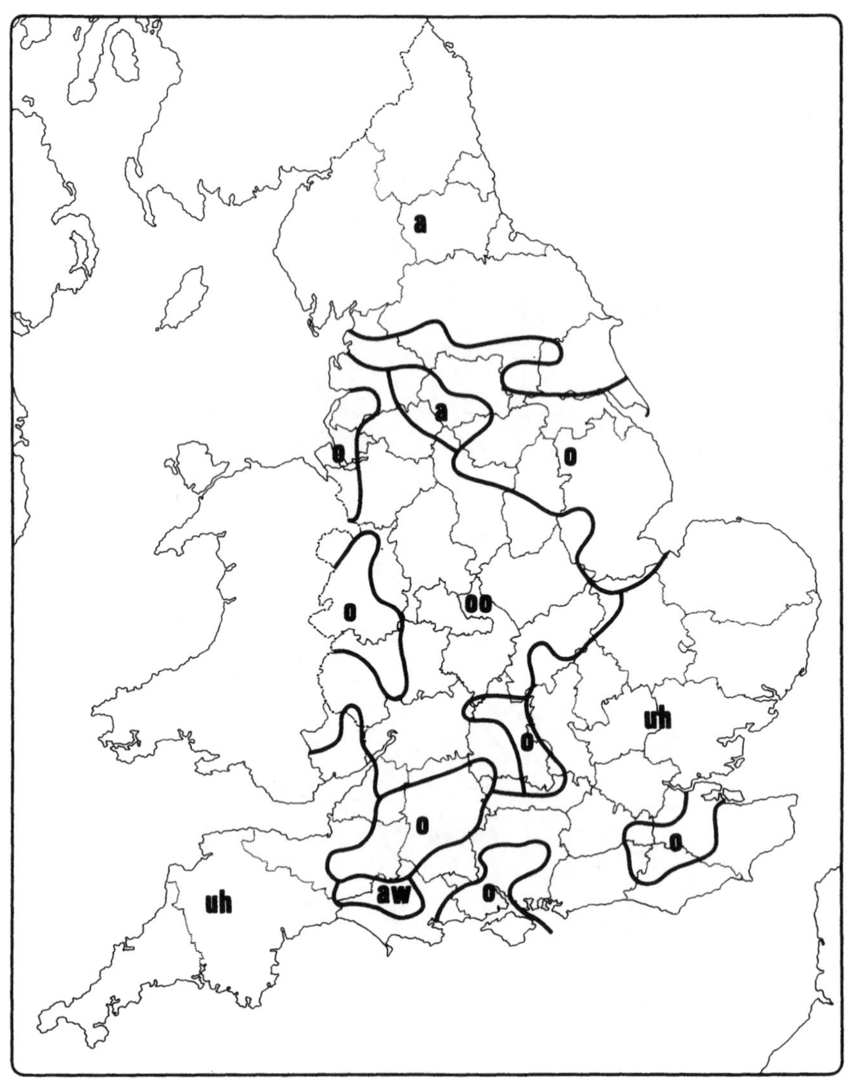

Map 9: AMONG

oo is the short vowel as in *put*.

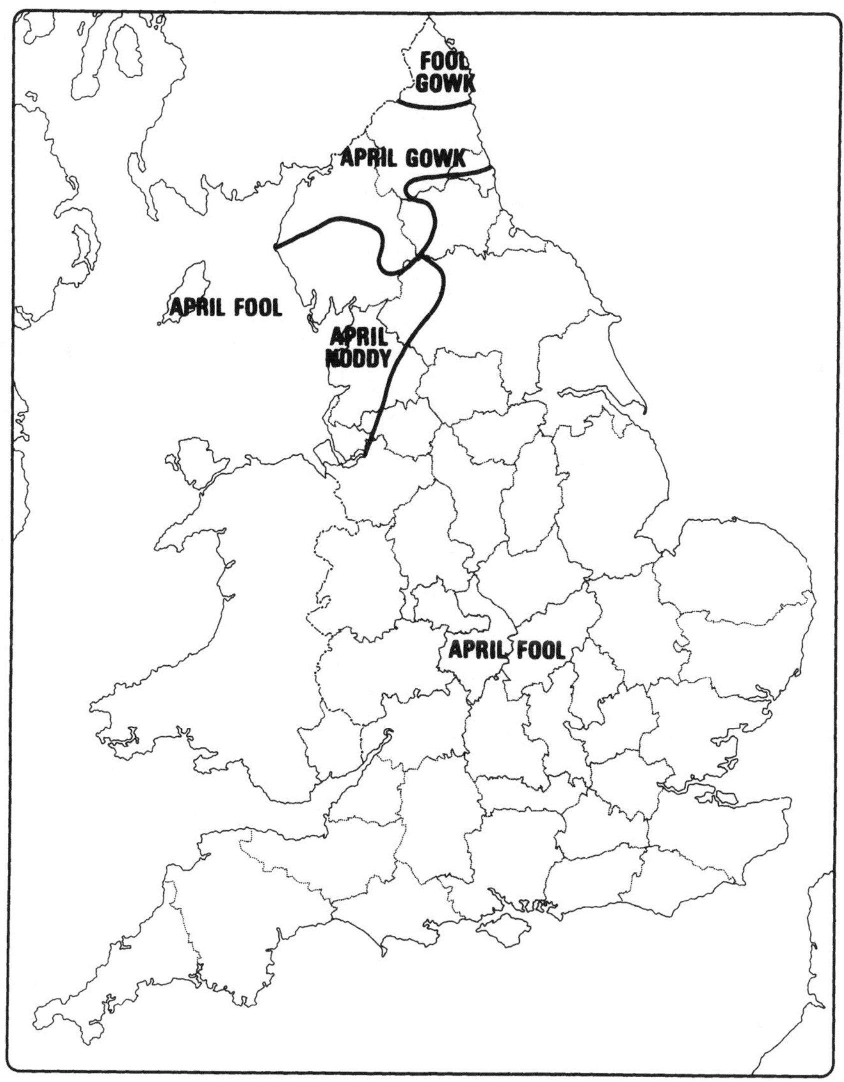

Map 10: APRIL FOOL
GOWK is derived from the Old Norse word for 'cuckoo'.

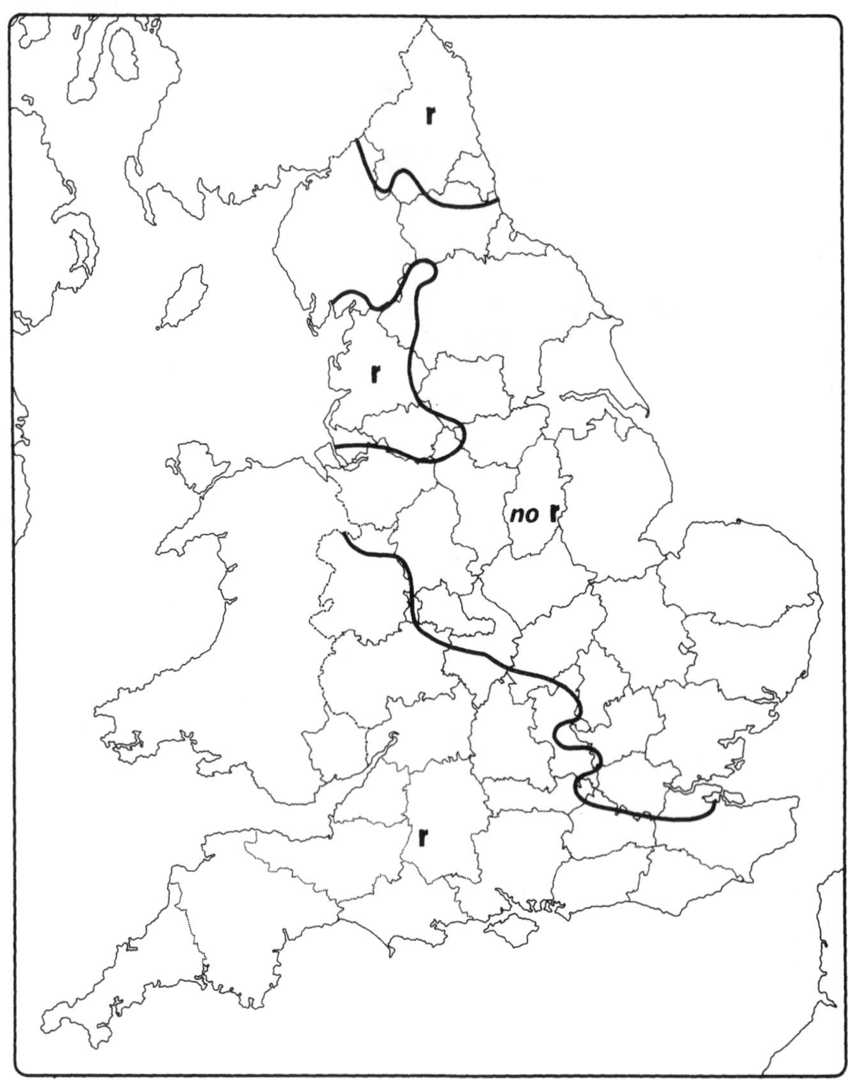

Map 11: A<u>R</u>M

Three different types of *r* occur:

(i) with tongue pulled back and tip curled up (South West and southwest Midlands)

(ii) with tongue flat and top curled back (Lancashire/Yorkshire and Kent)

(iii) 'throaty', the 'Northumberland burr' (North East)

Southeast Wales has the Standard pronunciation without *r*

For varieties of *r*, see also Map 51.

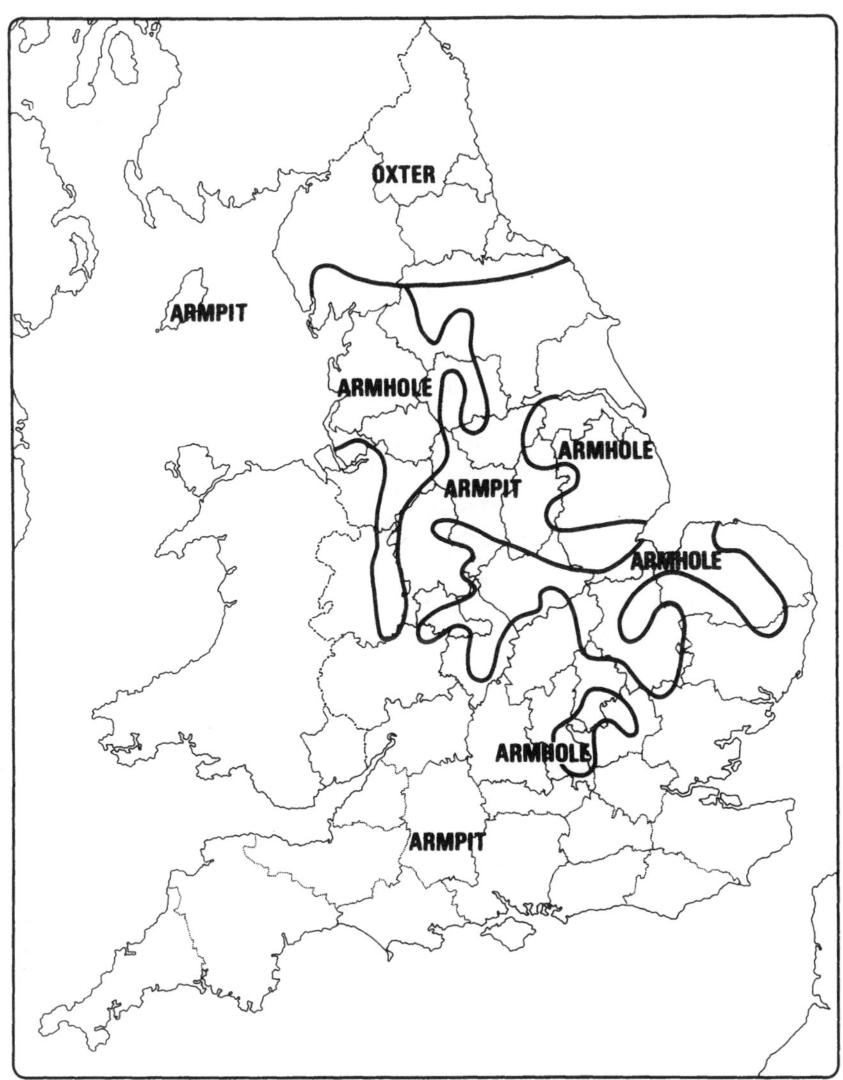

Map 12: ARMPIT
The Old English Northern dialect word **OXTER** remains dominant in the northernmost counties. In those areas where forms with **ARM-** are the most usual, such phrases as *under the arm* are sometimes used, especially in the Midlands.

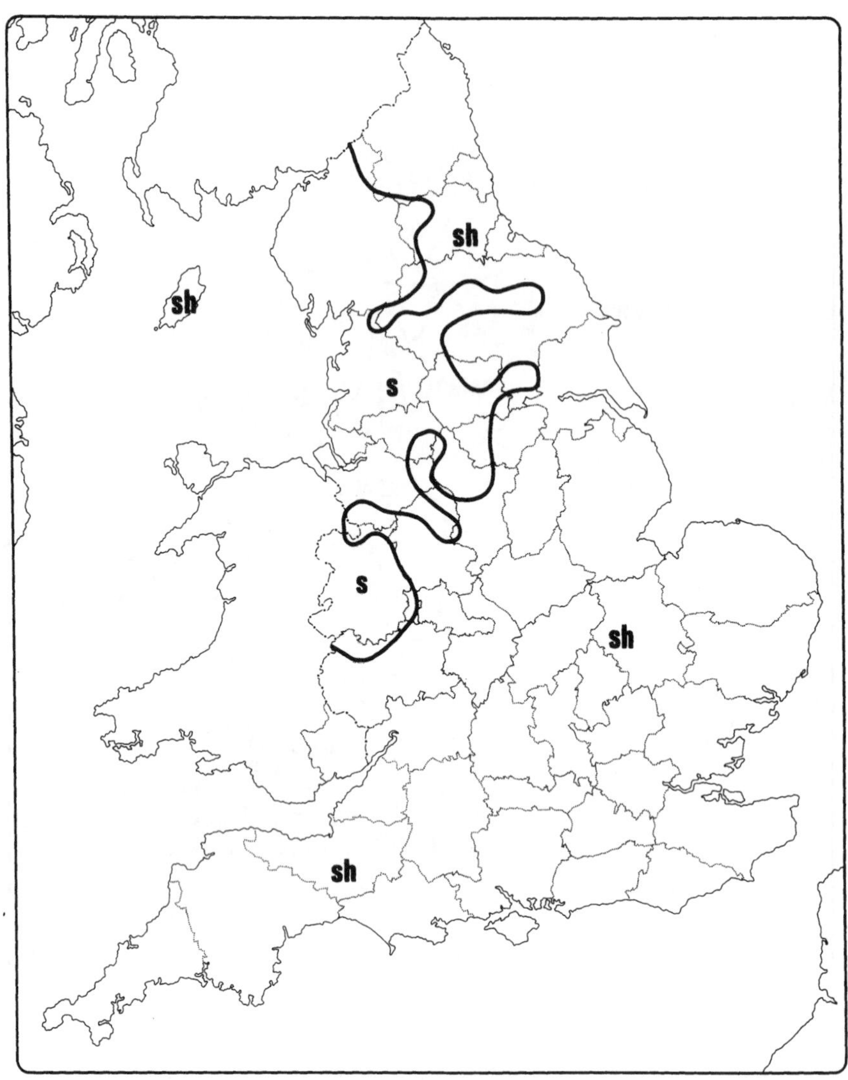

Map 13: A<u>SH</u>(ES) (in a burning fire)

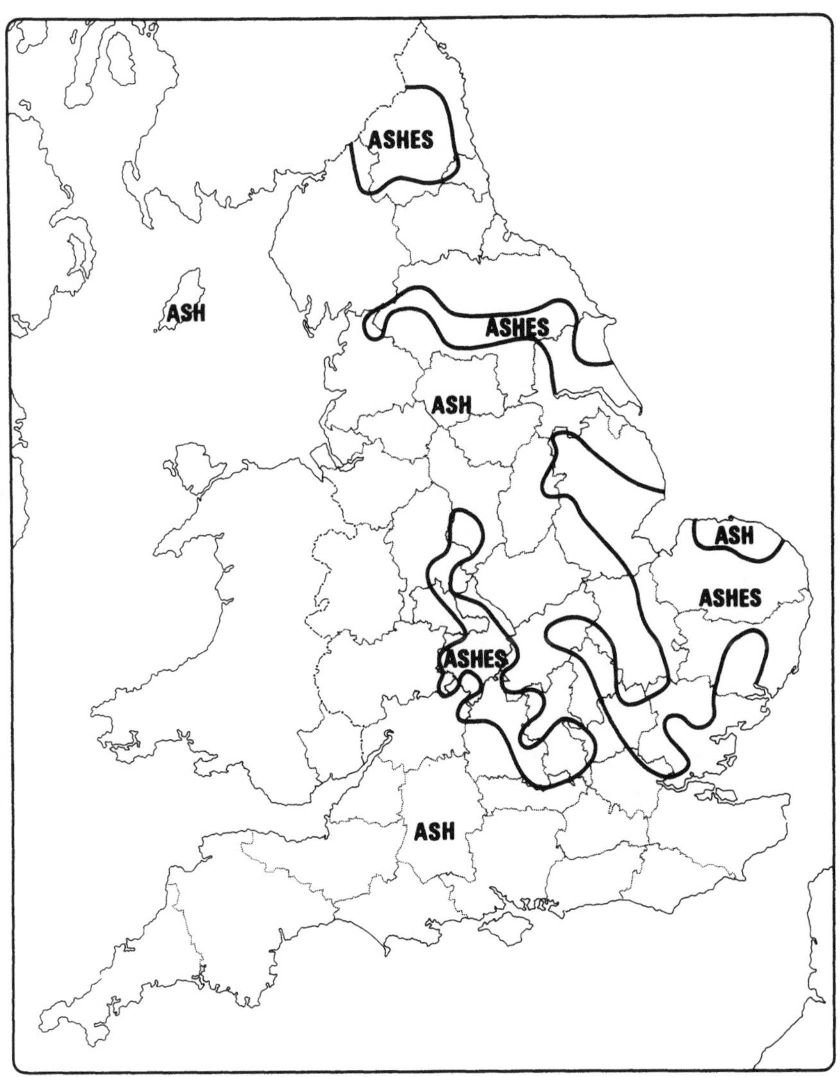

Map 14: ASH (in a burning fire)

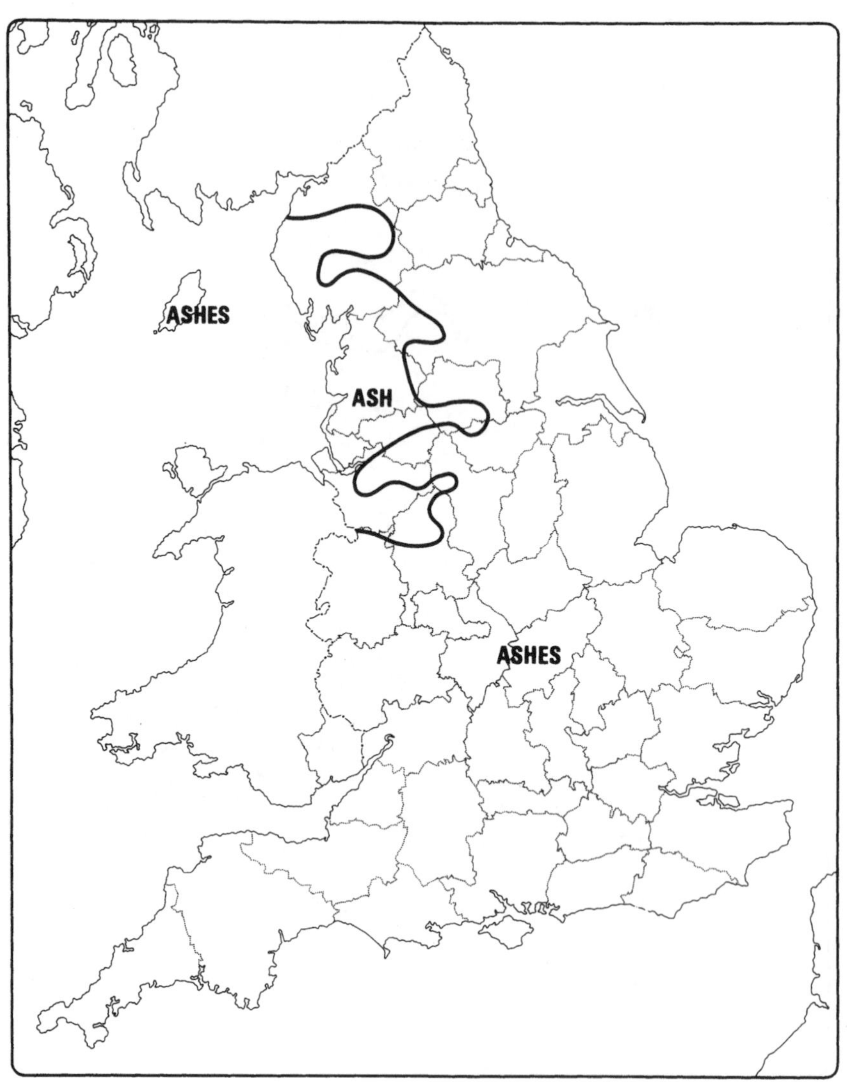

Map 15: ASHES (taken from a cold fire)

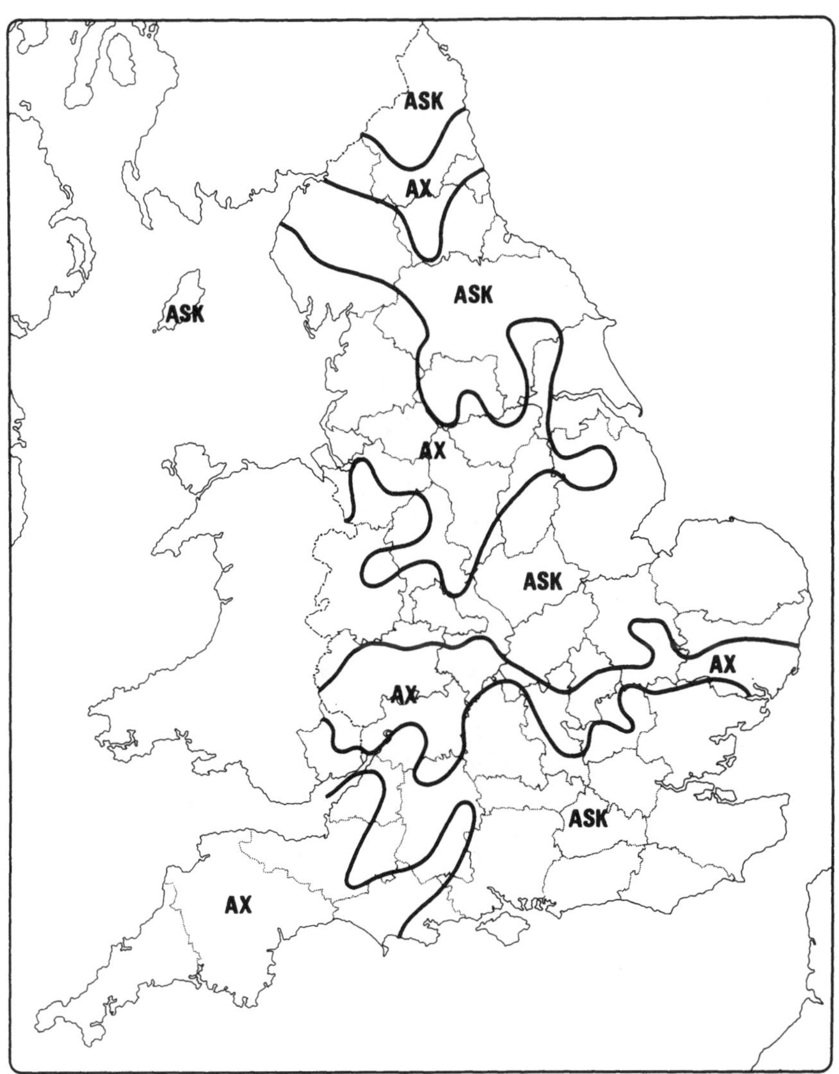

Map 16: ASK
Many speakers use both forms.

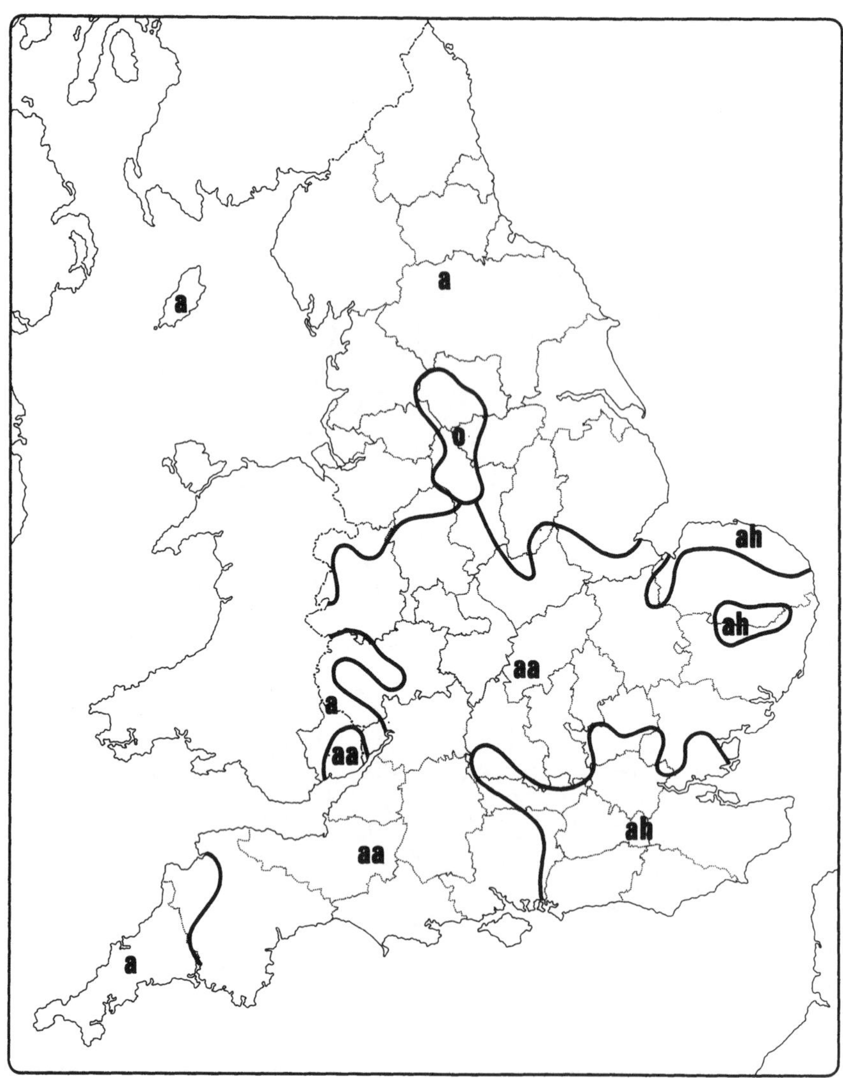

Map 17: AUNT(IE)

Although *aunt* is the most widely used word, *auntie* is also found, especially in the South West. This sometimes influences the boundaries of different pronunciations, e.g. the boundary between short **a** and long **aa** in Devon and Cornwall is also essentially the boundary between *aunt* (Devon) and *auntie* (Cornwall). The form *naunt* (from *an aunt*) occurs in small pockets in the west Midlands and on the Derbyshire-Yorkshire border.

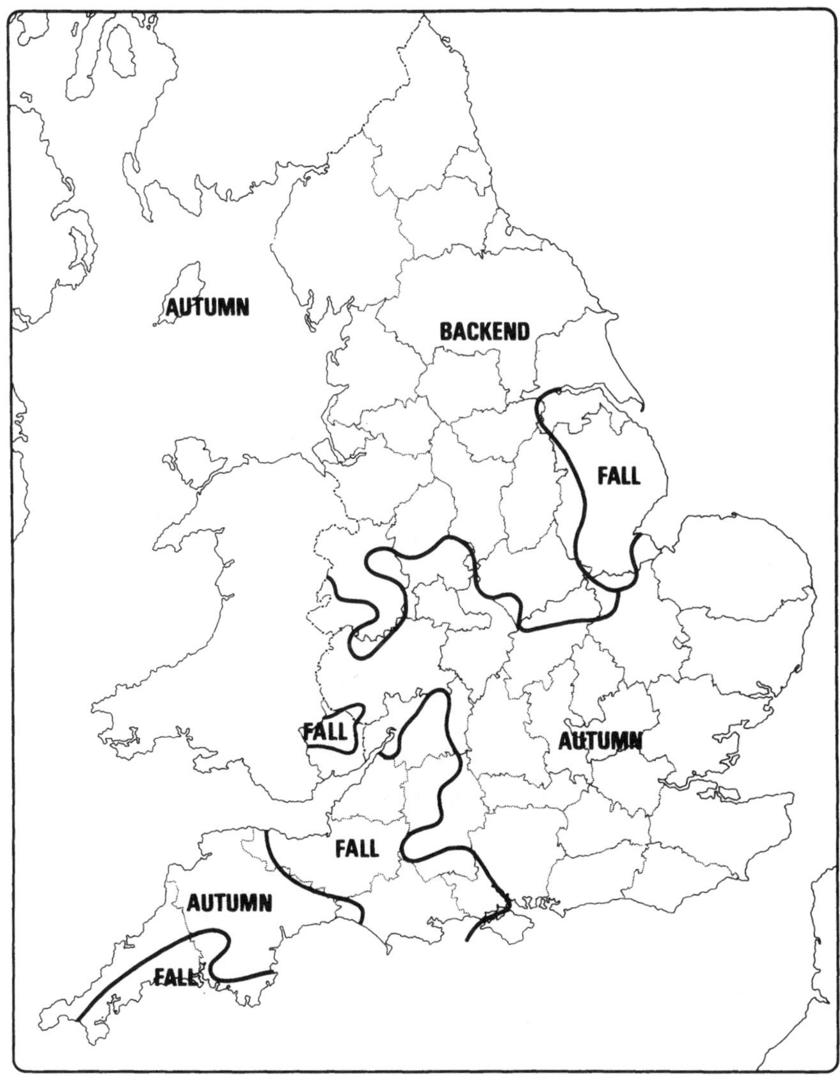

Map 18: AUTUMN
The Old English word **FALL**, the normal form in North America, is still found scattered in other areas, and in parts of Lincolnshire and the West Country occurs as *fall of the leaf/year*. The French **AUTUMN**, now the Standard form in England, continues to advance against the other terms.

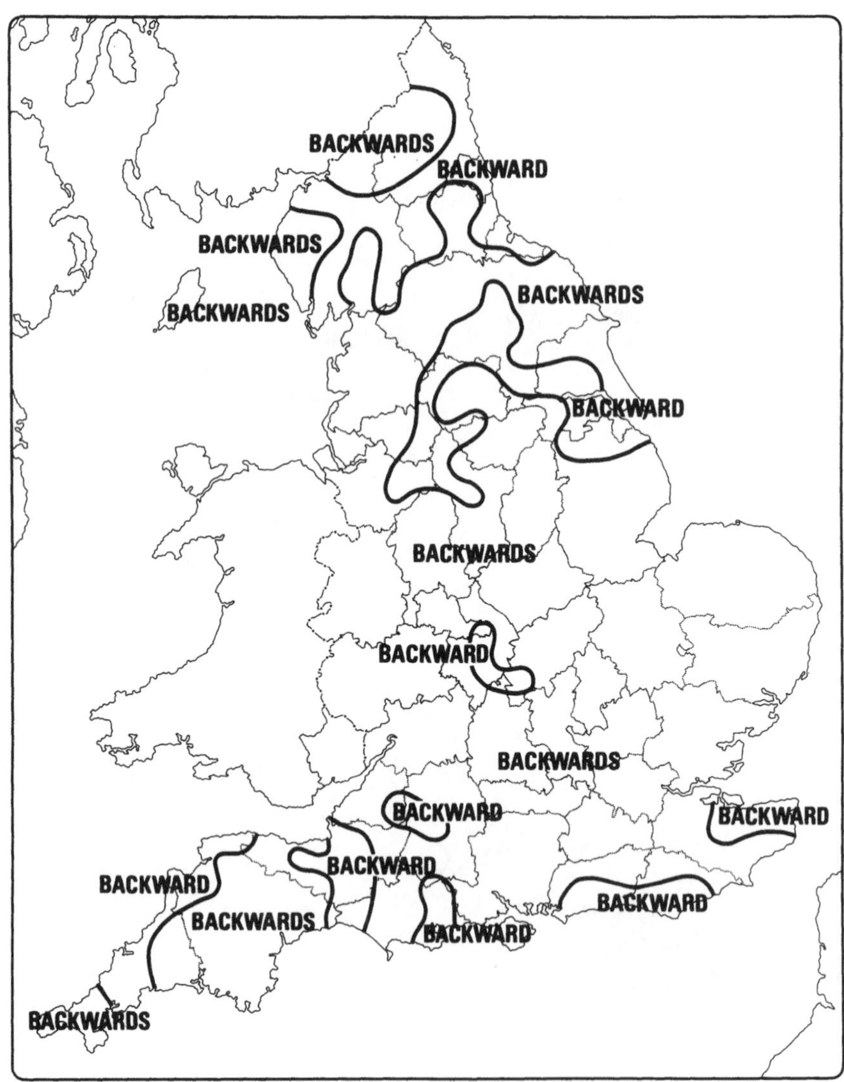

Map 19: BACKWARDS

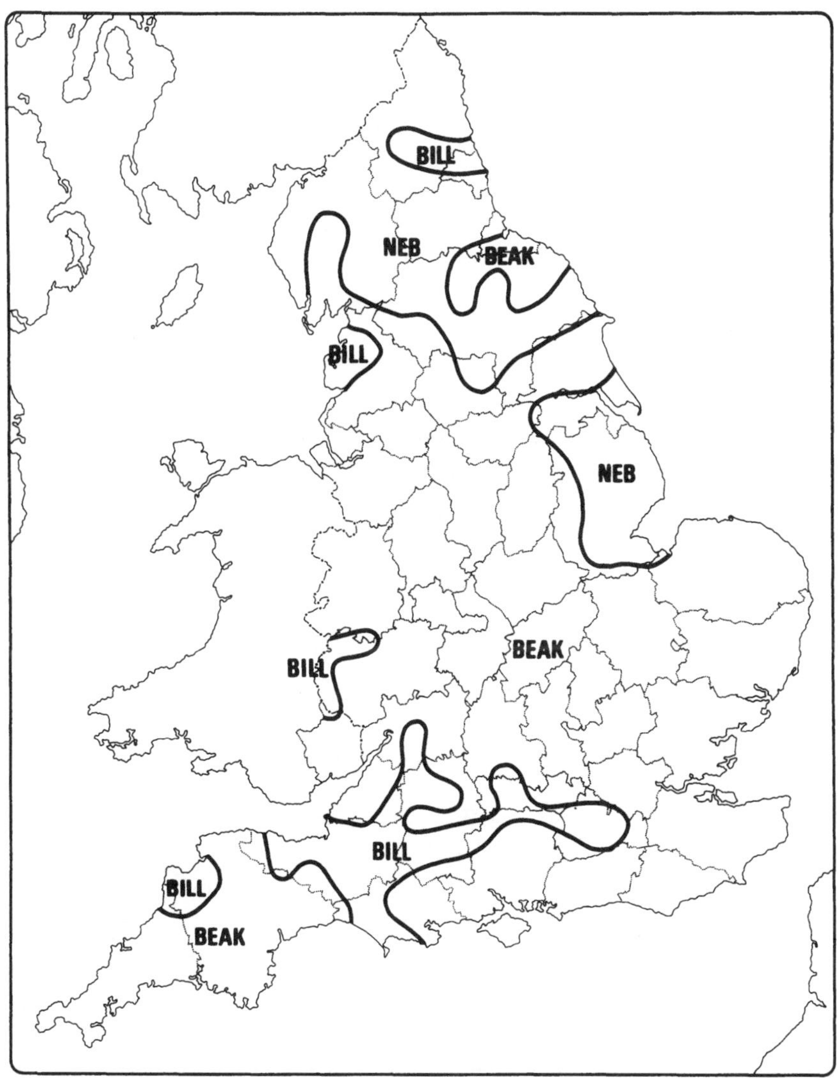

Map 20: BEAK

BILL comes from Old English, **NEB** from Old English and Old Norse, and **BEAK** (a newer word from medieval times) is from French. The distribution of forms on this map illustrates how words of different origins contribute to the vocabulary of English and how certain words, in this case the comparative newcomer, **BEAK**, establish themselves and become Standard usage, while older words linger in the regional dialects of clearly defined areas.

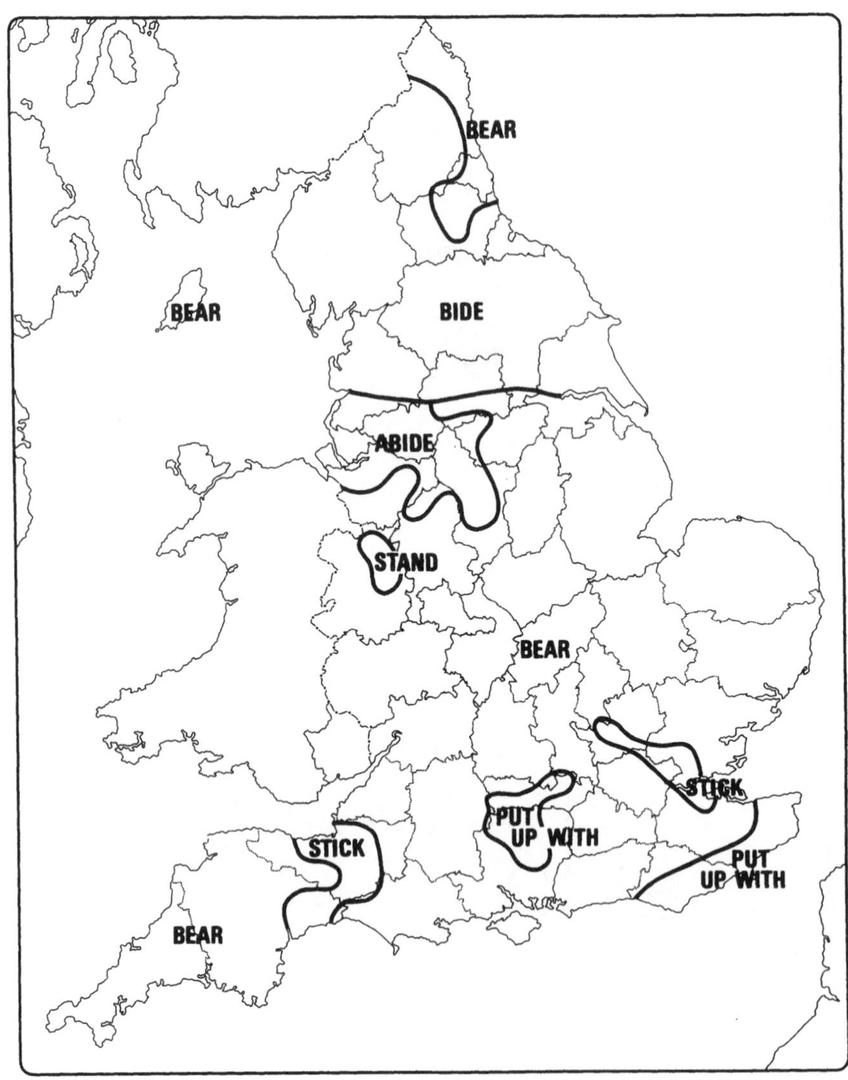

Map 21: BEAR (to . . ., pain)
bear with it and *abide with it* are occasionally found in the North and the north Midlands, *stand it* is scattered in the South and the Midlands, and *stick it* occurs particularly in the South.

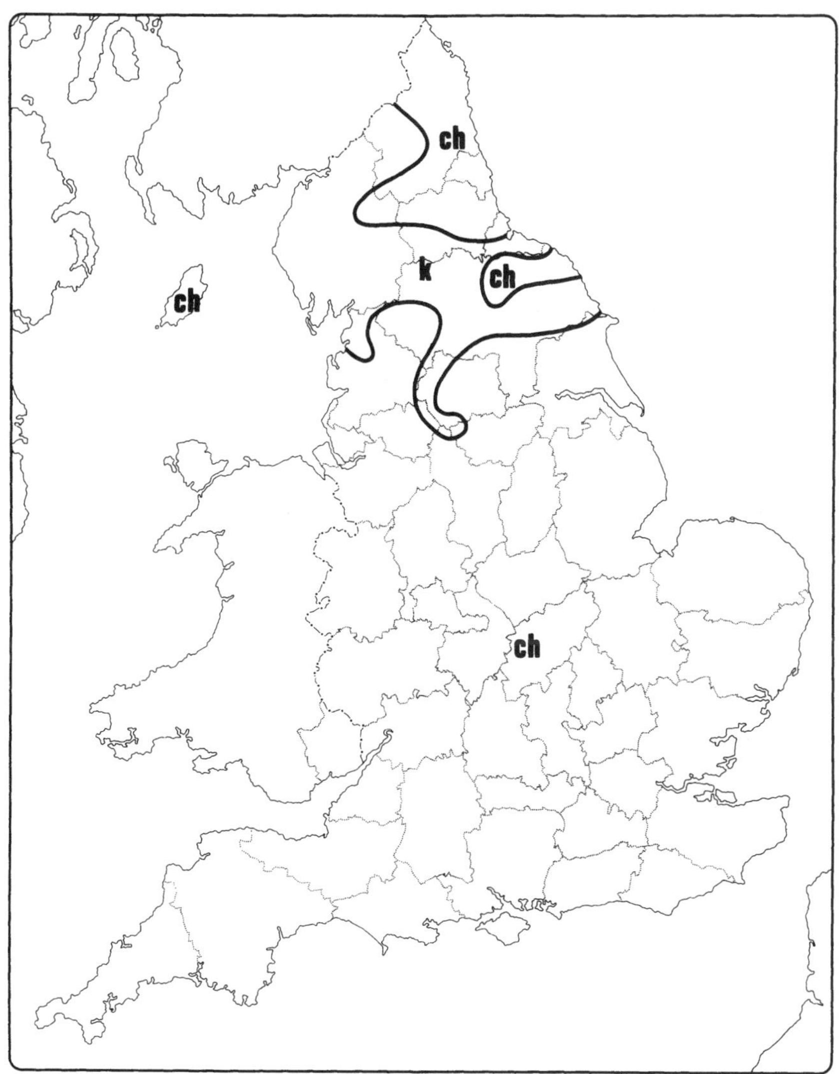

Map 22: BIRCH

Although isolated examples of **-k** are found in Lincolnshire and Norfolk, it is losing popularity in favour of **-ch**. The **-k** forms derive from Old Norse and the contrast between them and **-ch** is most obviously seen in the words *kirk* and *church*; see also Map 59.

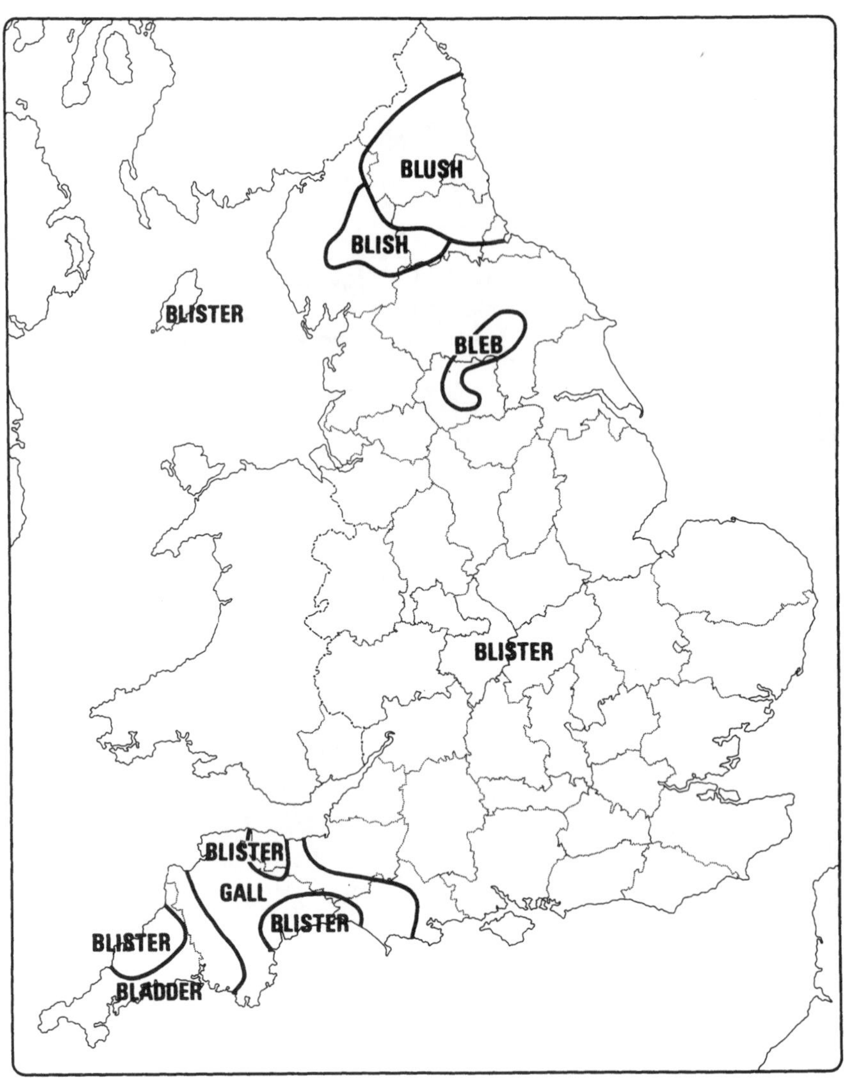

Map 23: BLISTER
BLEB is found sporadically throughout the North. Note how all but one of the terms begin with *bl-*, giving them an element in common despite their diversity.

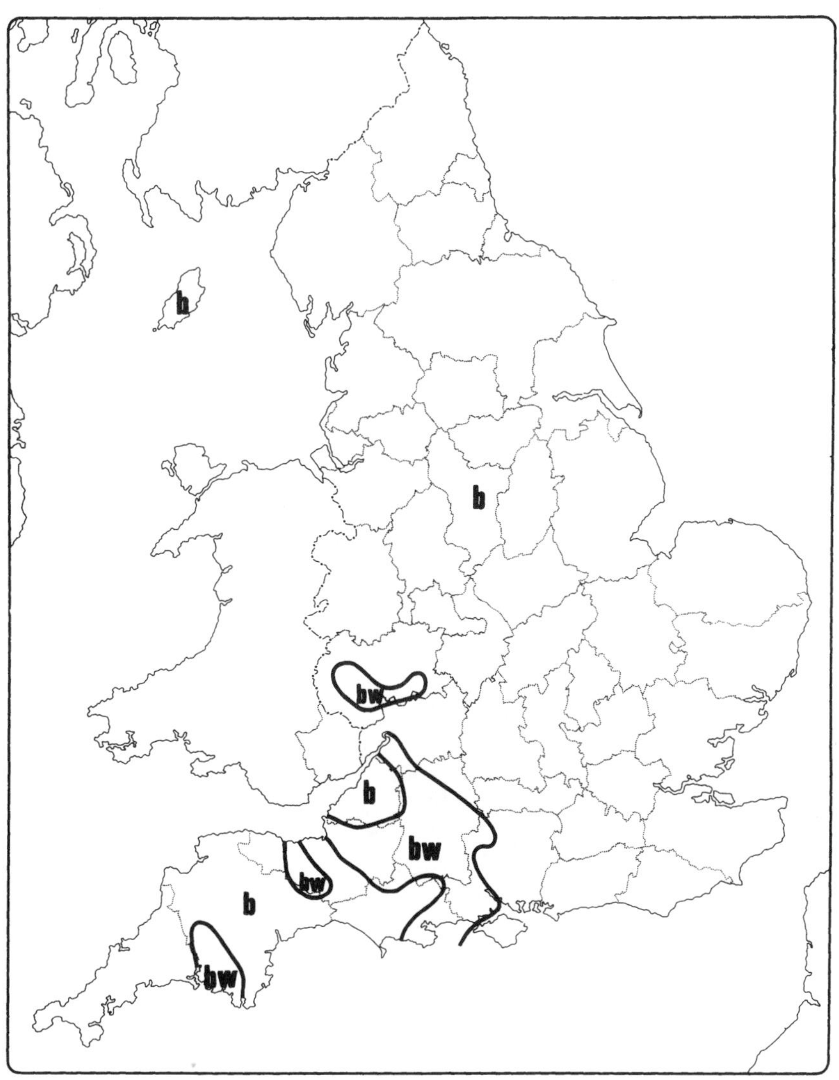

Map 24: BOILING

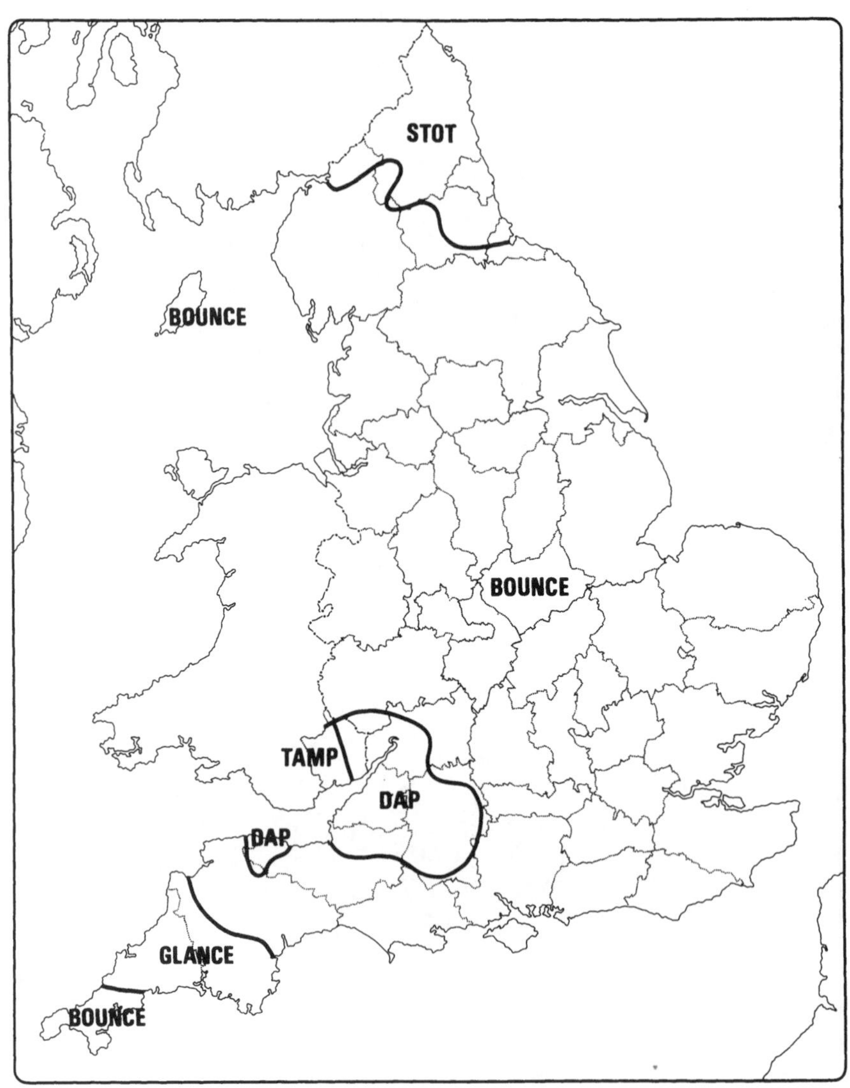

Map 25: BOUNCE (to …, describing a ball)

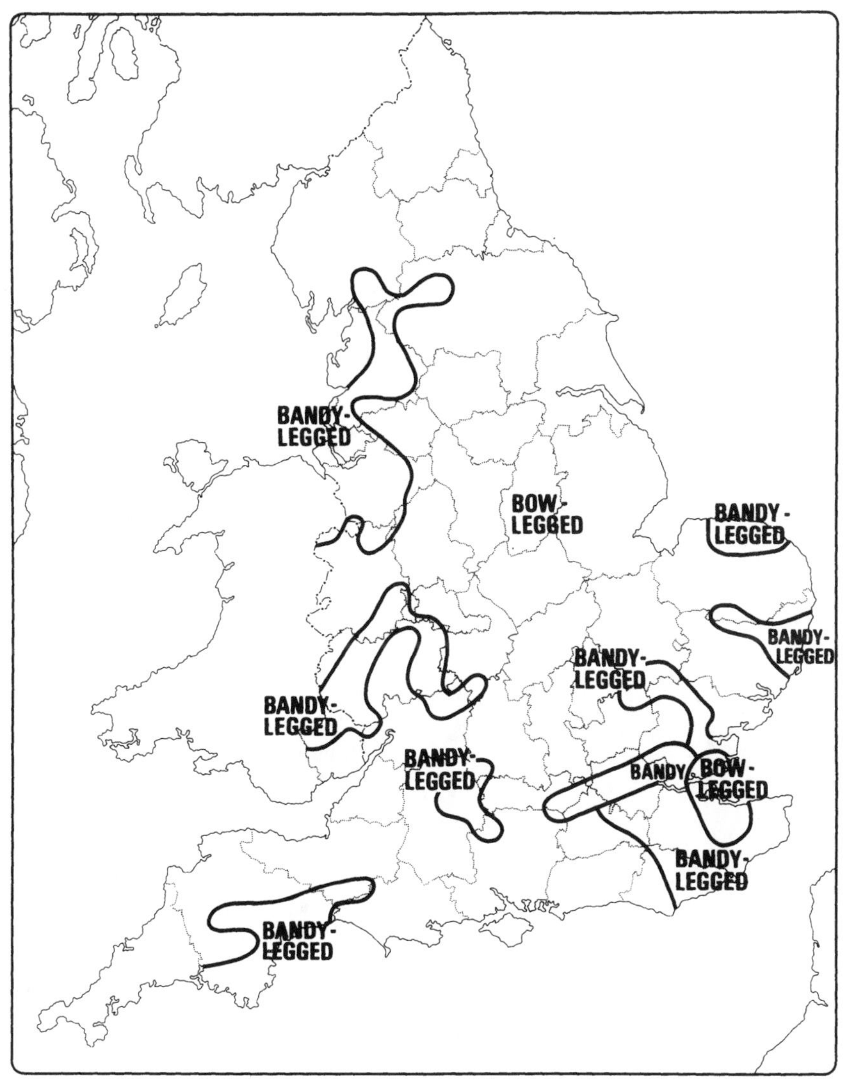

Map 26: BOW-LEGGED

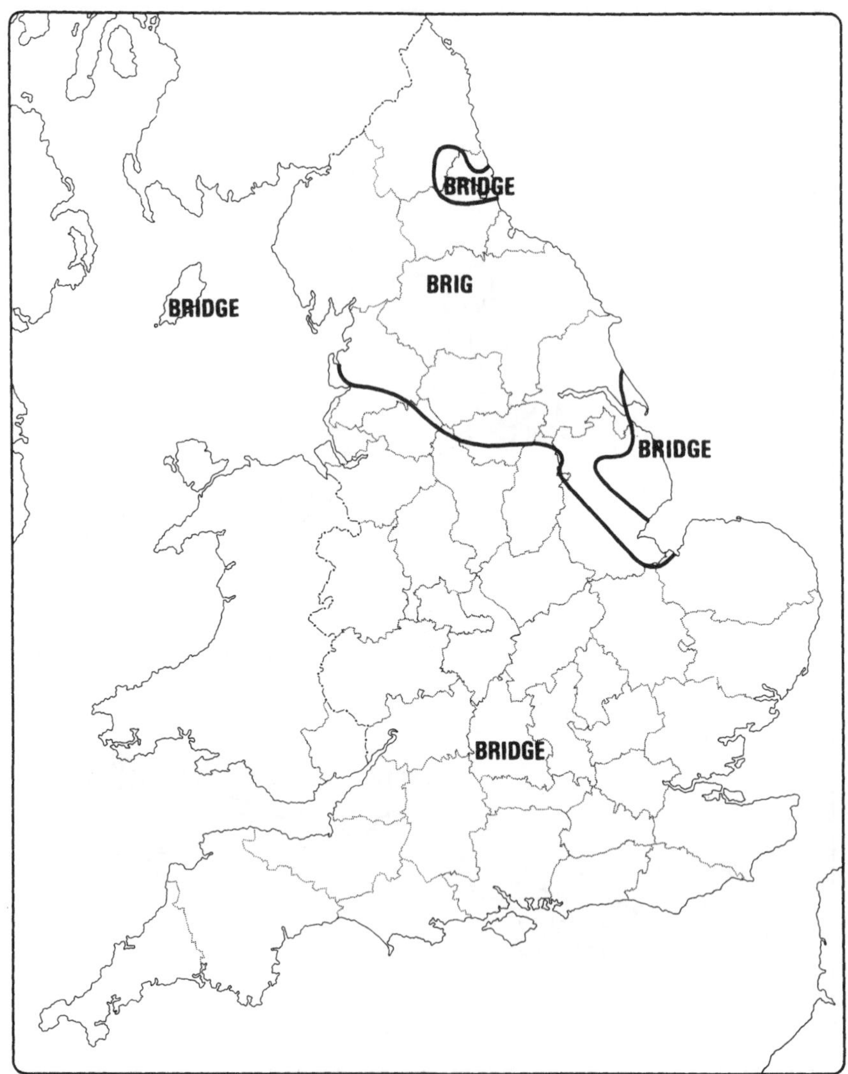

Map 27: BRIDGE

The dominant Old English **BRIDGE** contrasts with the Old Norse **BRIG**. In Somerset and parts of Wiltshire and Devon the form *birge* occurs; this is an example of a historical process (metathesis) in which the *-r-* changes position in a word, e.g. Old English *brid* became Modern English *bird*.

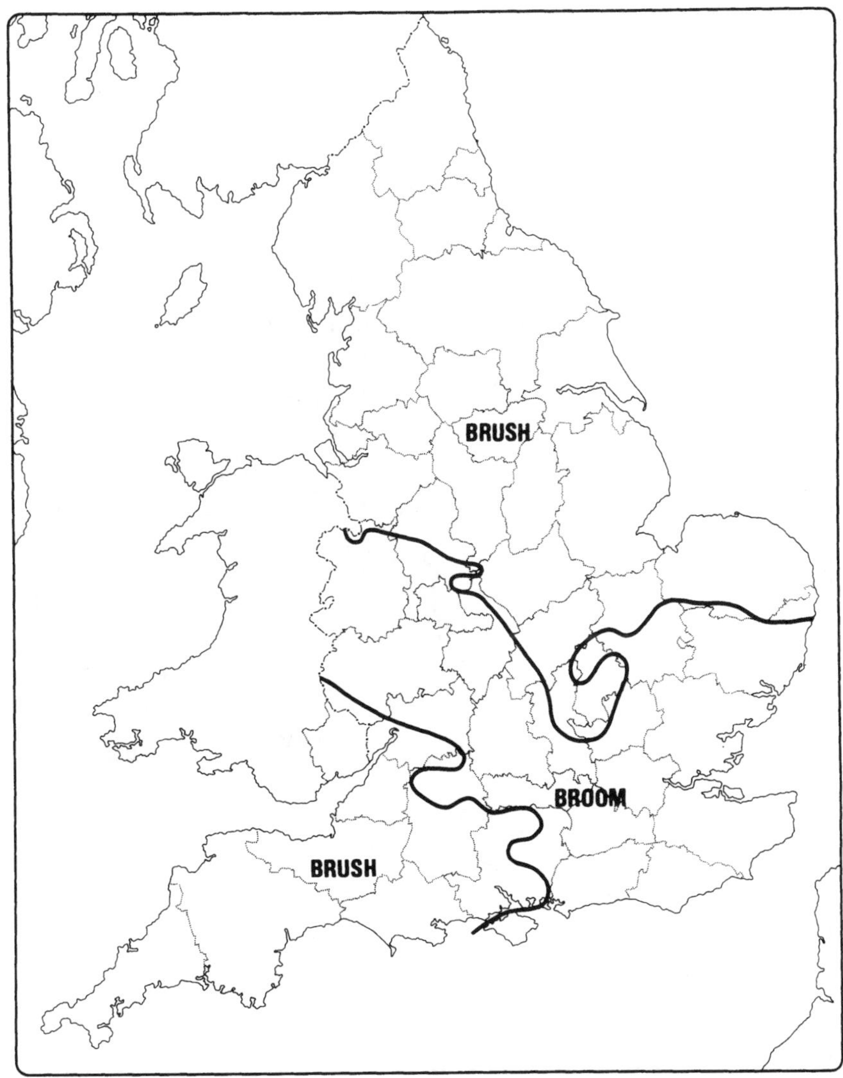

Map 28: BRUSH (for sweeping)
BROOM, an older word in English than **BRUSH** (Old English as opposed to Middle English), is found scattered through areas where **BRUSH**, of French derivation, is dominant.

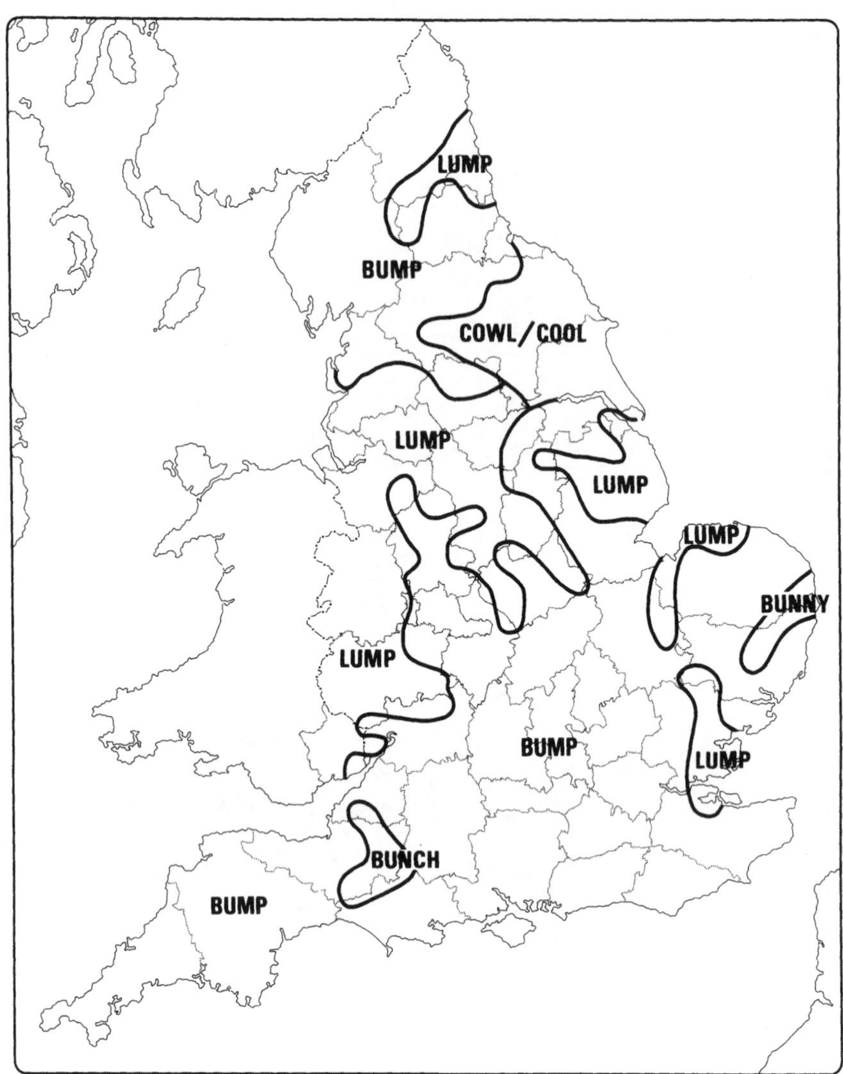

Map 29: BUMP (swelling on forehead)

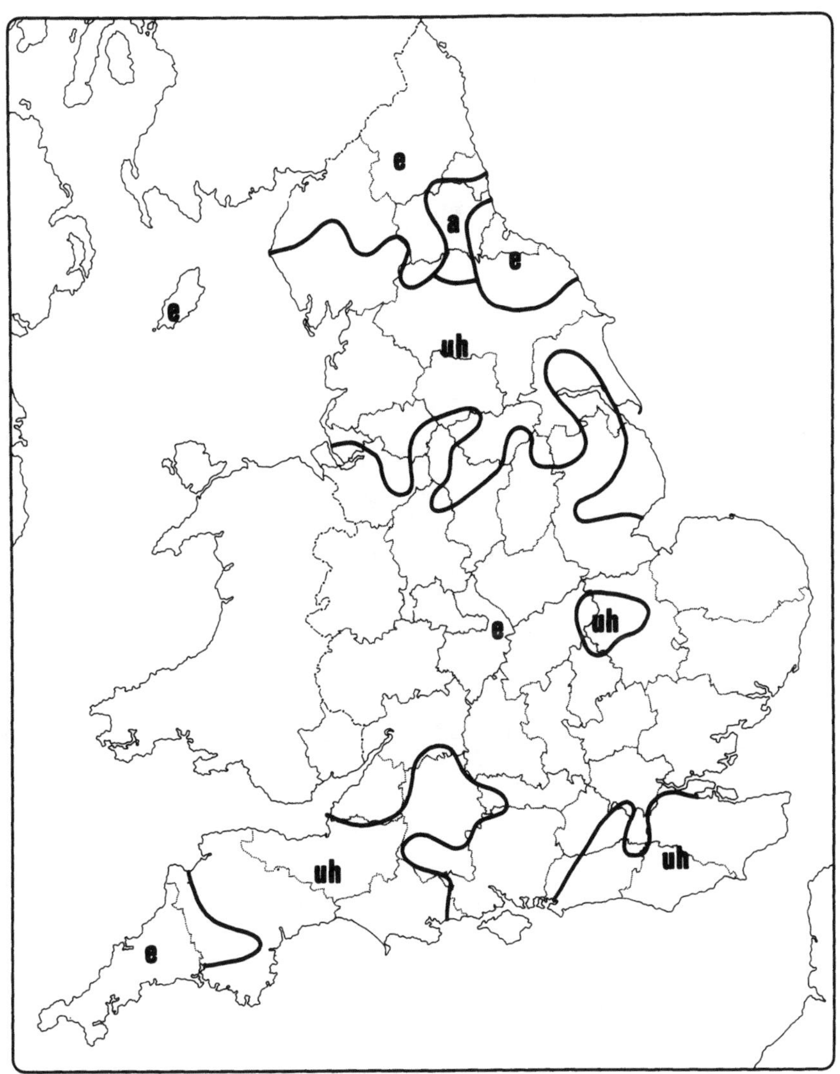

Map 30: B<u>U</u>RIED

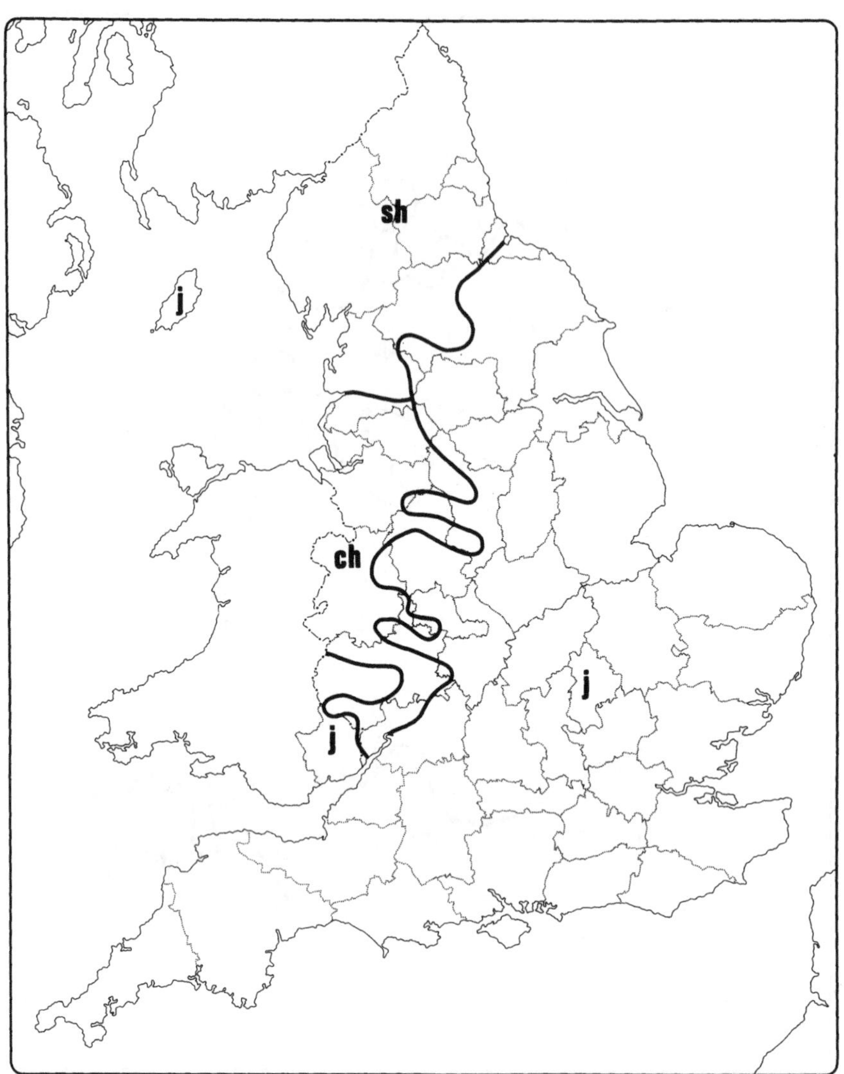

Map 31: CABBA<u>GE</u>

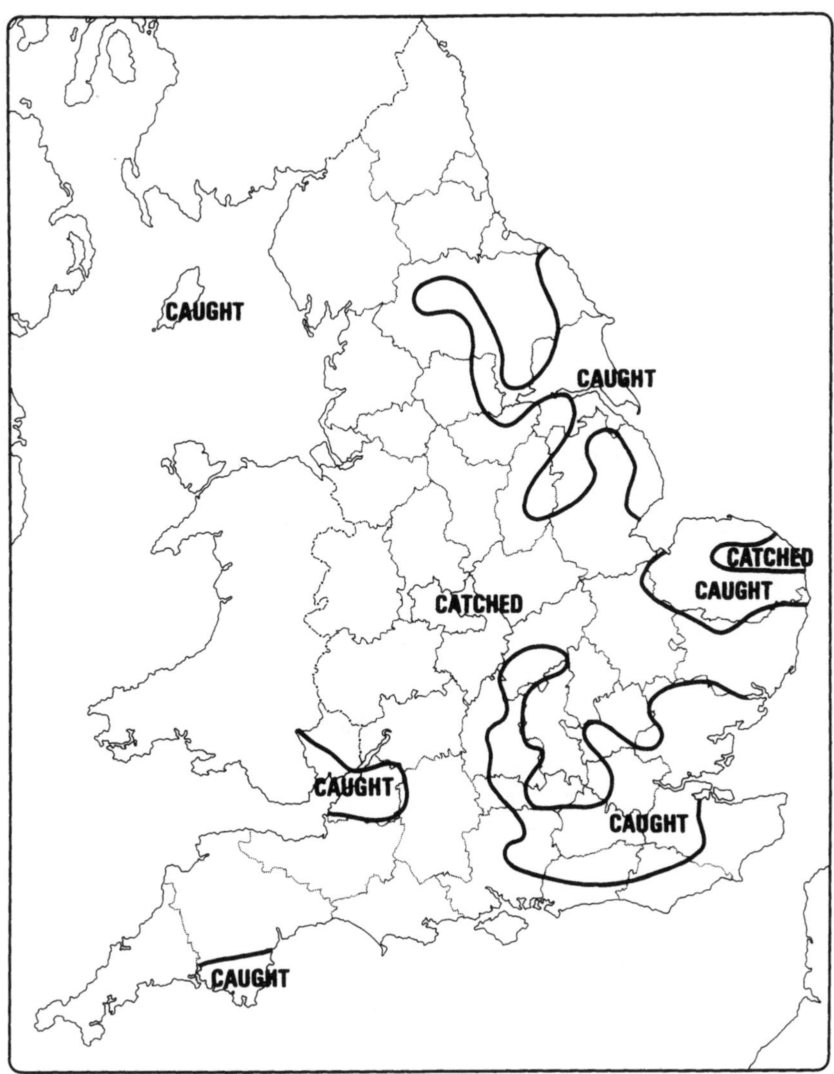

Map 32: CAUGHT (cat . . . a mouse)

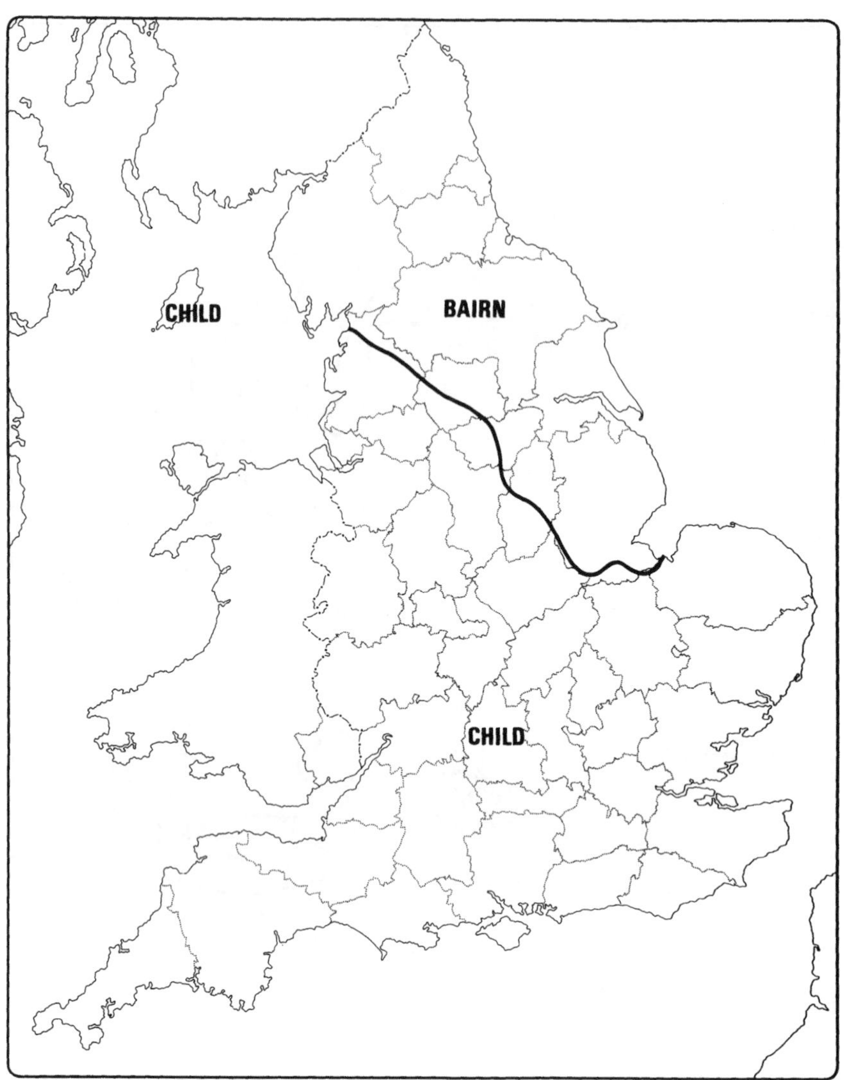

Map 33: CHILD
BAIRN is evidently receding northwards.

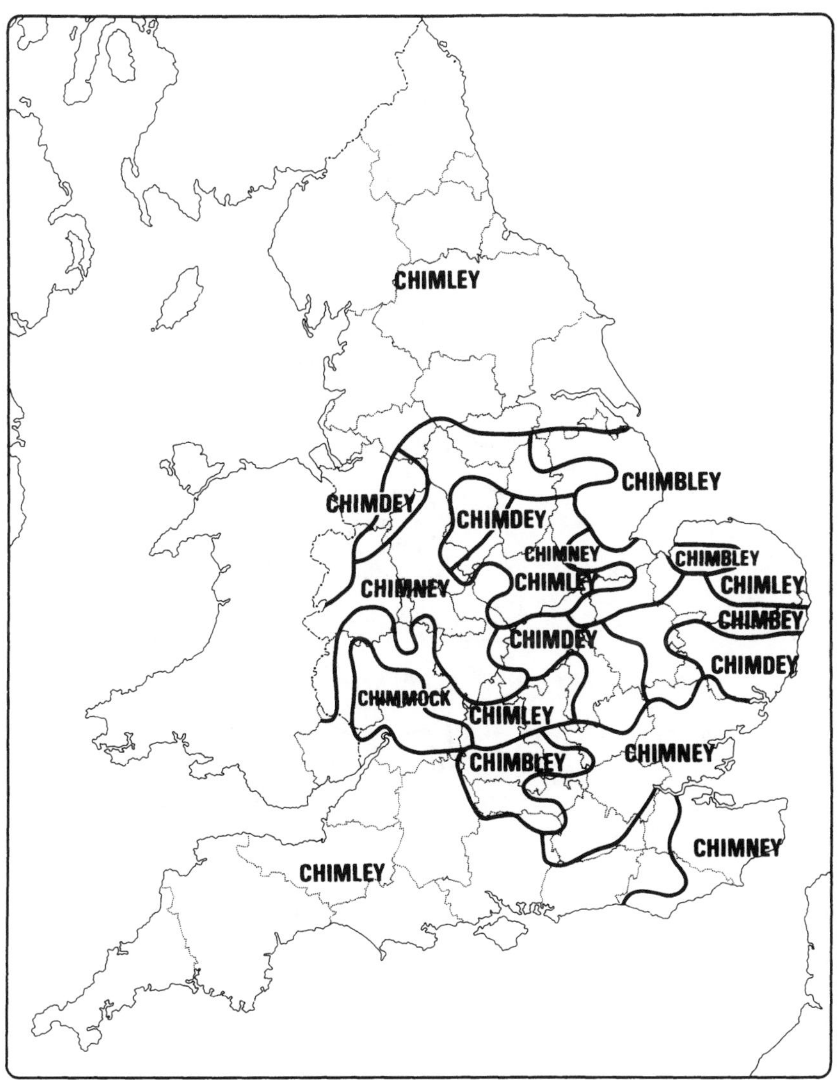

Map 34: CHIMNEY

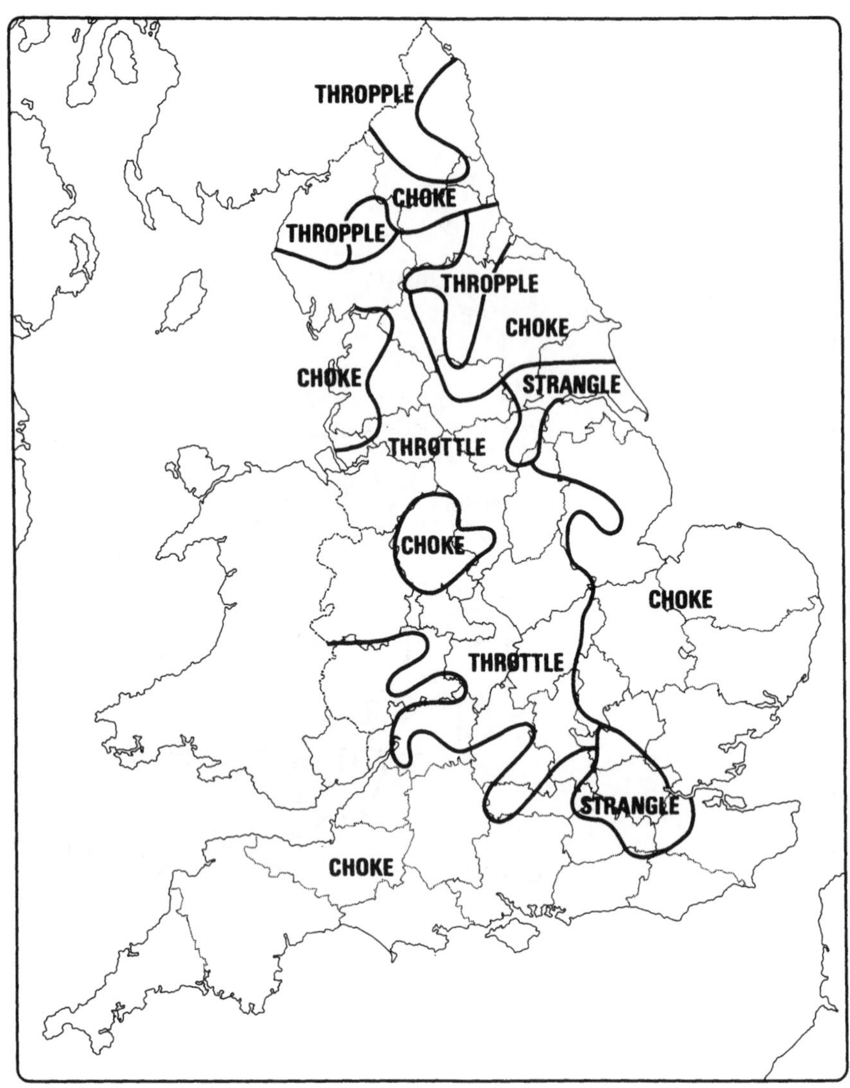

Map 35: CHOKE (or strangle someone, with hands)
Both **CHOKE** and **THROTTLE** tend to be used in many places in the east Midlands and the South East.

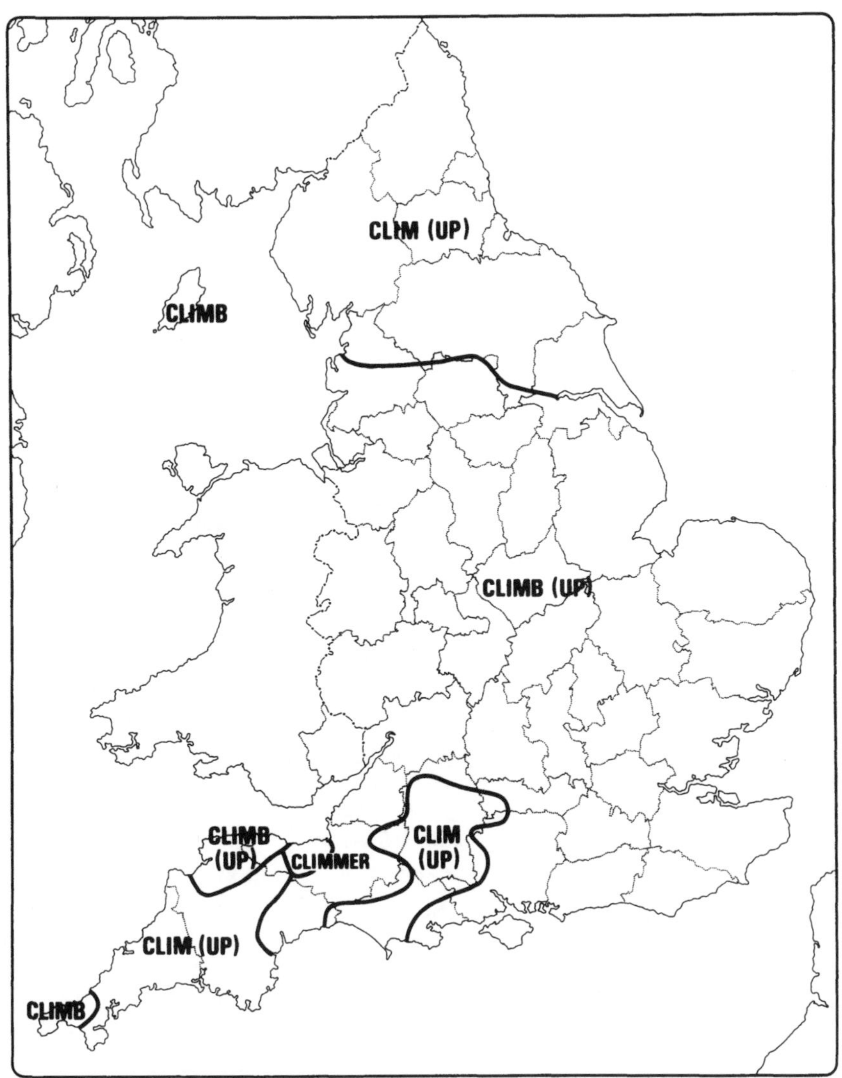

Map 36: CLIMB (a tree)

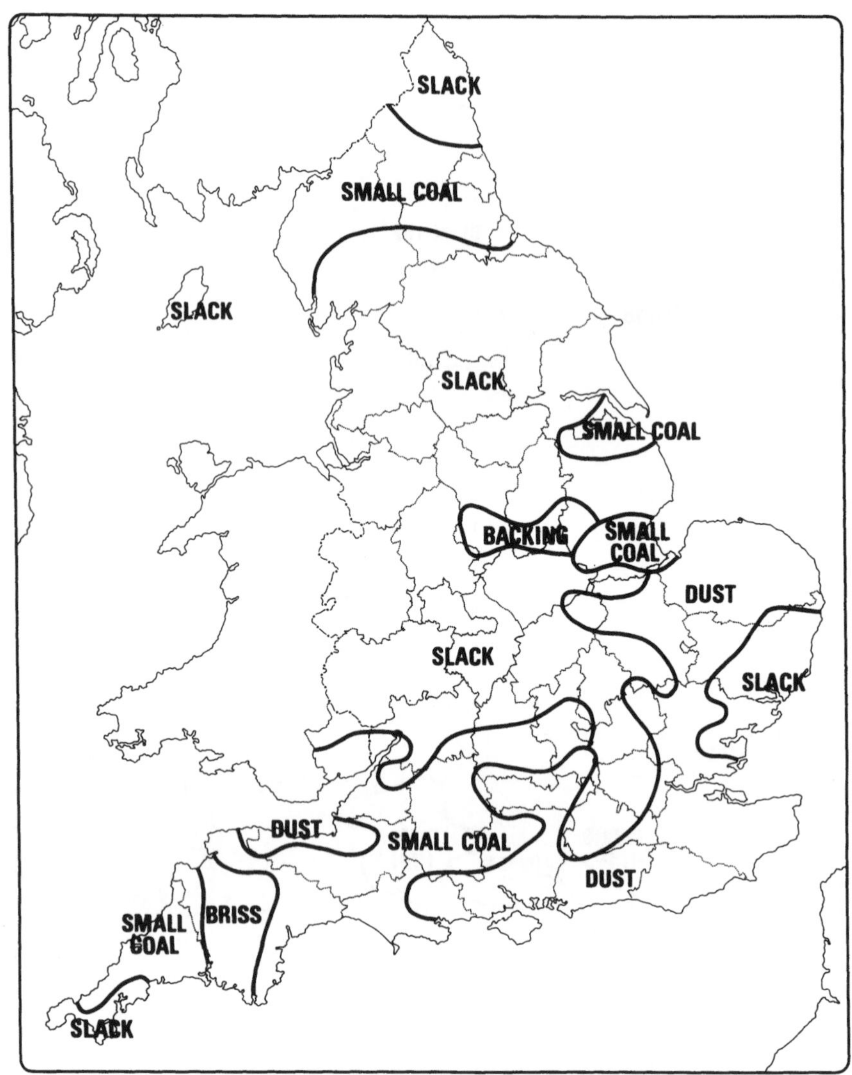

Map 37: COAL DUST

The areas in which **DUST** is predominant also include instances of *coal-dust*, *dust-coal*, *dusty-coal*. The form *coal-dust* is especially popular in Kent and Sussex, while *dusty-coal* is common in East Anglia. The **BRISS** area of Devon incorporates instances of *briss-coal* and *brissy coal*.

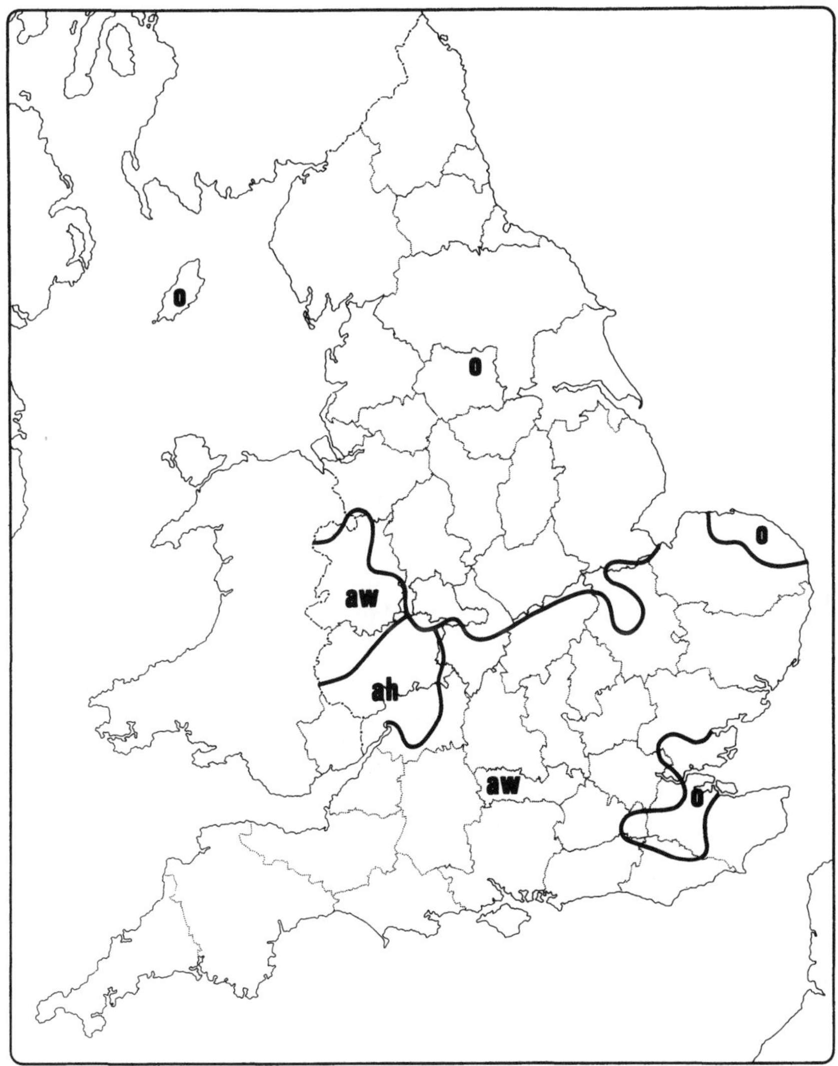

Map 38: CR<u>O</u>SS

A clear contrast is seen between the short **o**, predominantly north of the Wash, and the long **aw** sound to the south. This **aw** came into use in the seventeenth century, and is now found among some older speakers of Received Pronunciation, but seems to be on the decline both in Standard speech and dialects. The **ah** form to the north of the Severn estuary has parallels in North American pronunciation.

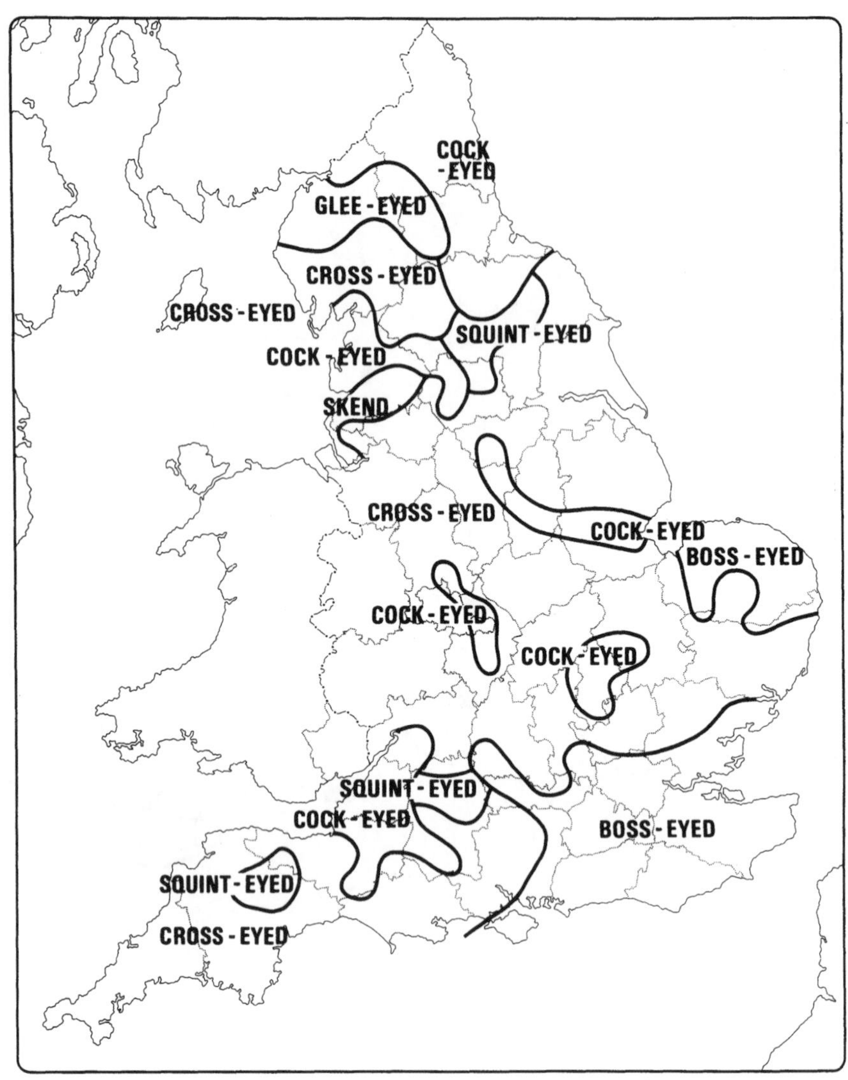

Map 39: CROSS-EYED
Some of those interviewed regarded **BOSS-EYED** as an older or less polite word than **CROSS-EYED**.

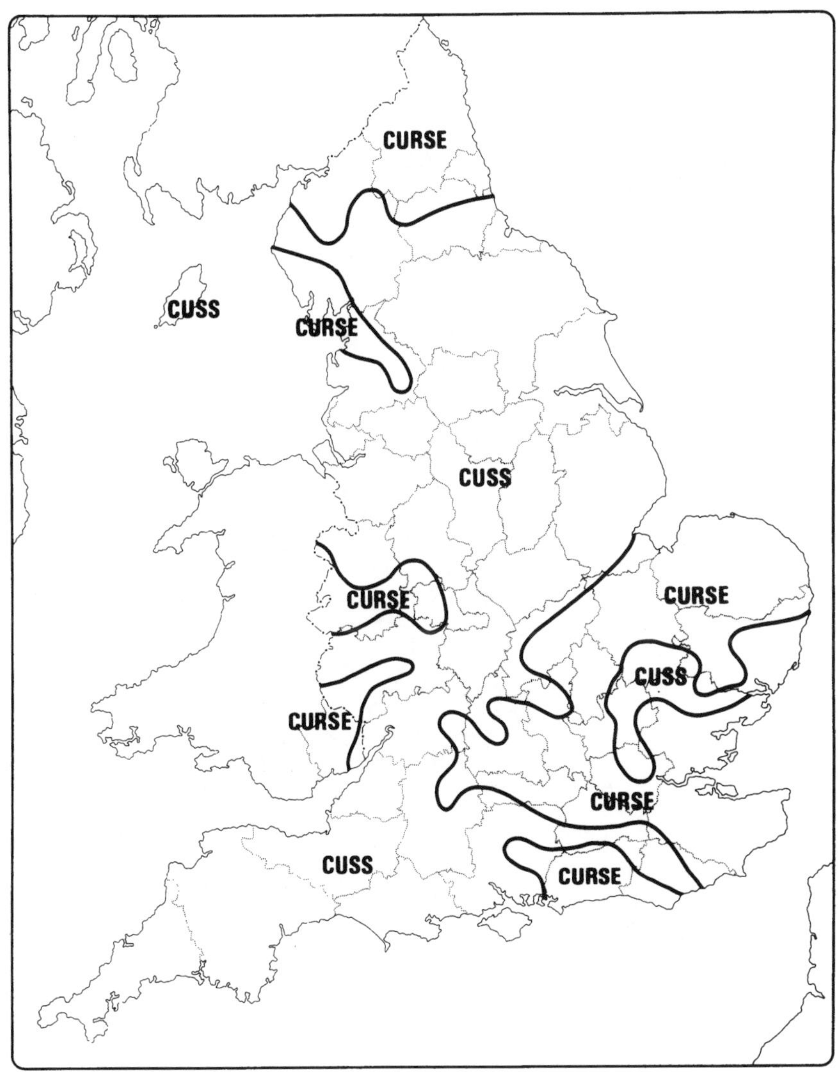

Map 40: CURSE (to . . . and swear)

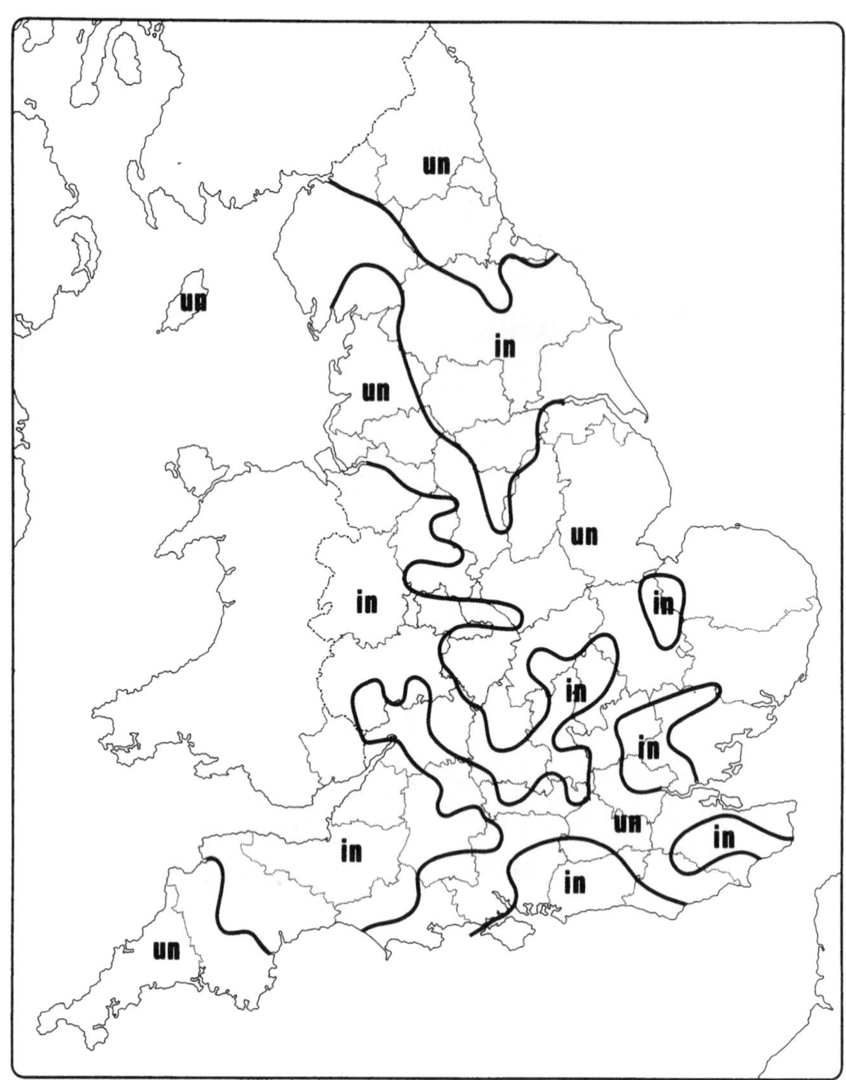

Map 41: CUSHION

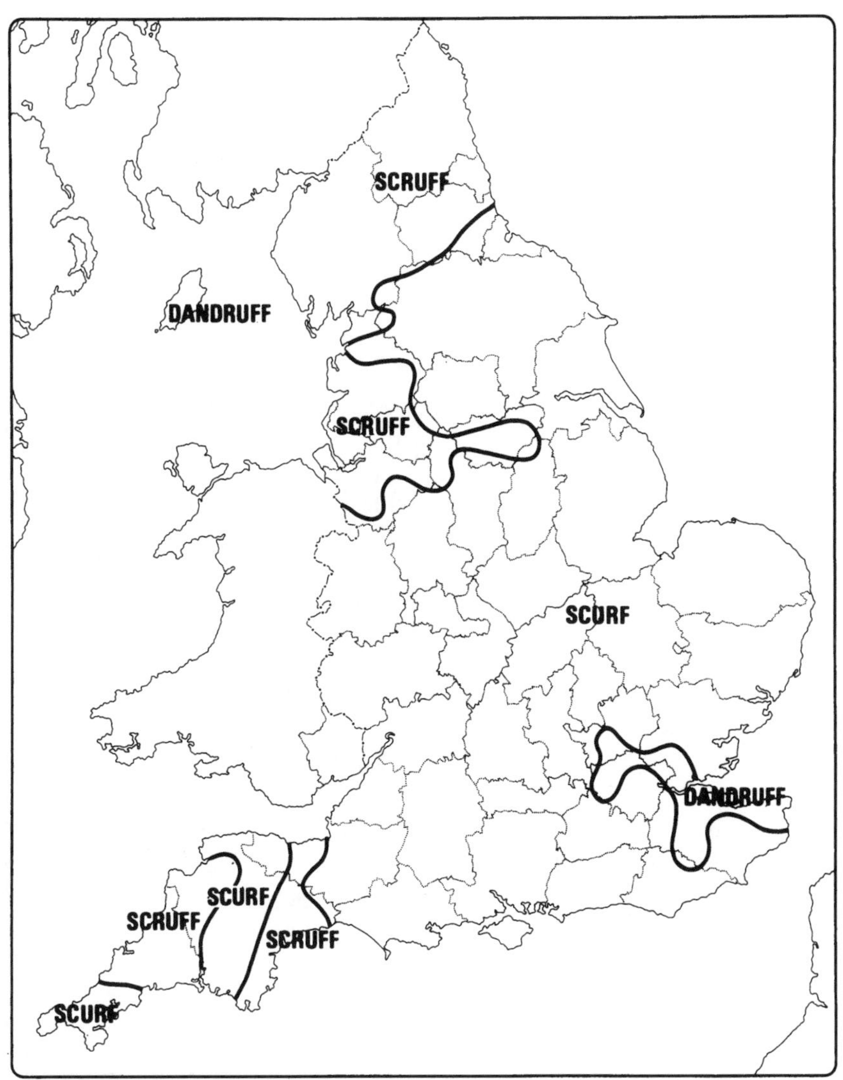

Map 42: DANDRUFF

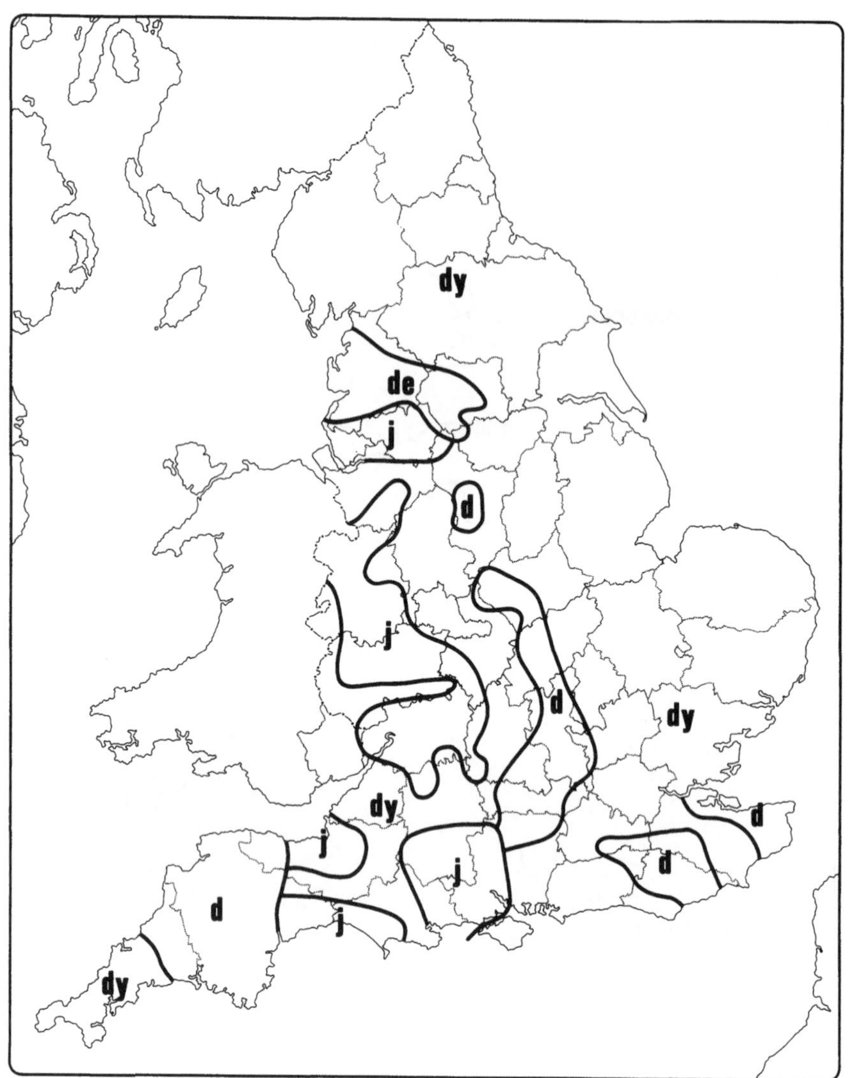

Map 43: D̲EW

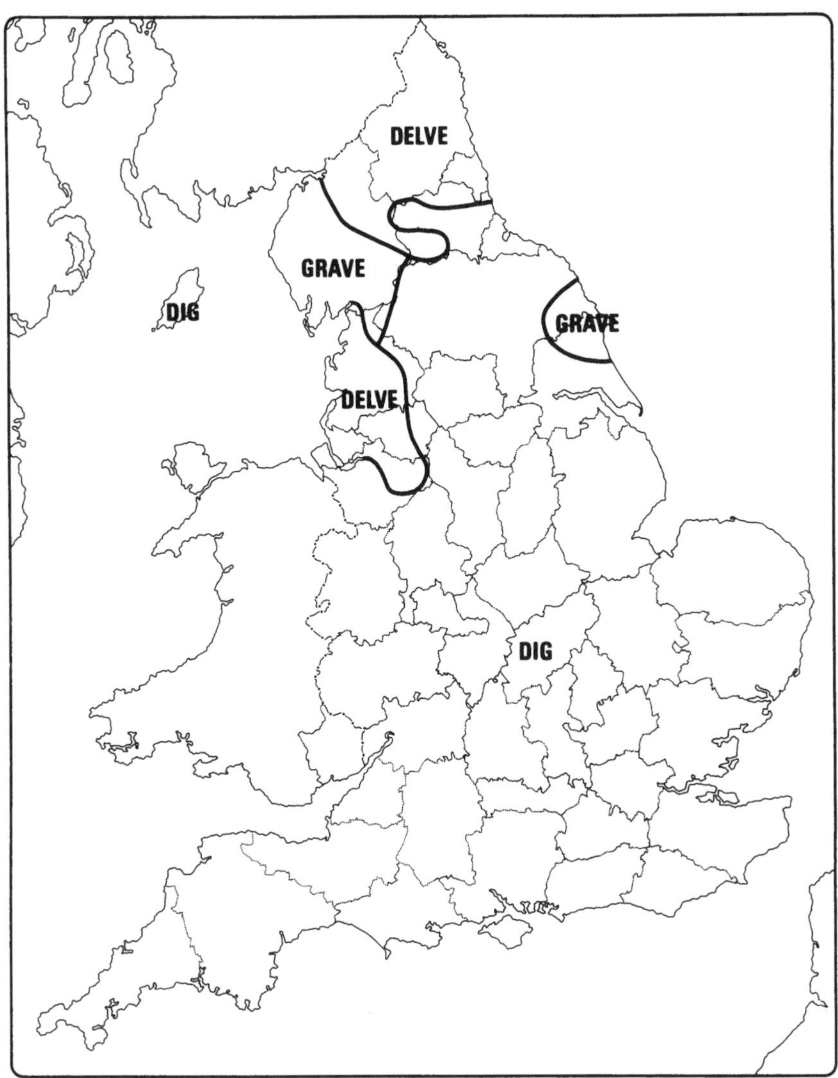

Map 44: DIG

DIG is widely used in all areas, but is a newer (Middle English) word than **DELVE** and **GRAVE**, both of which come from Old English. Some speakers prefer phrases such as *turn the ground up/earth over*, especially in the South West and in Norfolk. **SPIT** occurs occasionally in the South West and **HOWK** (pronounced *hoke*) in two localities in Northumberland.

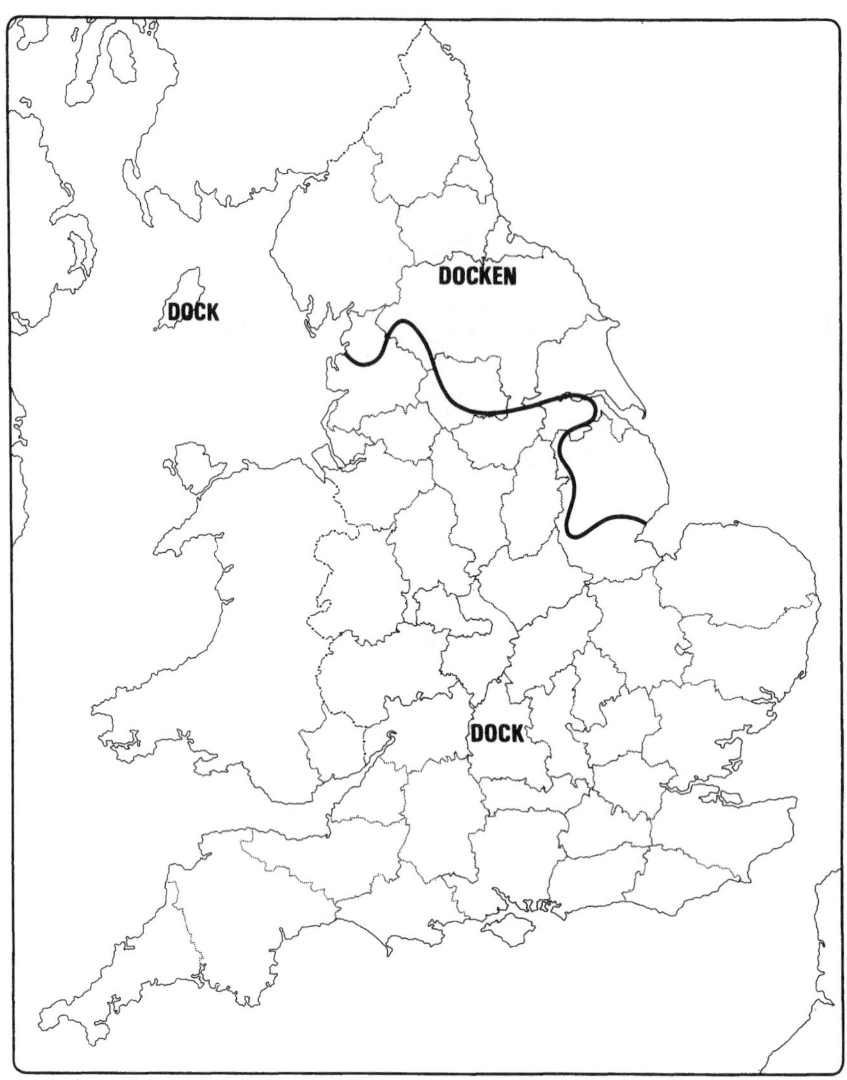

Map 45: DOCK (plant)
The **-EN** form is derived from an old plural ending as in *oxen*.

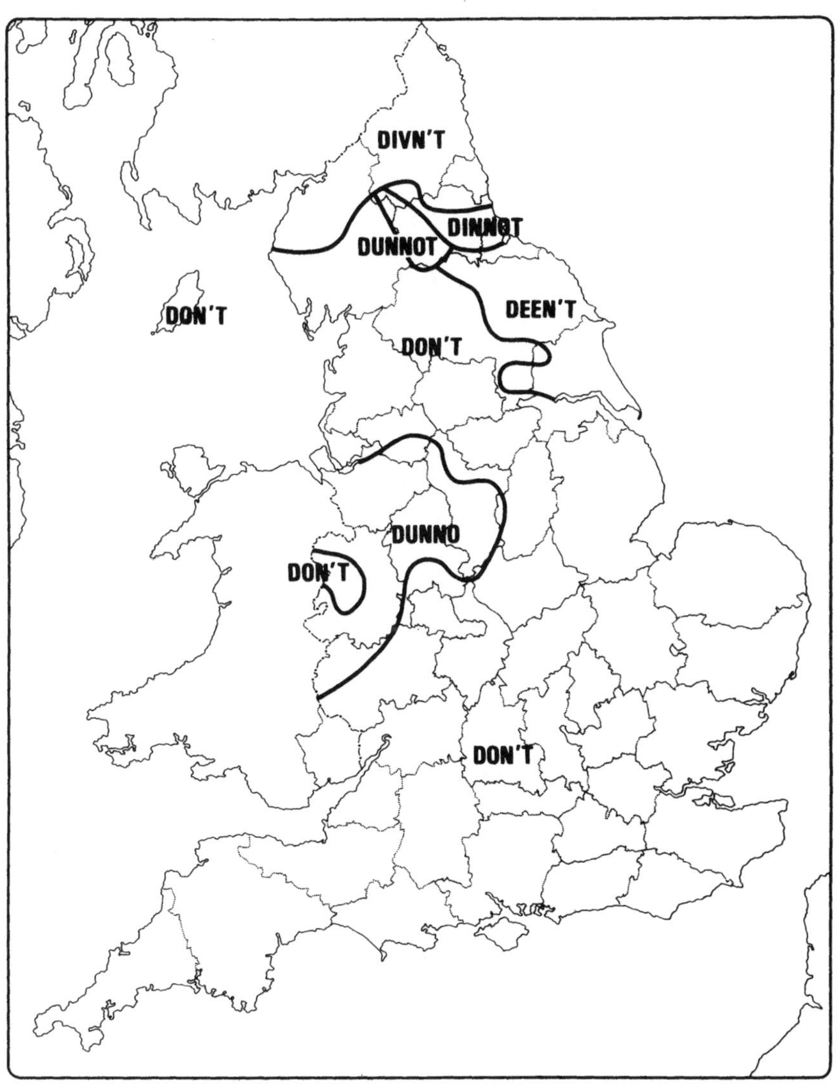

Map 46: DON'T (they . . .)

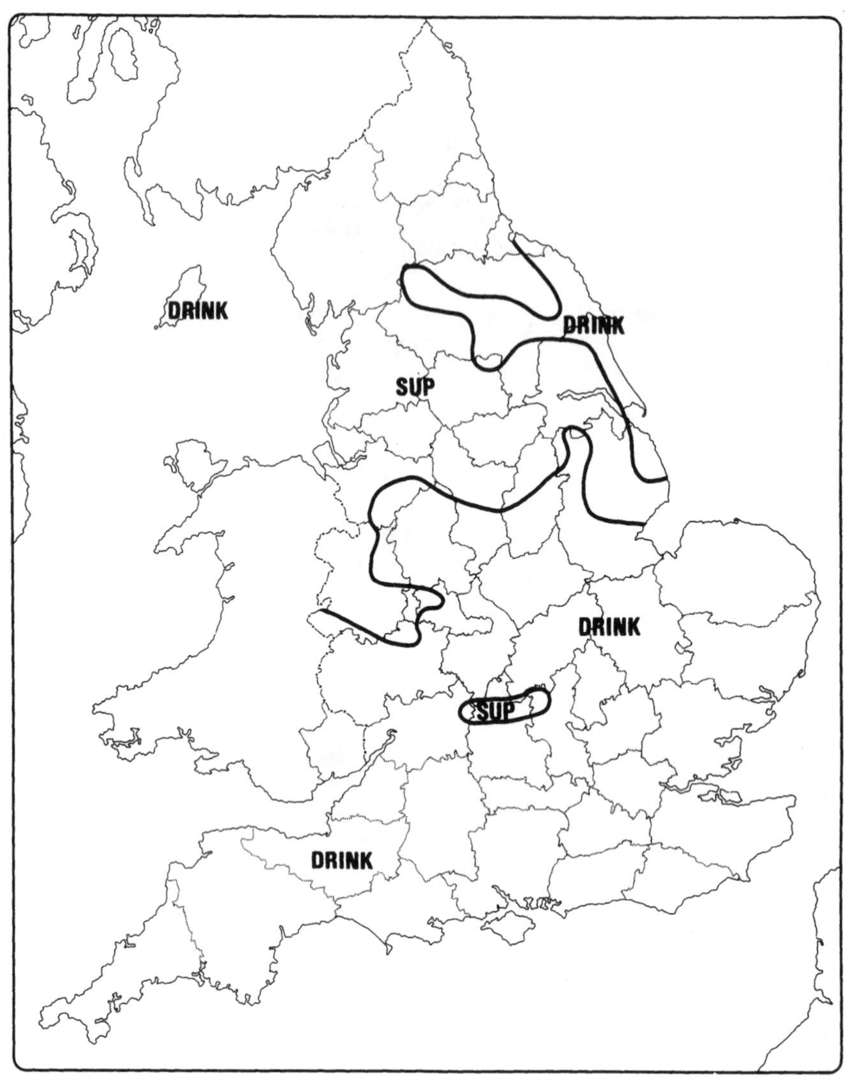

Map 47: DRINK (to . . .)

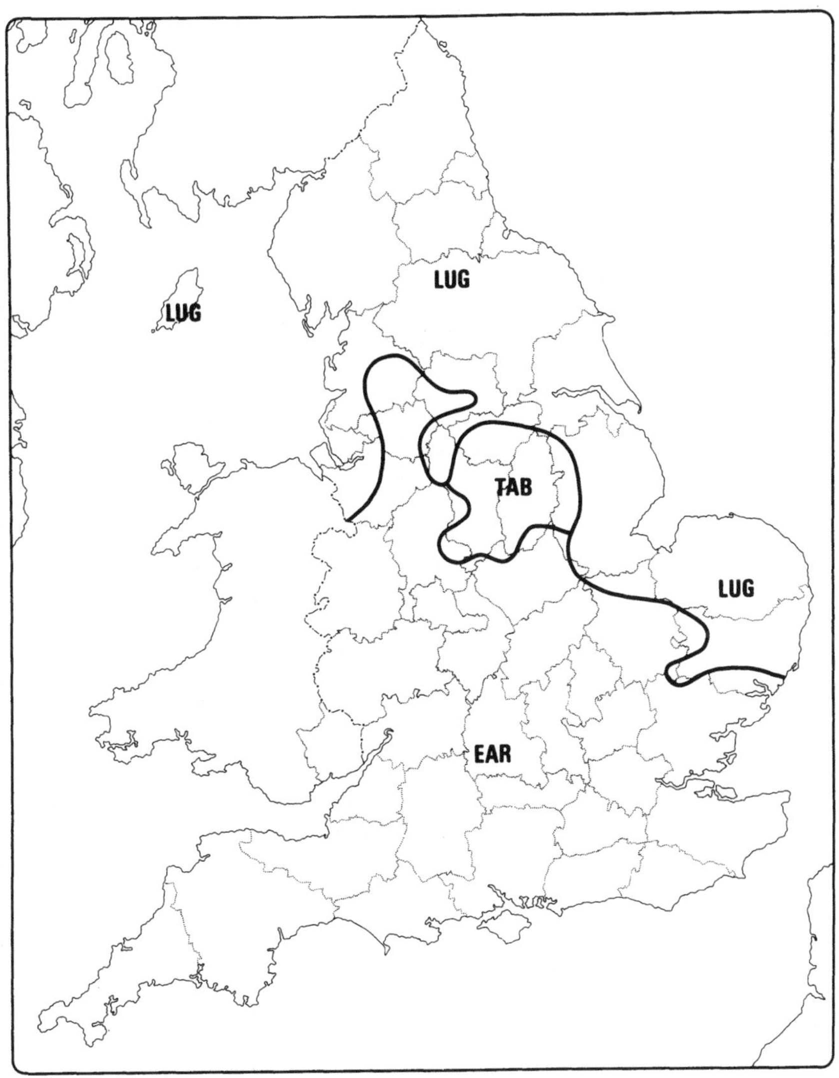

Map 48: EAR (human)
The Standard form **EAR** is of course widely used in the North and East where other words predominate.

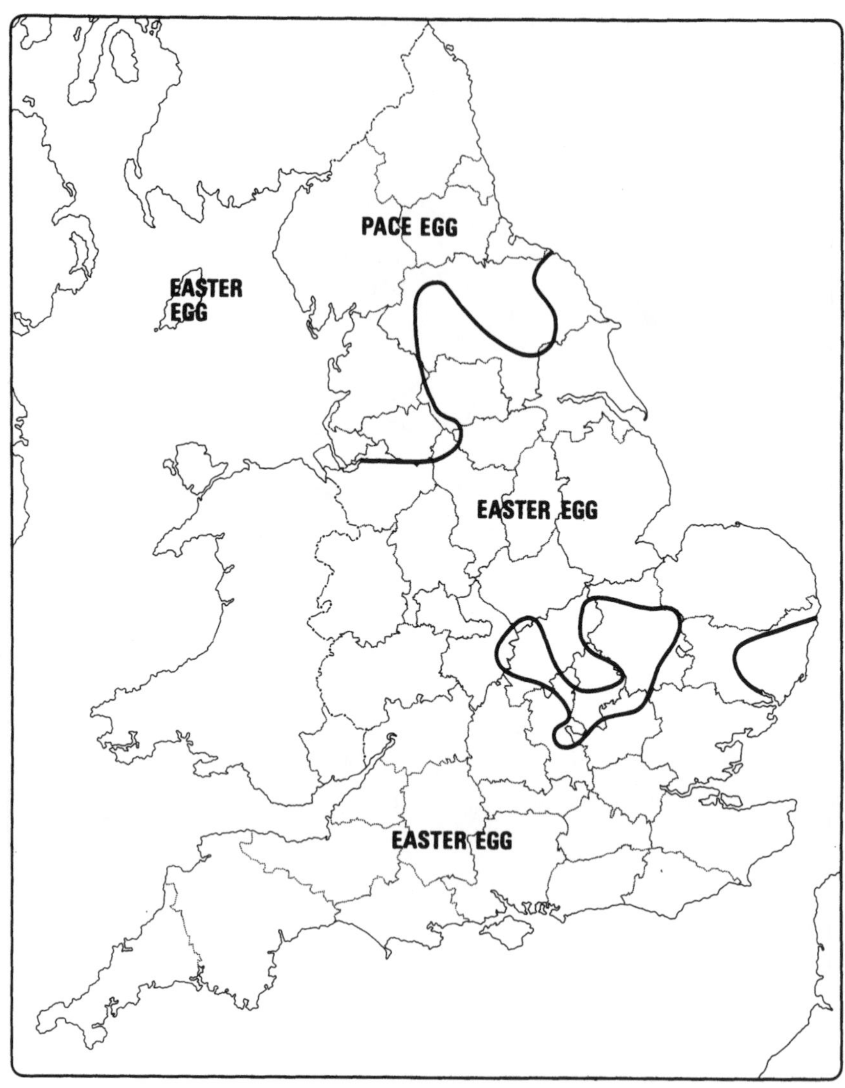

Map 49: EASTER EGG

In some parts of the East Midlands, east Warwickshire and East Anglia some speakers said that Easter eggs were not known traditionally.

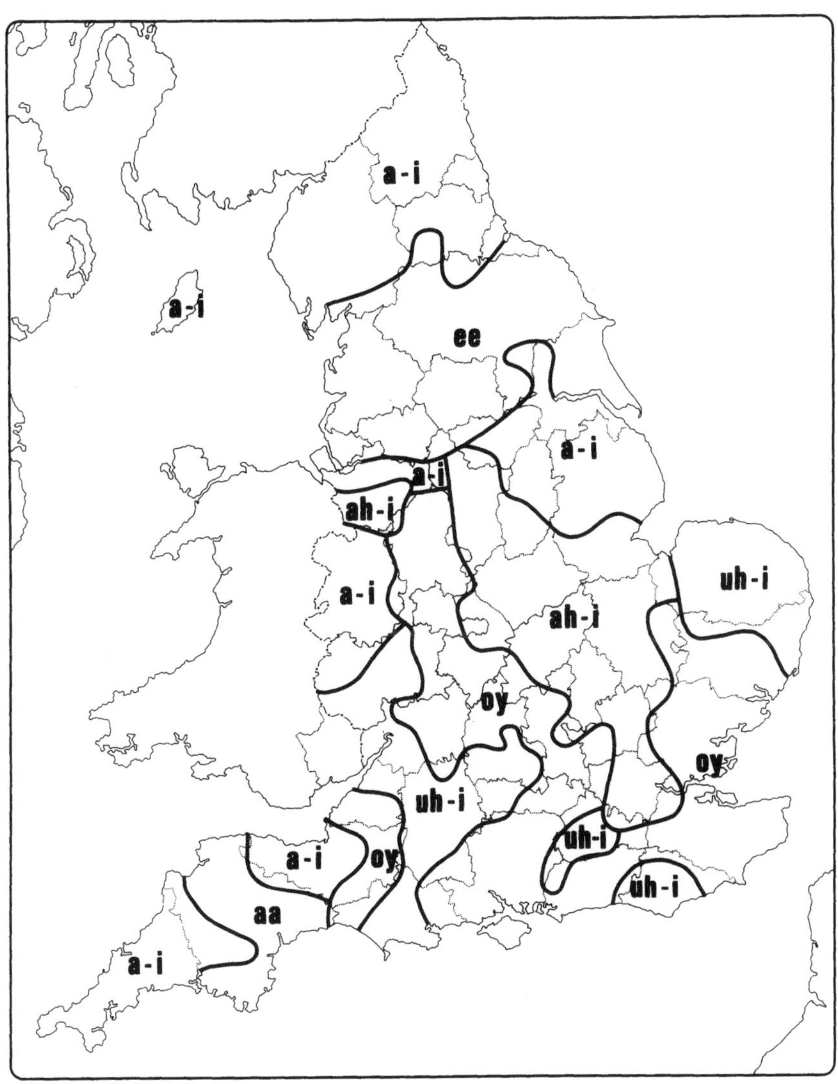

Map 50: EYE (human)

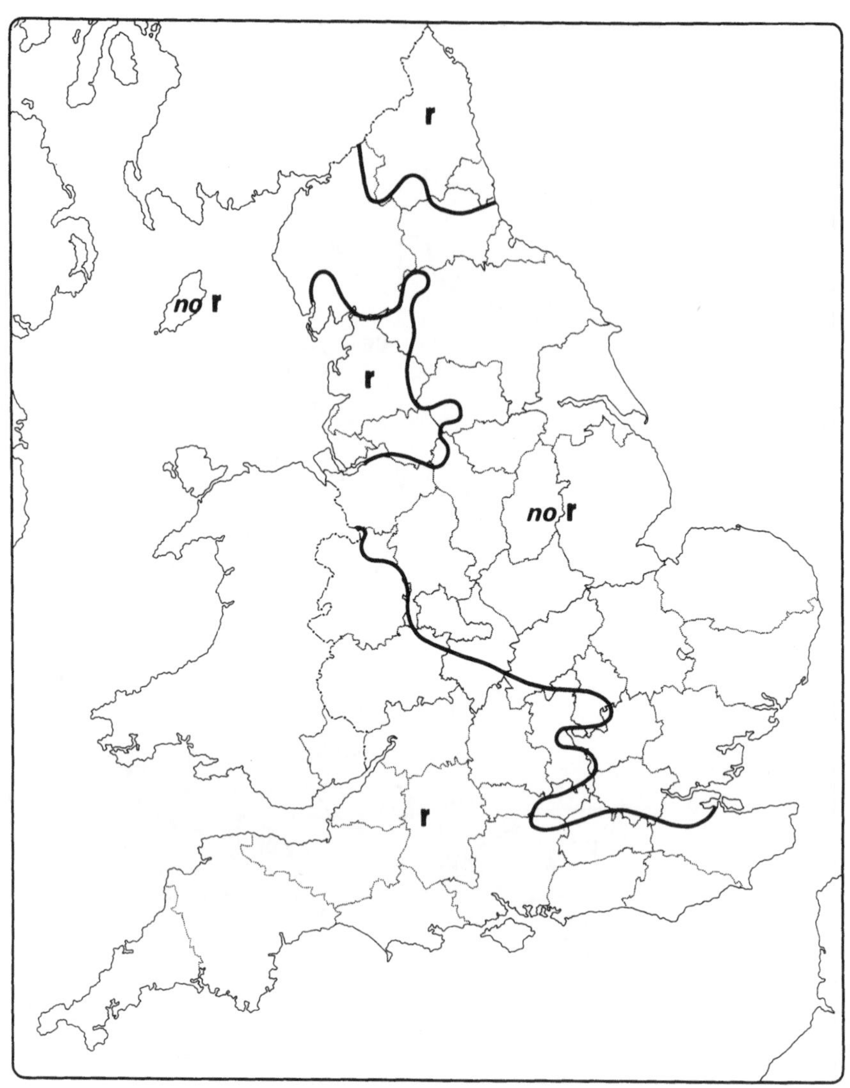

Map 51: FA<u>R</u>MER
For varieties of *r* see notes to Map 11.

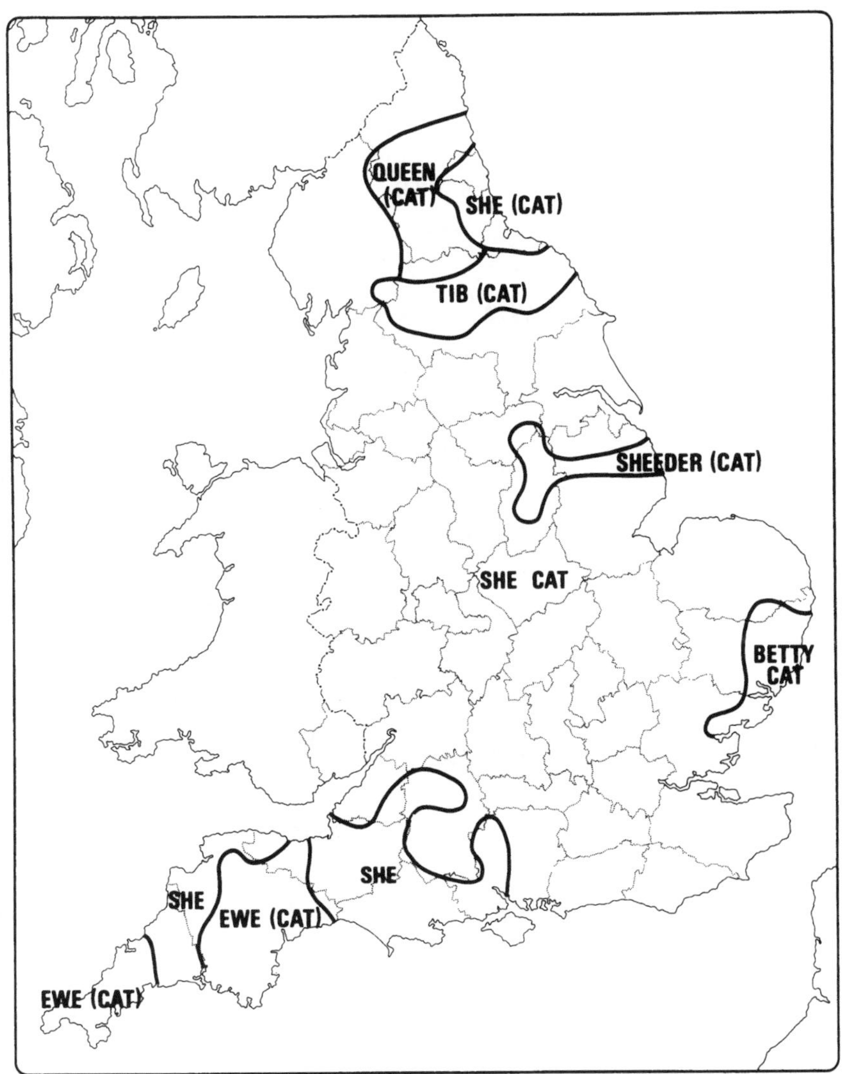

Map 52: FEMALE CAT

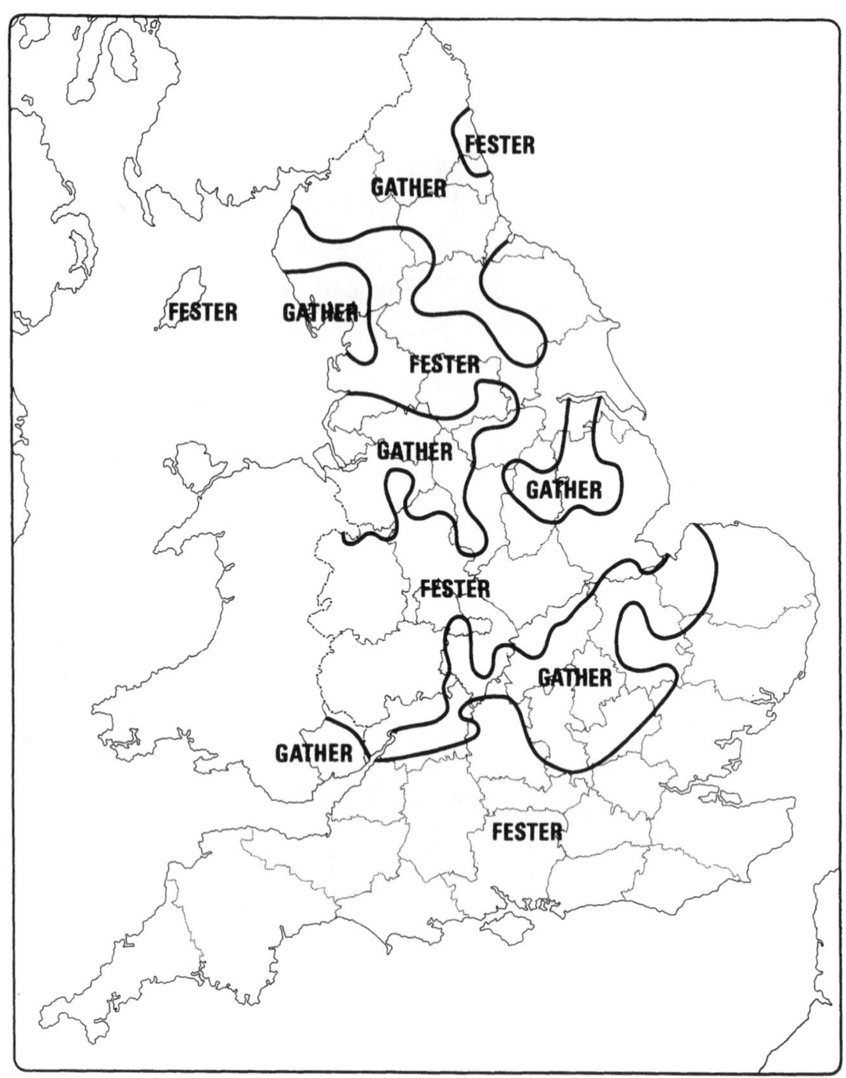

Map 53: FESTER
gather up and *fester up* were occasionally found.

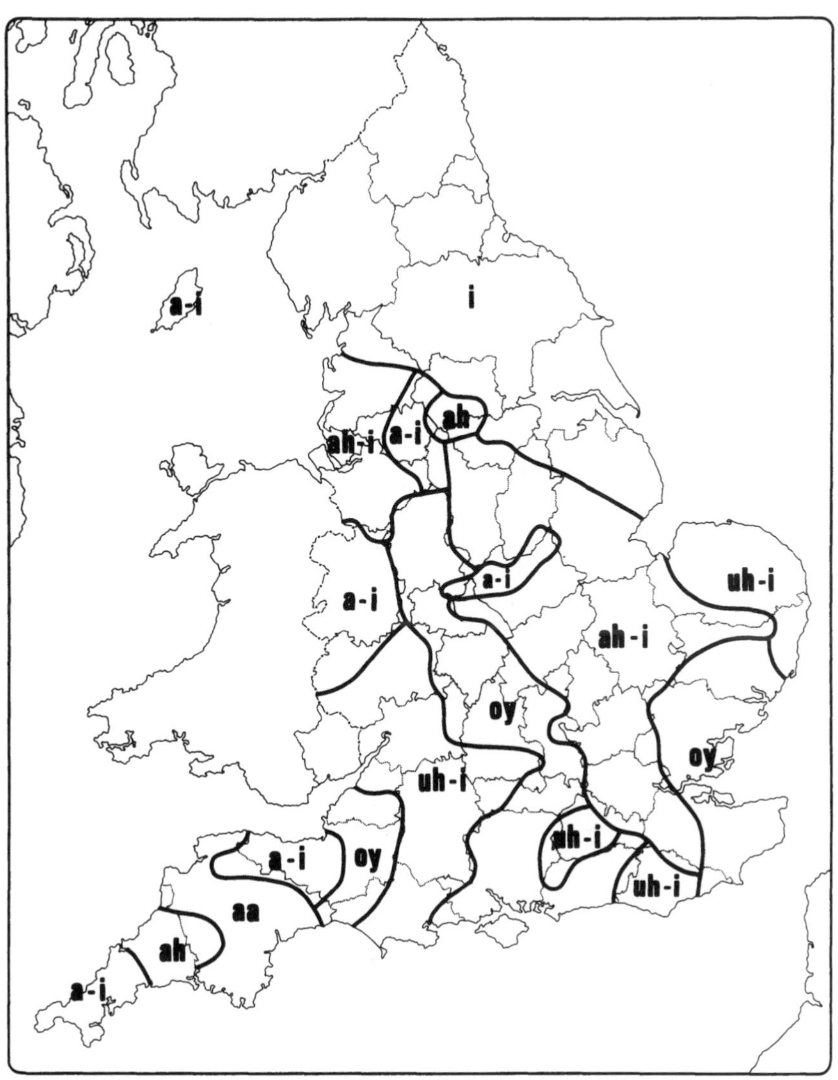

Map 54: FIND

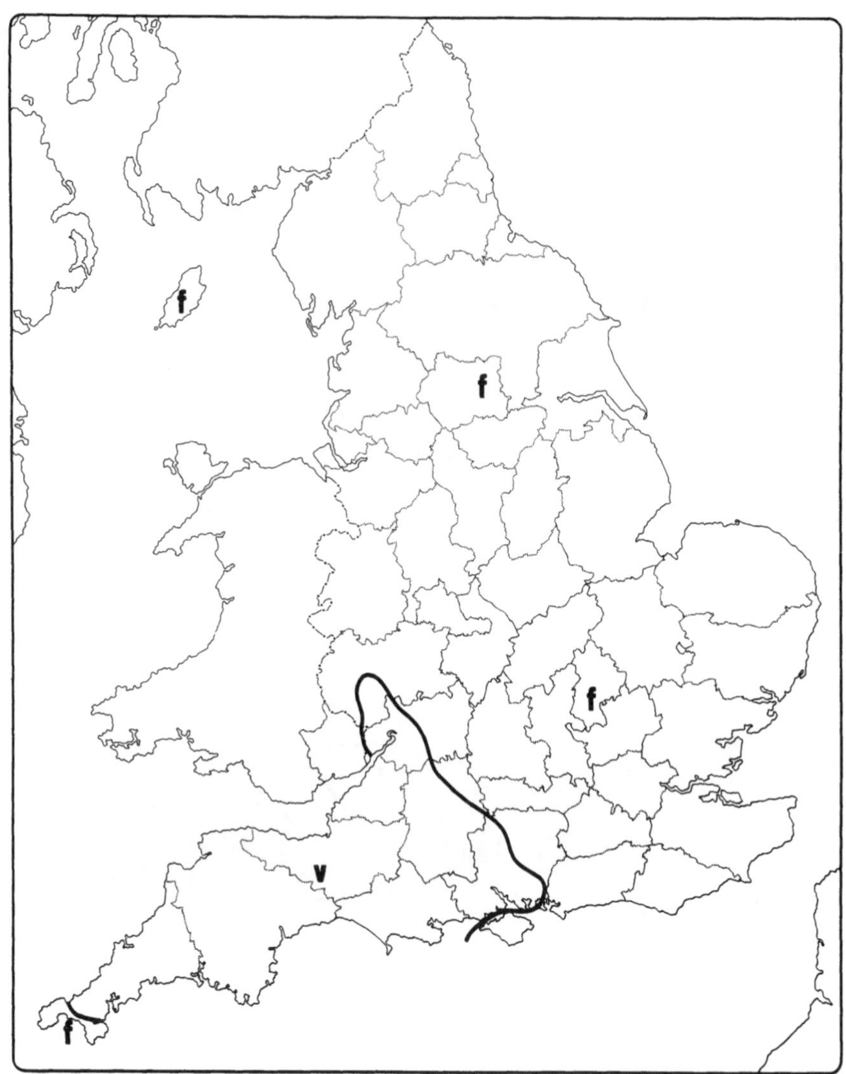

Map 55: FINGER

The 'voicing' of initial consonants is a well known and typical feature of West Country speech. Here **f** becomes **v**. For other examples see Map 60 (**fl** to **vl**); Map 61 (**f** to **v**); Map 64 (**fr** to **vr**); Map 141 (**s** to **z**); Map 156 (**sh** to **zh**); Map 159 (**sw** to **zw**); Map 164 (**thr** to **dr**) and Map 167 (**th** to **dh**).

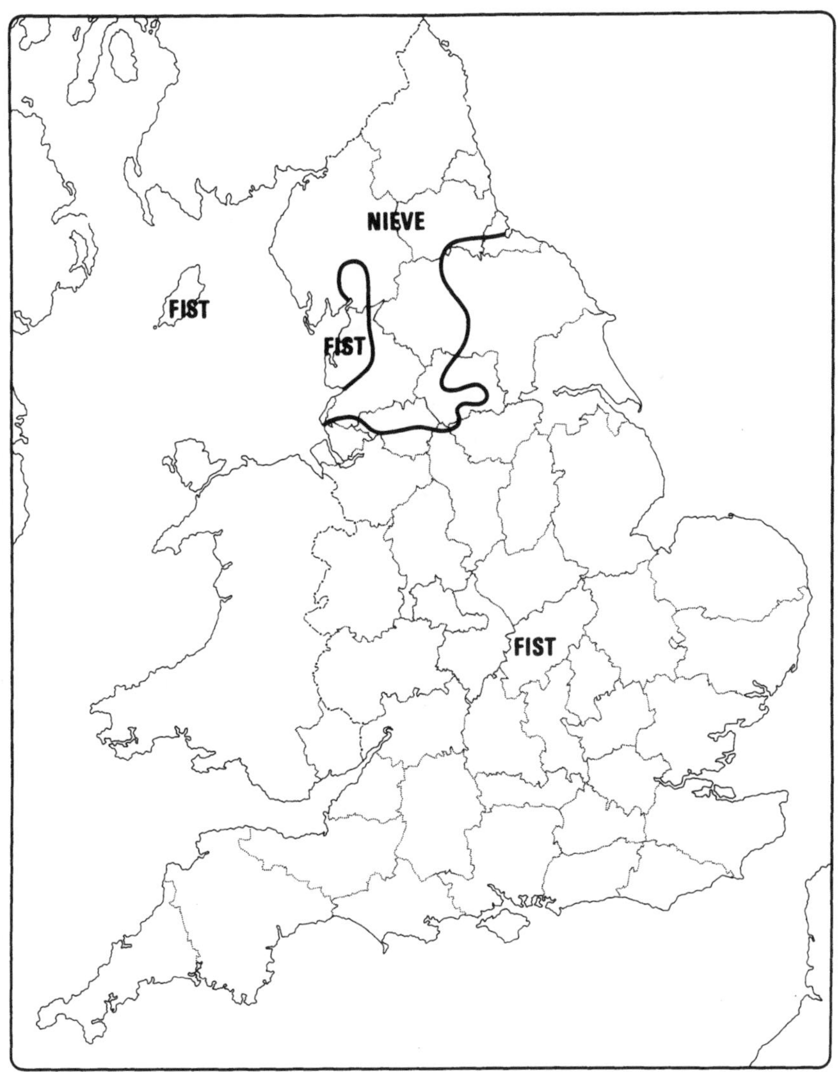

Map 56: FIST
The Old Norse **NIEVE** is yielding to the Standard **FIST** from Old English.

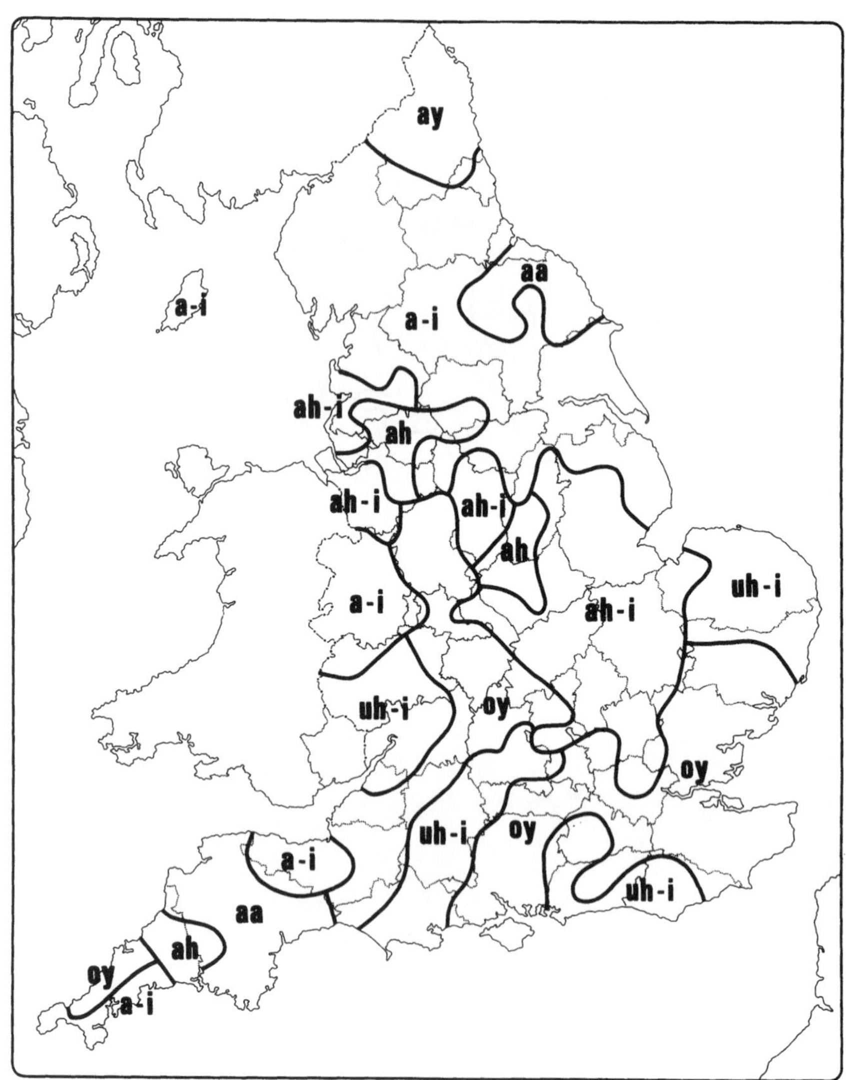
ay
aa
a-i
a-i
ah-i
ah
ah-i
ah-i
ah
uh-i
a-i
ah-i
uh-i
oy
oy
uh-i
oy
a-i
uh-i
aa
ah
oy
a-i

Map 57: FIVE

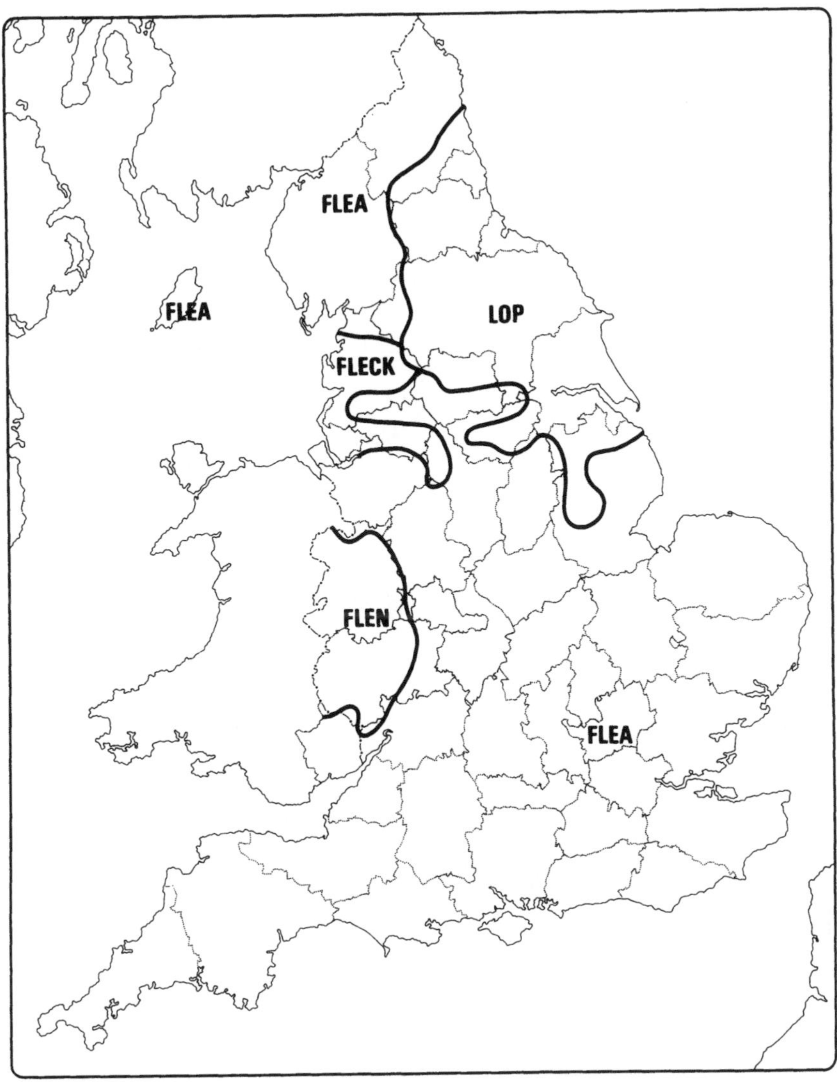

Map 58: FLEA

FLEA (occasionally *flef* in Lancashire and Cheshire) is an Old English word while **LOP** is from Old Norse and is shown to be dominant in much of the area settled by the Danes.

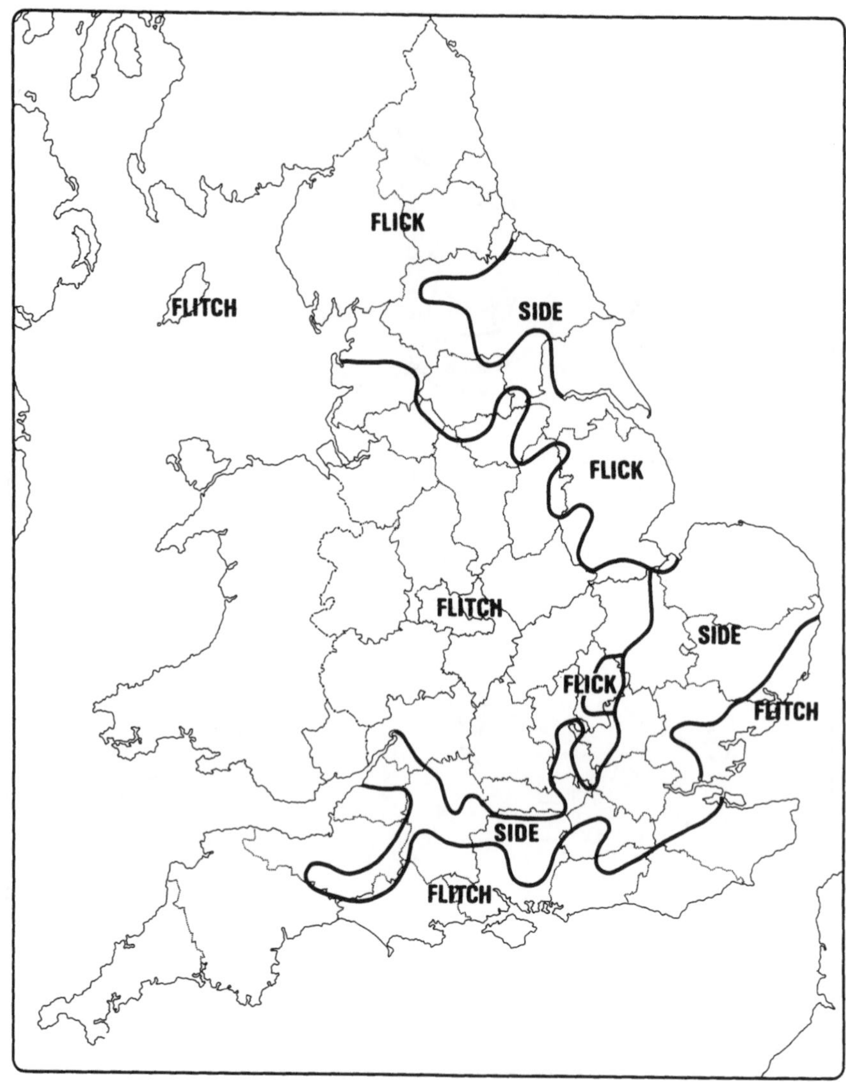

Map 59: FLITCH (of bacon)

FLICK represents the Old Norse form, still very common in areas of the old Danelaw, while **FLITCH** derives from Old English. **SIDE** often has *of bacon* added to it, especially in the South West. Compare Map 22 for the alternation of the final consonants in **FLICK** and **FLITCH**.

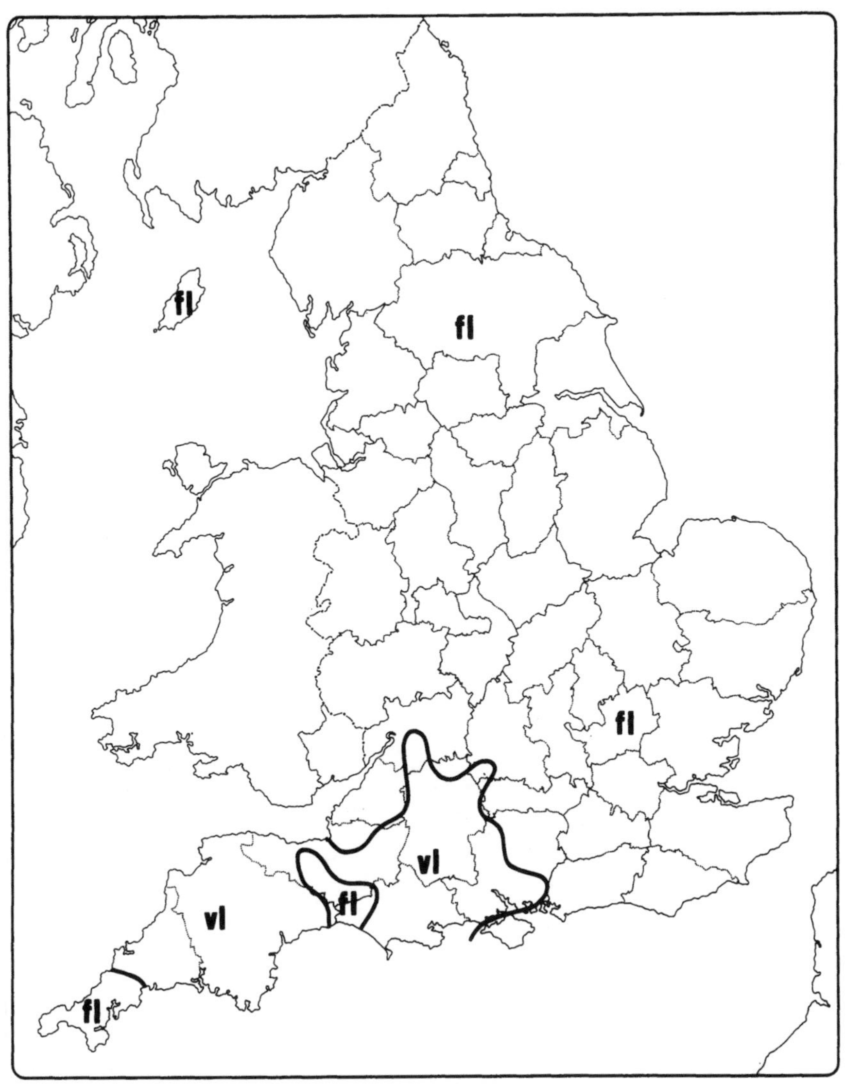

Map 60: FLOOR
For the 'voicing' of initial consonants see Map 55.

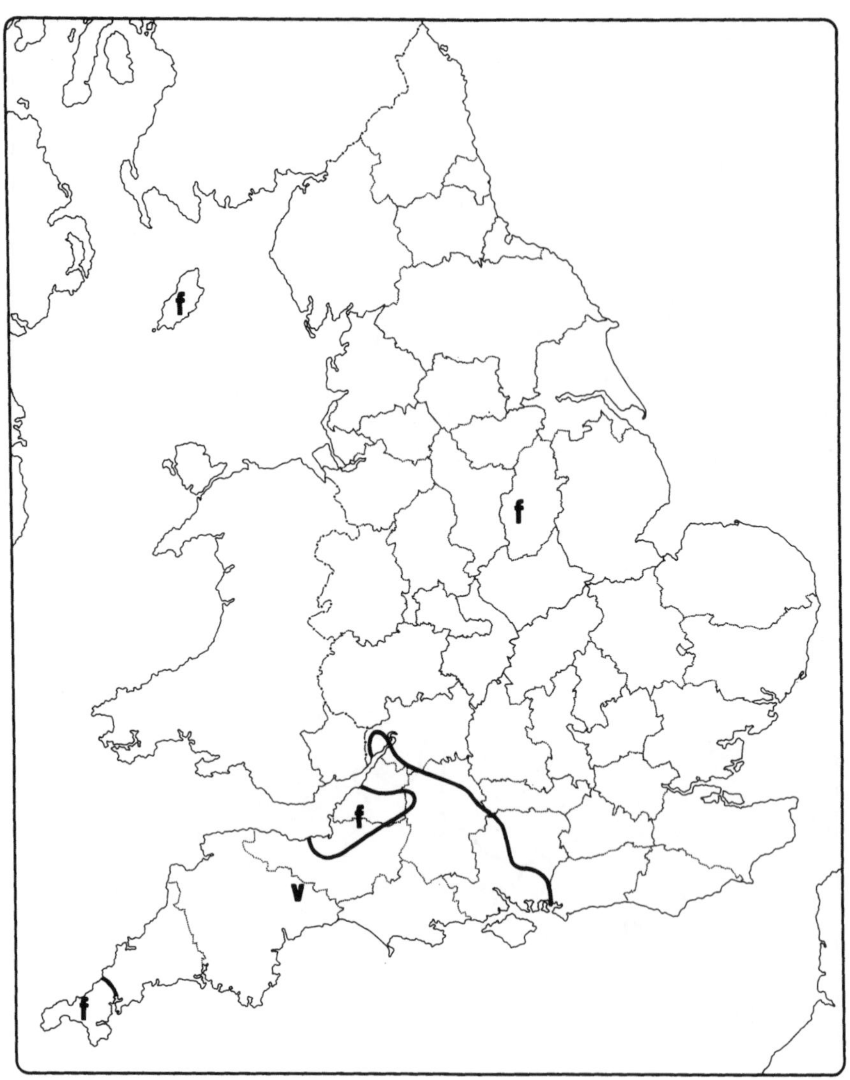

Map 61: FOG
For the 'voicing' of initial consonants see Map 55.

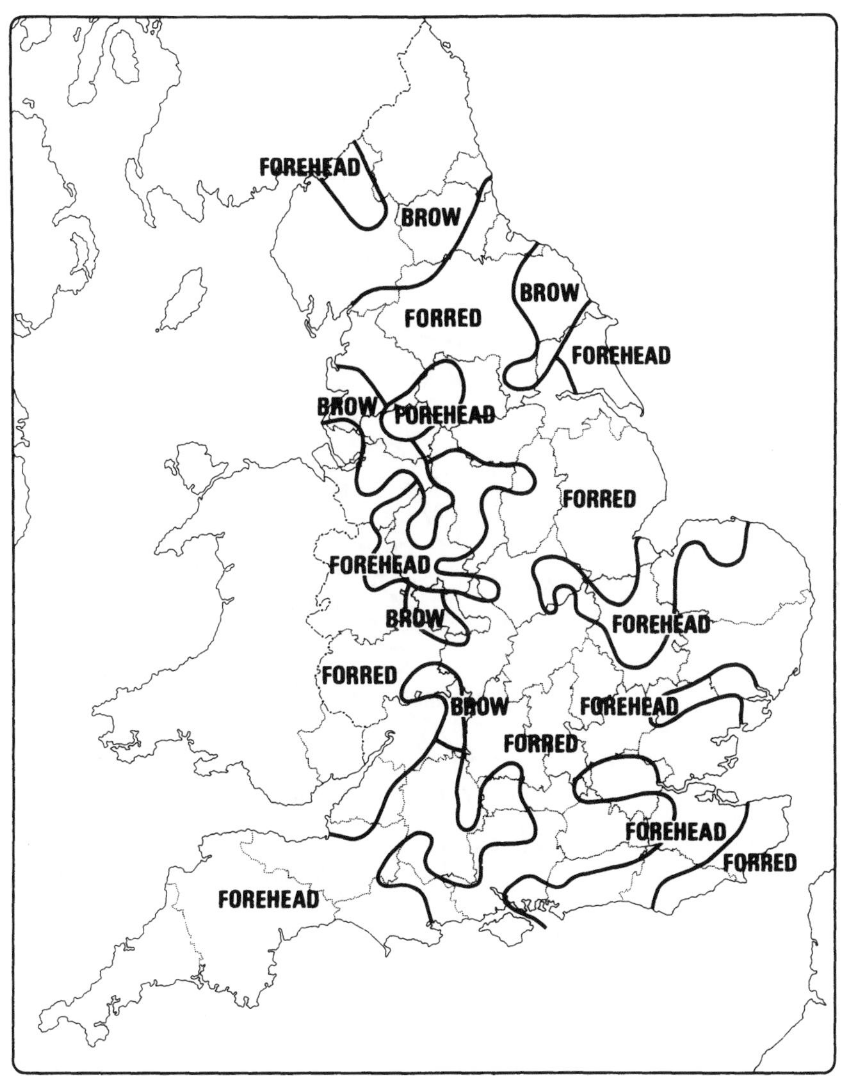

Map 62: FOREHEAD

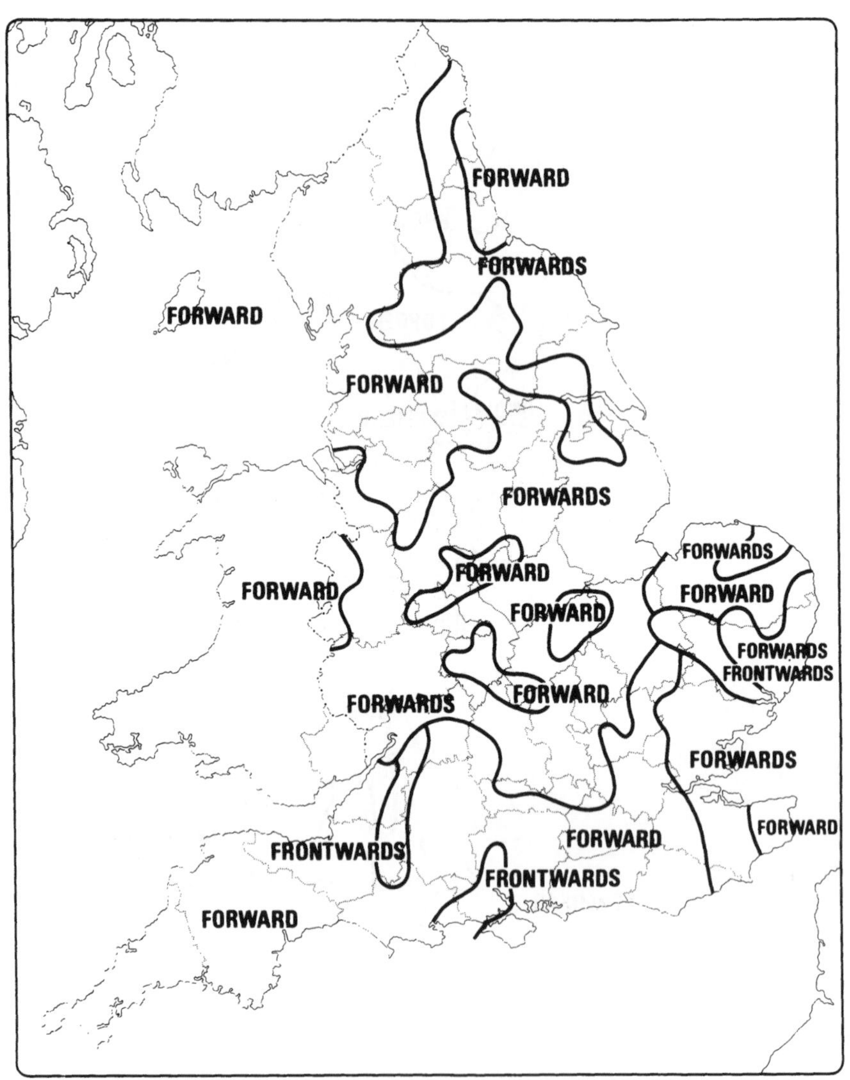

Map 63: FORWARDS

FORWARD(S) is generally pronounced *forrard(s)*.

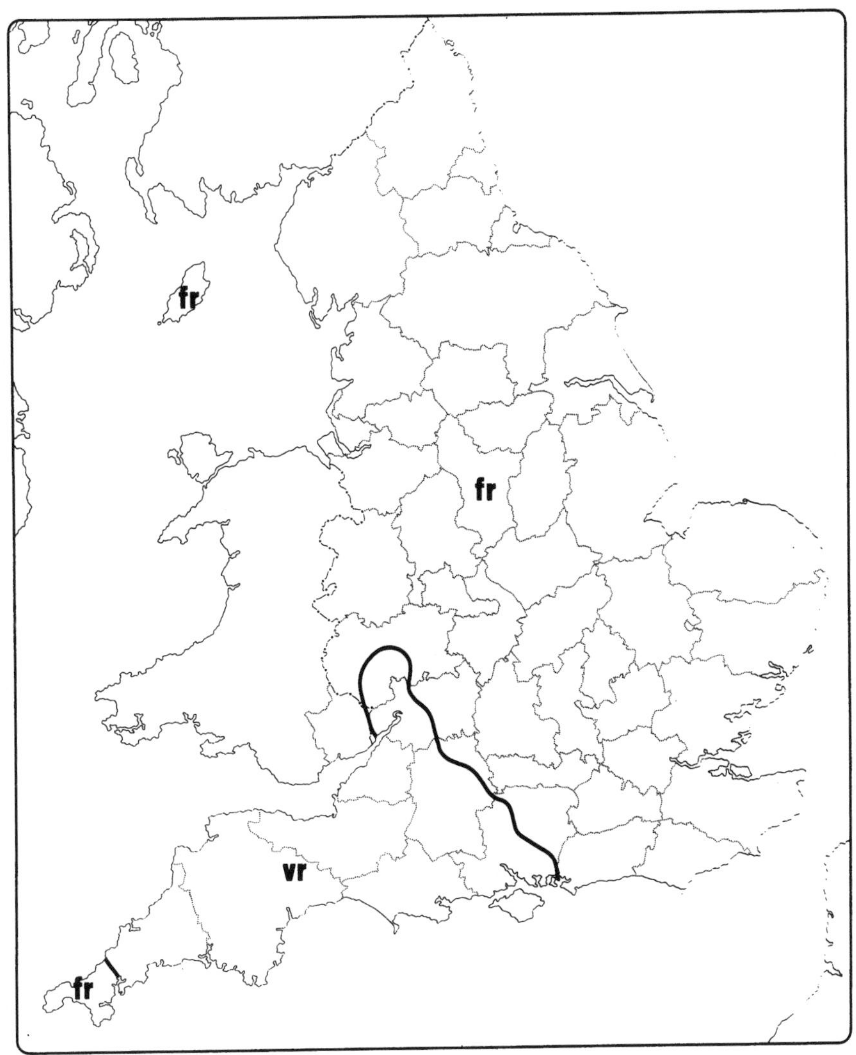

Map 64: FRIDAY
For the 'voicing' of initial consonants see Map 55.

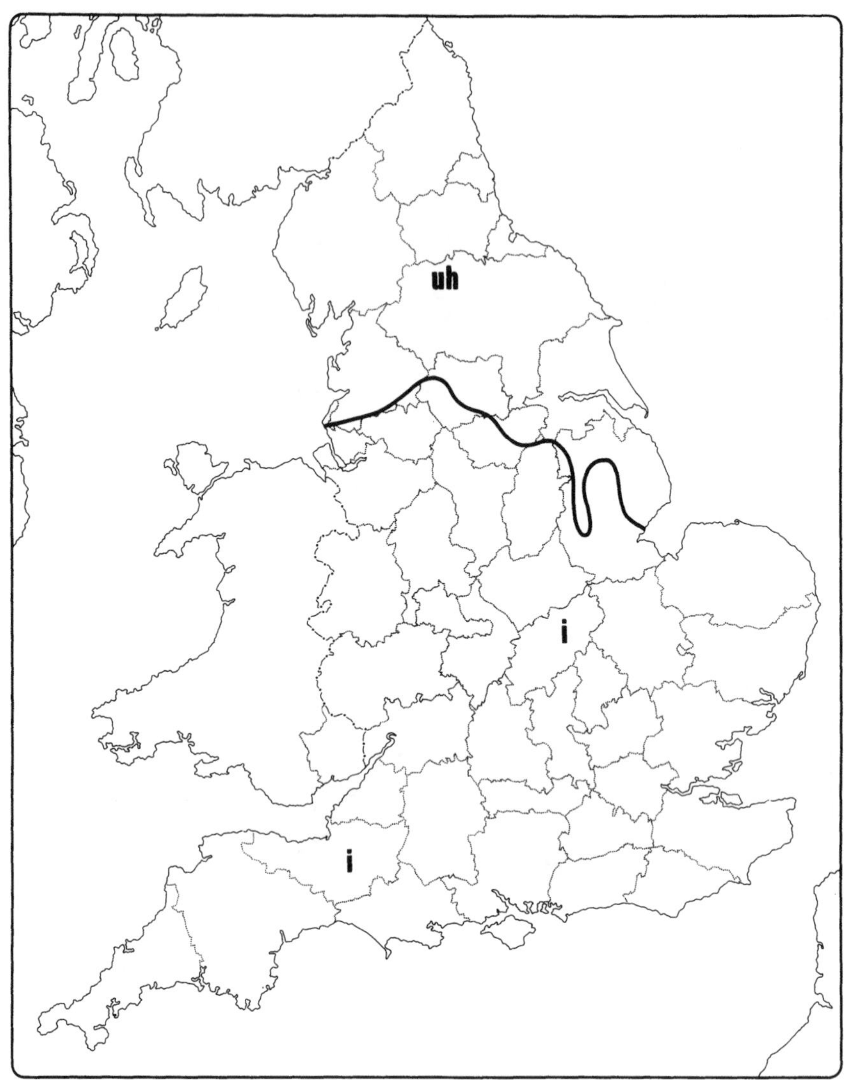

Map 65: FRID<u>AY</u>

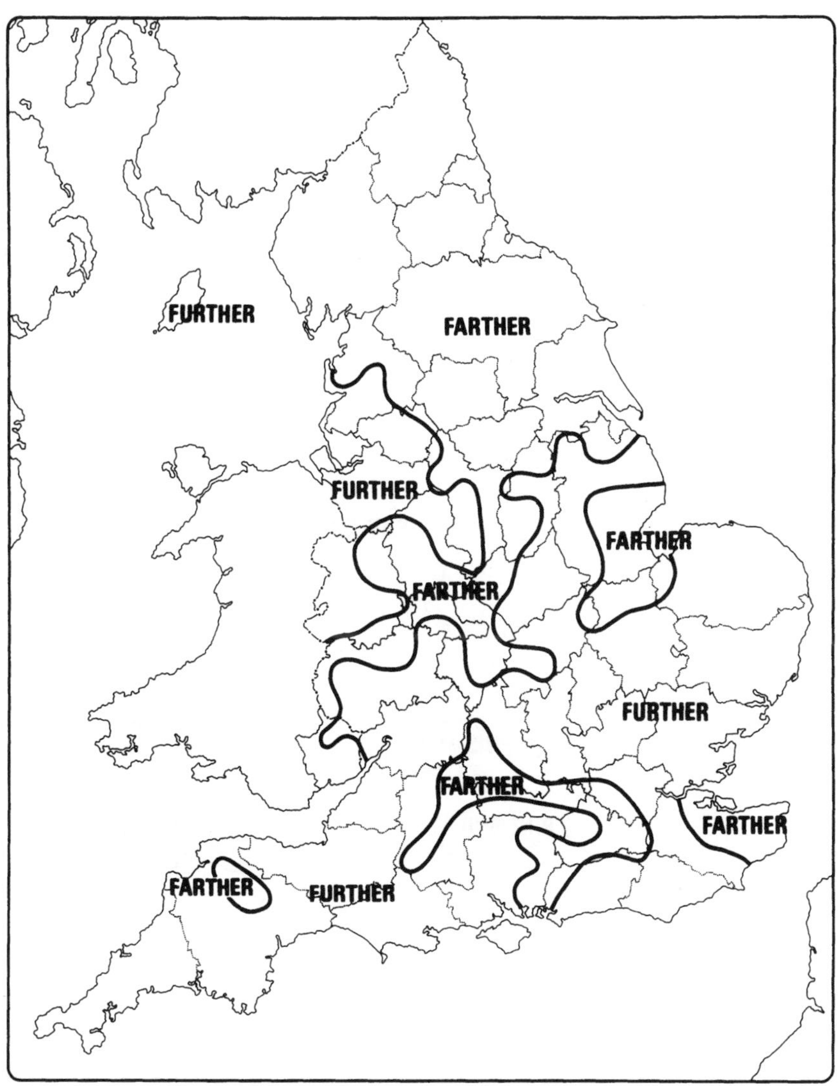

Map 66: FURTHER

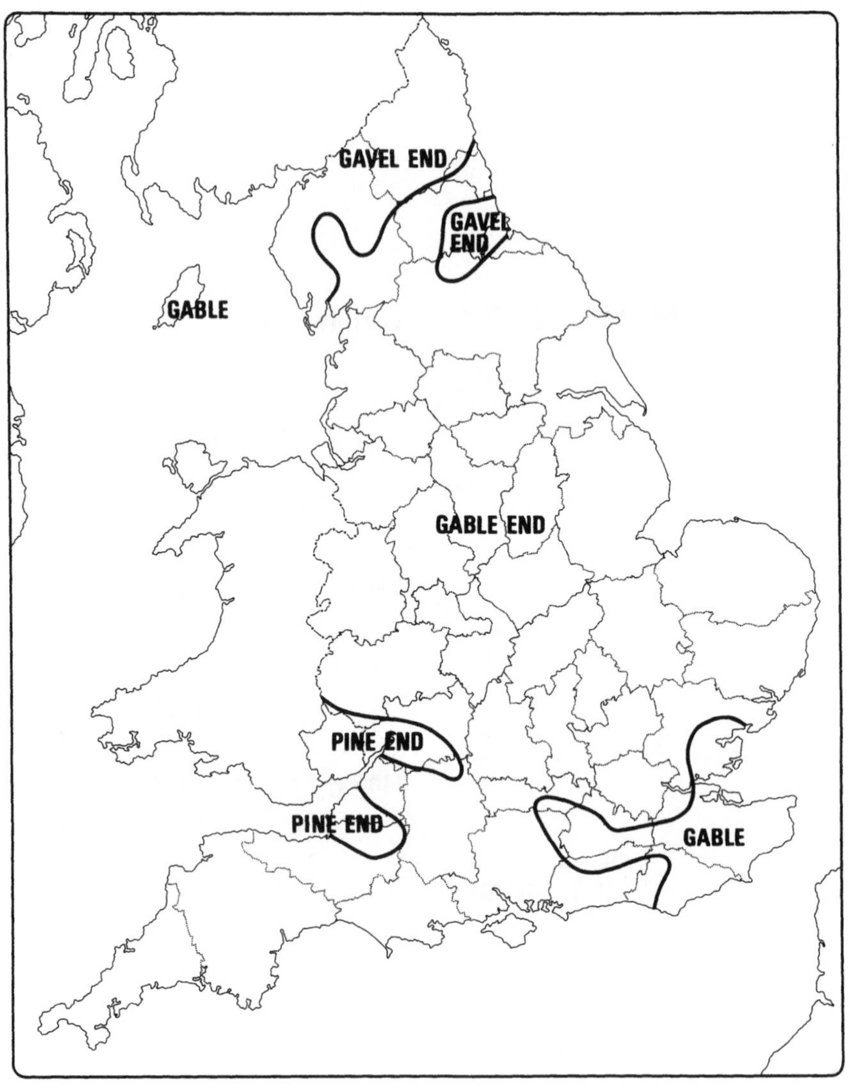

Map 67: GABLE END (of house)
GABLE and *house-end* are found scattered in various dialect areas where other terms predominate.

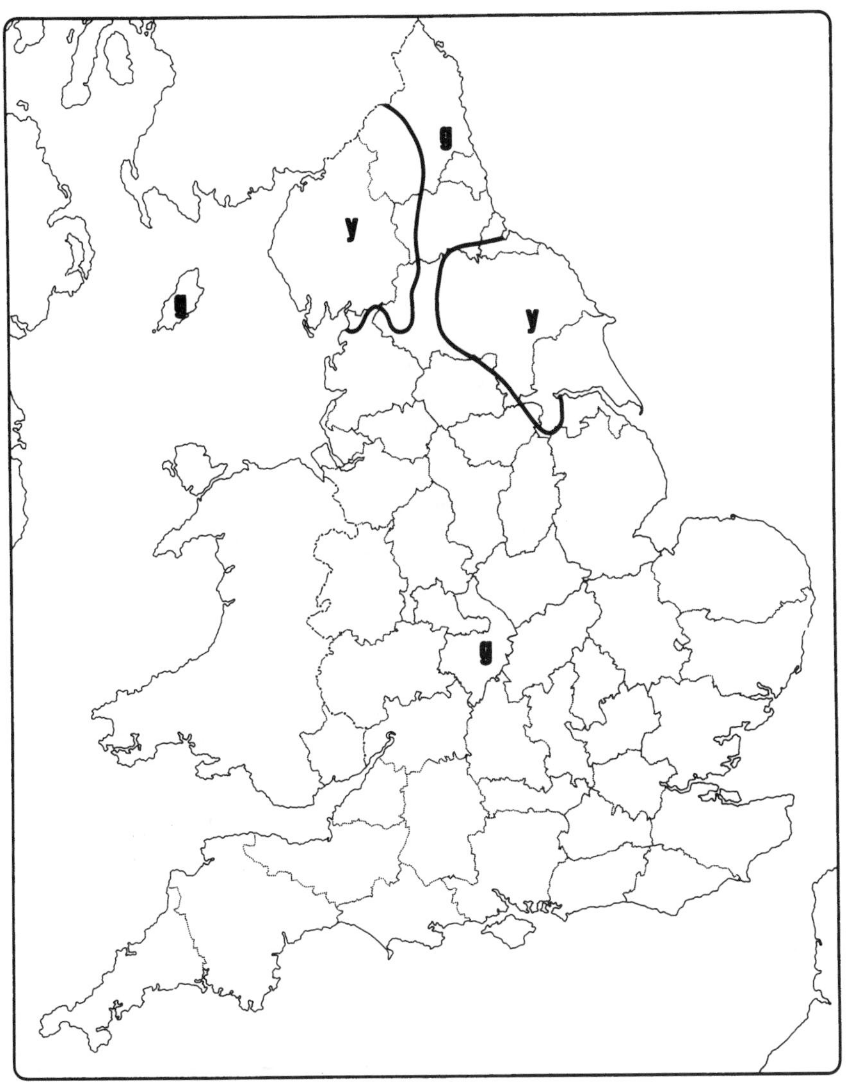

Map 68: GATE

g occurs in places in the **y** areas, notably in east Yorkshire, suggesting that the **y** forms are declining there.

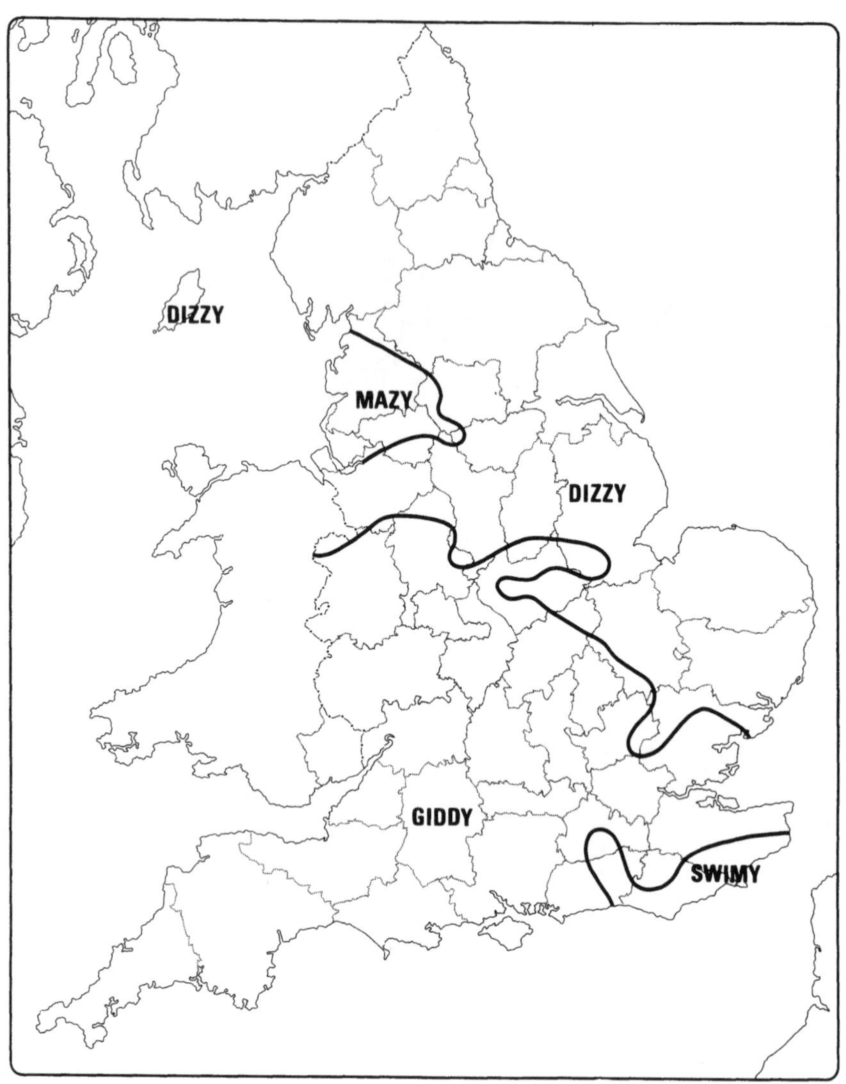

Map 69: GIDDY

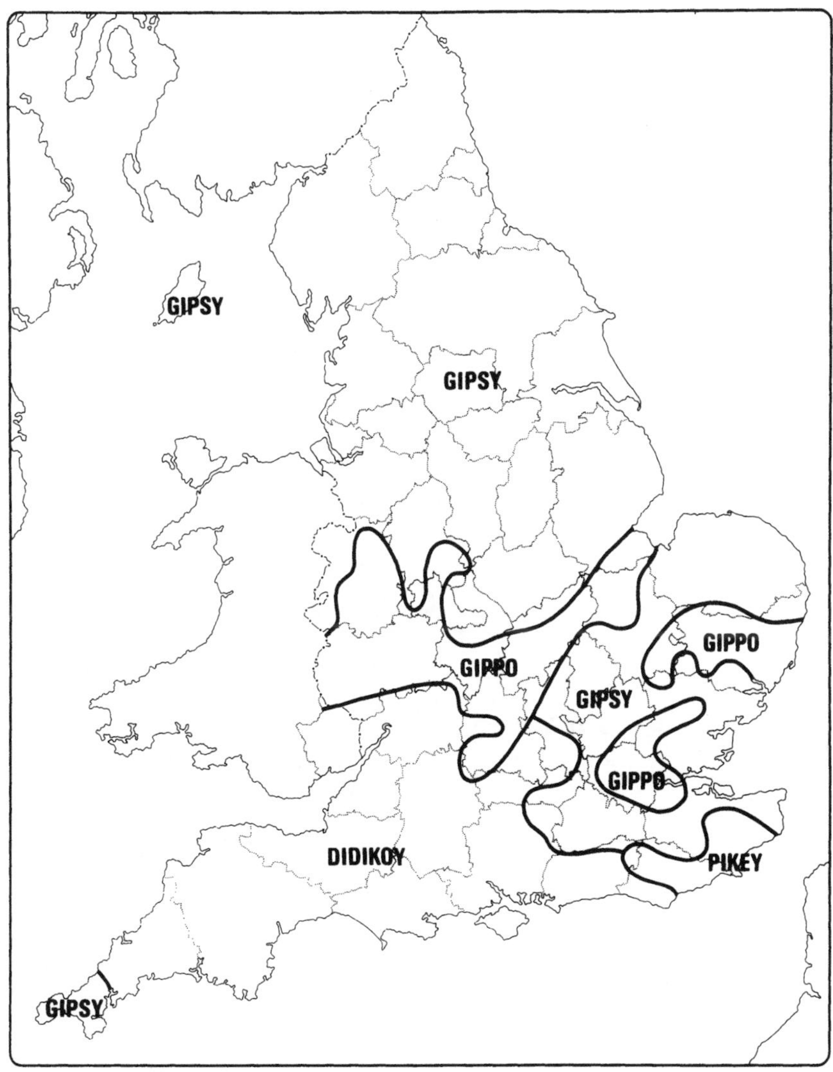

Map 70: GIPSY

DIDIKOY, **GIPSY** and **GIPPO** occur frequently in the South in those areas where they do not predominate.

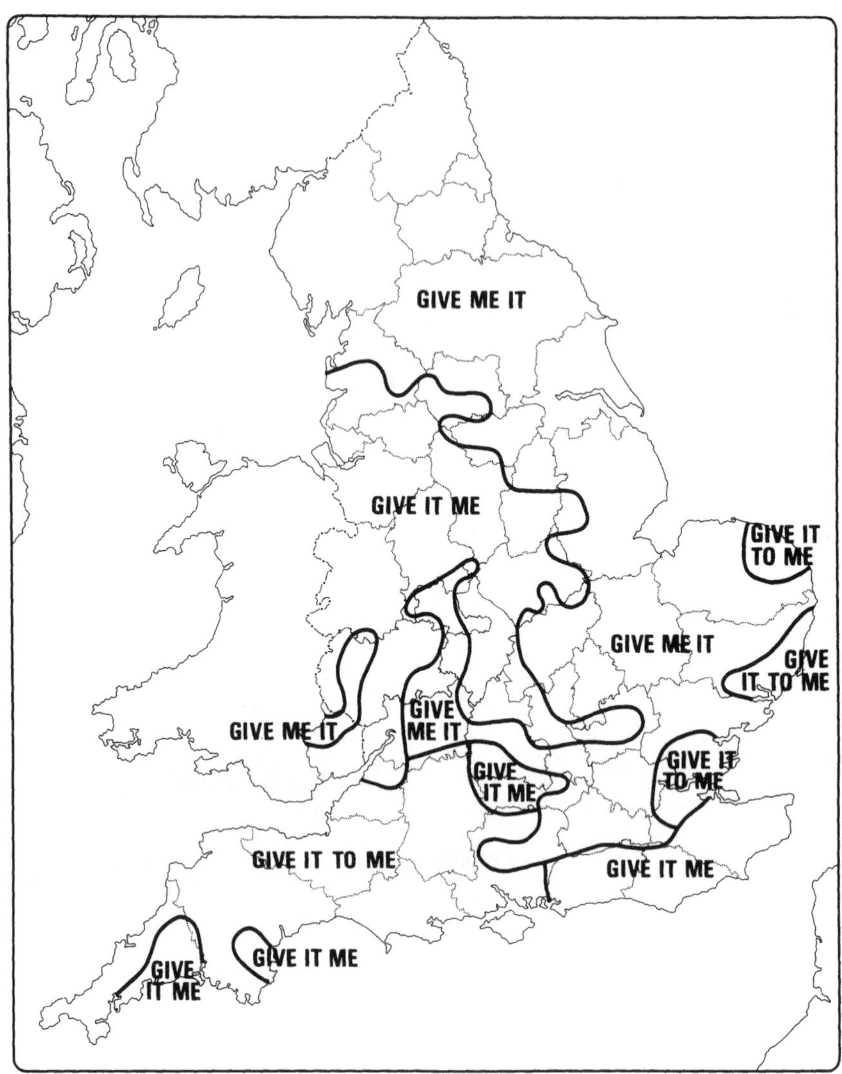

Map 71: GIVE IT ME
Regional dialects differ in word order as well as in pronunciation, vocabulary and grammar. This map is a good illustration of variation in word order and shows how a particular form may be found consistently across quite a wide area.

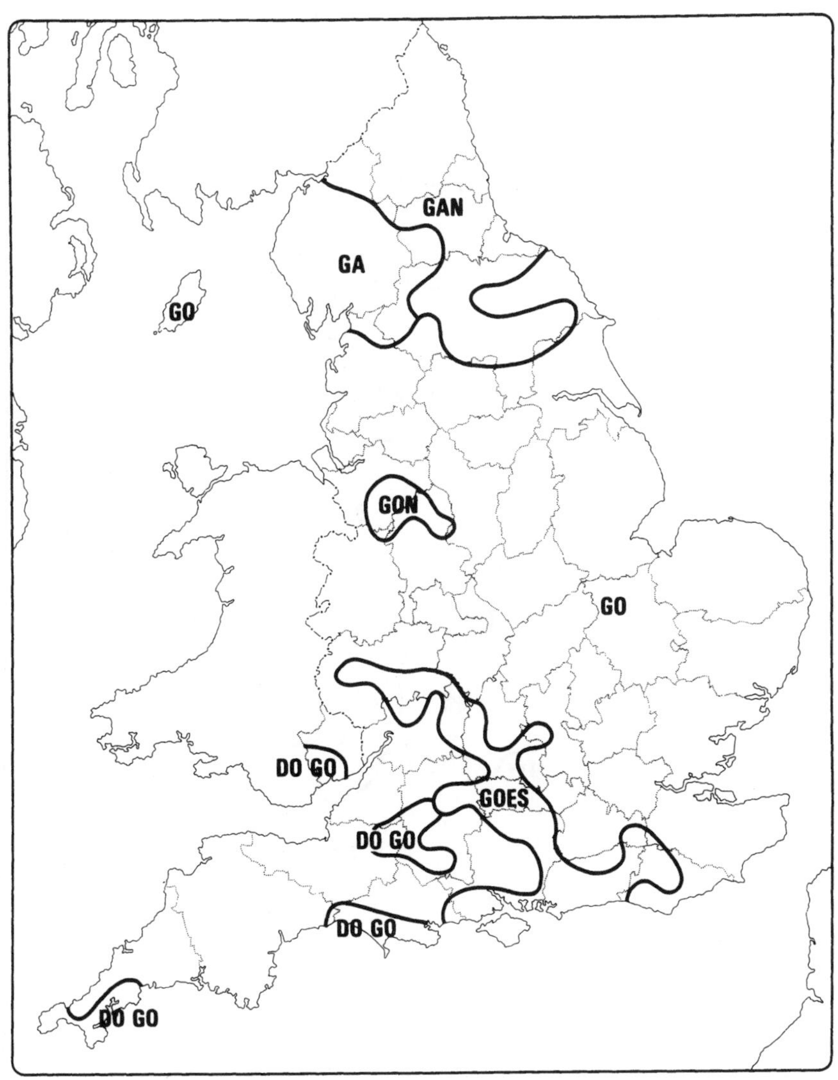

Map 72: GO (they . . .)

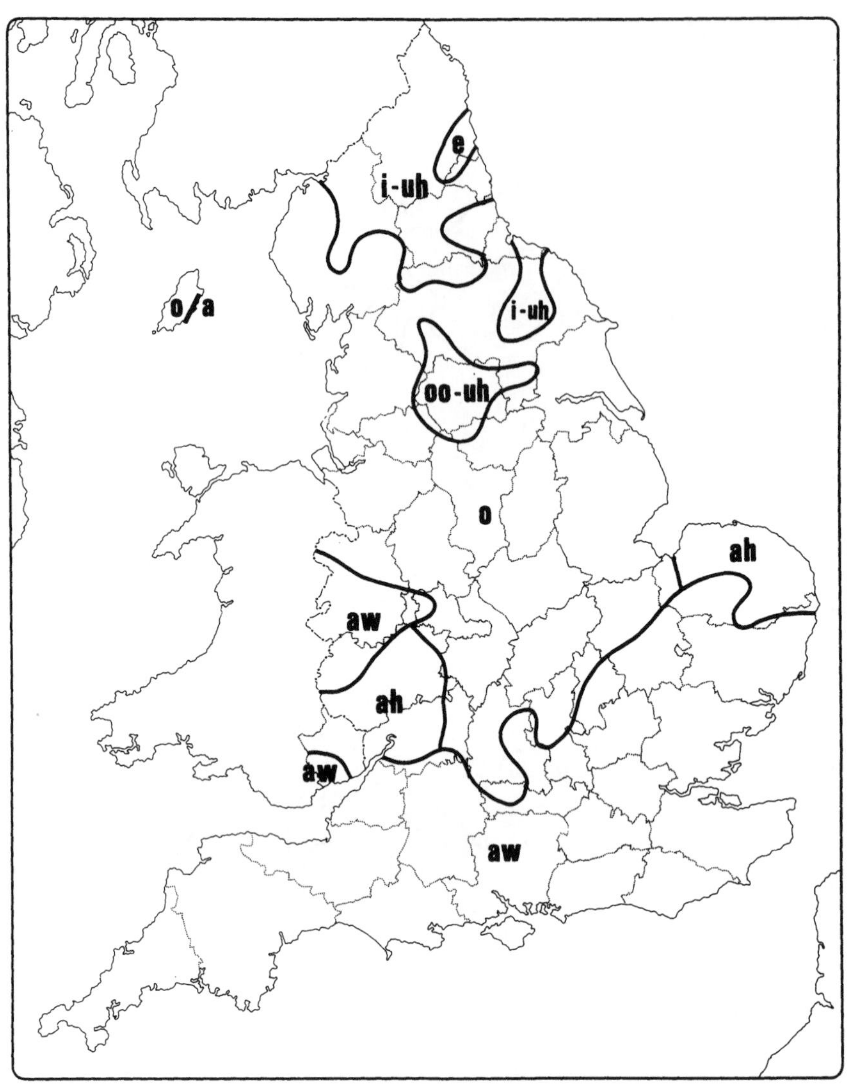

Map 73: G<u>O</u>NE

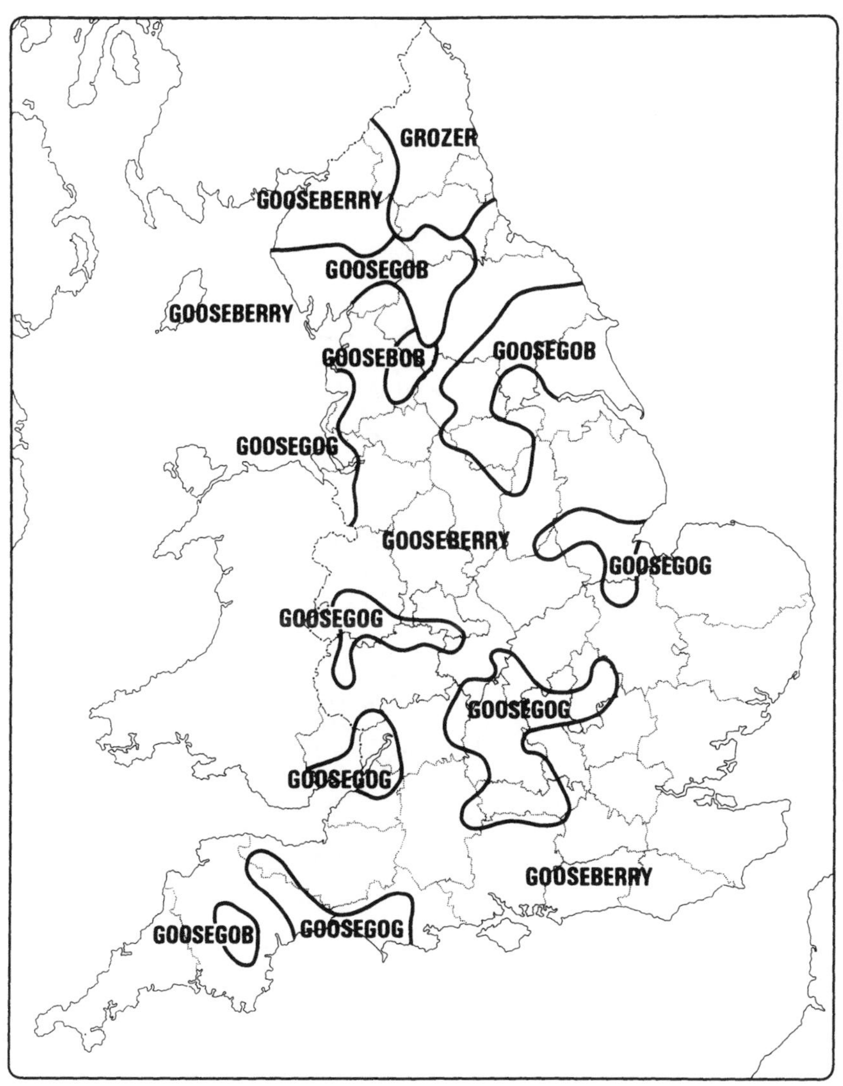

Map 74: GOOSEBERRY

GOOSEBERRY is a newer term in many of the dialects, while **GOOSEGOG** is nowadays often regarded as a children's word and is referred to as such by many dialect speakers, especially in East Anglia.

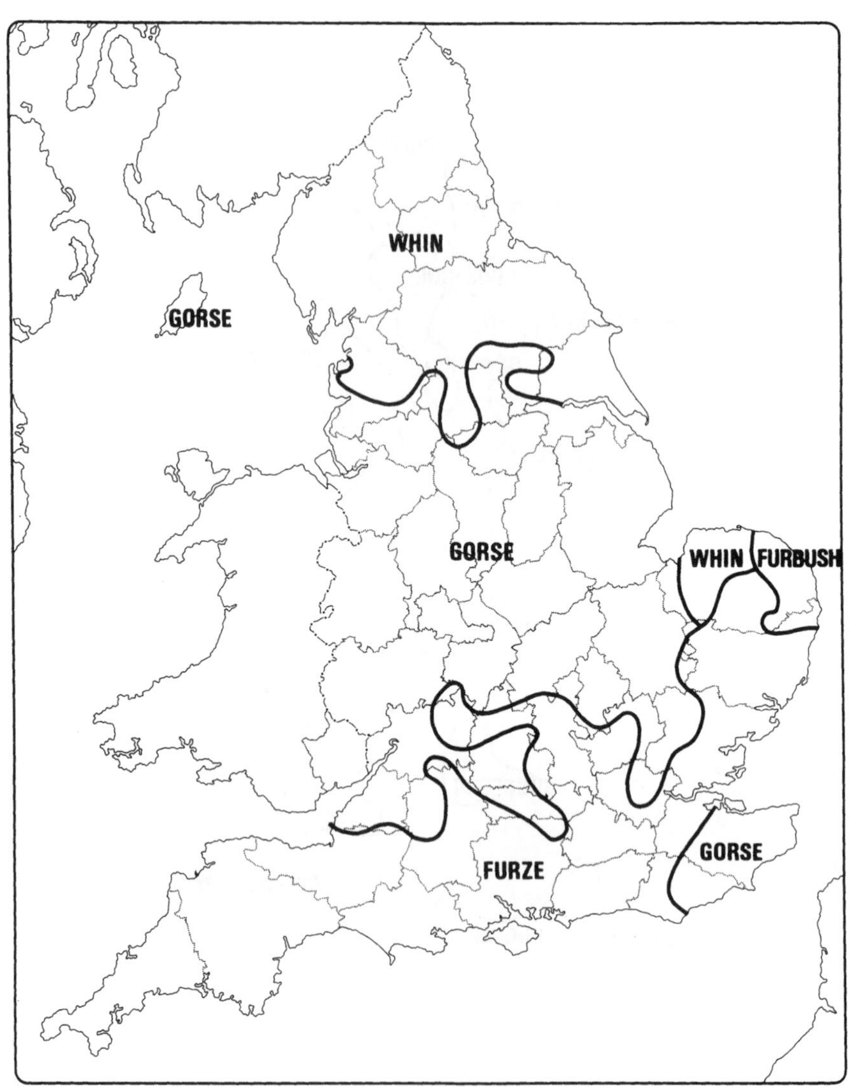

Map 75: GORSE

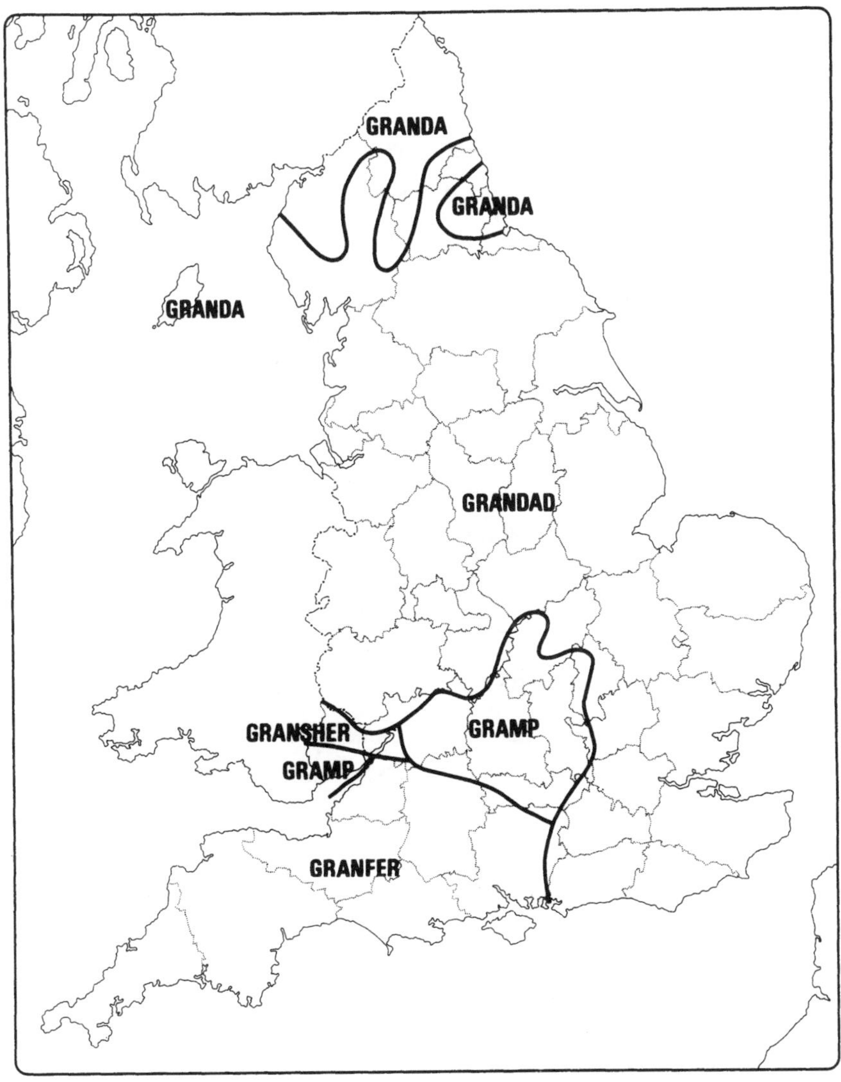

Map 76: GRANDAD
The basic forms mapped here include such variants as *gramfer* and *gramfy* (for **GRANFER**), *grampy* and *gramps* (for **GRAMP**) and *granshy* (for **GRANSHER**).

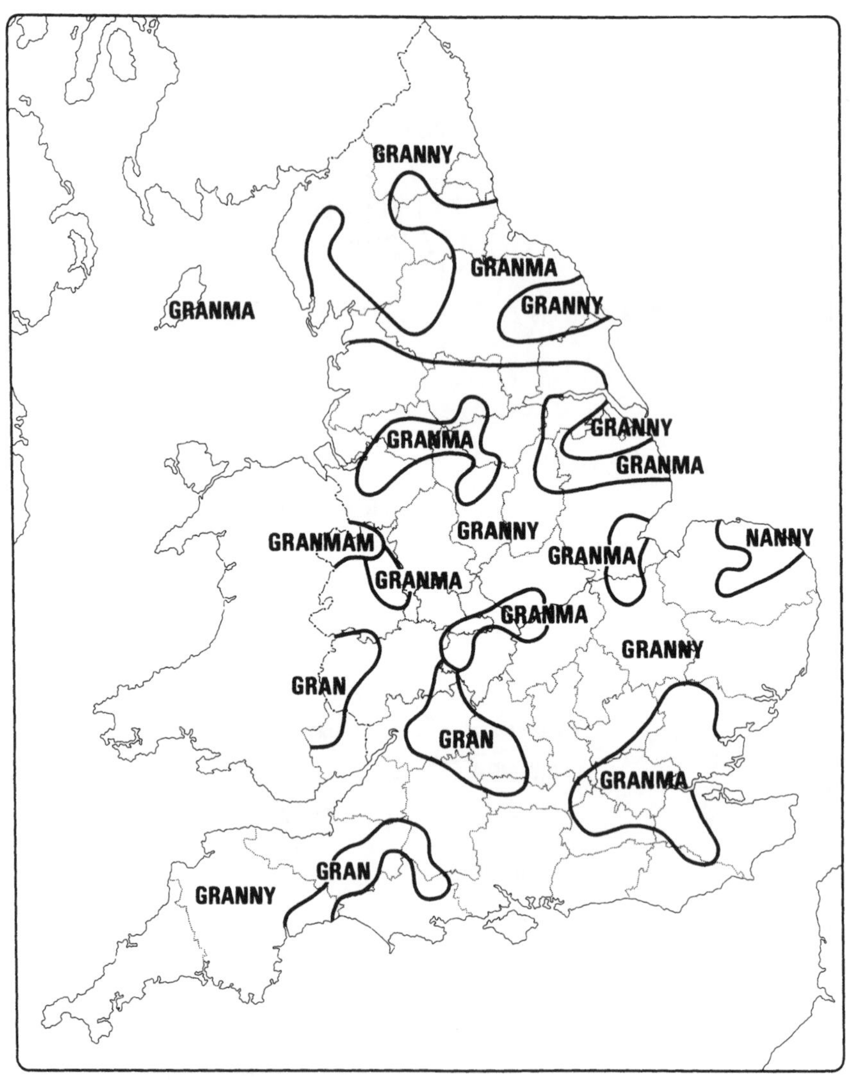

Map 77: GRANNY
Variations on the basic forms shown include *nan* and *nanna* (for NANNY).

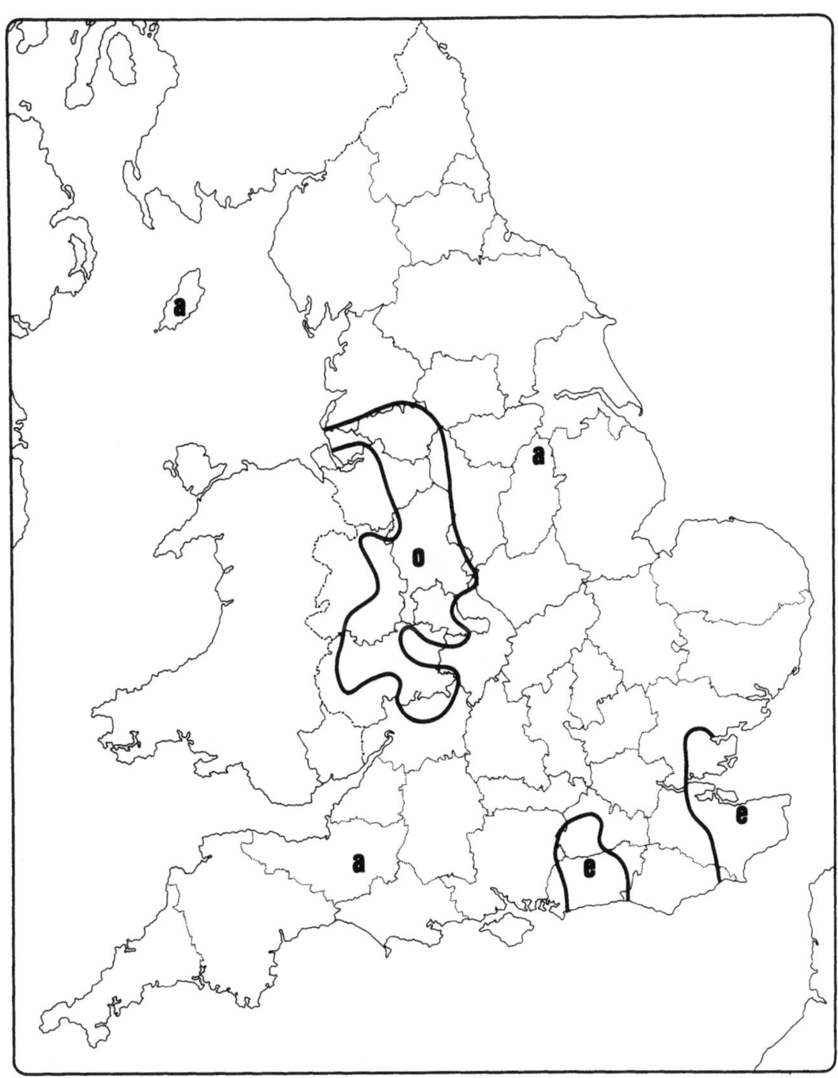

Map 78: H<u>A</u>ND

The **o** pronunciation is apparently contracting and **a** is found in the **o** area. **a** is sometimes pronounced rather like **e**, especially on the fringes of the **e** areas in the South East; in other southern areas it is sometimes long **aa**.

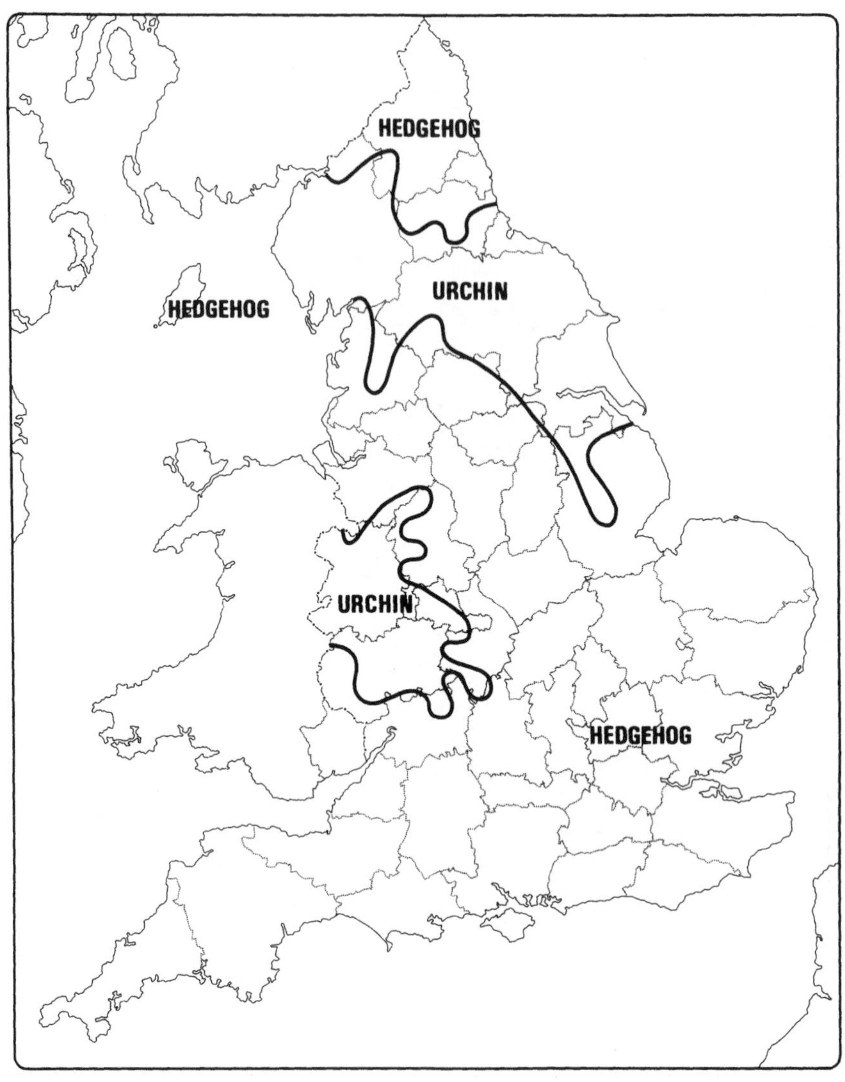

Map 79: HEDGEHOG

URCHIN, from Old French *herichon* (compare *sea-urchin*), is often preceded by such words as *prickly* in the North. **HEDGEHOG** is encroaching on the **URCHIN** area in the west Midlands.

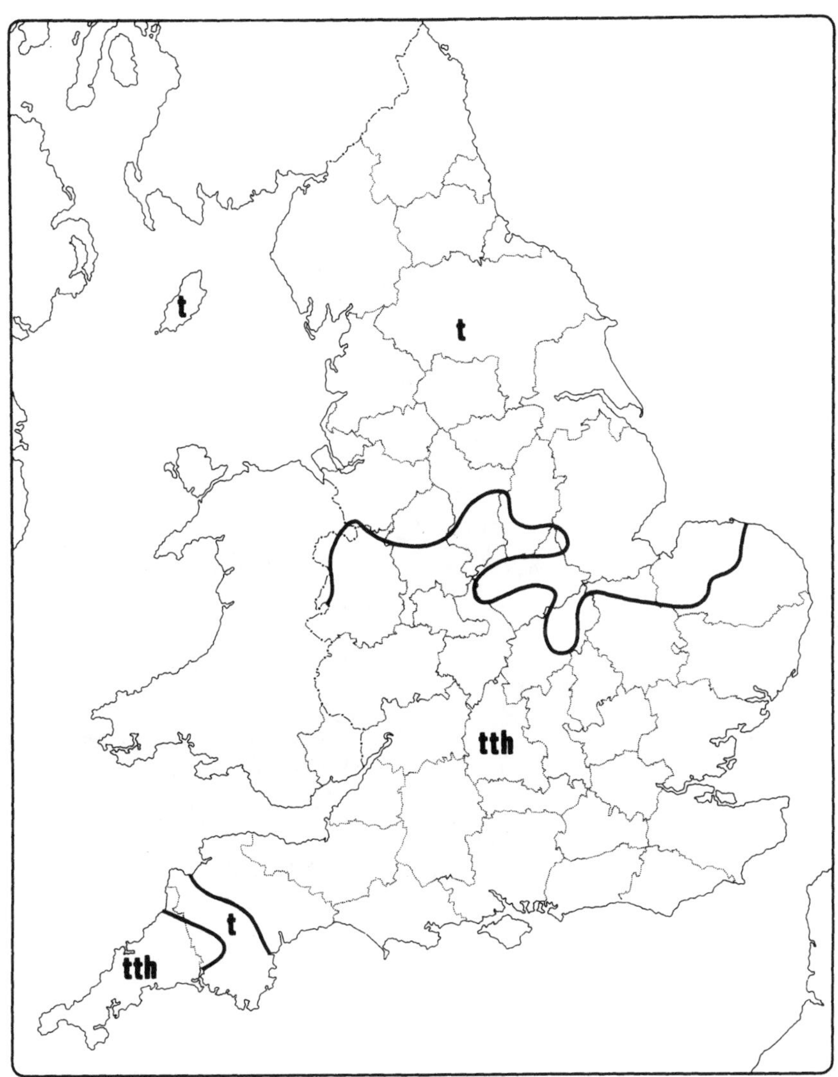

Map 80: HEIGHT

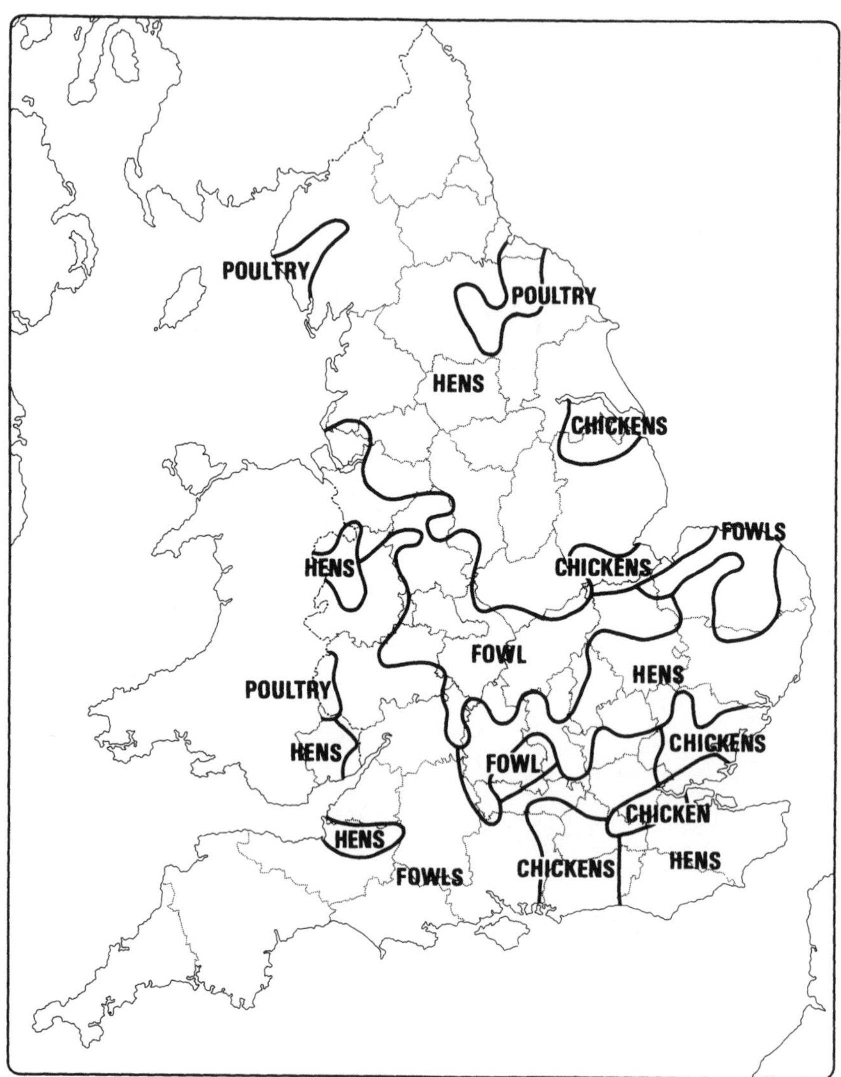

Map 81: HENS (people keep . . .)

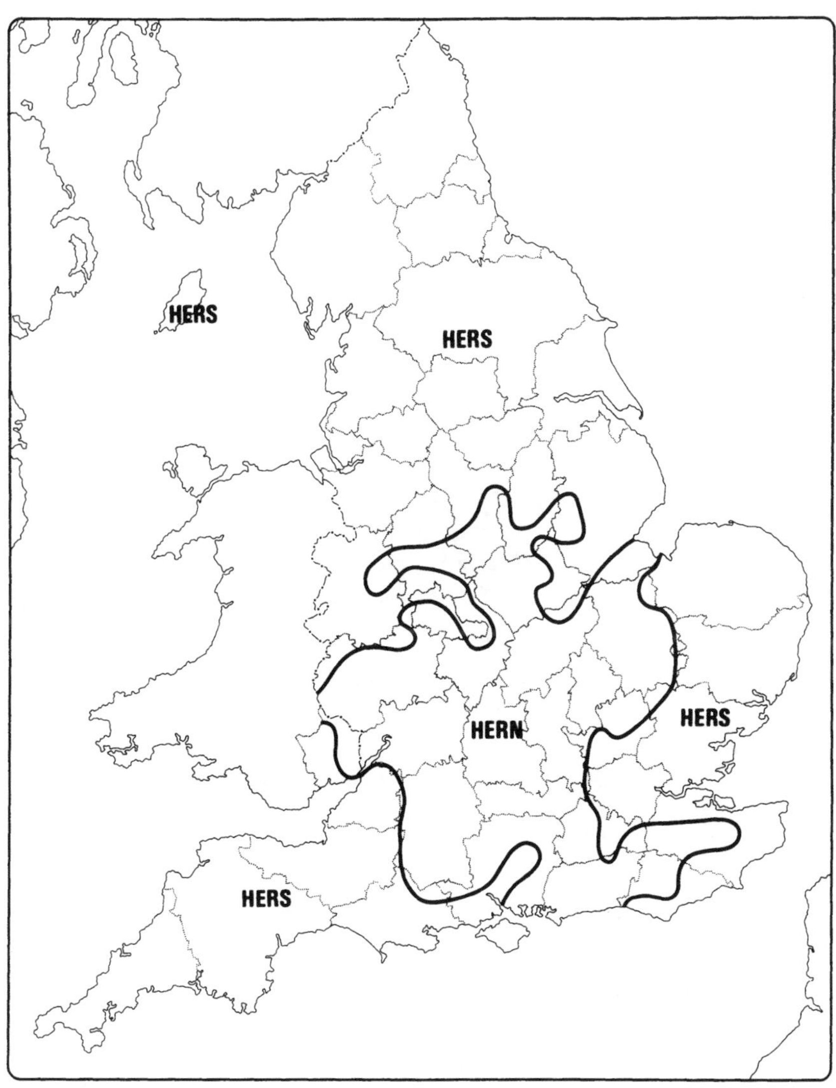

Map 82: HERS

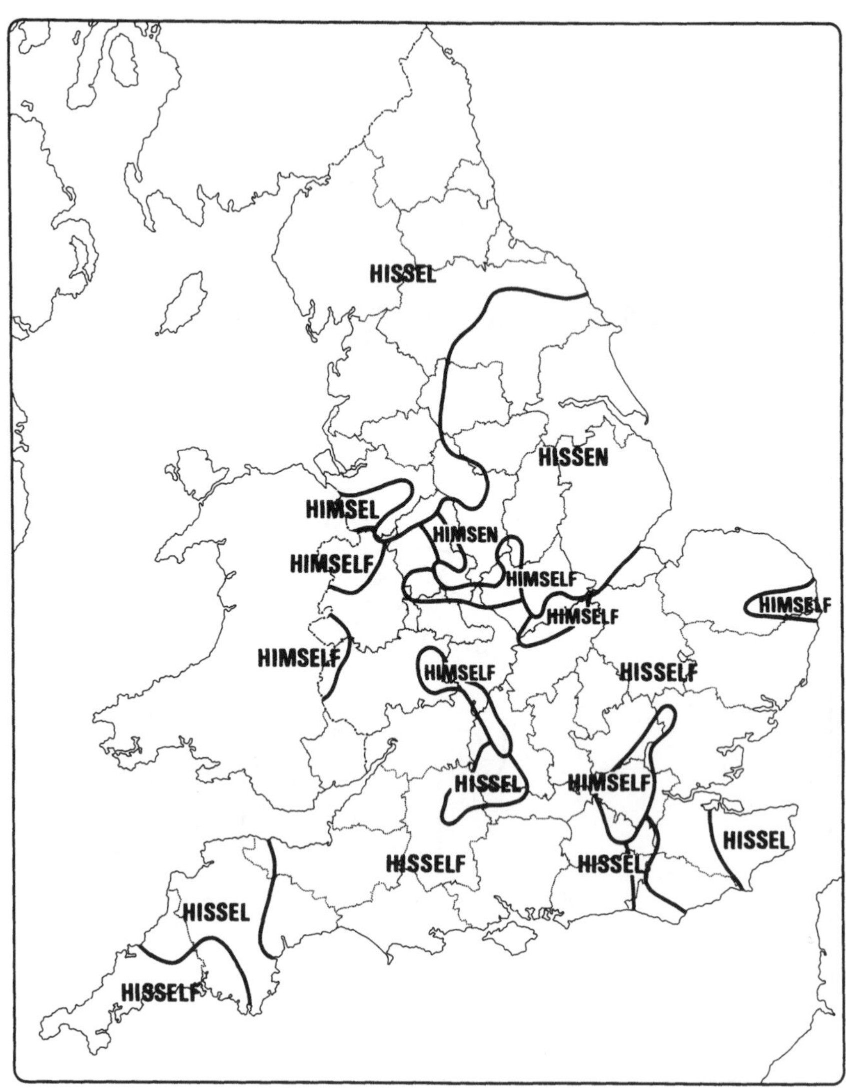

Map 83: HIMSELF

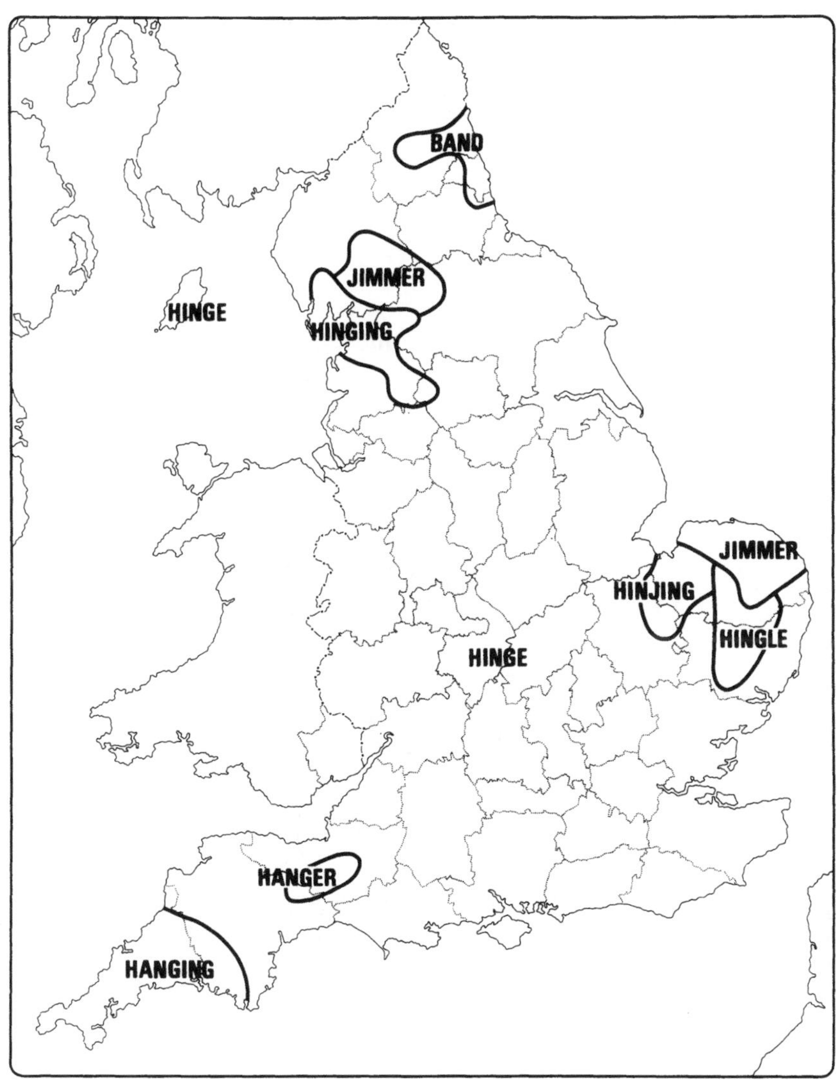

Map 84: HINGE (of door)

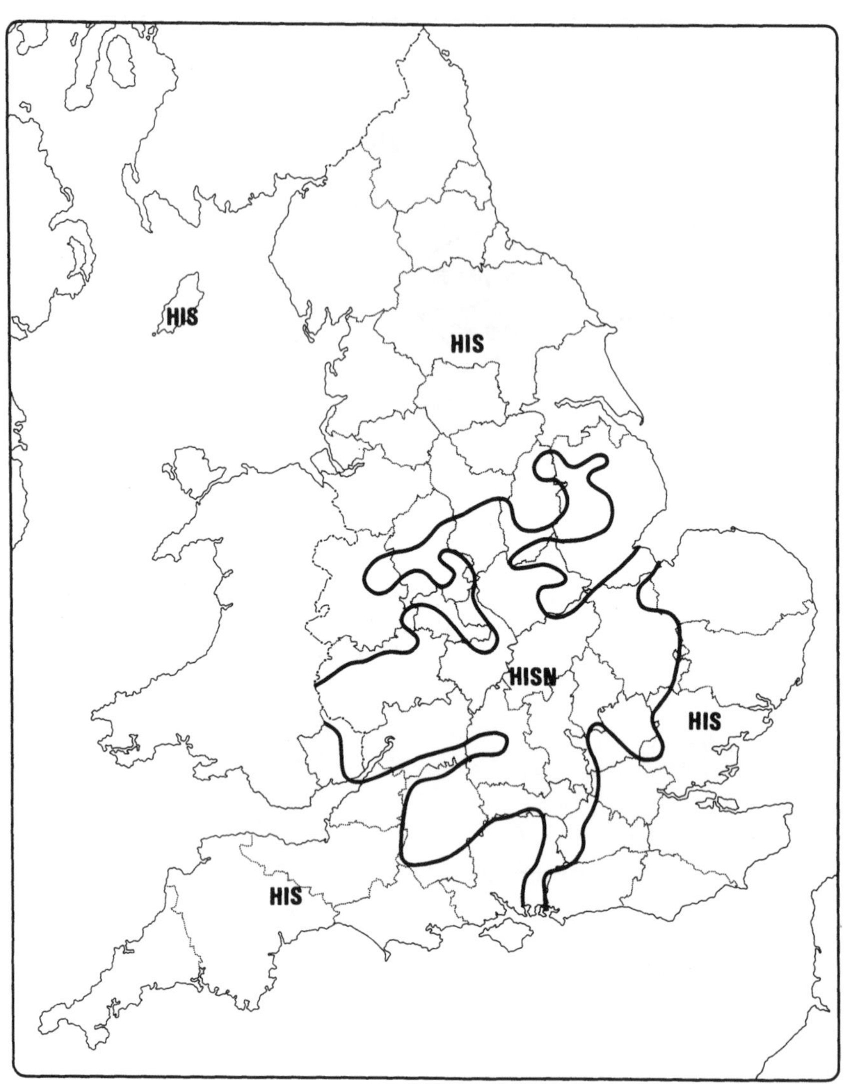

Map 85: HIS (he has ...)

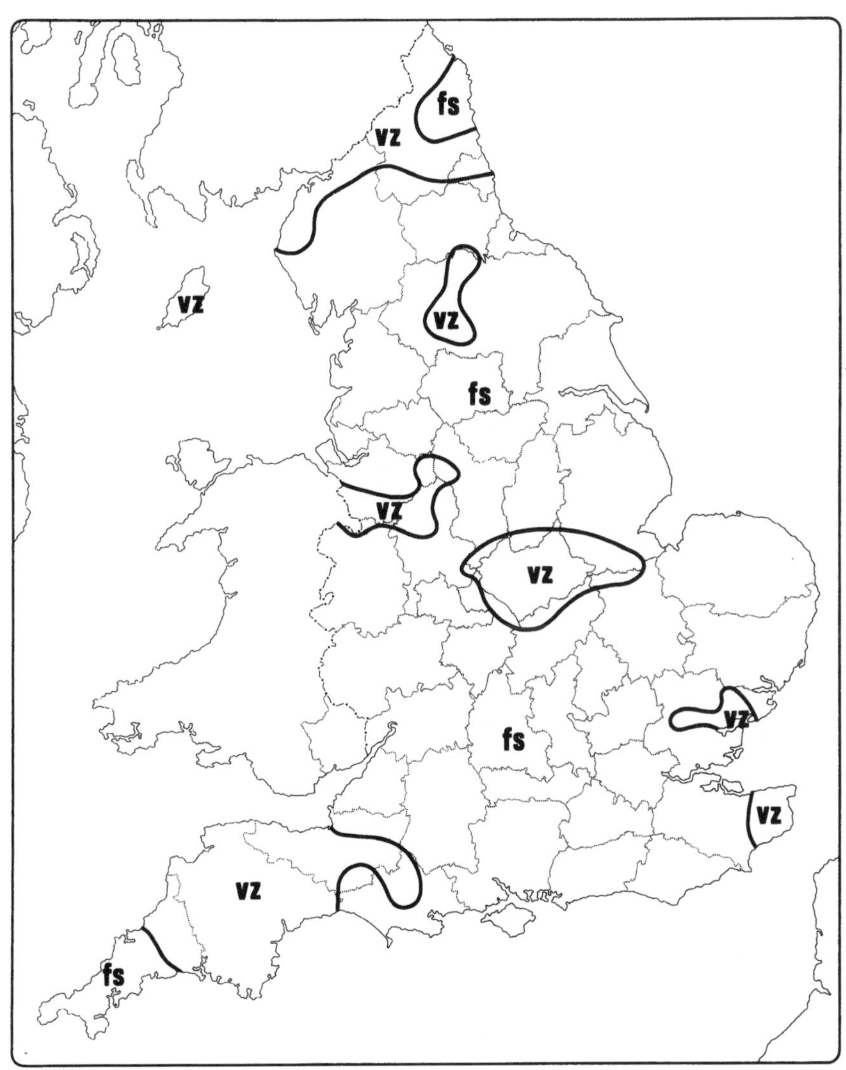

Map 86: HOOFS

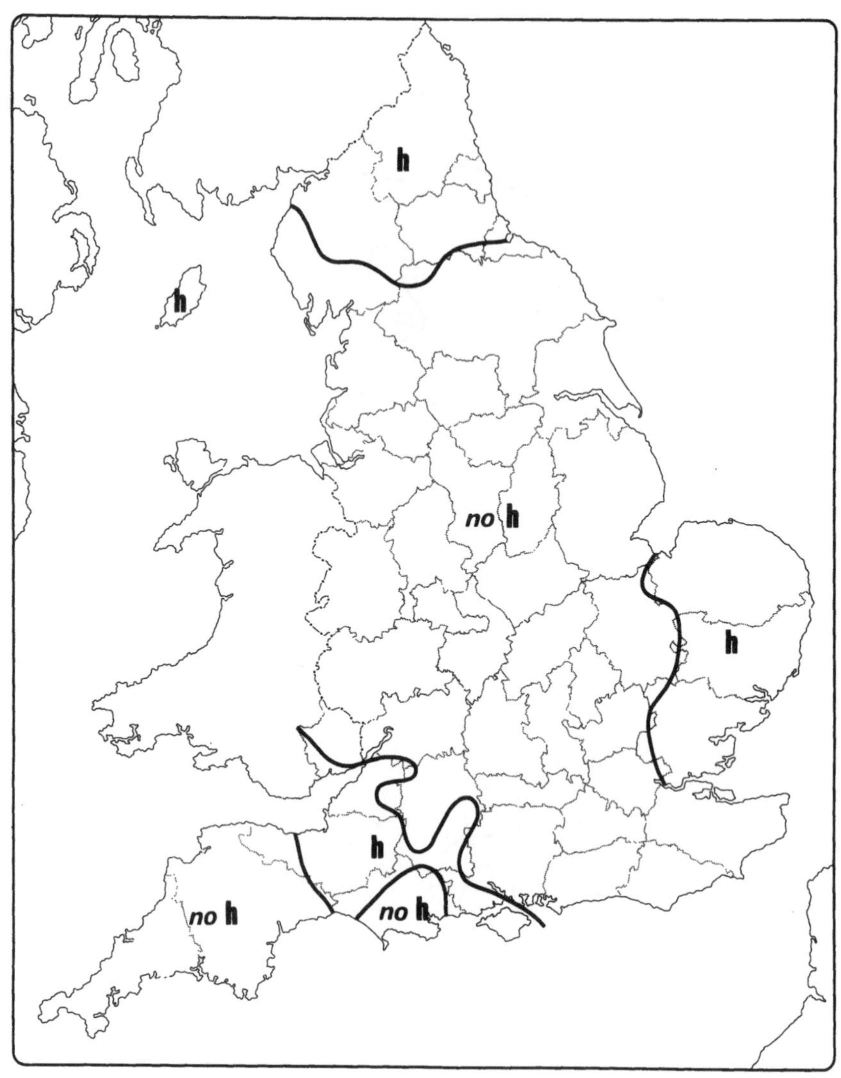

Map 87: <u>H</u>OUSE

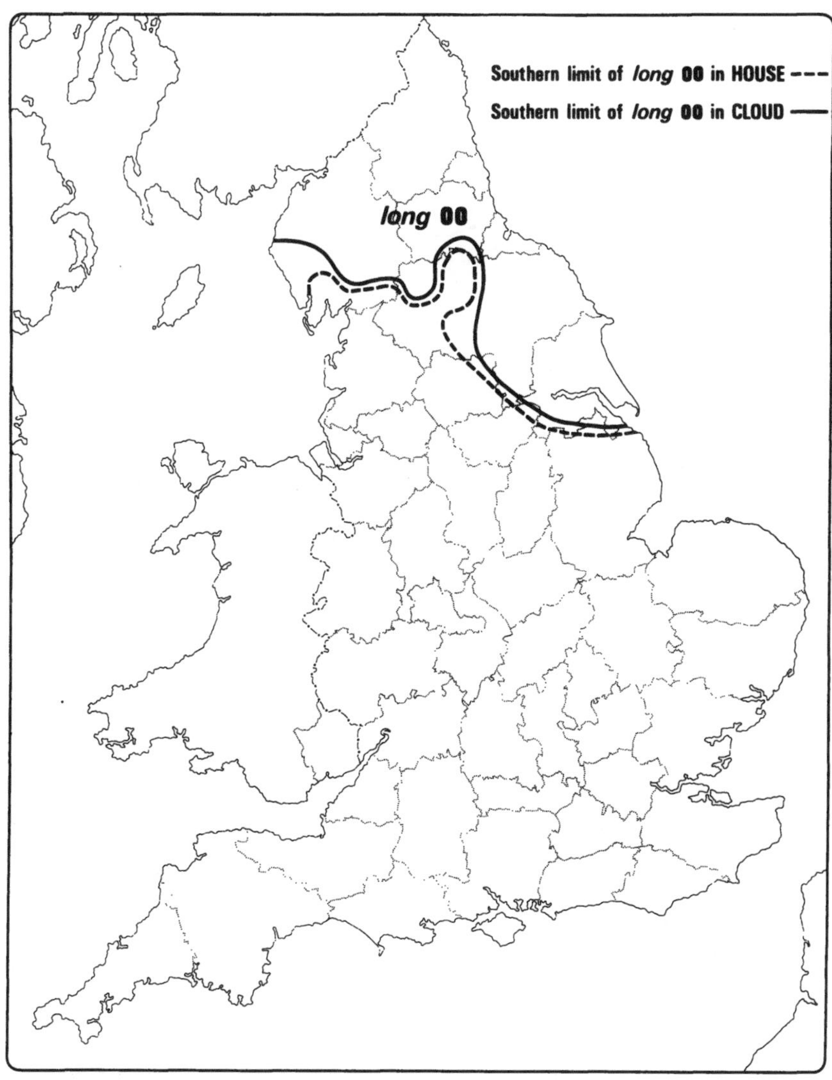

Map 88: H<u>OU</u>SE/CL<u>OU</u>D

The boundary lines separate what are usually referred to as the Northern and North Midland dialect areas. The long **oo** in these words is retreating northwards, though it still extends surprisingly far down the eastern side of the country.

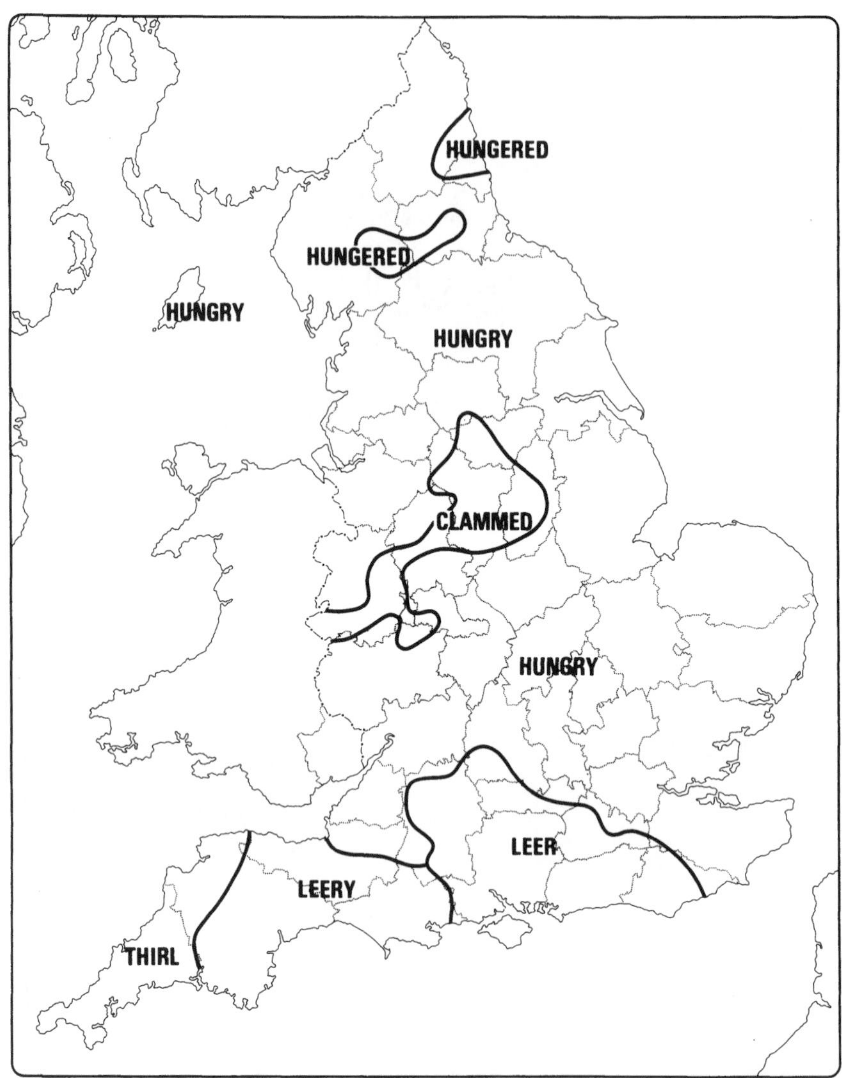

Map 89: HUNGRY

LEER, which is recorded from the Middle English period, literally means 'empty' and **THIRL** goes back to an Old English word for 'hole'. **HUNGRY** occurs widely in the areas where **CLAMMED** and **LEER** predominate.

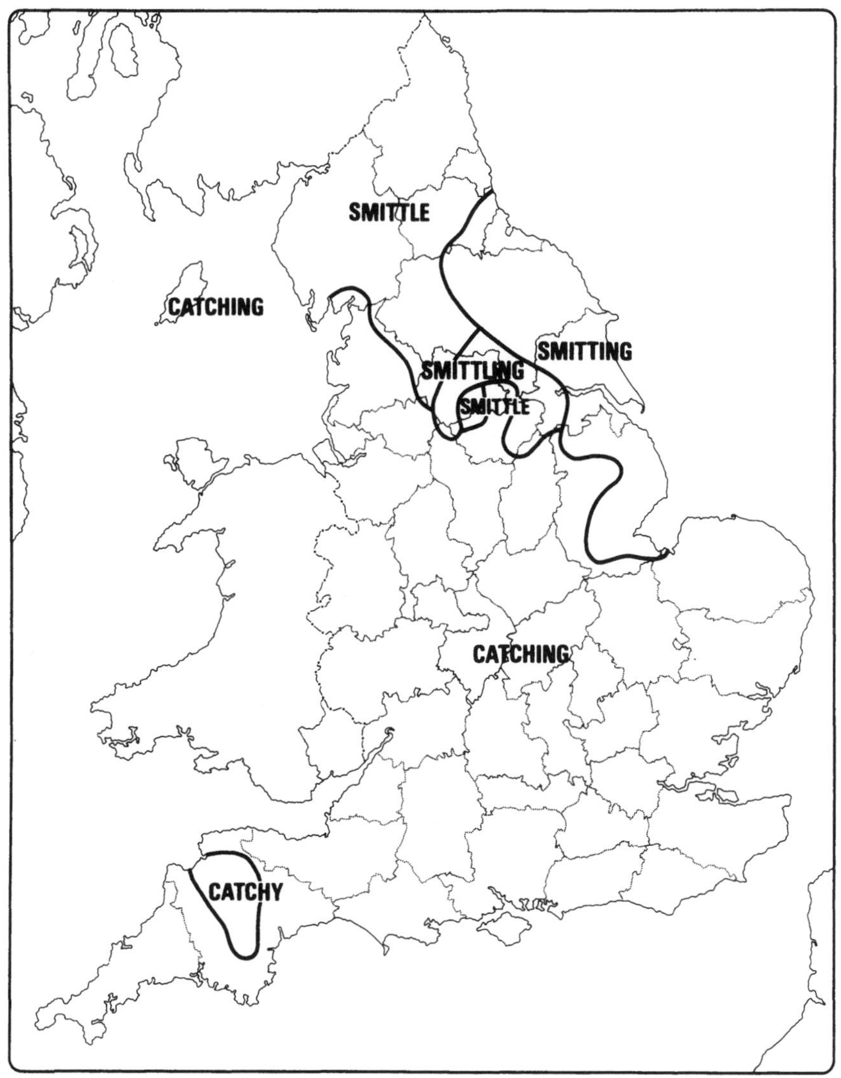

Map 90: INFECTIOUS (disease)
The origin of the forms with SMIT- lies in the Old English word *smitte*, meaning 'spot, stain, smear'.

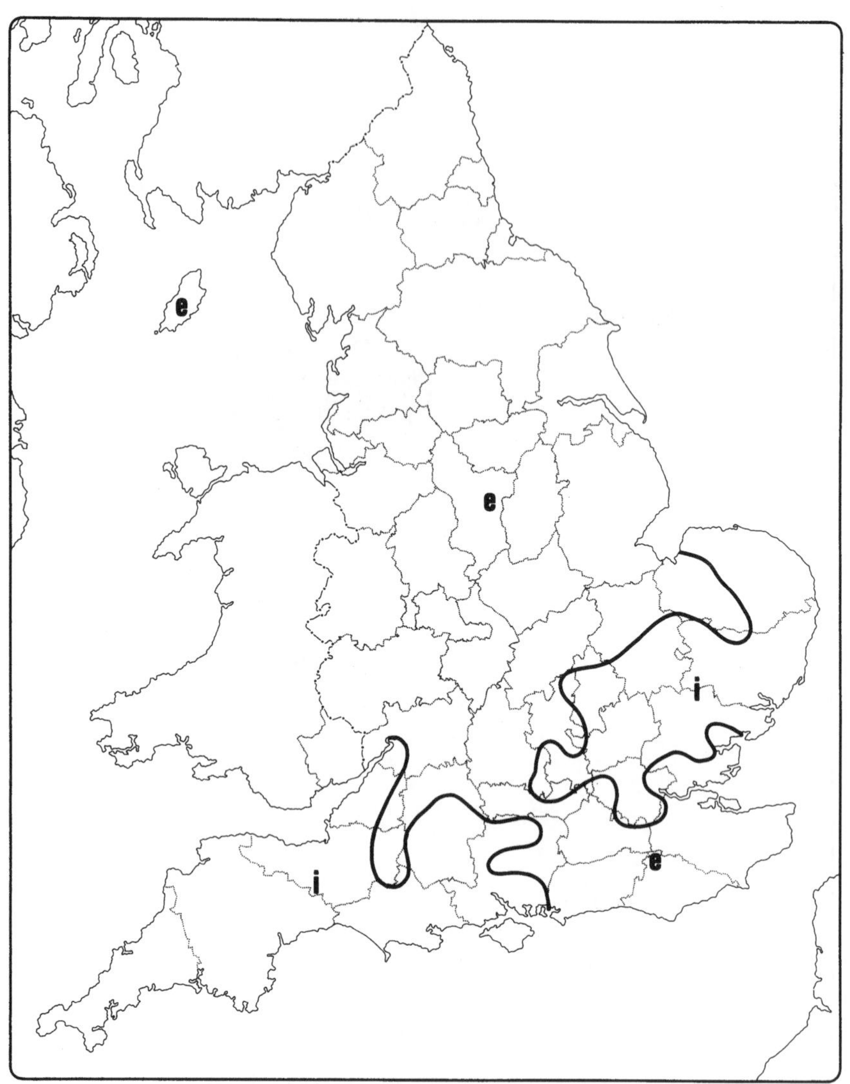

Map 91: KE̲TTLE

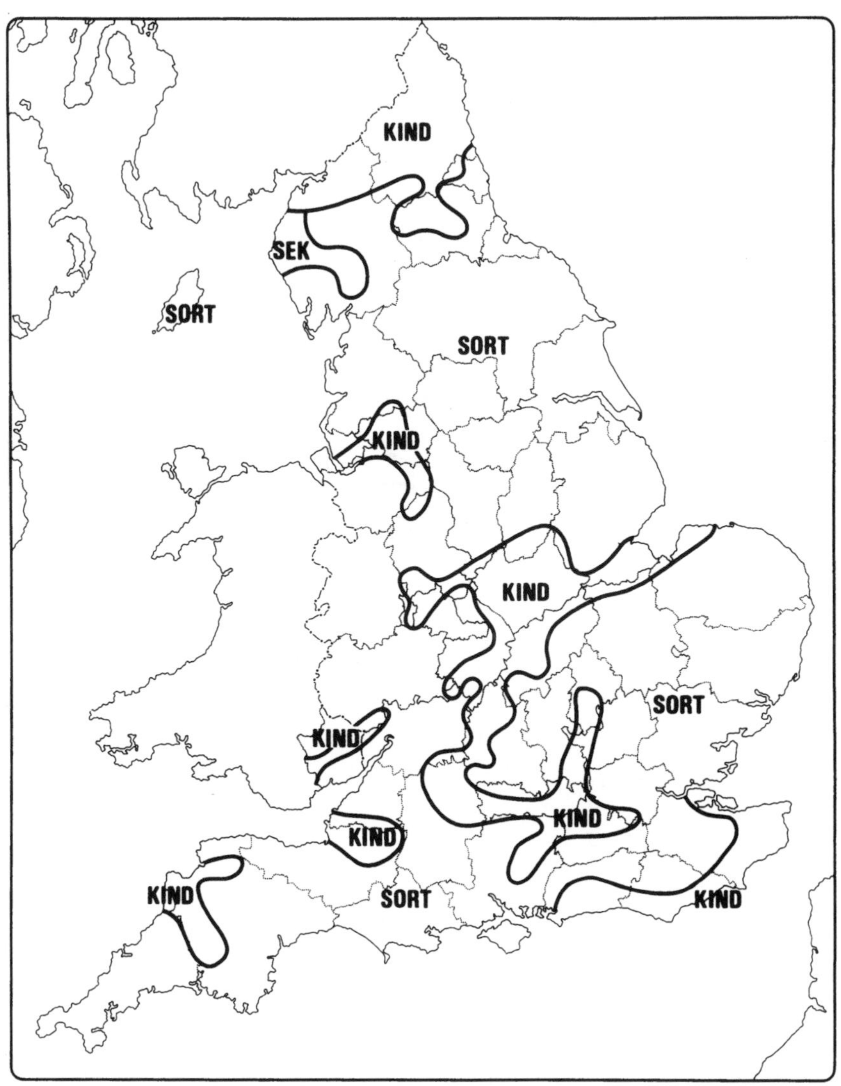

Map 92: KIND (what . . .?)

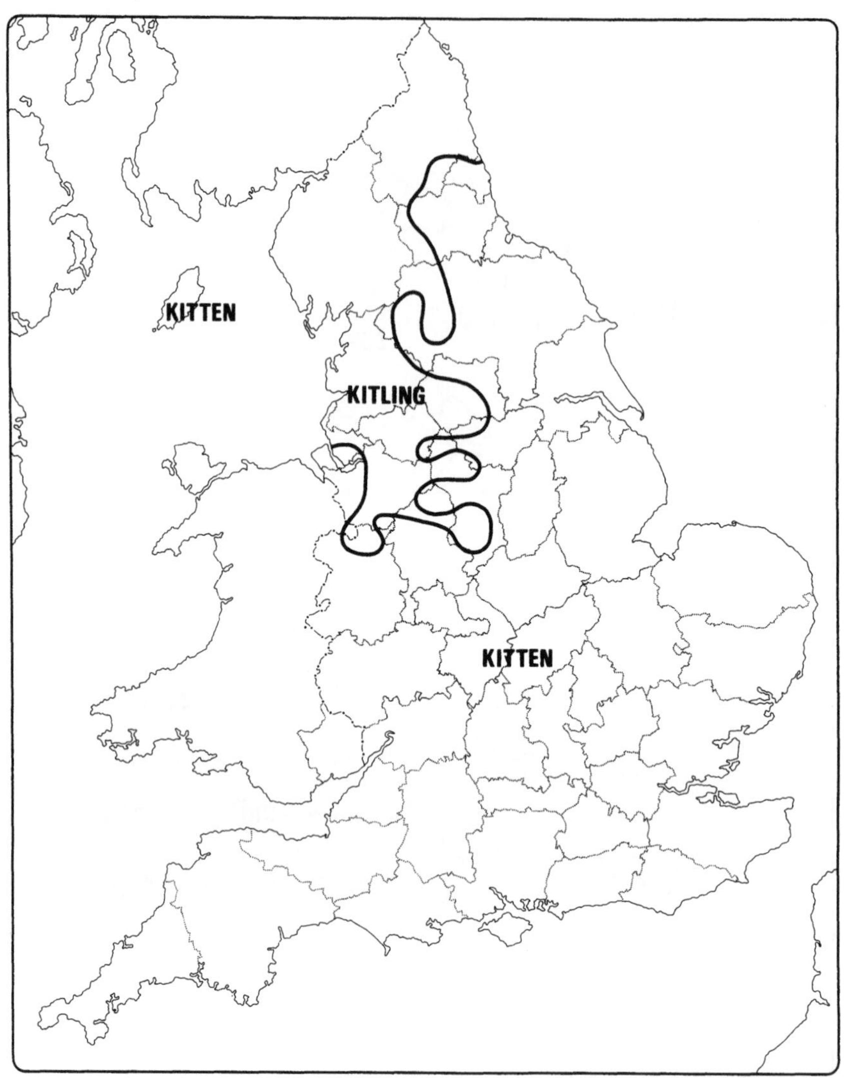

Map 93: KITTEN

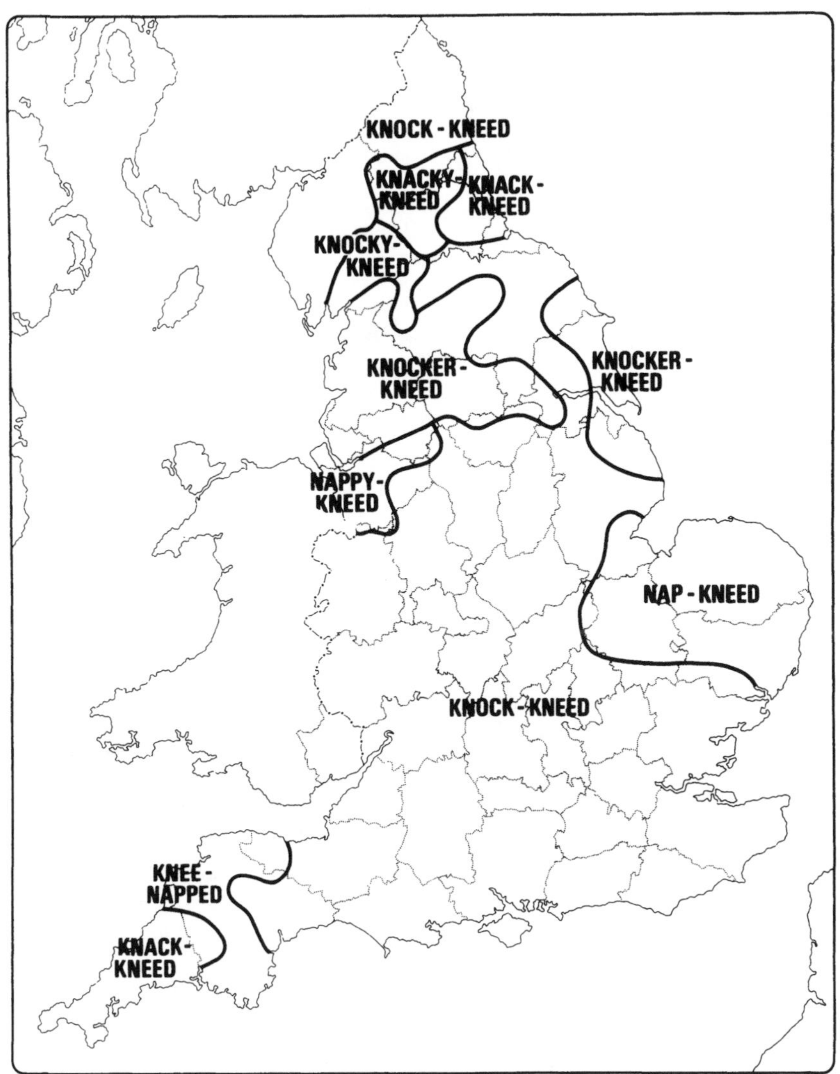

Map 94: KNOCK-KNEED

The **NAPPY-KNEED** area in Cheshire and northwest Derbyshire includes *napper-kneed* and *nap-kneed*. Historically, the forms beginning **NAP-** would have been written *knap*; we have written them here without the **k-** to avoid any suggestion that the **k-** should be pronounced.

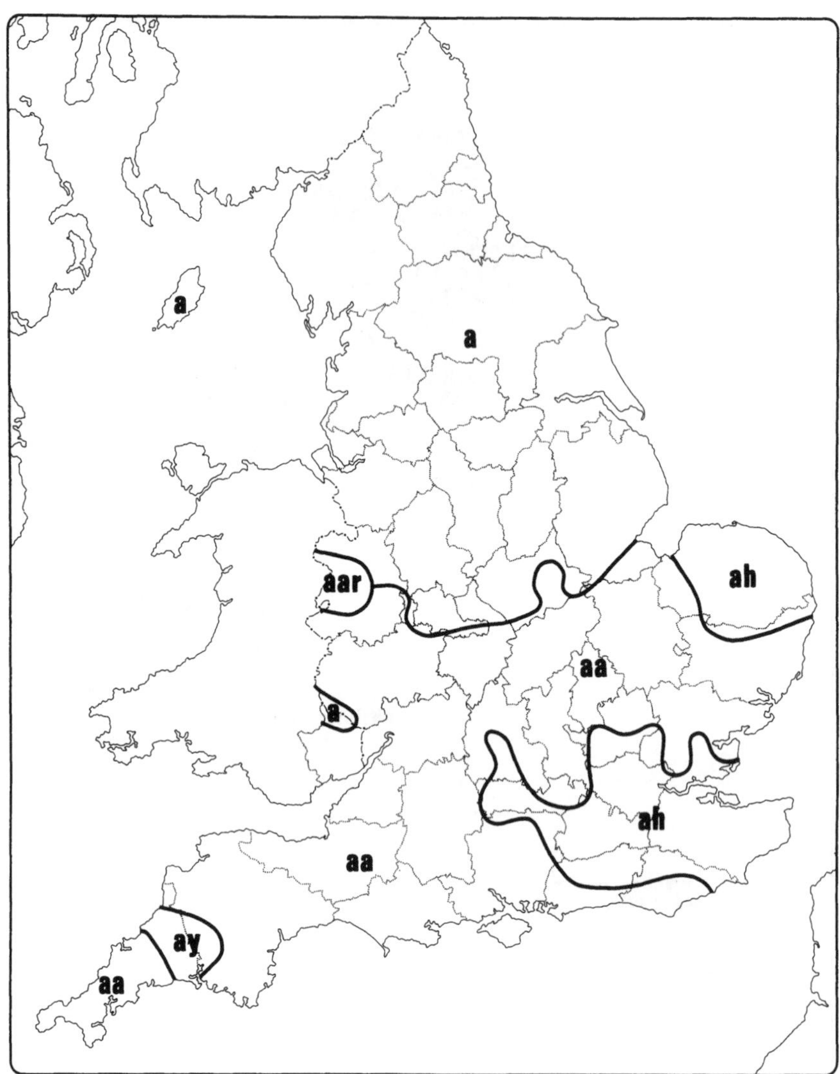

Map 95: L<u>A</u>ST

This map shows the main division between short *a* (**a**) north of the Wash and varieties of long *a* (**aa**) to the south. The long *a* (**ah**) of Received Pronunciation which became established as late as the eighteenth century is found only in the Home Counties and Norfolk. The **aa** sound typical of much of the South was established in the seventeenth century. Historically, short *a* occurs in front of *-s*, *-f* and *-th*.

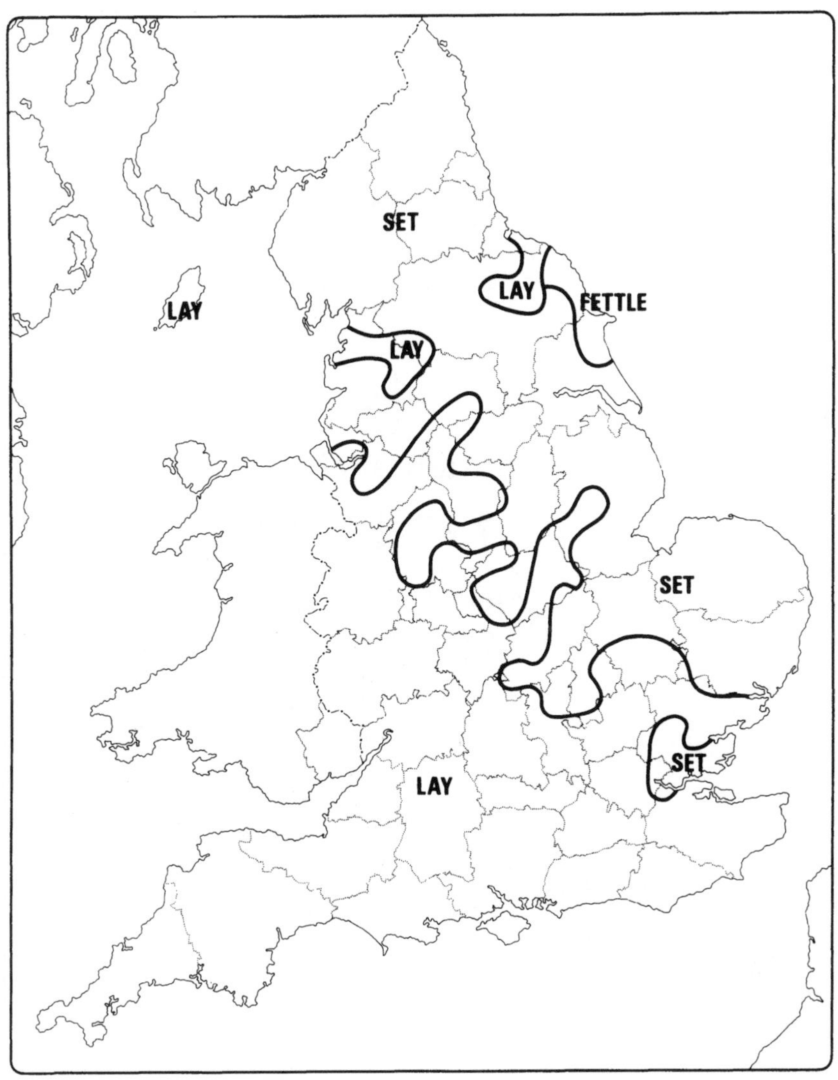

Map 96: LAY (to … the table)

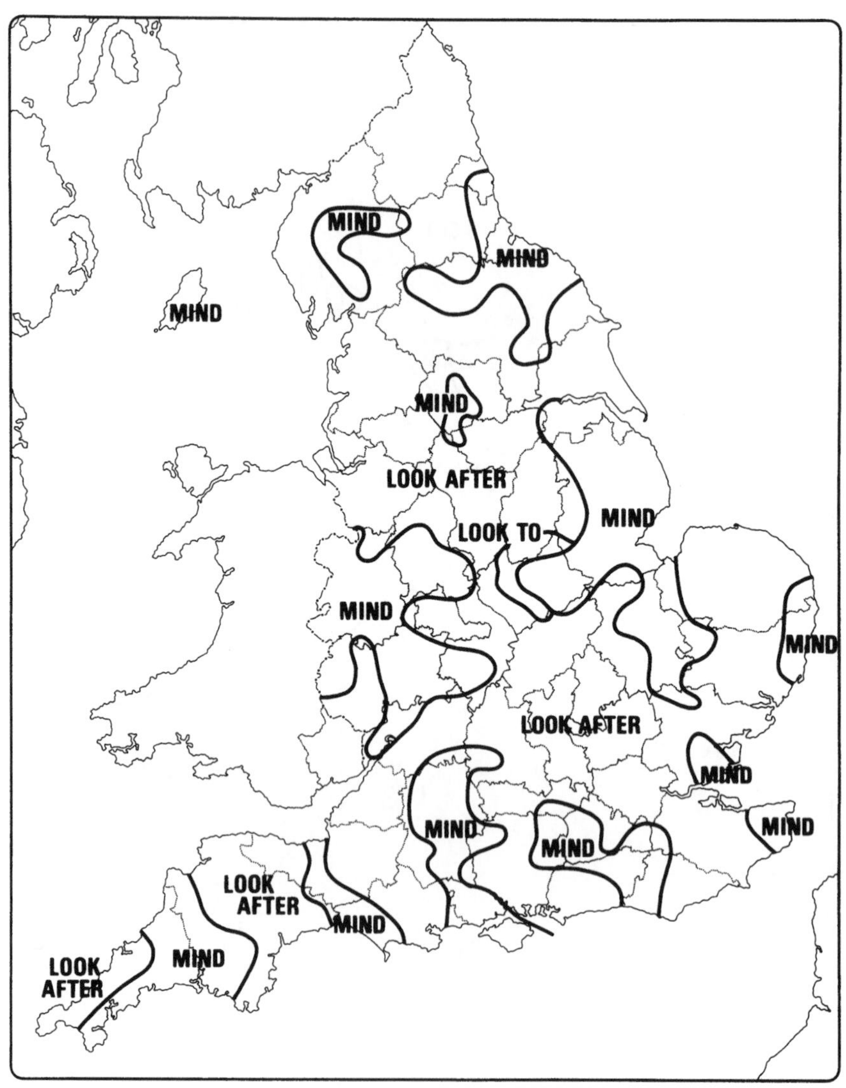

Map 97: LOOK AFTER (to . . . the baby)

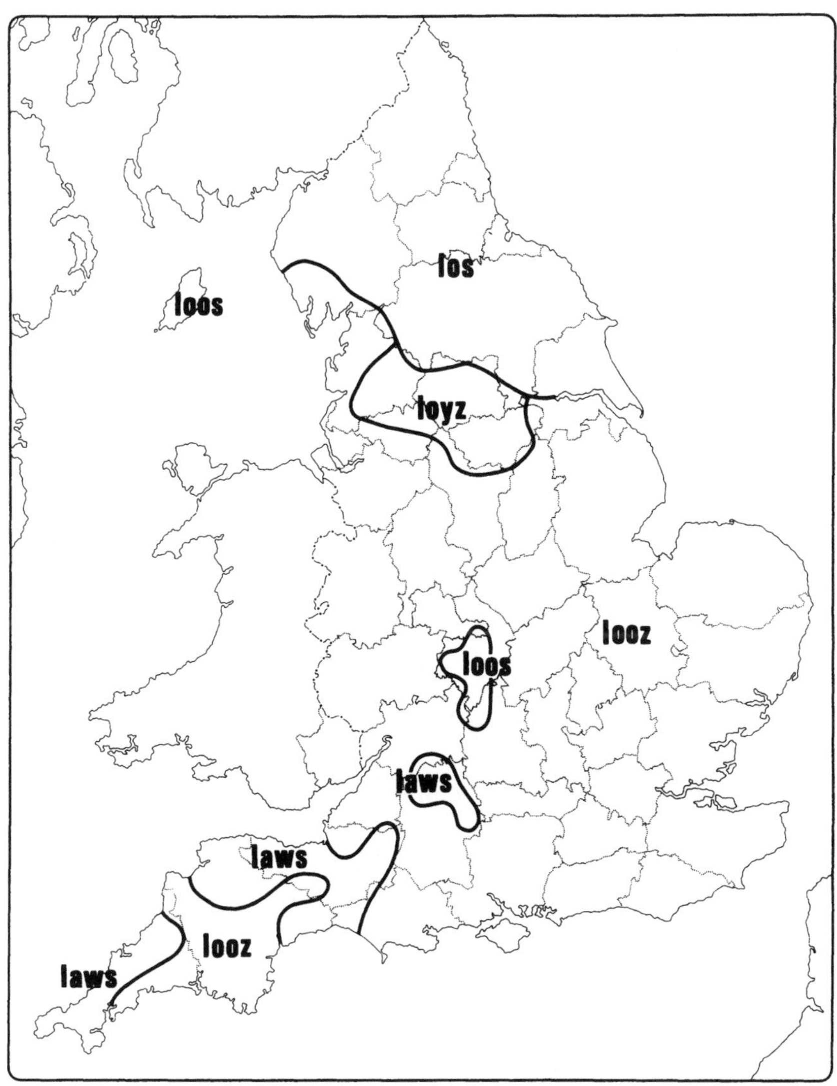

Map 98: LOSE

Historically, the normal pronunciation of *lose* in Modern English would be expected to rhyme with *rose*, but its association with the verb *loose* has led to its present form with the long **oo**. However, a number of dialects retain pronunciations derived from the original Old English form.

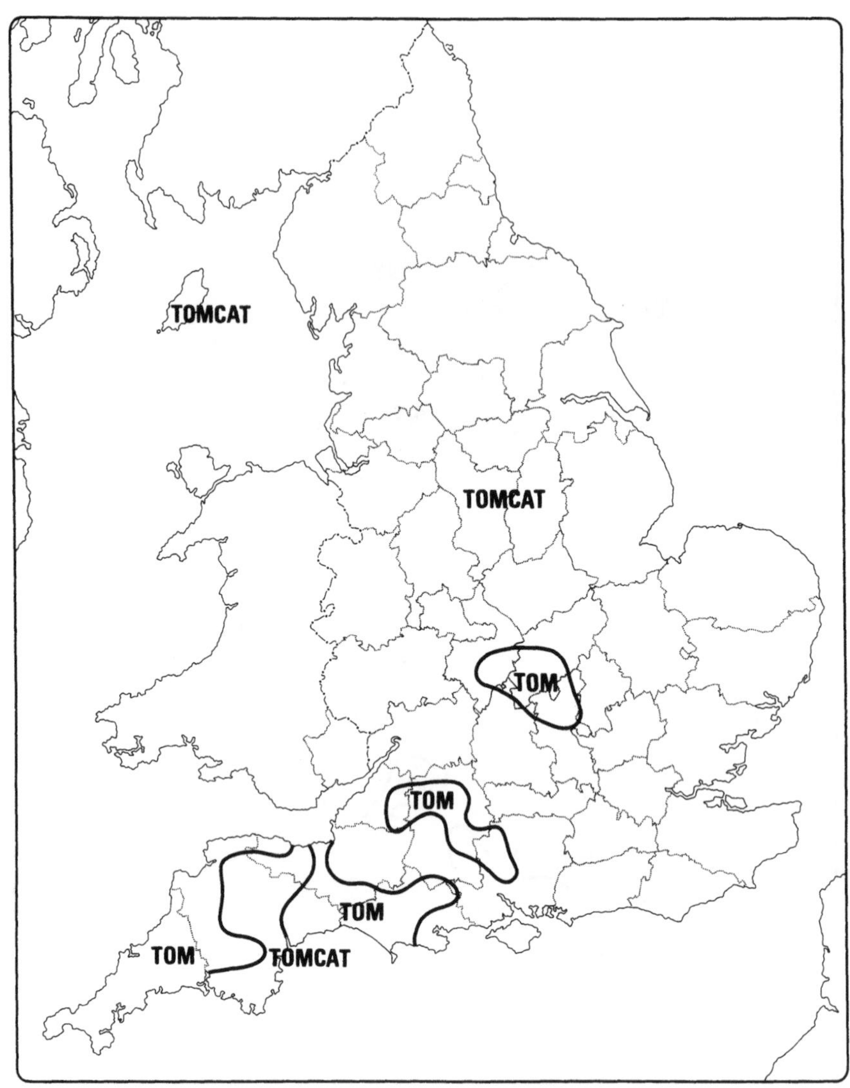

Map 99: MALE CAT

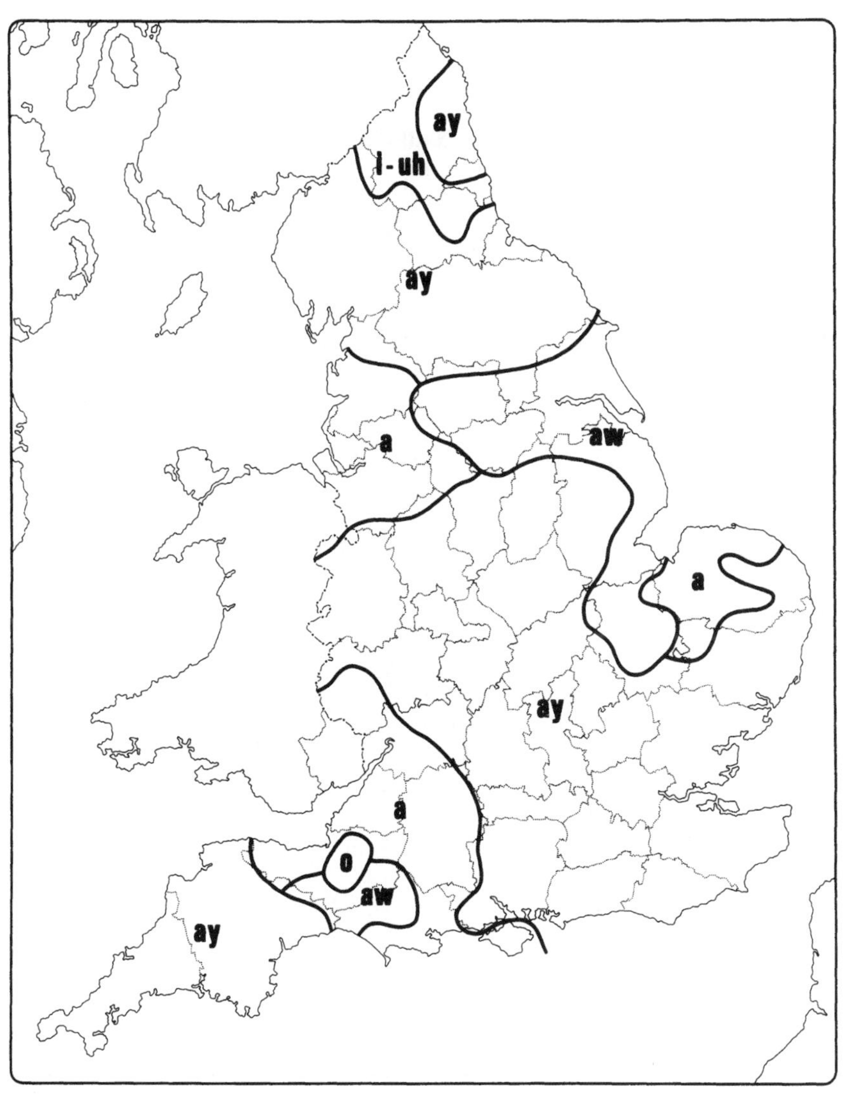

Map 100: M<u>A</u>NGE

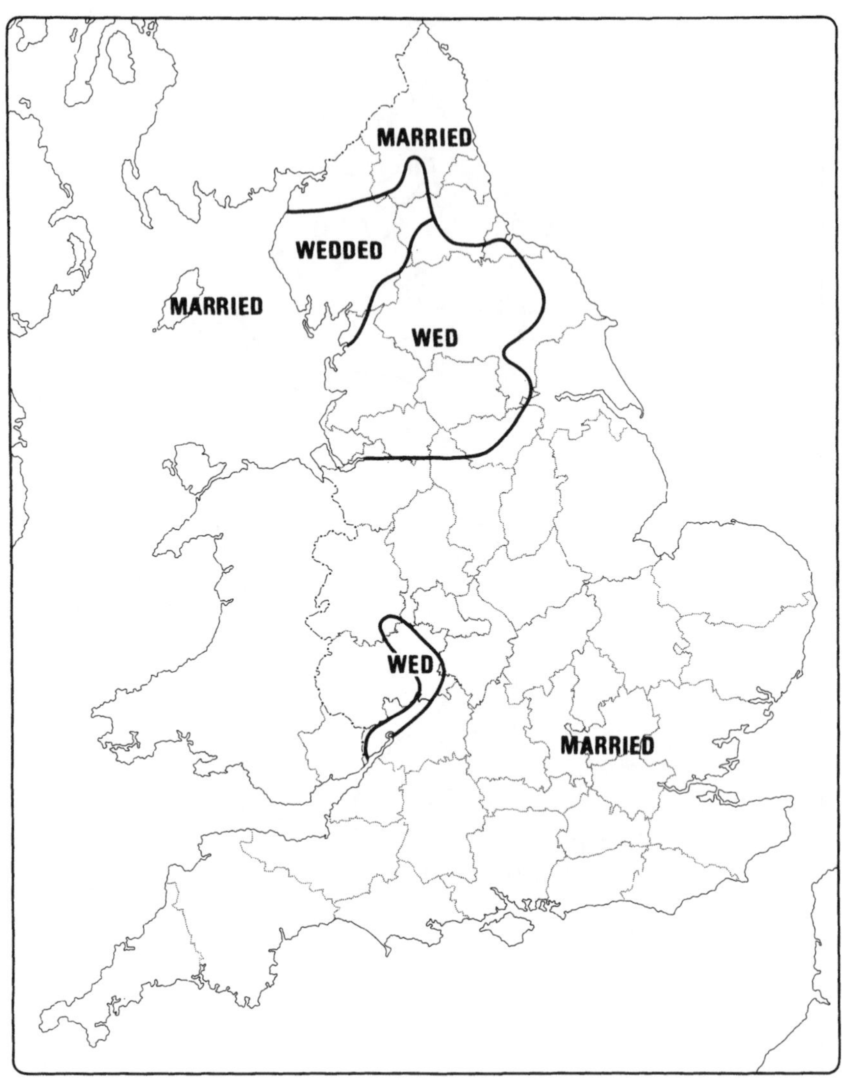

Map 101: MARRIED
WED is the Old English form; **MARRIED** is a later word from French.

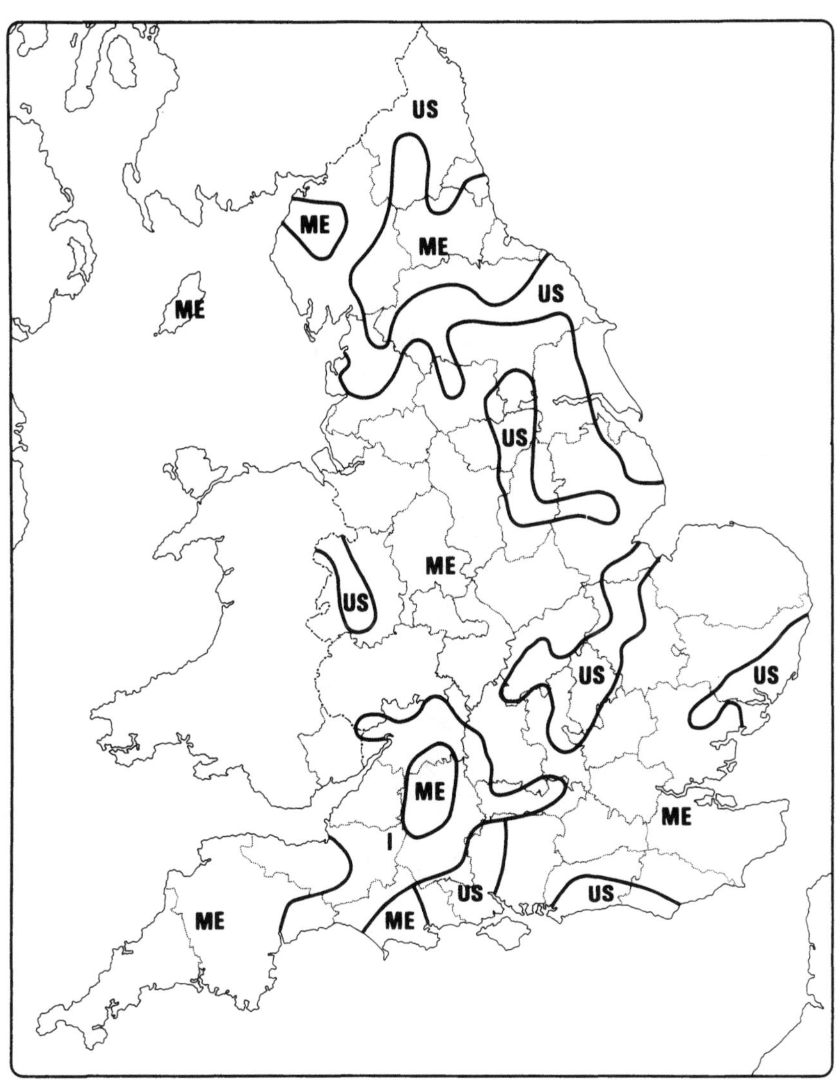

Map 102: ME (with ...)

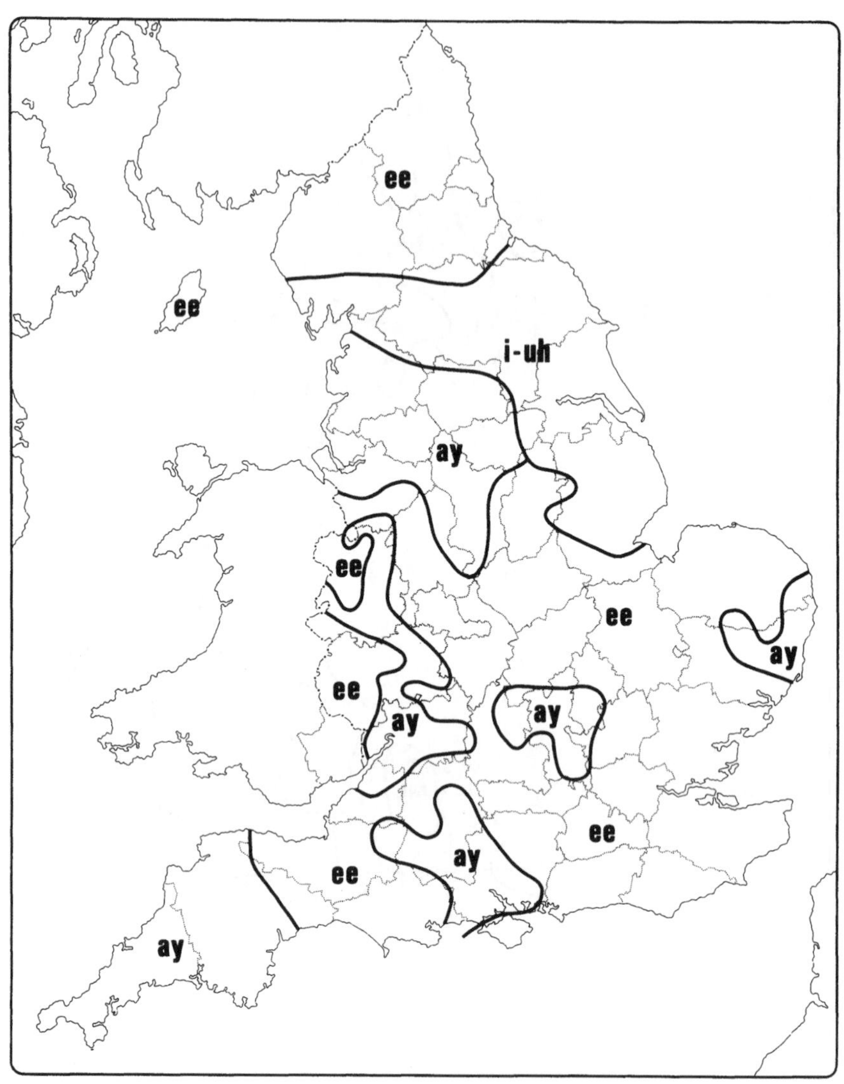

Map 103: MEAT

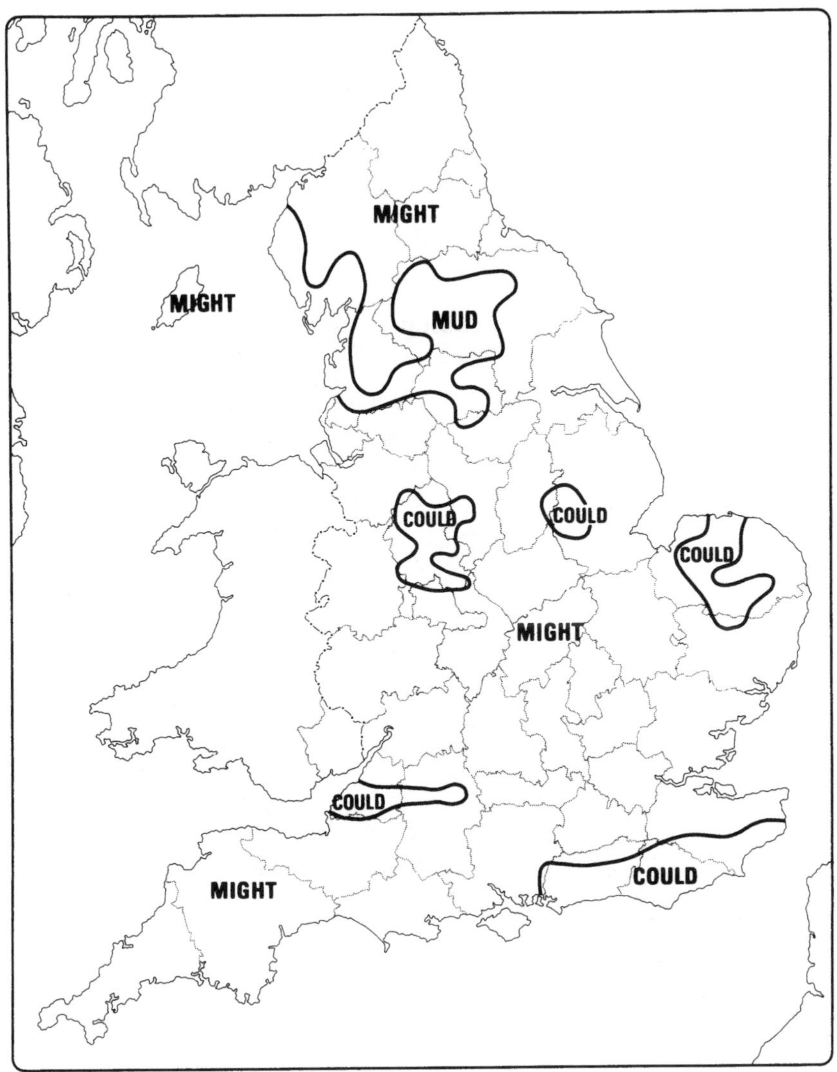

Map 104: MIGHT (it . . . have done)

MIGHT is found in all areas and is clearly displacing the other forms.

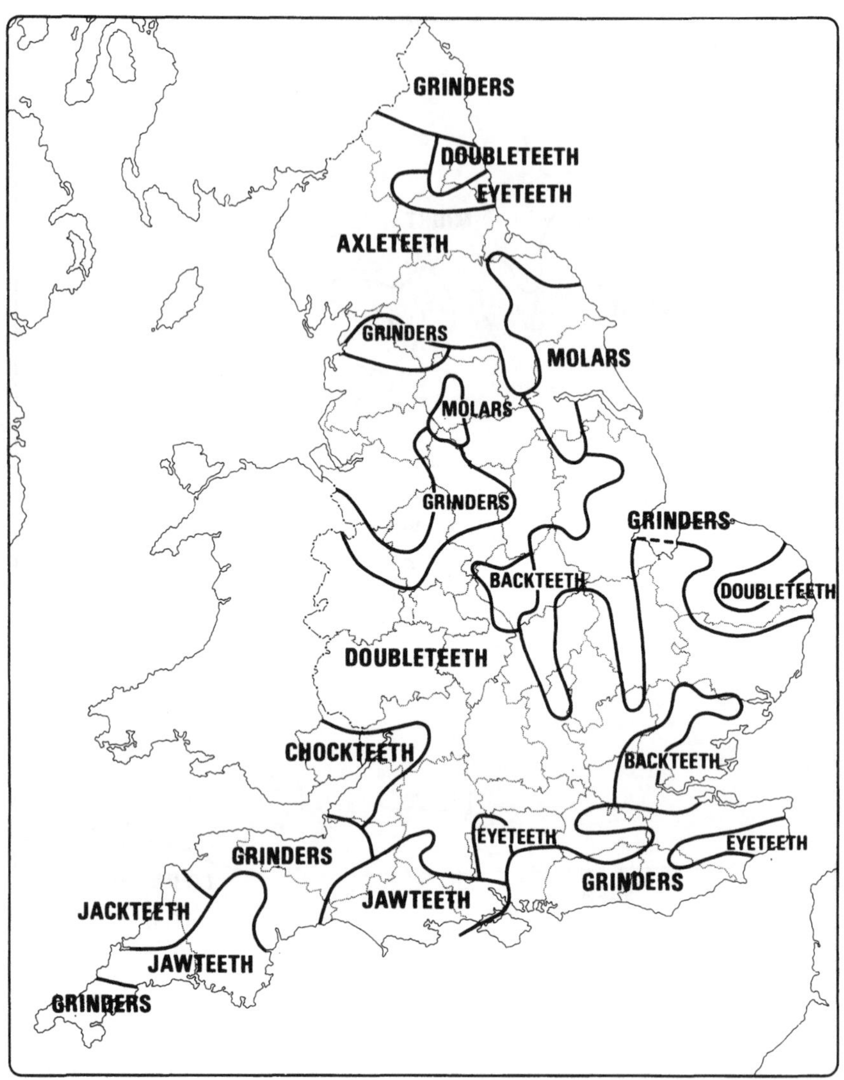

Map 105: MOLARS

MOLARS, which derives from the Latin word for milling or grinding, often occurs with the pronunciation *maulers*, which perhaps reflects a misunderstanding of its meaning ('folk etymology').

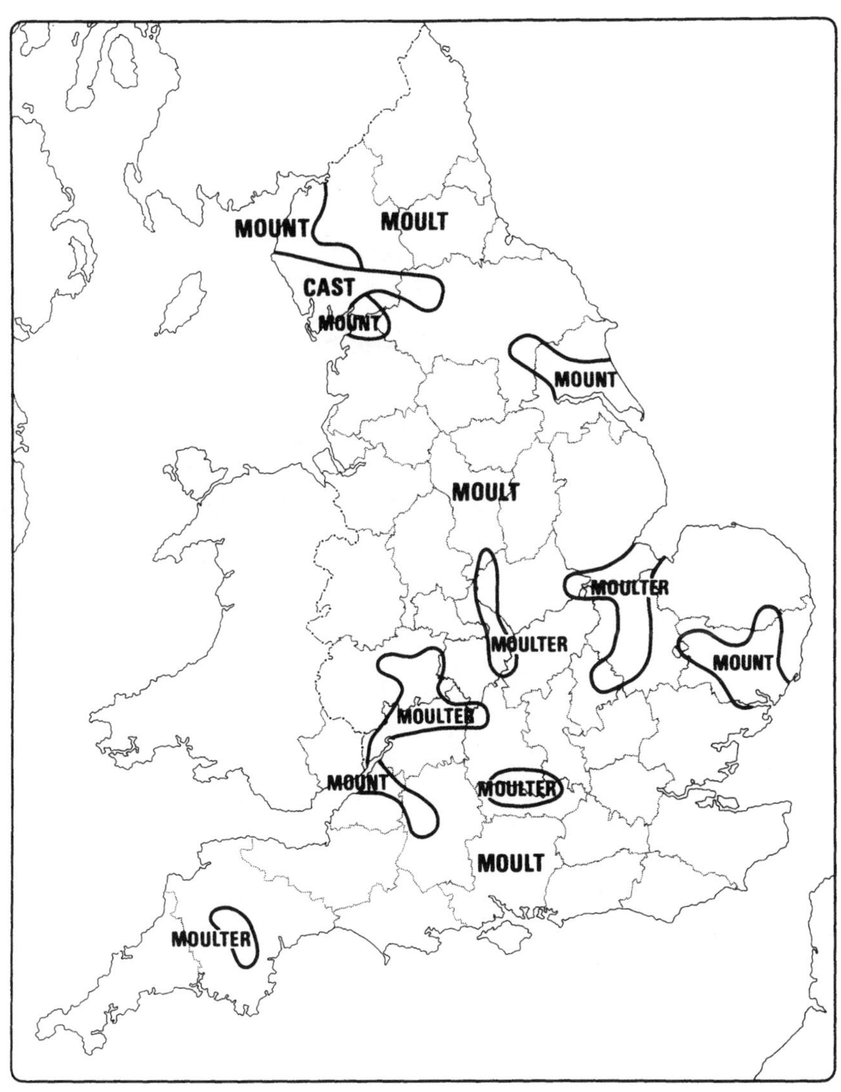

Map 106: MOULT (to ...)

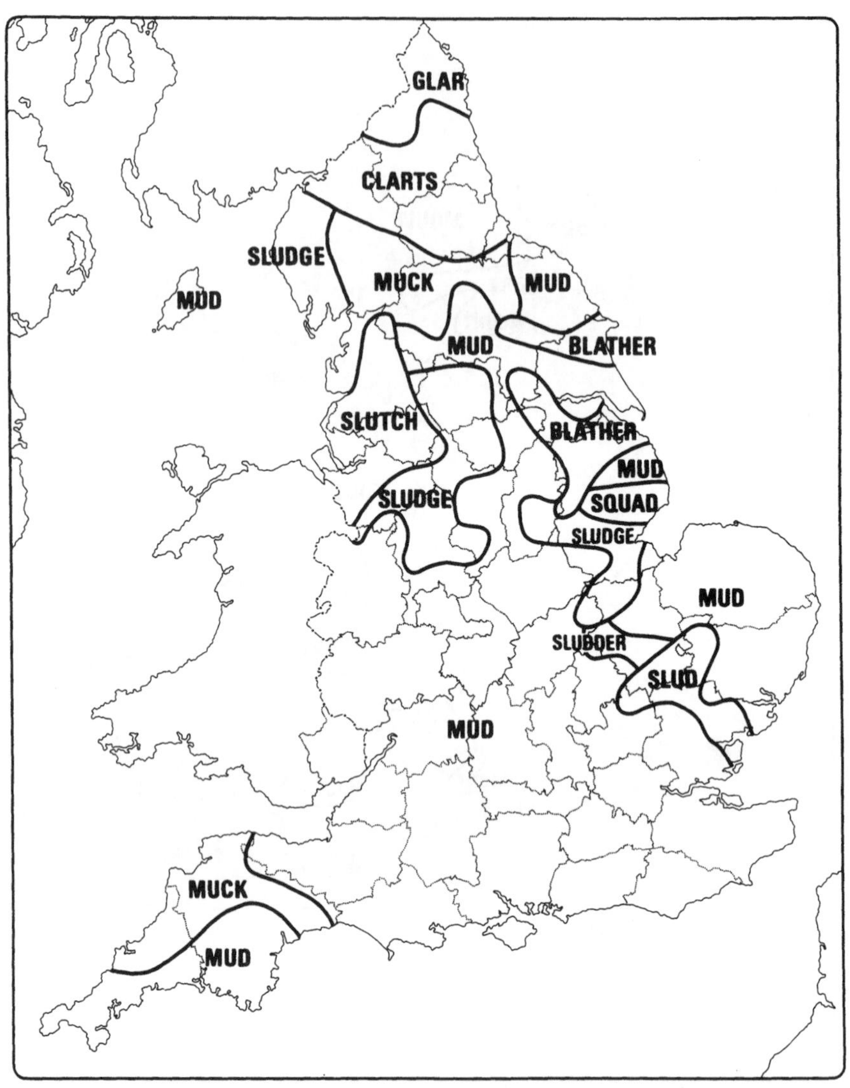
GLAR
CLARTS
SLUDGE
MUCK
MUD
MUD
MUD
BLATHER
SLUTCH
BLATHER
MUD
SLUDGE
SQUAD
SLUDGE
MUD
SLUDDER
SLUD
MUD
MUCK
MUD

Map 107: MUD

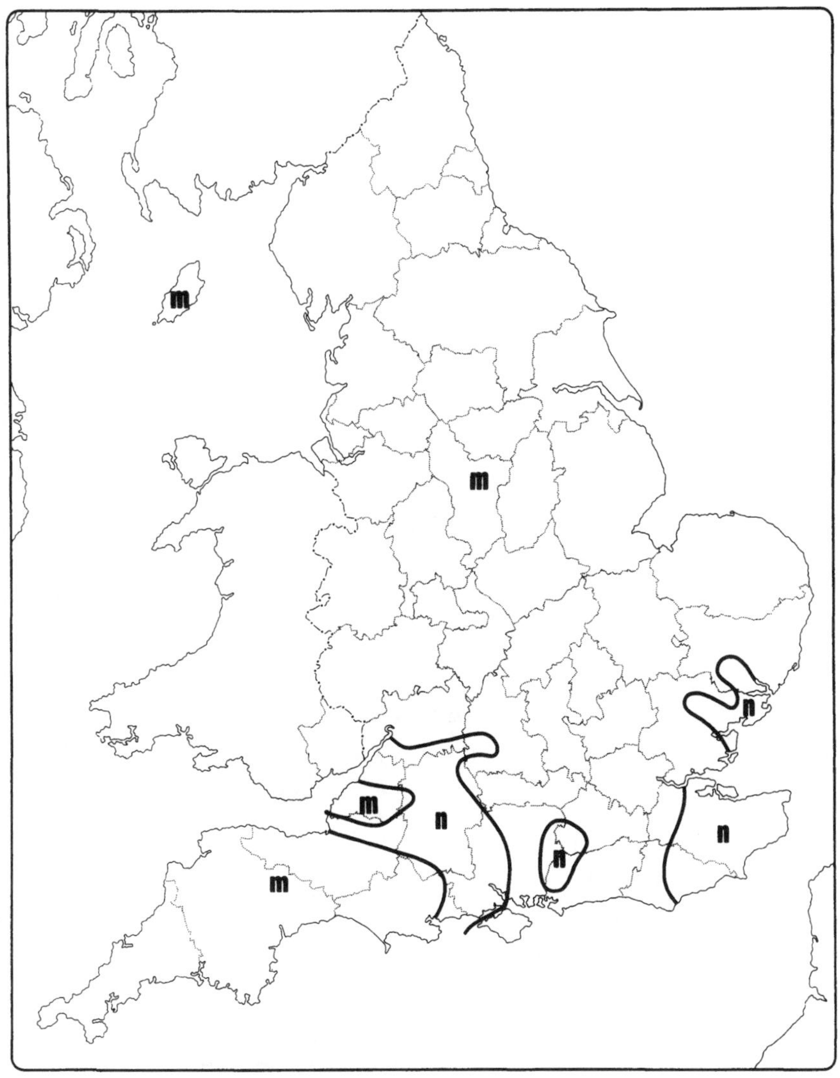

Map 108: MUSHROOM

Sometimes the word is pronounced as if there was a third syllable between the *sh* and *r*, giving the variant pronunciations *musheroom* and *musheroon.*

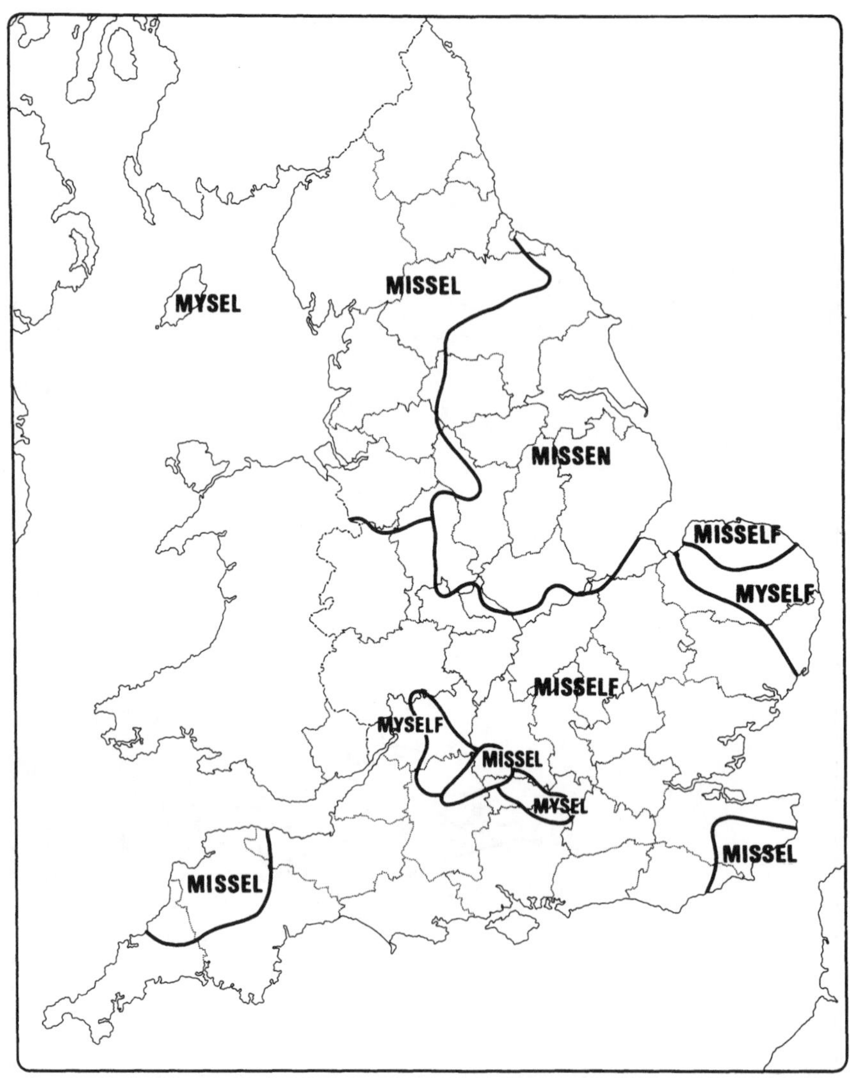

Map 109: MYSELF (by ...)

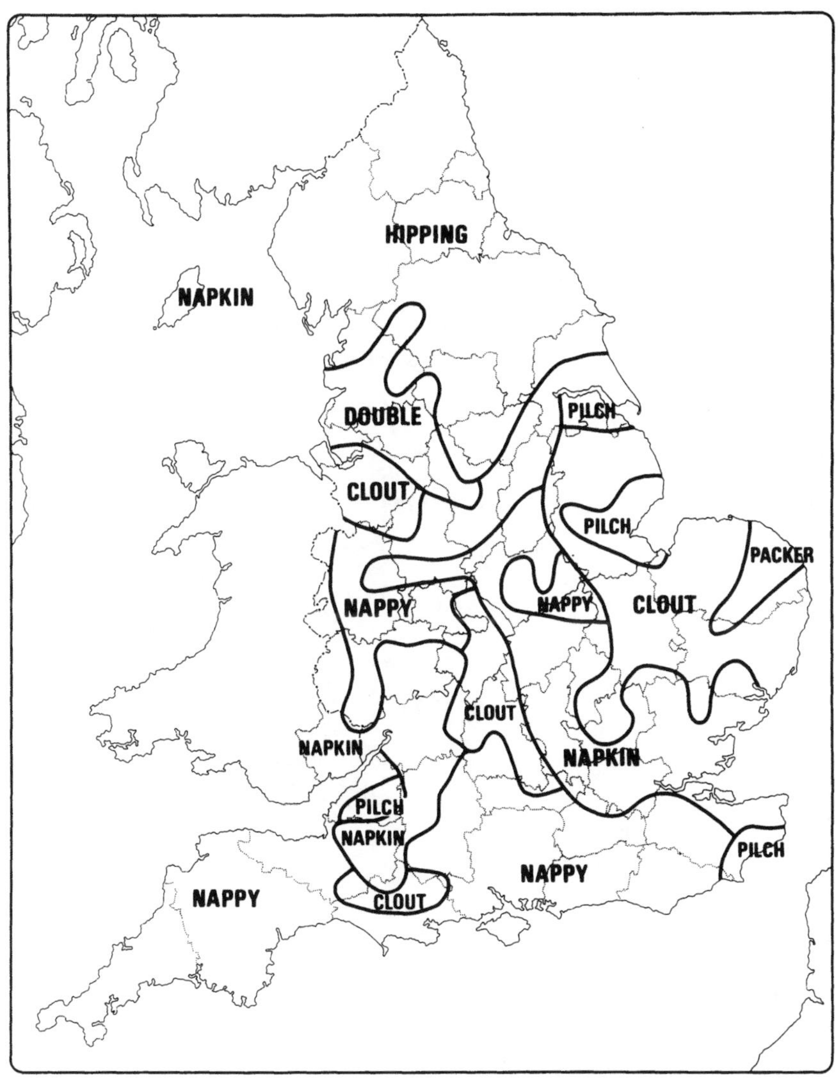

Map 110: NAPPY

Older forms such as **PILCH, HIPPING, CLOUT** and **PACKER** still dominate the dialects, but **NAPPY** is often found with **HIPPING** in Yorkshire. **HIPPING** alternates with *hippings* in the North.

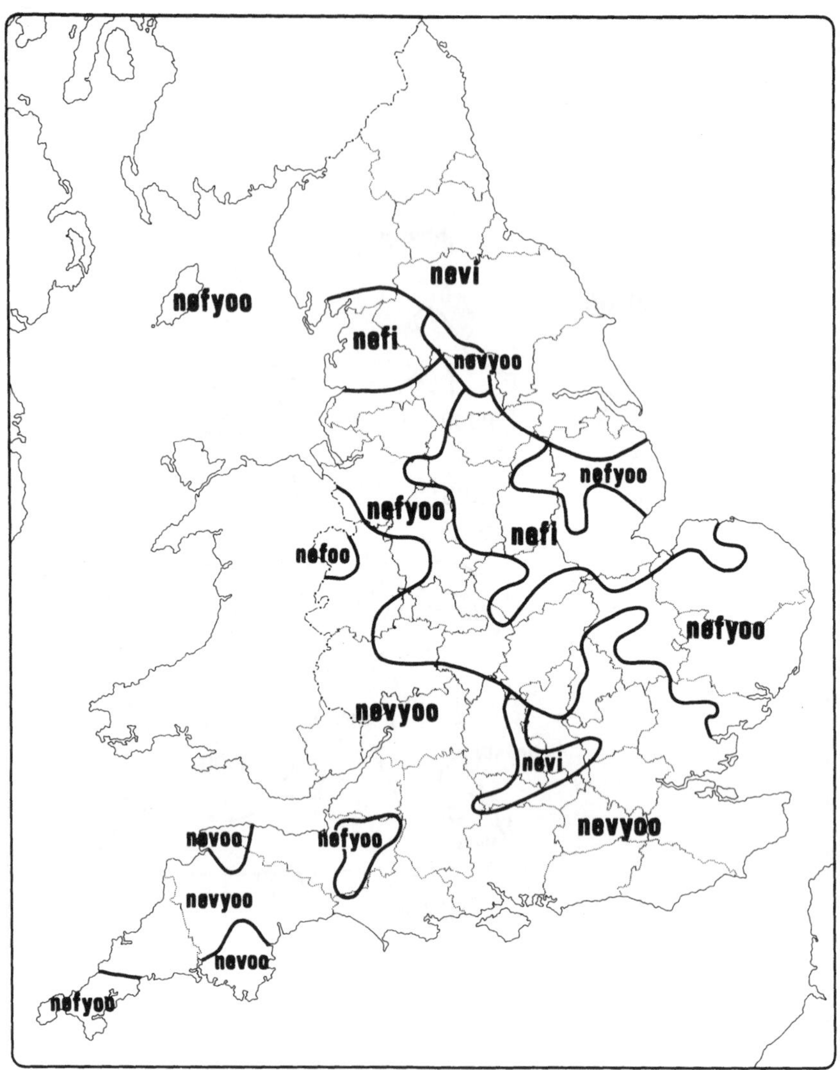

Map 111: NEPHEW

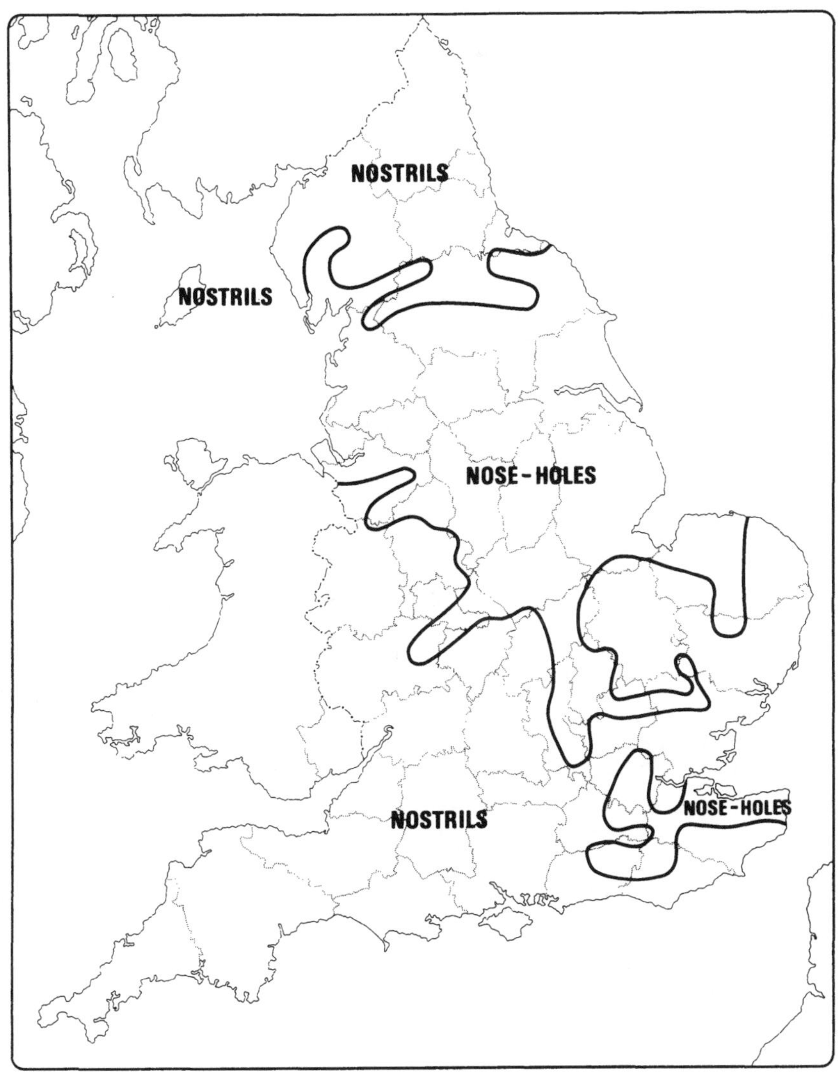

Map 112: NOSTRILS

NOSTRIL is made up of the Old English words for 'nose' and 'hole' (*thirl*) and is increasing in popularity over **NOSE-HOLE**.

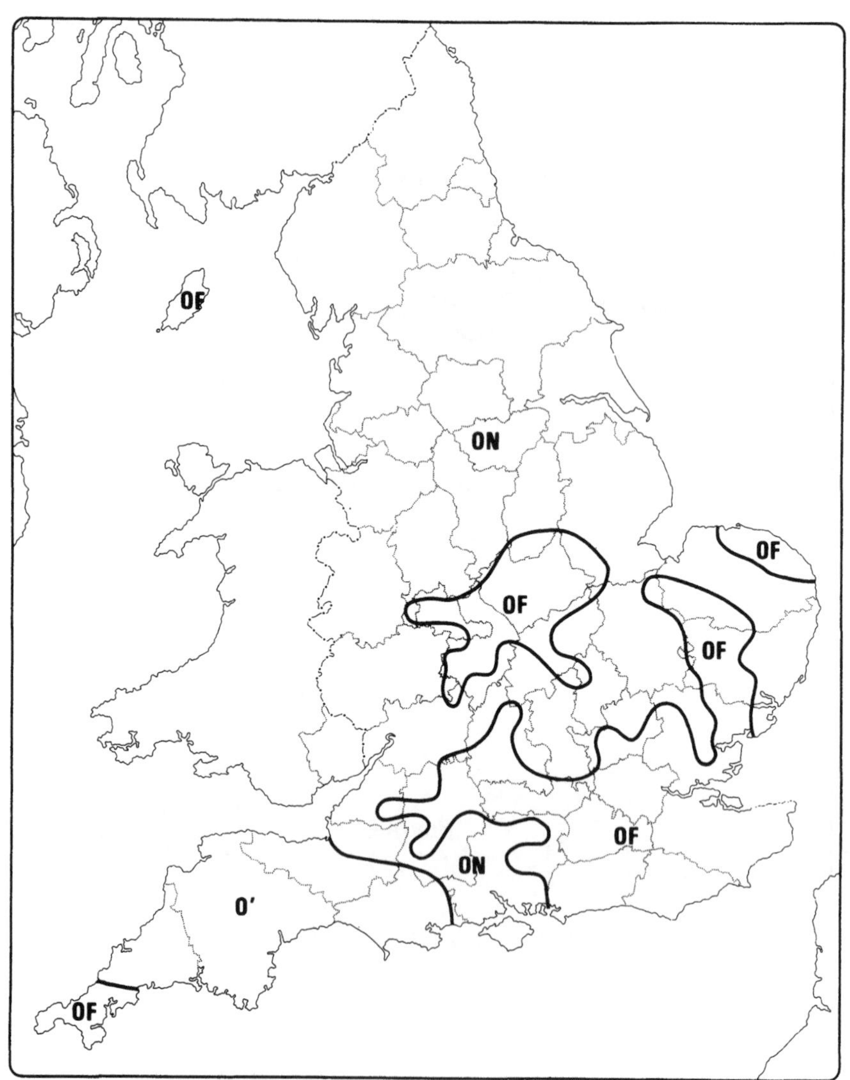

Map 113: OF (get out … it)

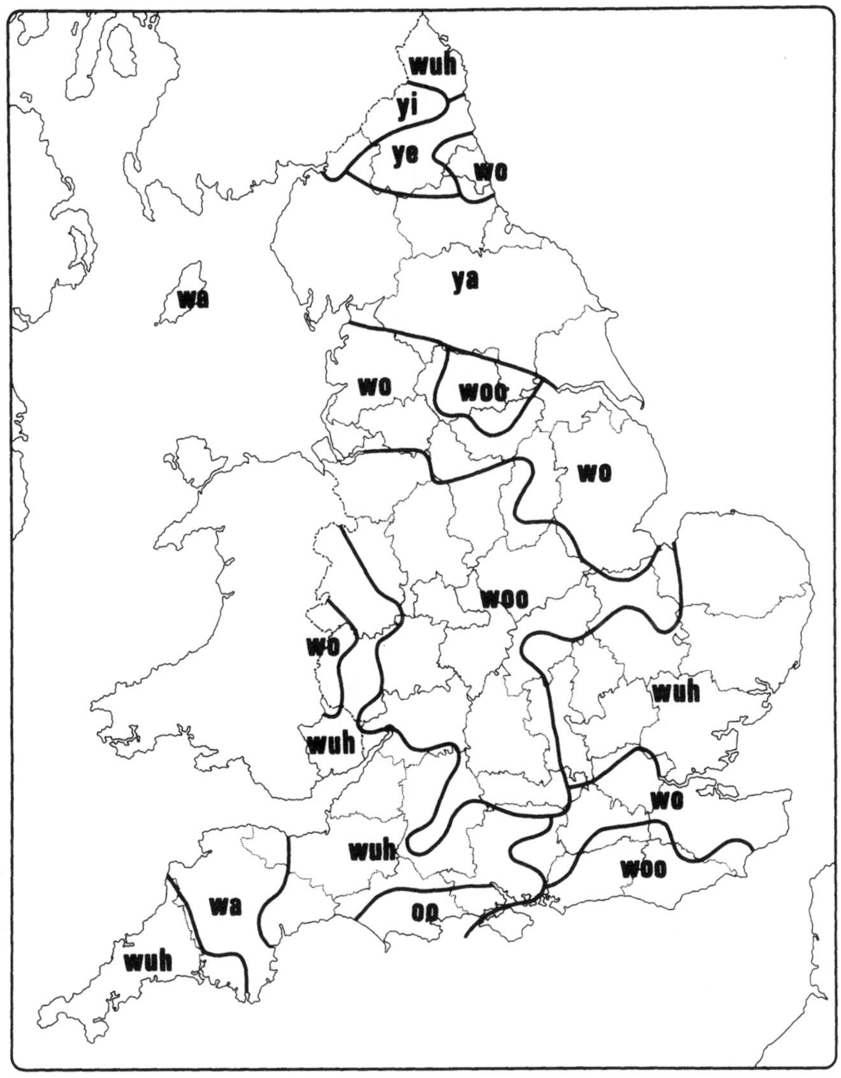

Map 114: <u>O</u>NCE

The **oo** in **woo** is a short sound, as in *put*; when not preceded by **w** the **oo** sound is long, as in *moon*.

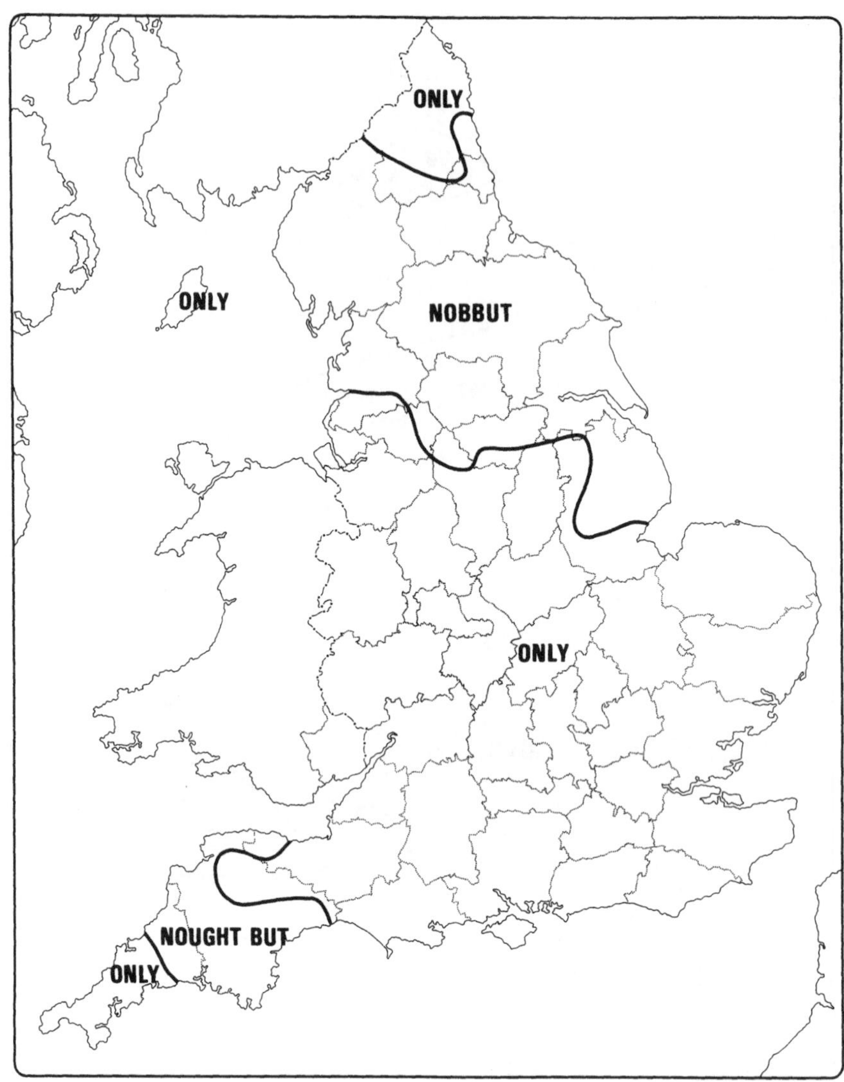

Map 115: ONLY (... a child)

ONLY occurs widely in **NOBBUT** areas. **NOBBUT** is a shortened form of *naught but/nought but*; the adverbs *naught* and *nought* persisted in Standard and literary English well into the nineteenth century.

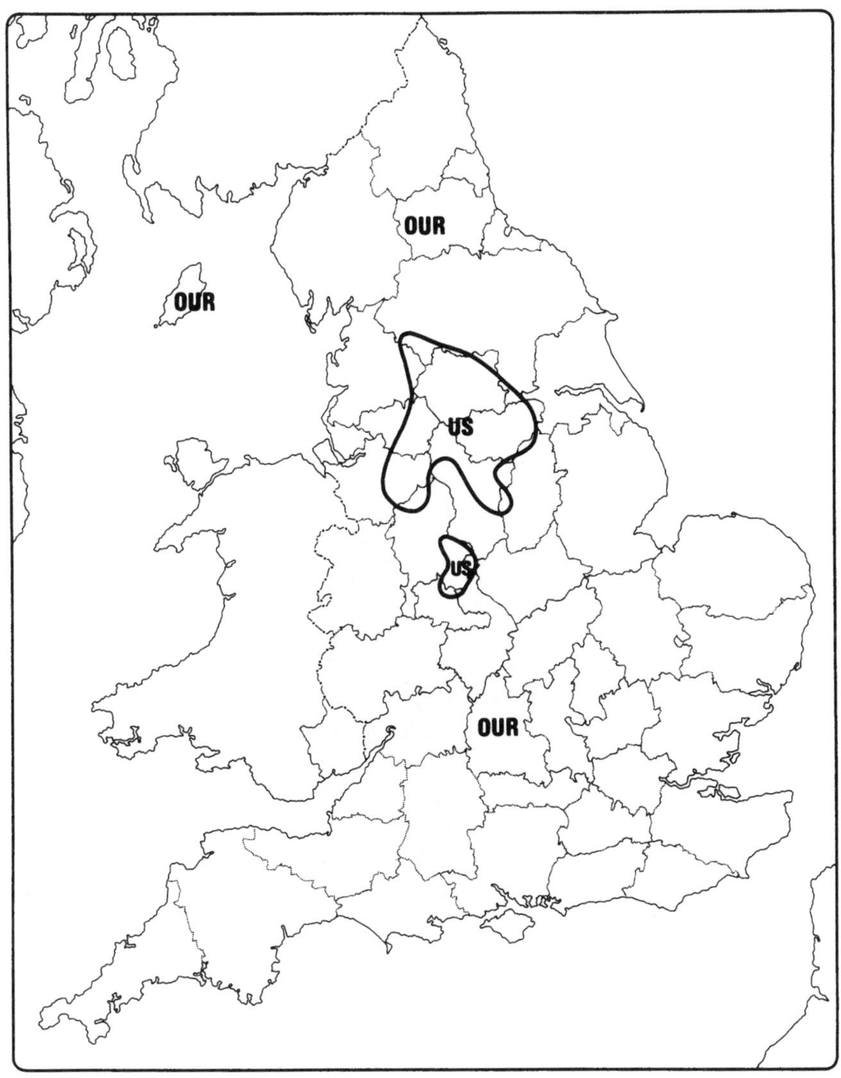

Map 116: OUR (we have ... own)

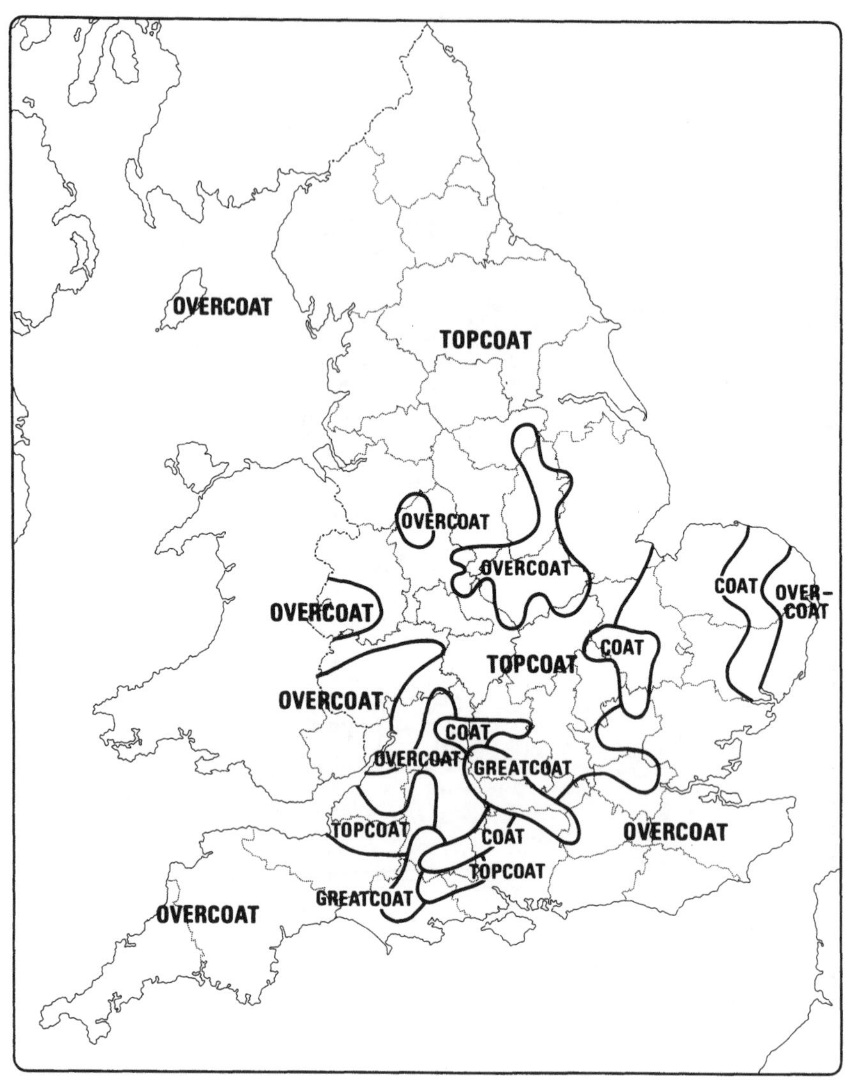

Map 117: OVERCOAT

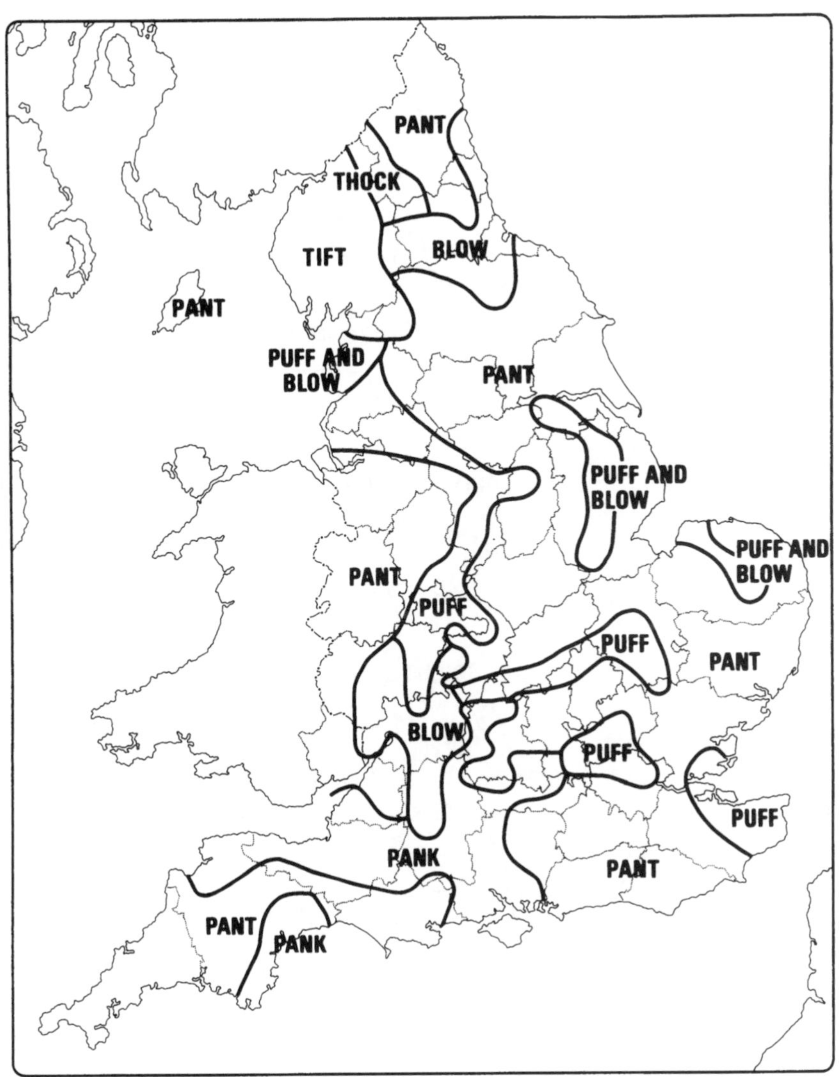

Map 118: PANT (to ...)

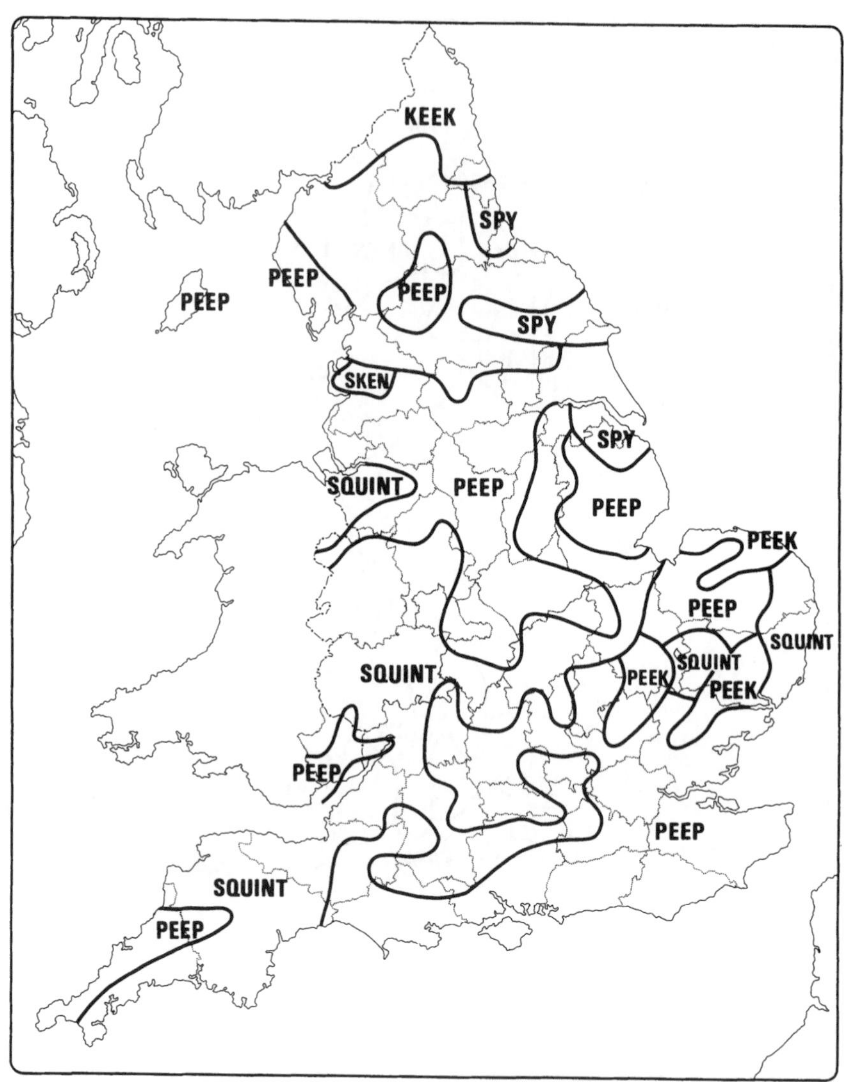

Map 119: PEEP (to ...)

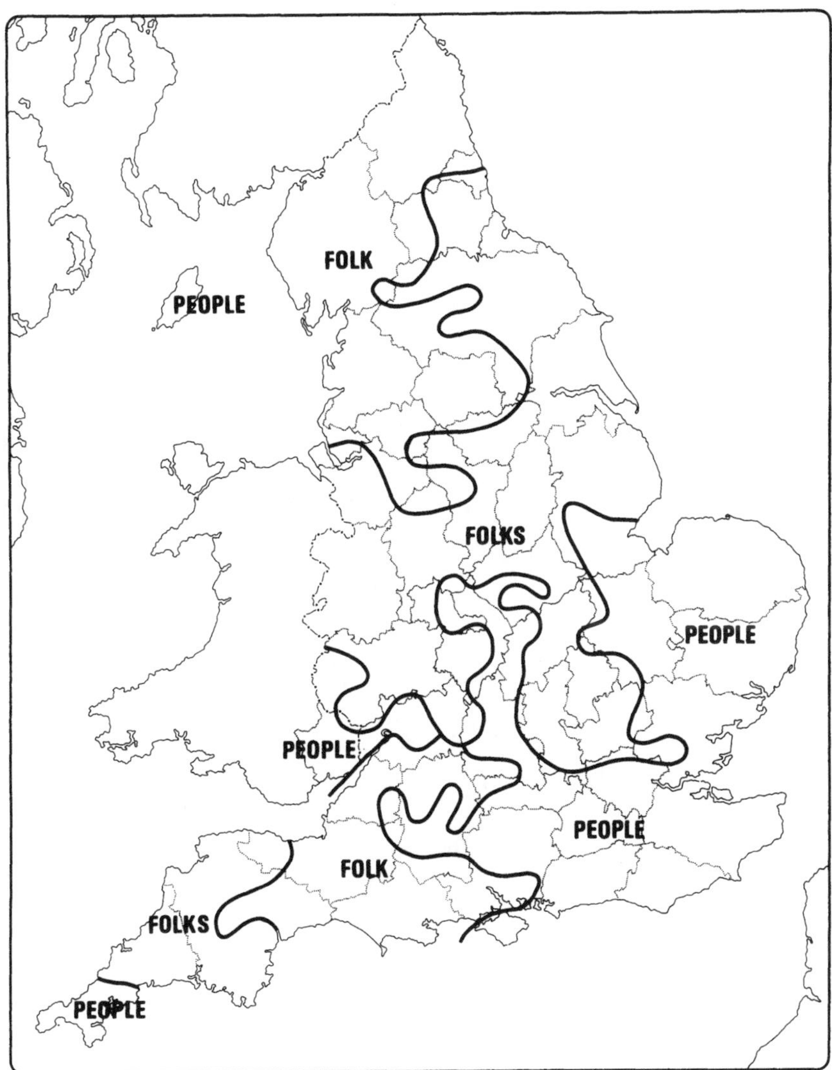

Map 120: PEOPLE

Here in the dialects we see the Old English word **FOLK(S)** maintaining its ground against the French word **PEOPLE** which has become the Standard term.

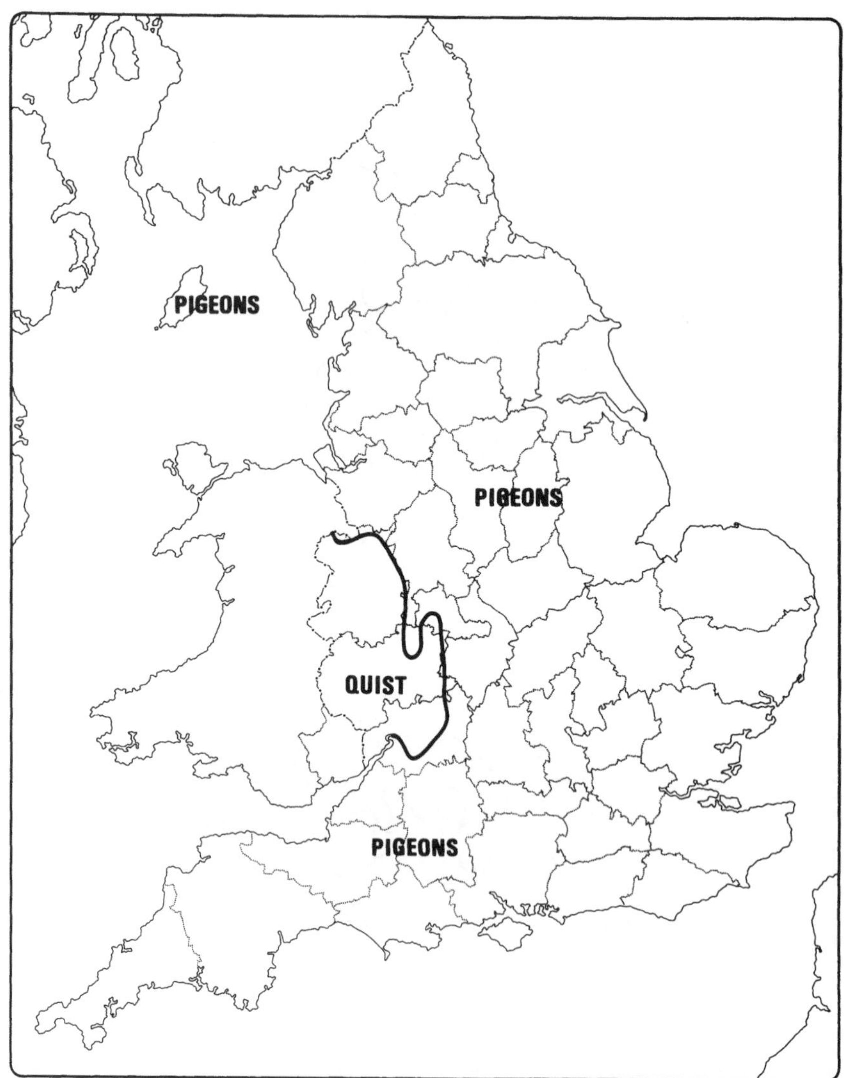

Map 121: PIGEONS (tame)
There is some uncertainty about whether **QUIST** is sometimes a singular word; it can usually be regarded as a collective plural, meaning 'a number of pigeons' but some examples of a plural form *quists*, usually meaning 'tame pigeons', have also been recorded. In Cheshire and south Gloucestershire *quists* sometimes denotes 'woodpigeons', while in north Hereford and Worcester is can denote 'wild pigeons'.

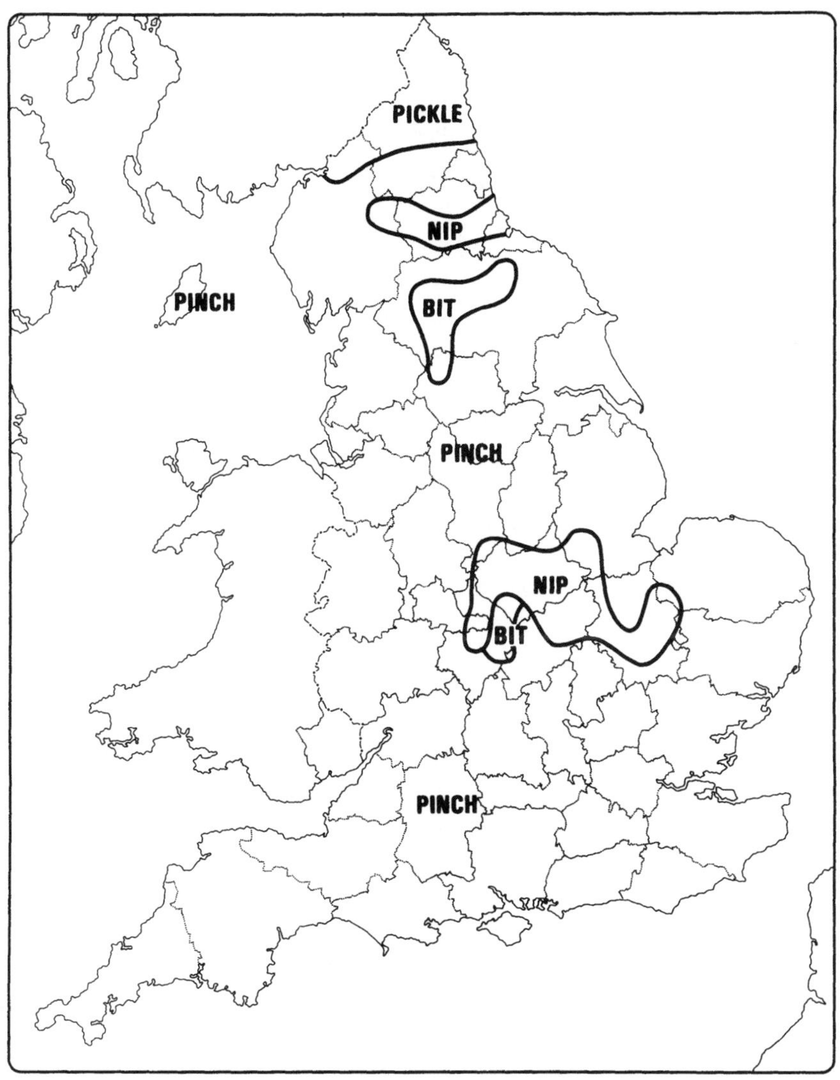

Map 122: PINCH (small quantity of salt or sugar)

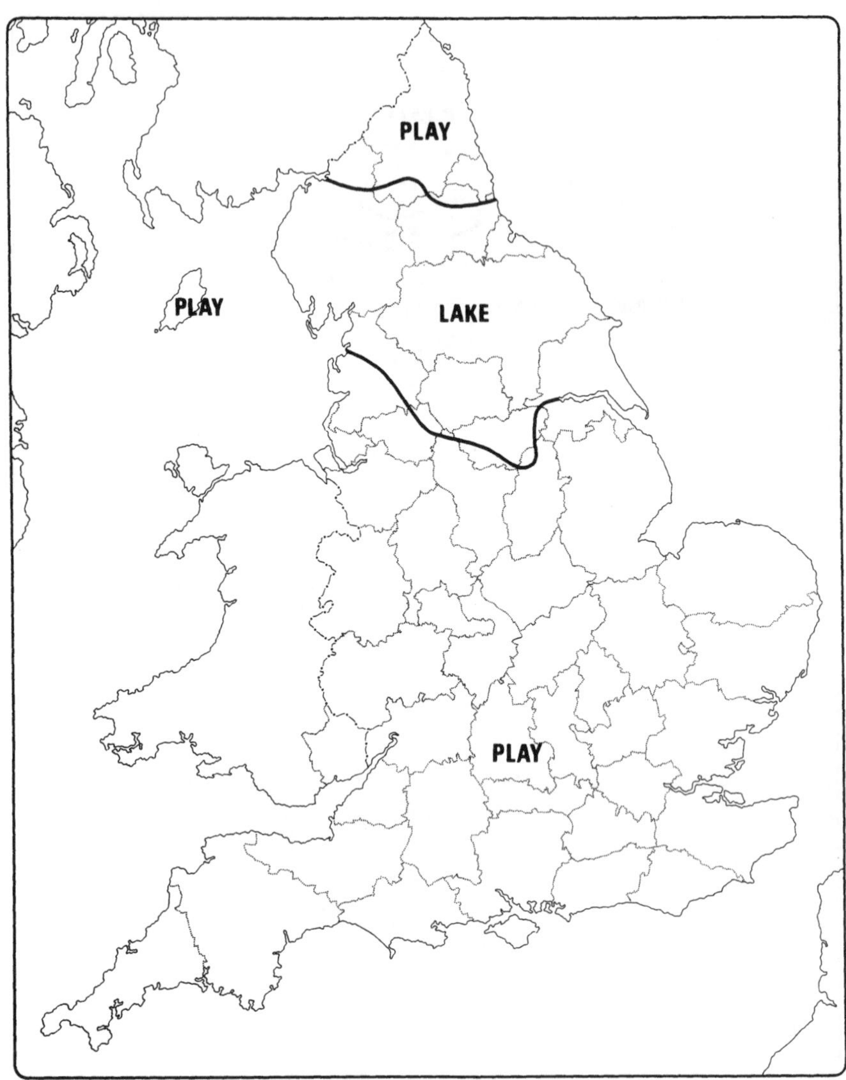

Map 123: PLAY (to . . .)

The Old English **PLAY** is obviously the dominant word and is found frequently in areas where **LAKE** is the more common form, especially in east Yorkshire. **LAKE** comes from Old Norse and still survives, under pressure, in part of the area settled by the Norwegians (the North West) and the Danes (the North East).

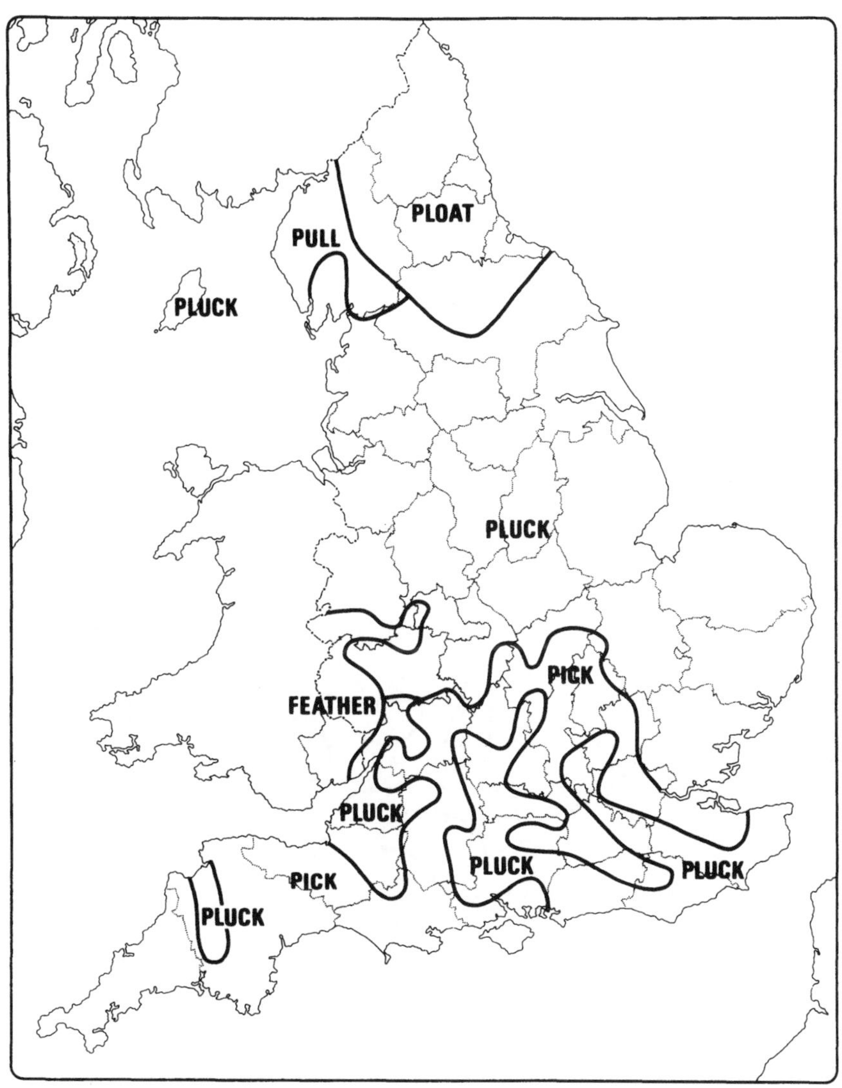

Map 124: PLUCK (to . . ., feathers)

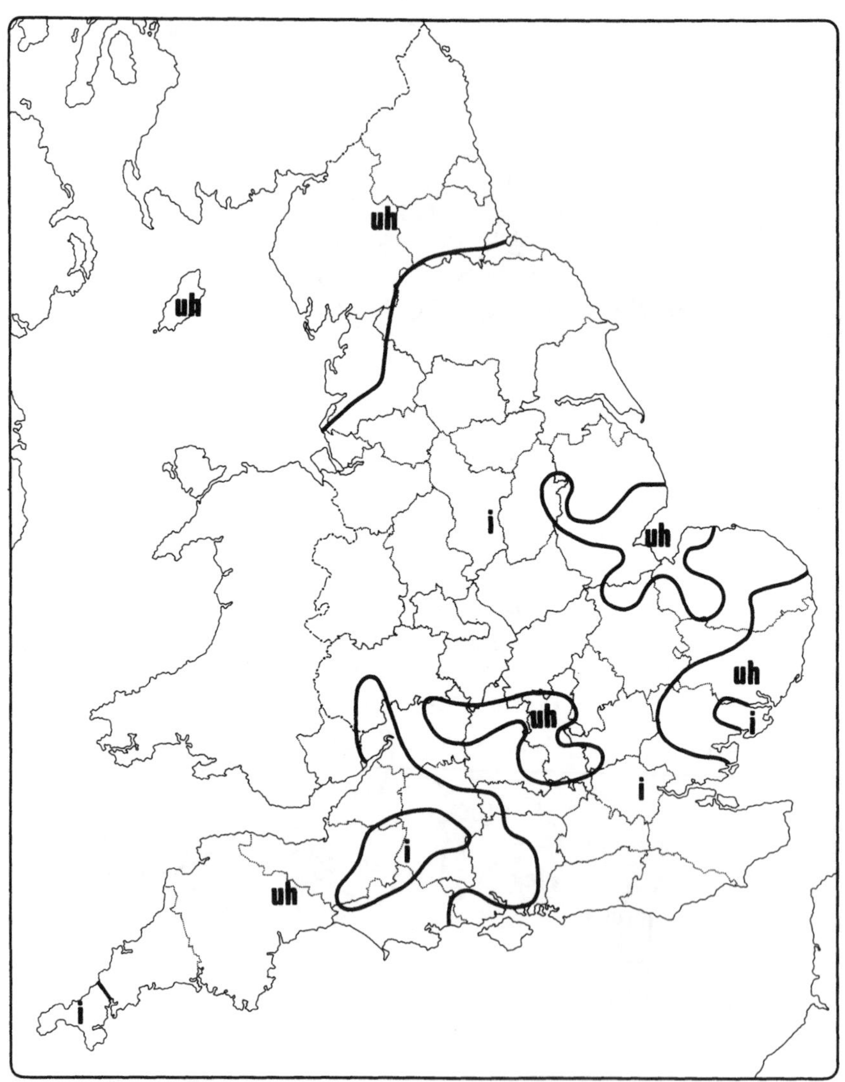

Map 125: POCKETS

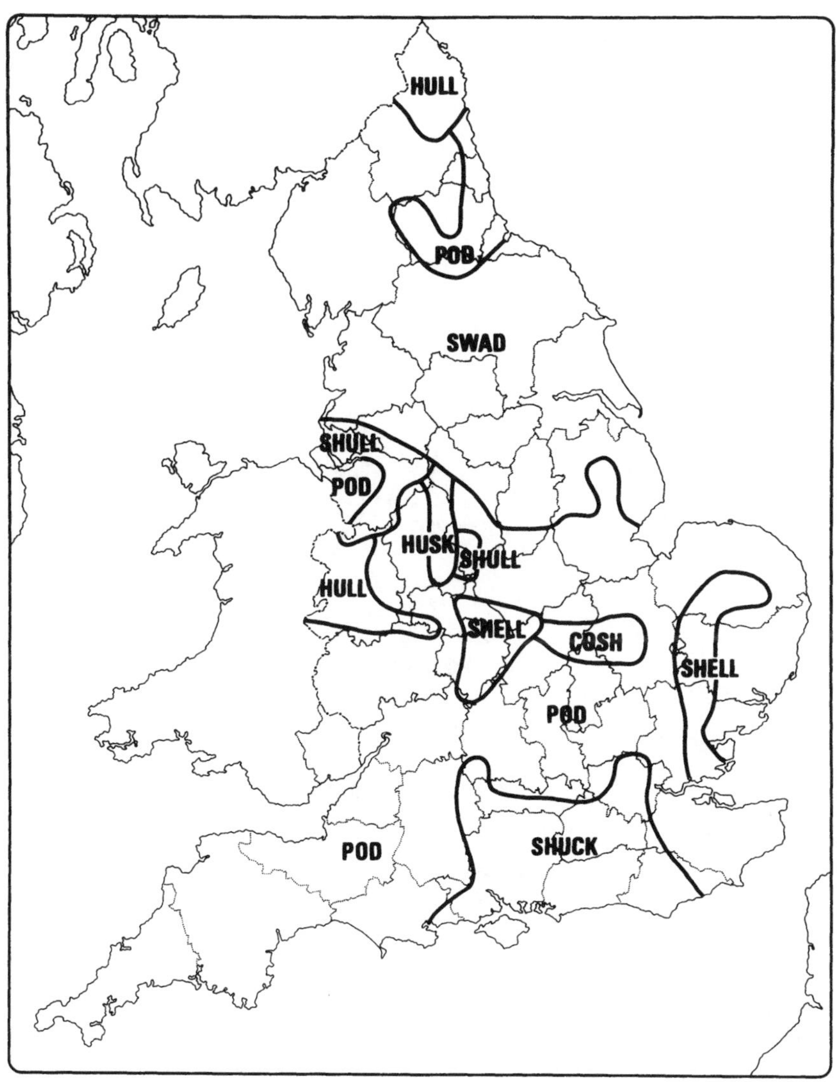

Map 126: POD (peas)

The Standard form **POD** is recorded widely throughout the country, but regional variants, notably **SWAD**, persist strongly.

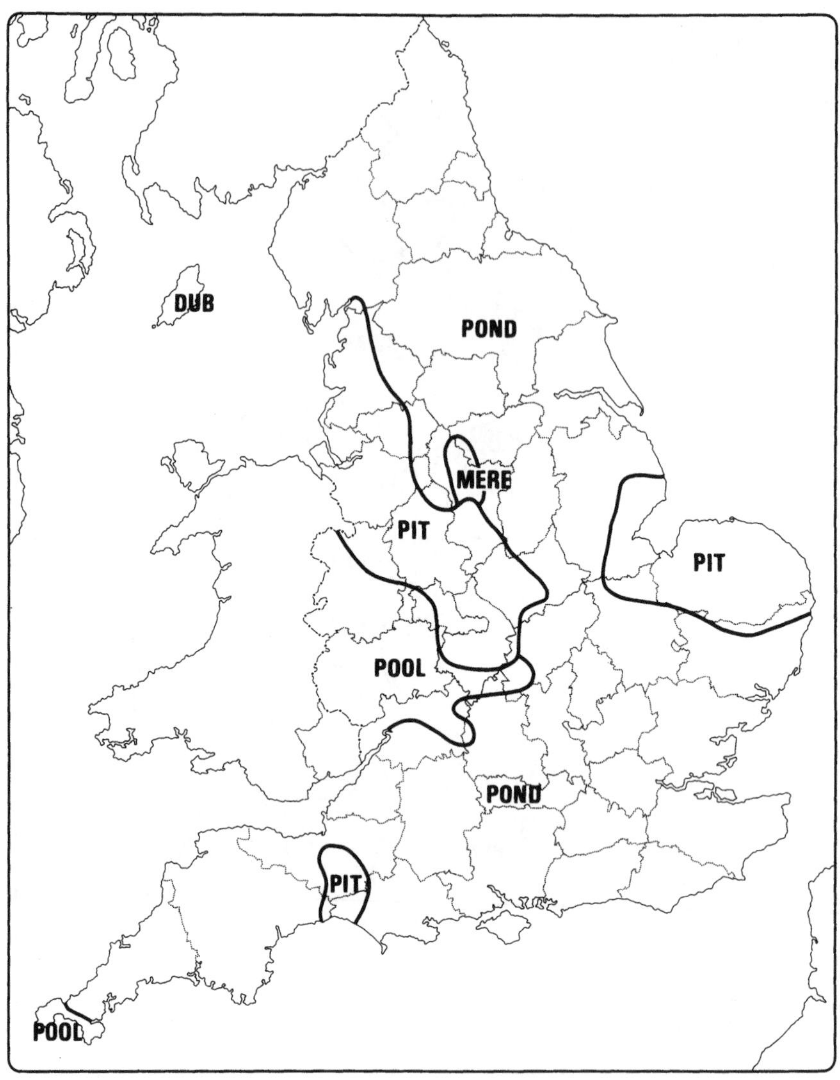

Map 127: POND

POND is clearly dominant and is found widely throughout the country, but variants, notably **PIT** and **POOL**, continue to hold their ground.

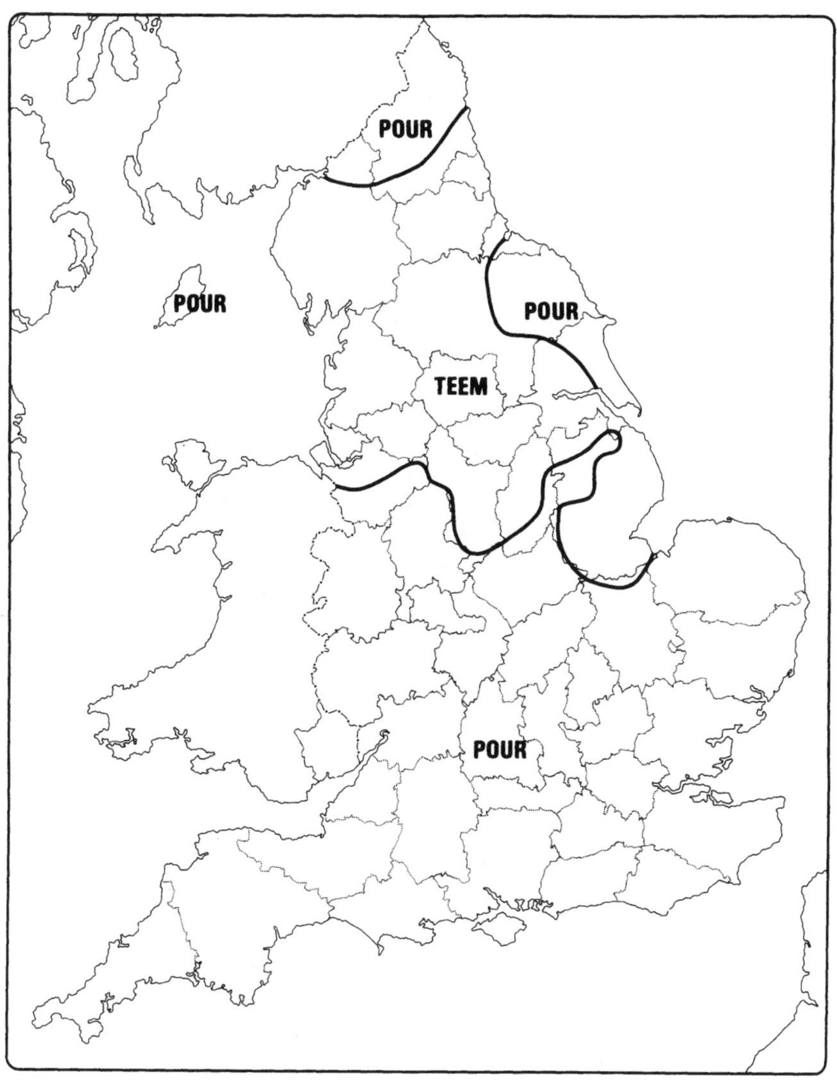

Map 128: POUR (tea)

POUR is clearly dominant, but **TEEM** persists strongly in the North and is used even more frequently with reference to rain.

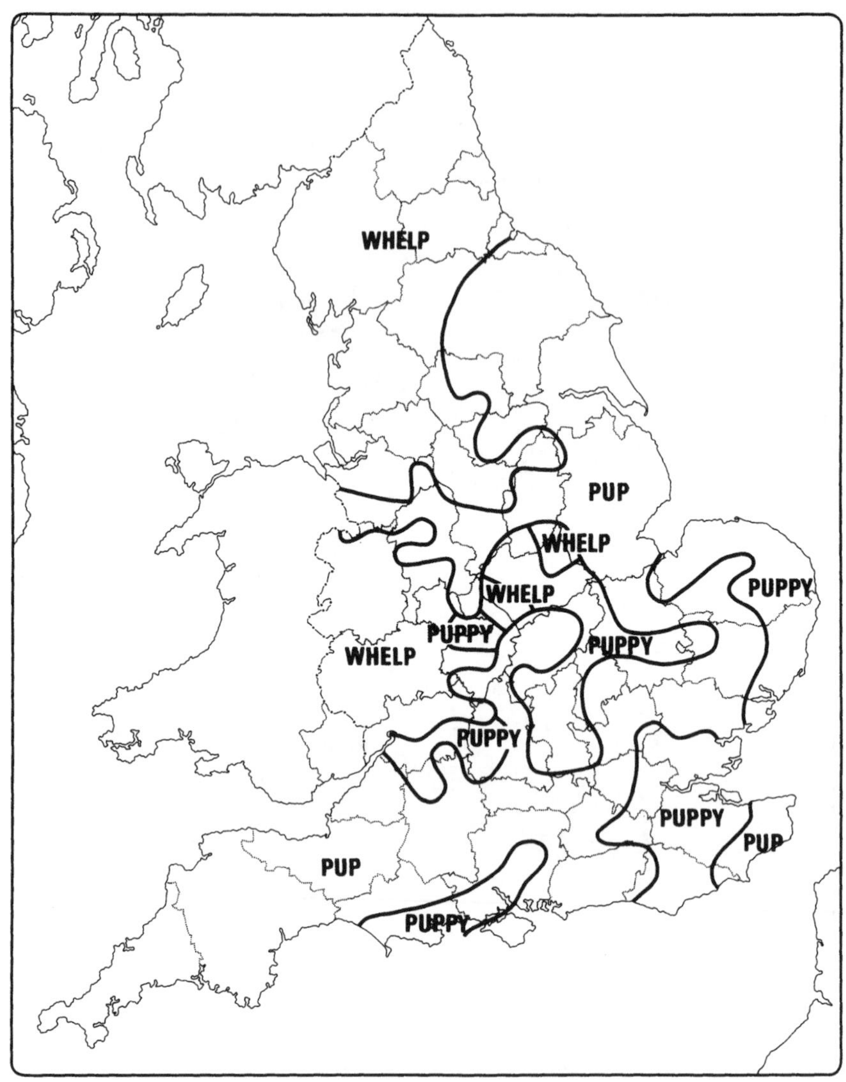

Map 129: PUP
This map illustrates the contrasting distribution of the interesting French word *pup(py)* (originally = a doll, plaything) and the Old English *whelp*.

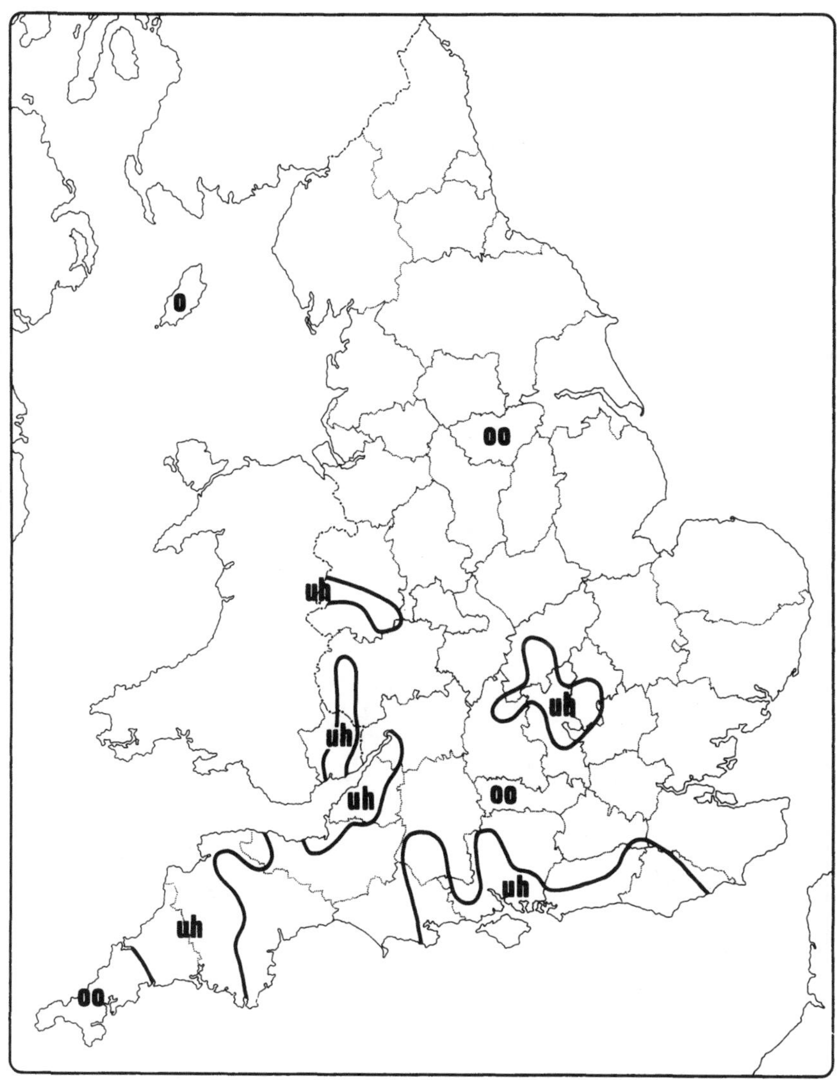

Map 130: P<u>U</u>T
oo is the short vowel in Standard English *put*. The **uh** forms are an interesting parallel with other examples in which speakers alter the Standard pronunciation **oo** to **uh** in such words as *put*, *foot*, *butcher* and *cushion*. This is known as 'hypercorrection'.

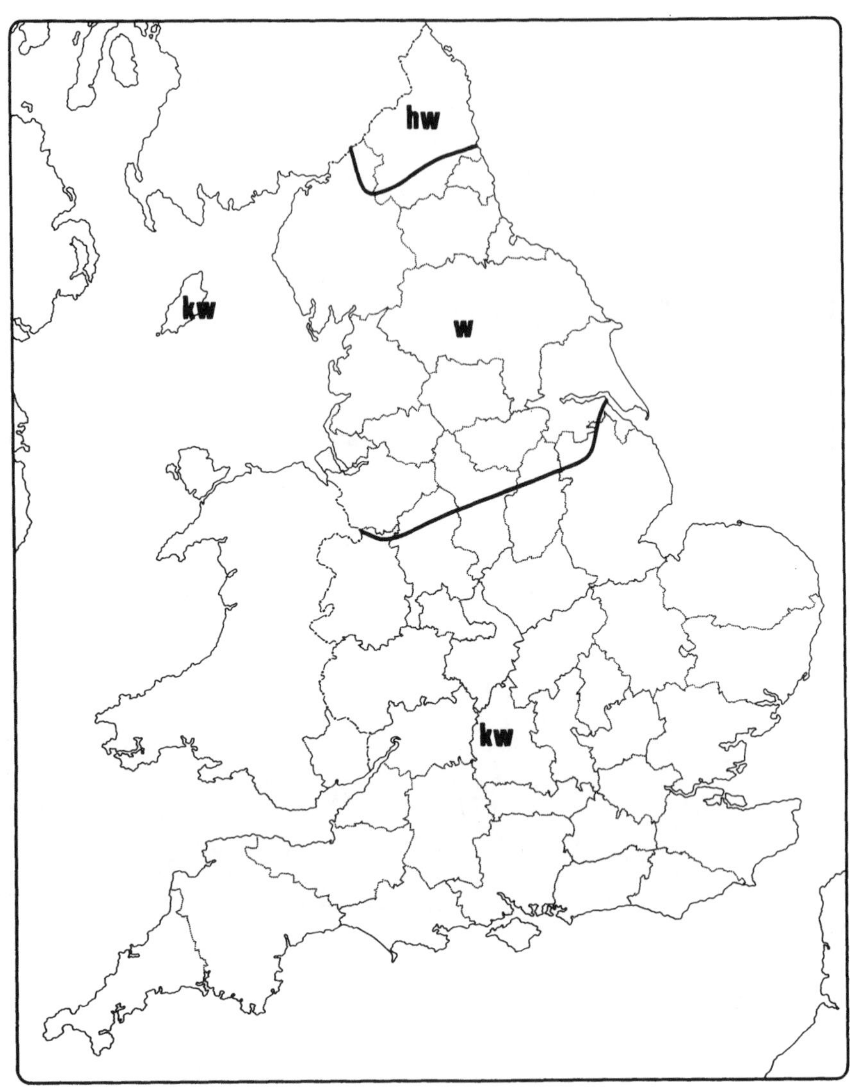

Map 131: QUICK (of fingernail)
While most of the country has the Standard form with **kw-**, the **w-** form *wick* continues to dominate in the North, no doubt strengthened by the similar adjective *wick*, meaning 'lively', in such proverbial comparisons as 'as wick as an eel'. The characteristic Scottish English pronunciation **hw-** is found predictably in the extreme North East. See also Map 186.

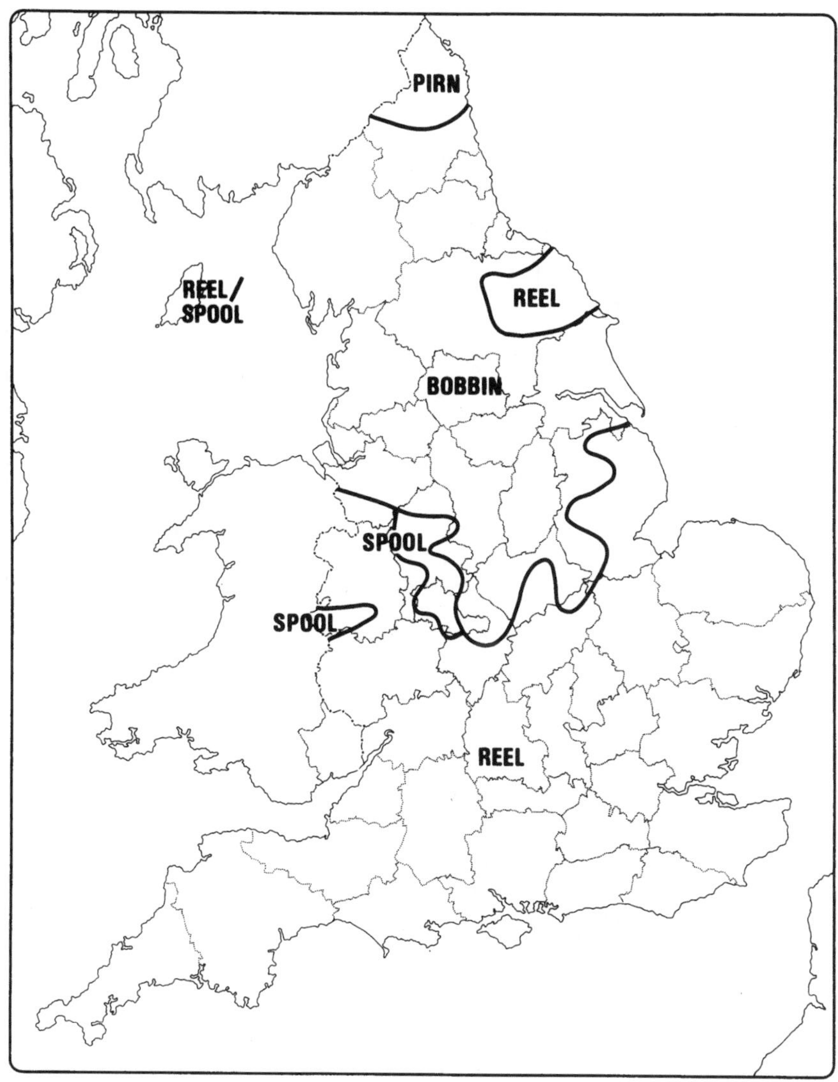

Map 132: REEL (of thread)
It is interesting to note that **BOBBIN**, derived from French, is dominant in the North; dialectal words of French origin are generally more common in the South.

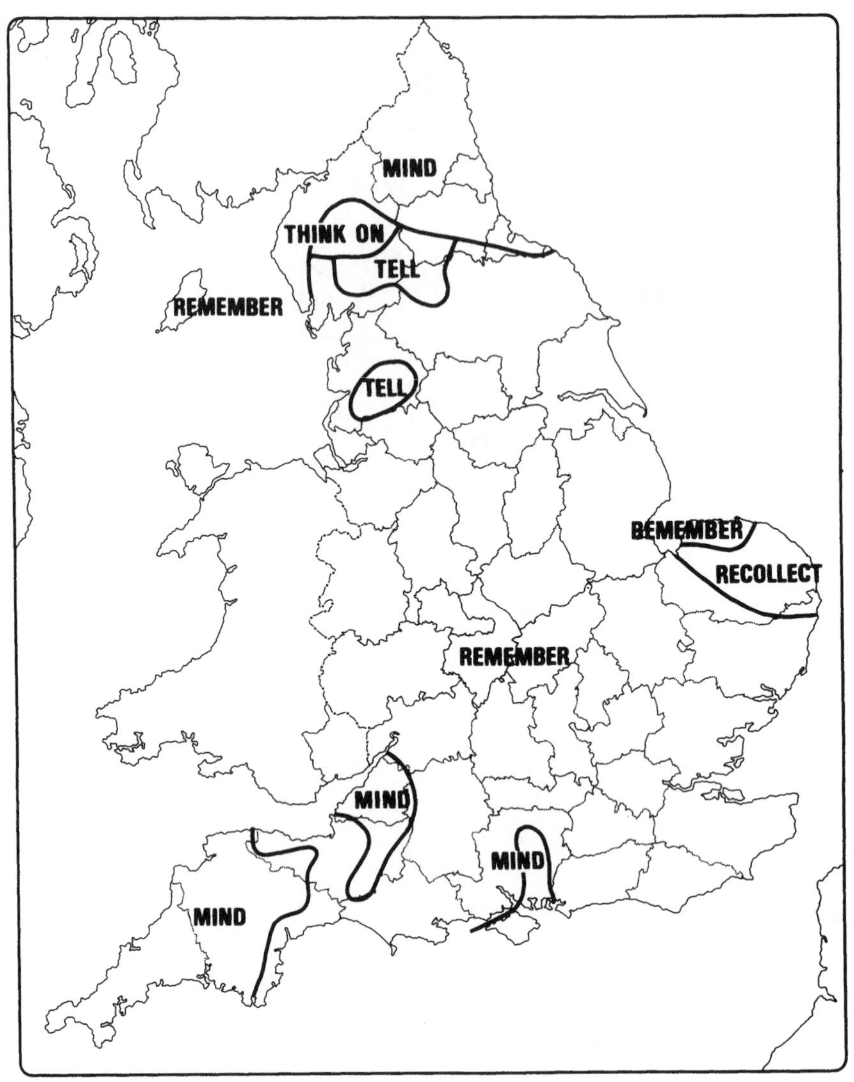

Map 133: REMEMBER (to . . .)

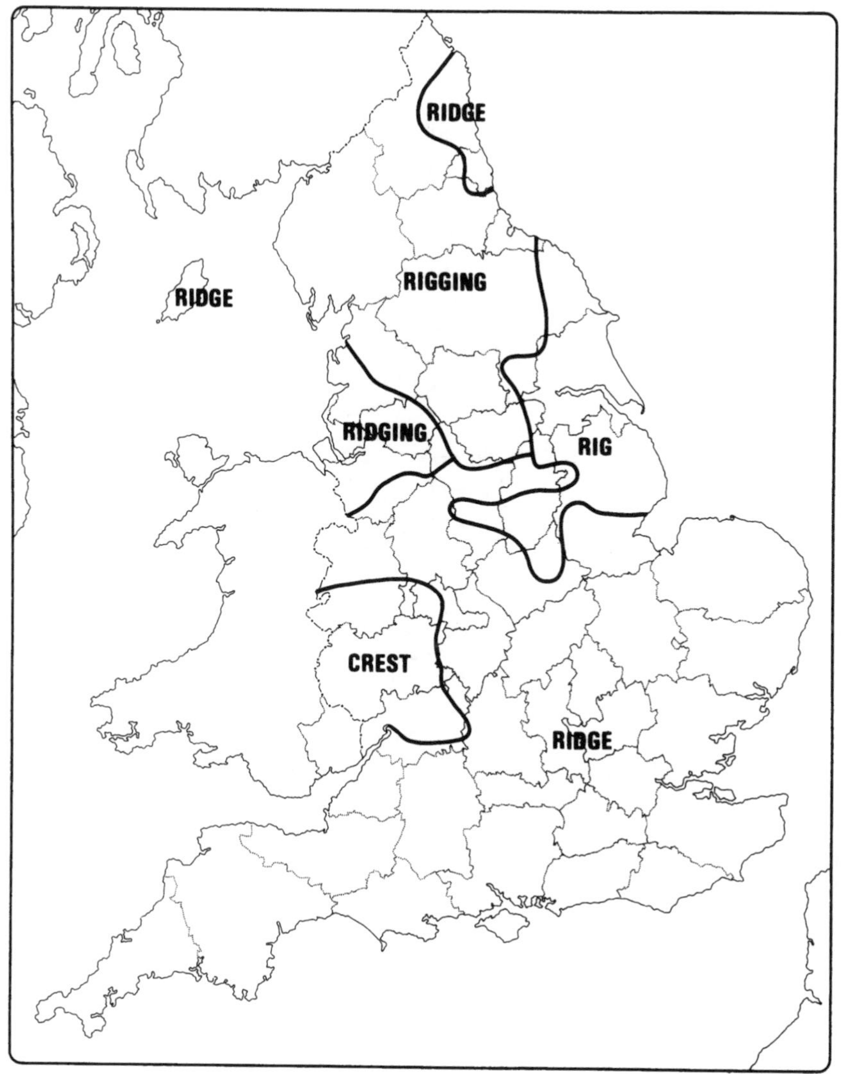

Map 134: RIDGE (of house roof)

CREST is often pronounced like *cress*; the final *g* is not pronounced in **RIGGING** and **RIDGING**.

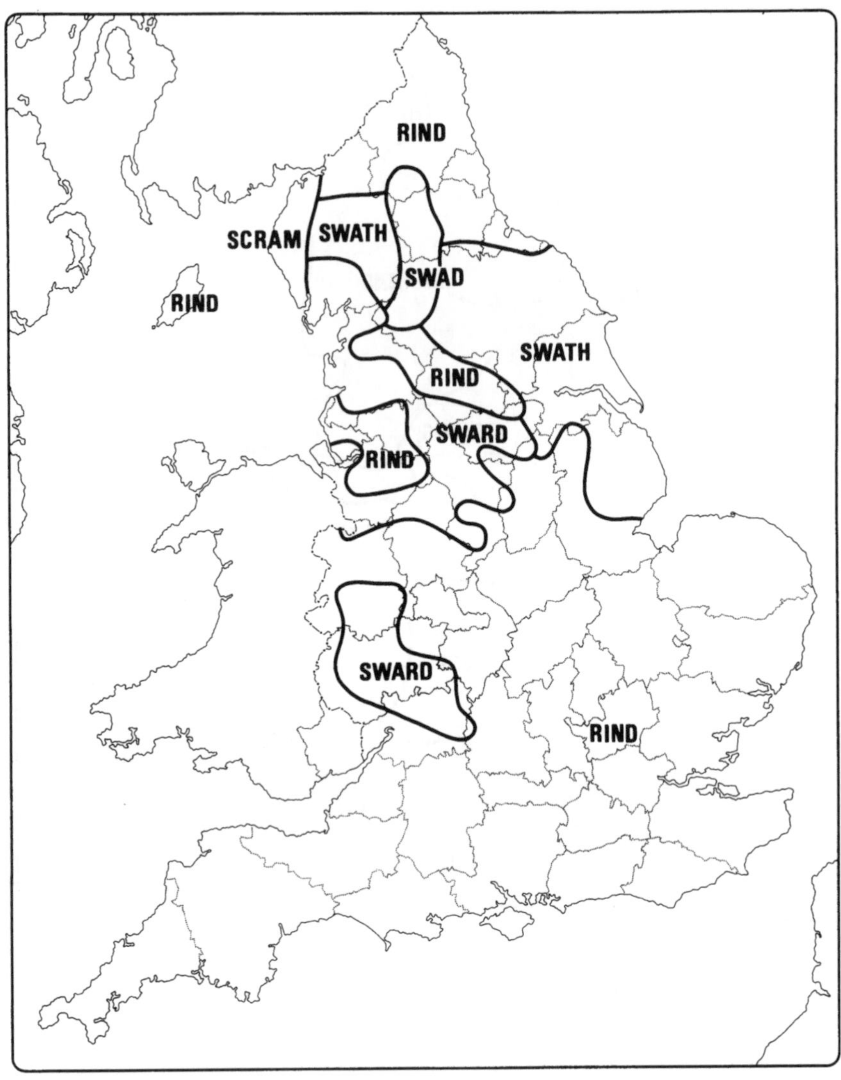

Map 135: RIND (of bacon)

RIND often occurs in areas where the alternative forms are the most common, and in these areas it is sometimes regarded as a newer word. **SWARD** and **SWATH** are derived from two parallel Old English words, *sweard* and *swearth*.

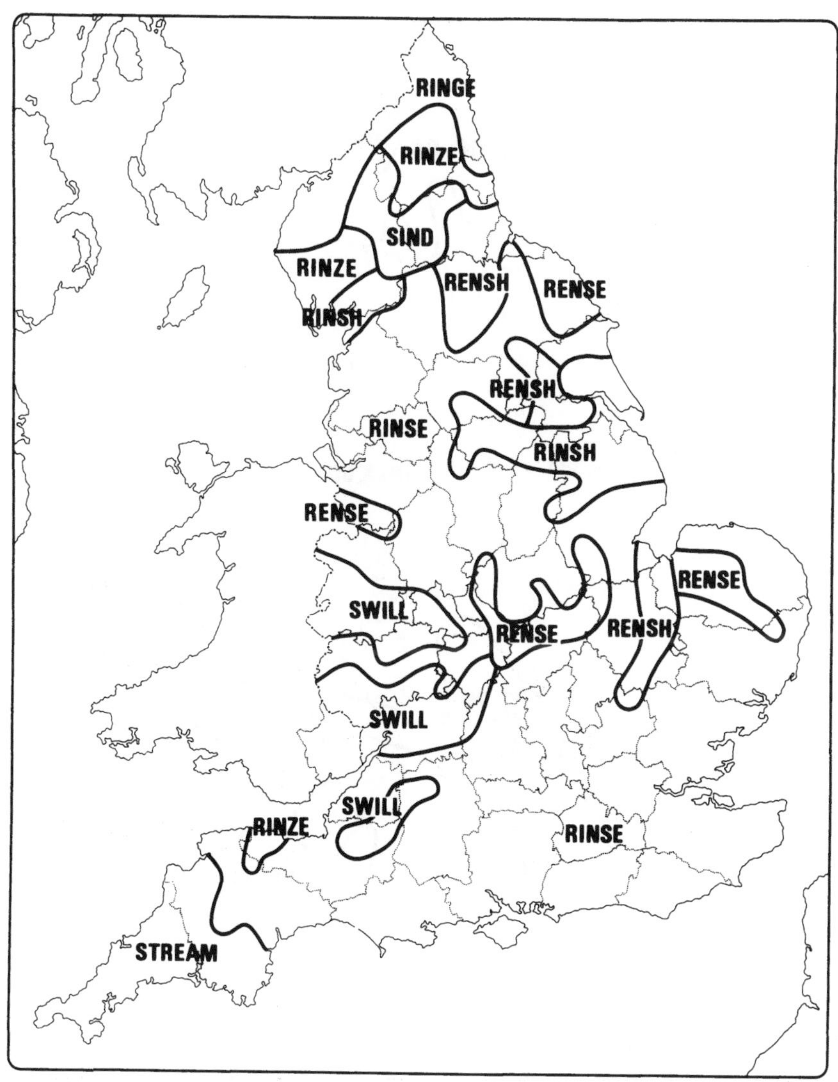

Map 136: RINSE (to . . ., clothes)
The final sound of **RINGE** in the far North is **zh**.

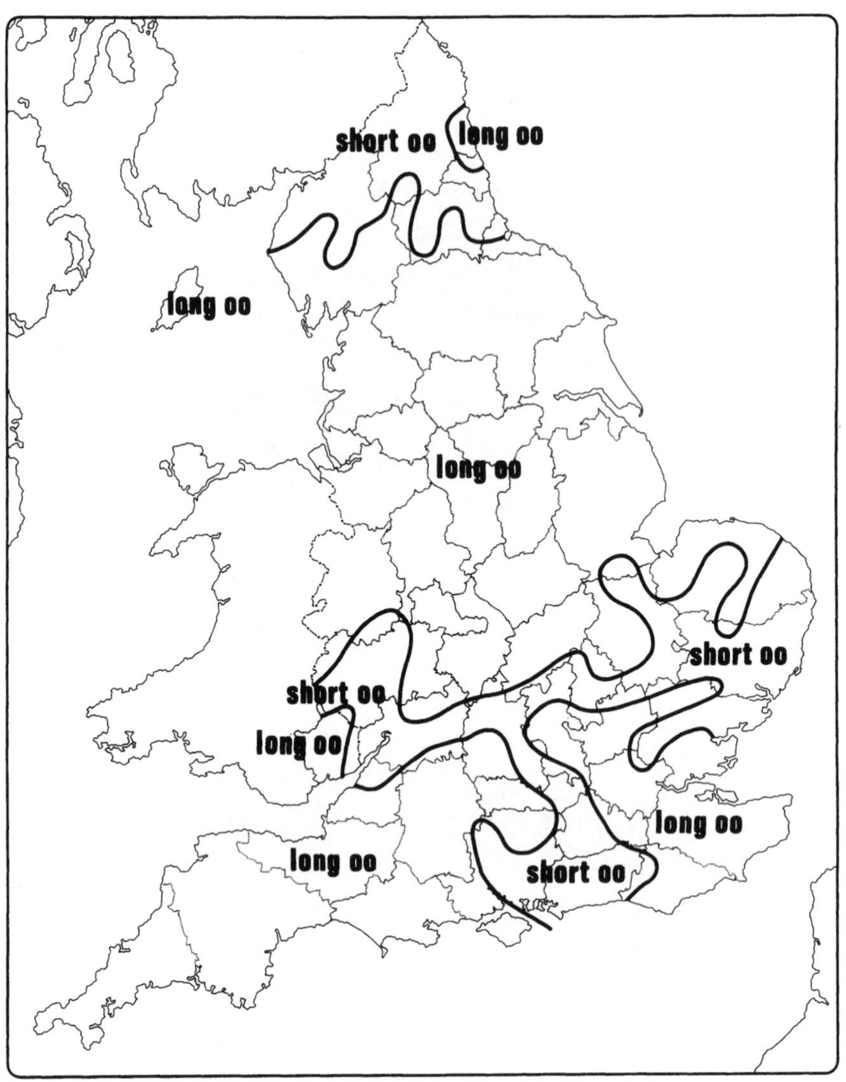

Map 137: R<u>OO</u>MS

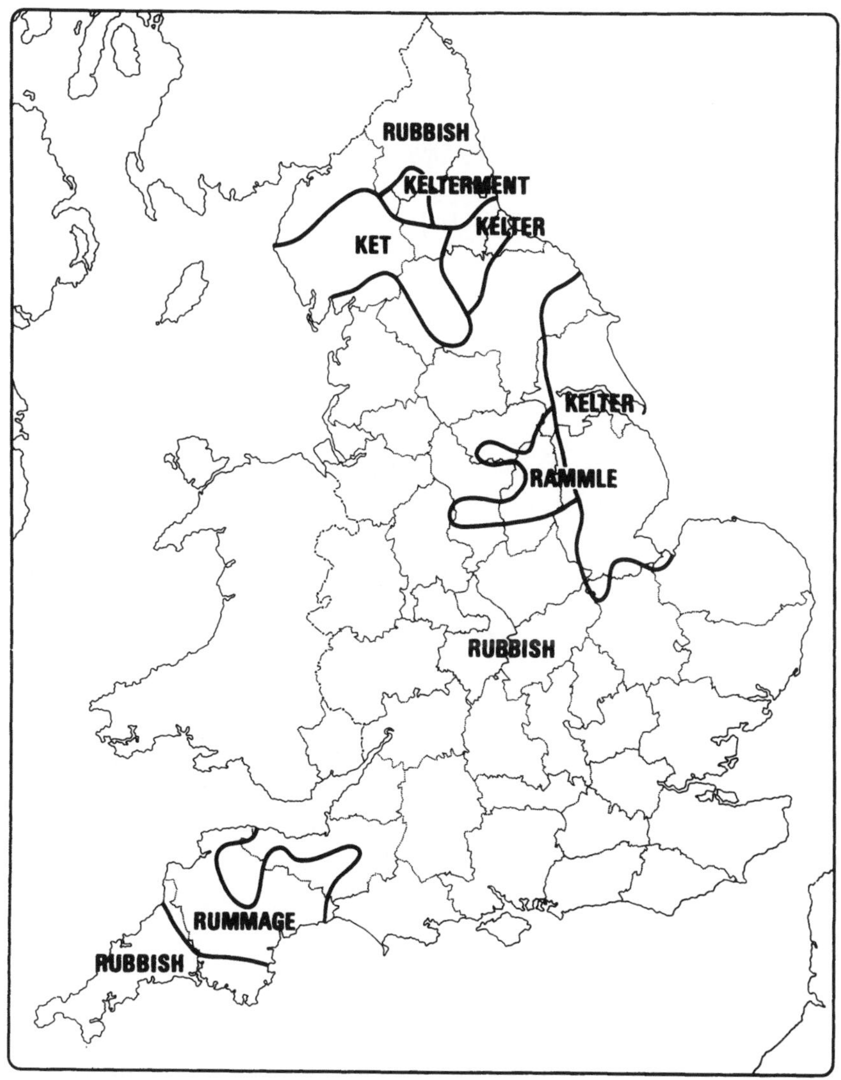

Map 138: RUBBISH (thrown away)
The Standard form **RUBBISH** is often found in the areas where **KET** and **KELTER** dominate.

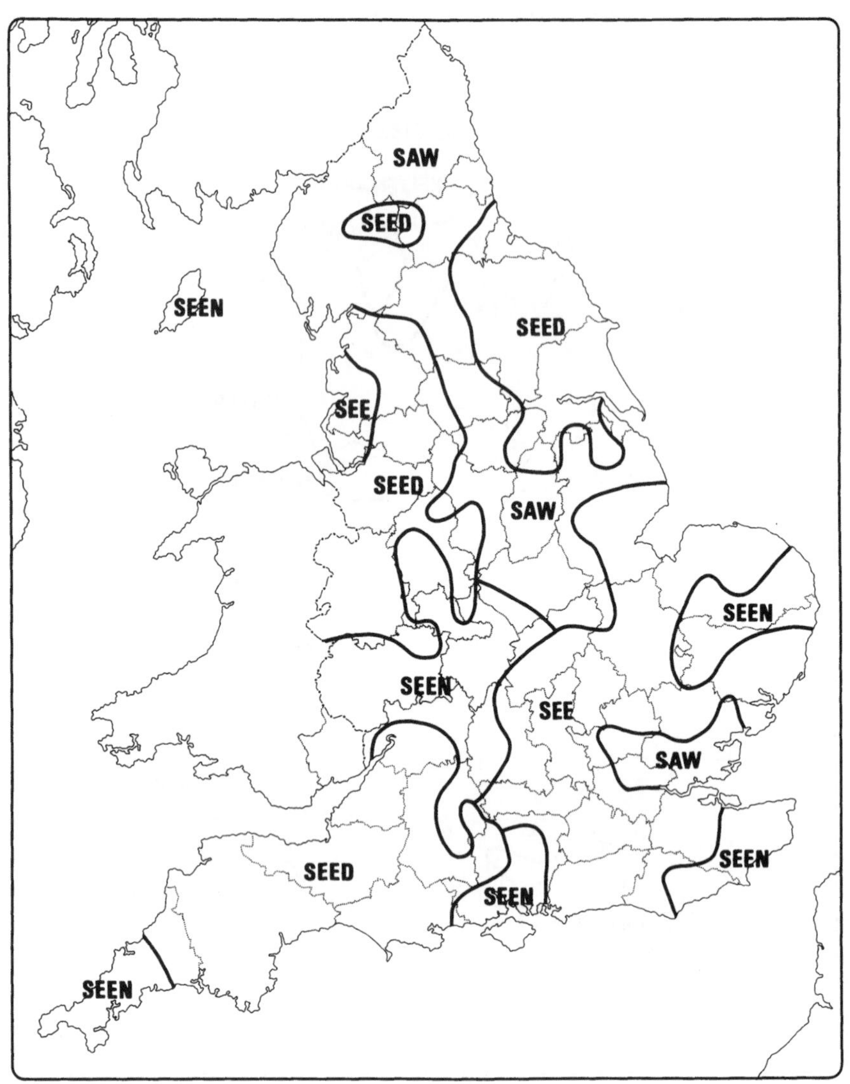
SAW
SEED
SEEN
SEED
SEE
SEED
SAW
SEEN
SEEN
SEE
SAW
SEEN
SEED
SEEN
SEEN

Map 139: SAW (I ...)

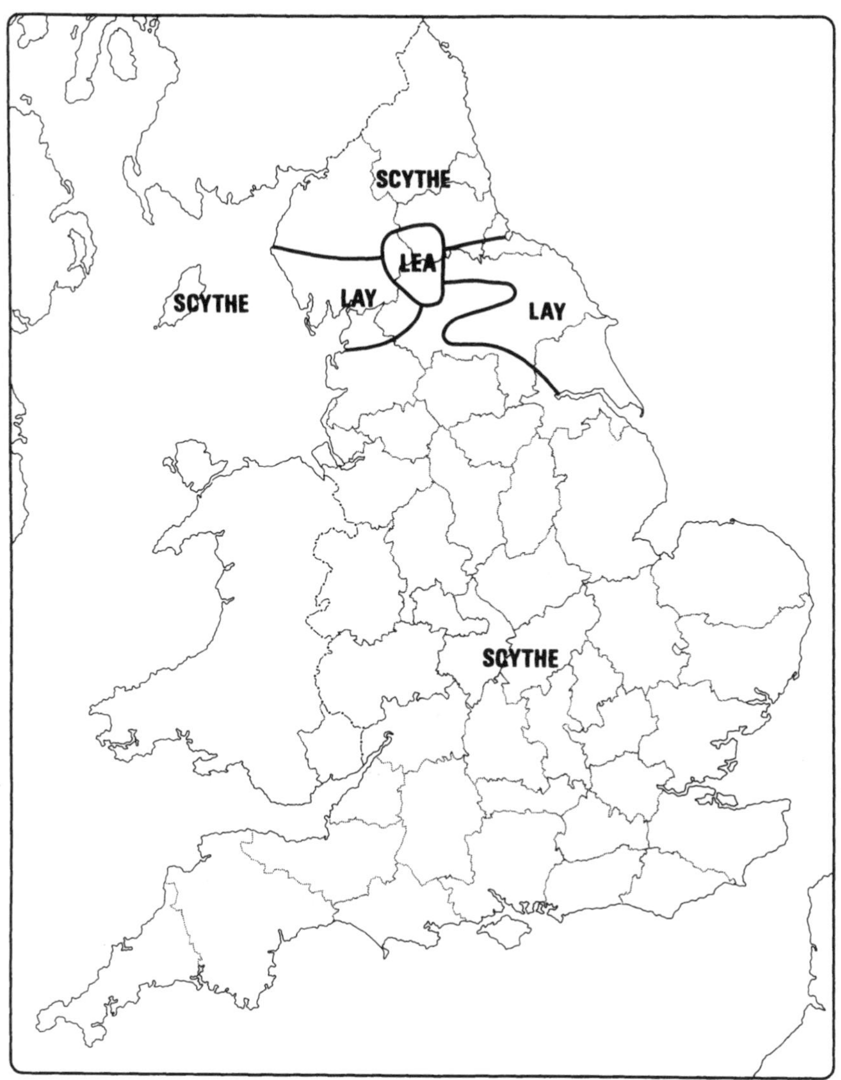

Map 140: SCYTHE

LAY and **LEA** are derived from Old Norse, but the Old English **SCYTHE** is clearly ousting them from the mid-northern areas of Viking settlement where they have held out until recently.

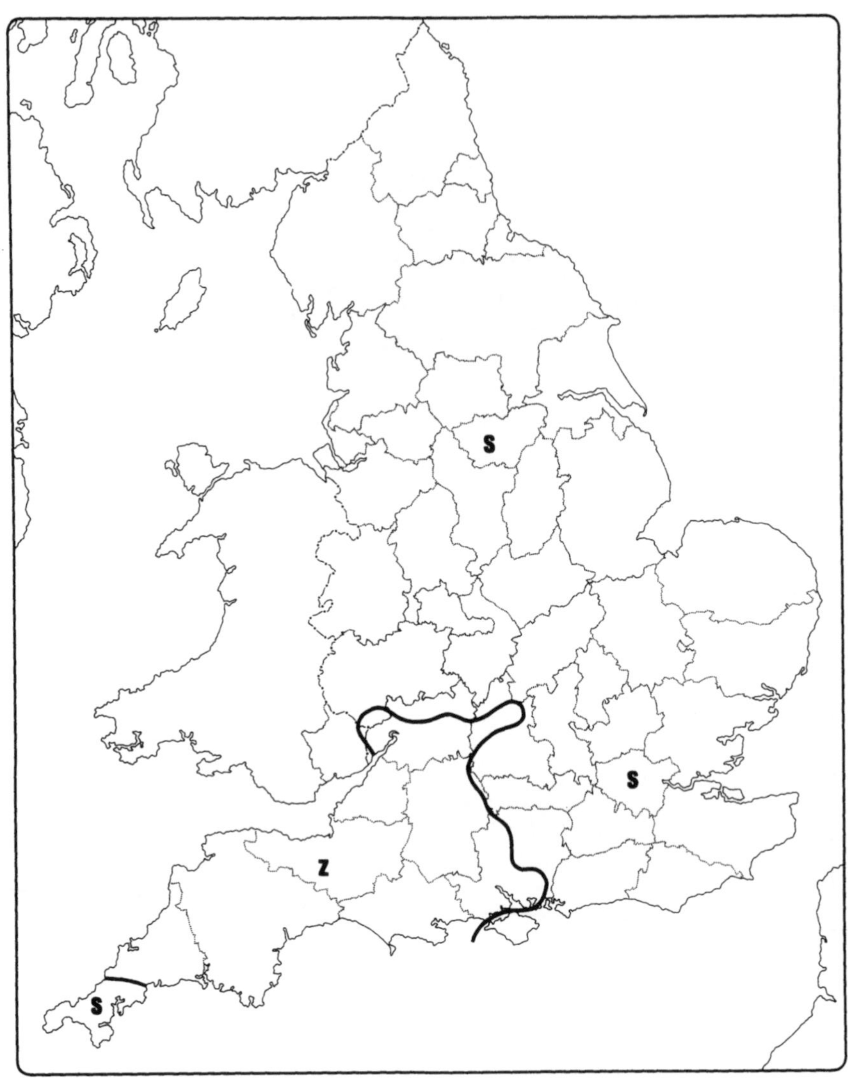

Map 141: SEVEN
For the 'voicing' of initial consonants see Map 55.

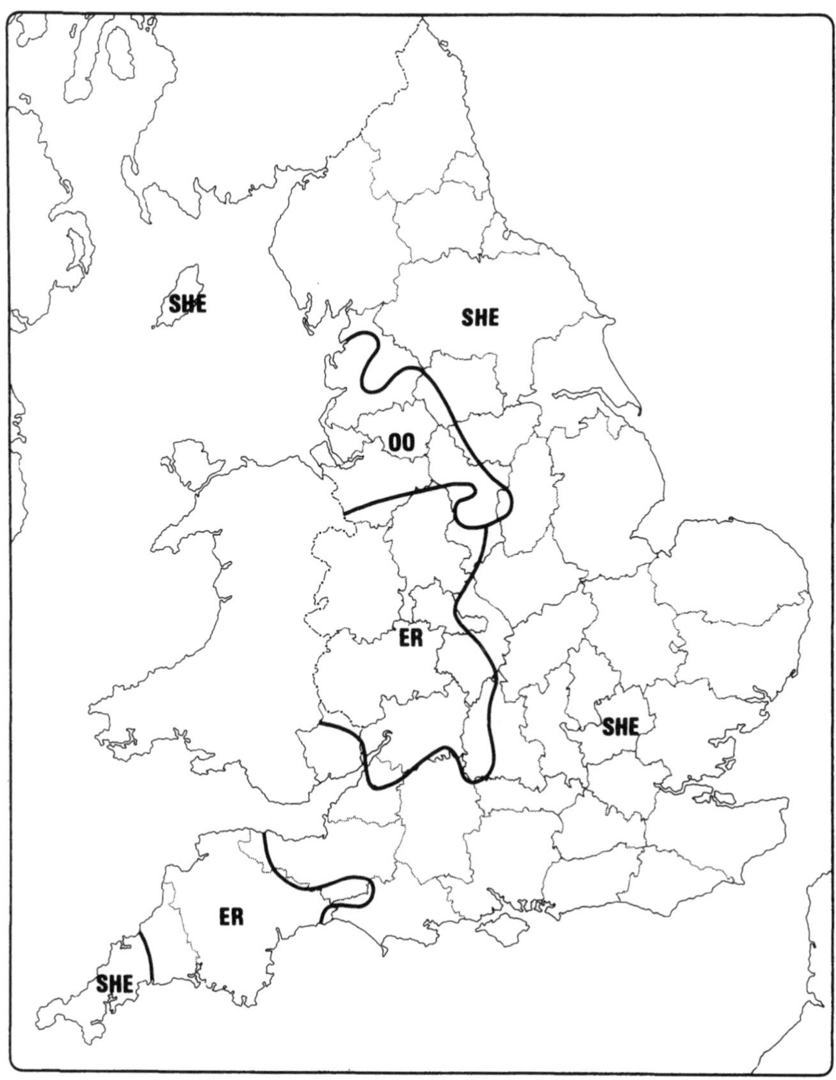

Map 142: SHE

The Standard form of the pronoun (**SHE**) did not emerge until medieval times, but now dominates. The interesting form **OO** is derived from the Old English *heo* ('she').

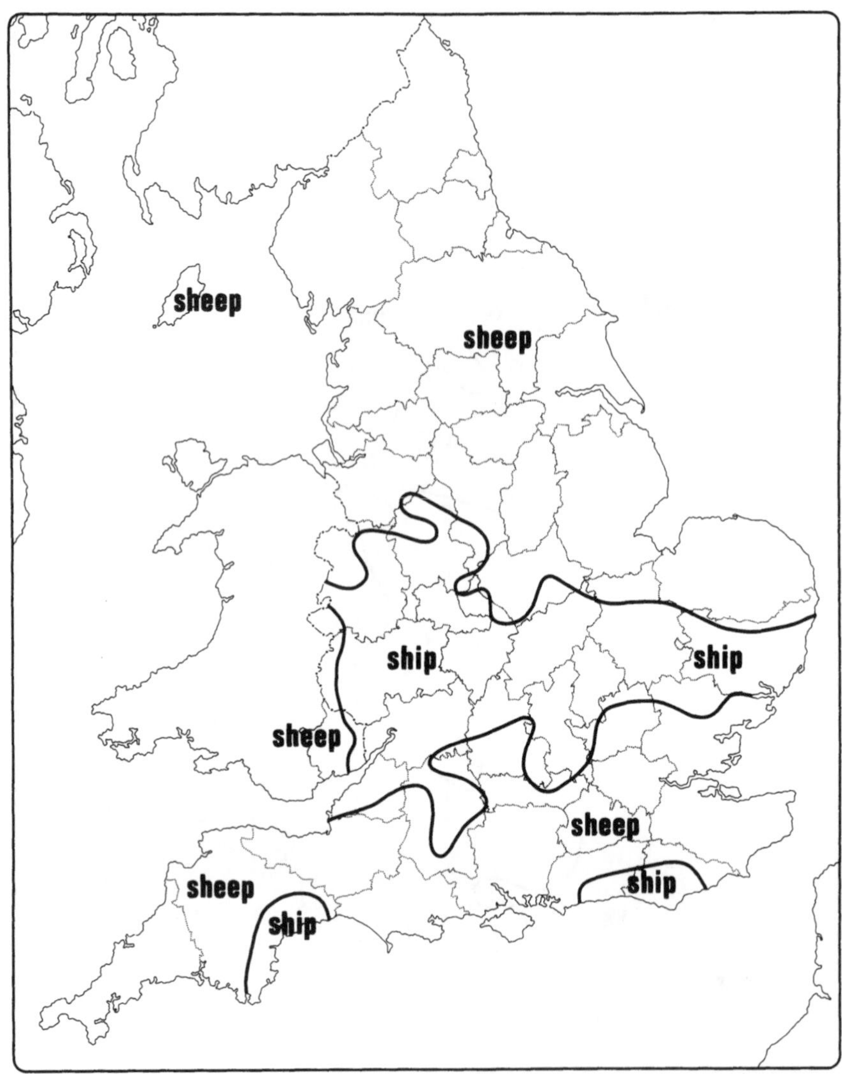

Map 143: SHEEP

It is a matter of debate whether the word *ship* in 'to spoil the ship for a ha'porth of tar' refers to a boat or a sheep; tar was frequently used in treating sores as well as for marking sheep to identify their owners. The confusion between the two words may well arise because of the pronunciation of *sheep* as *ship* in much of the Midlands and parts of the South as this map shows. There is considerable overlap between the two forms in Leicestershire and Northamptonshire.

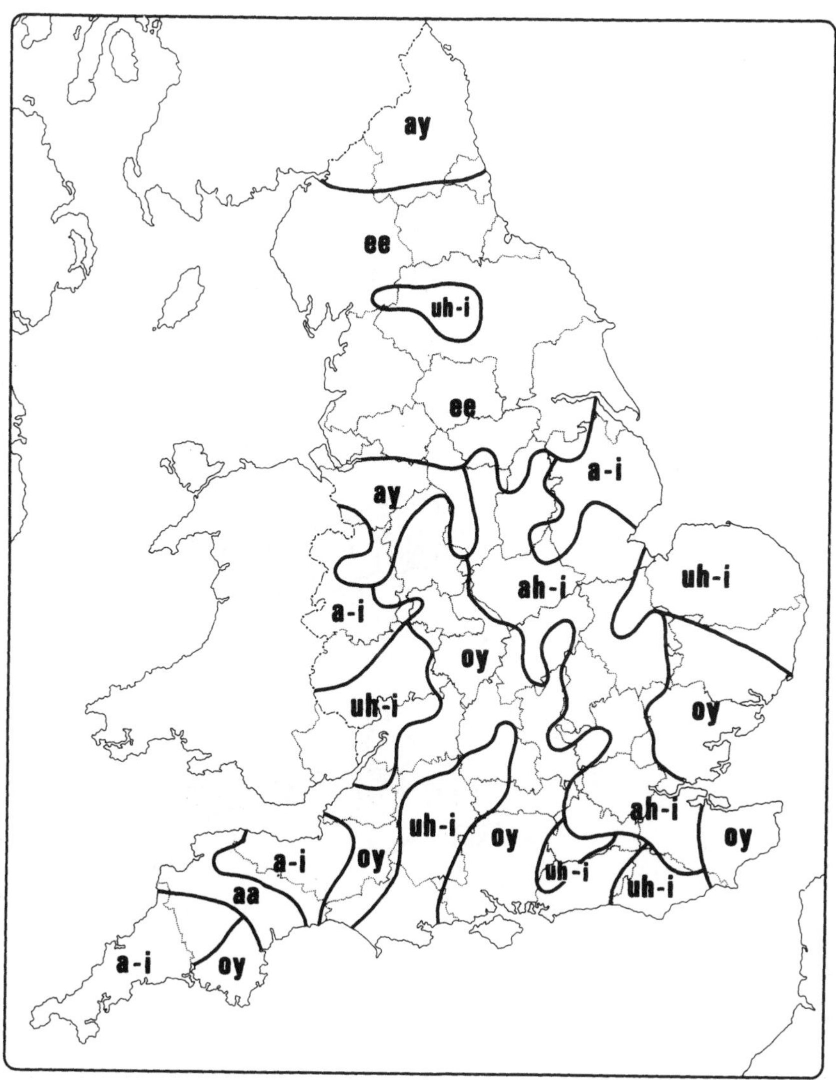

Map 144: SIGHT

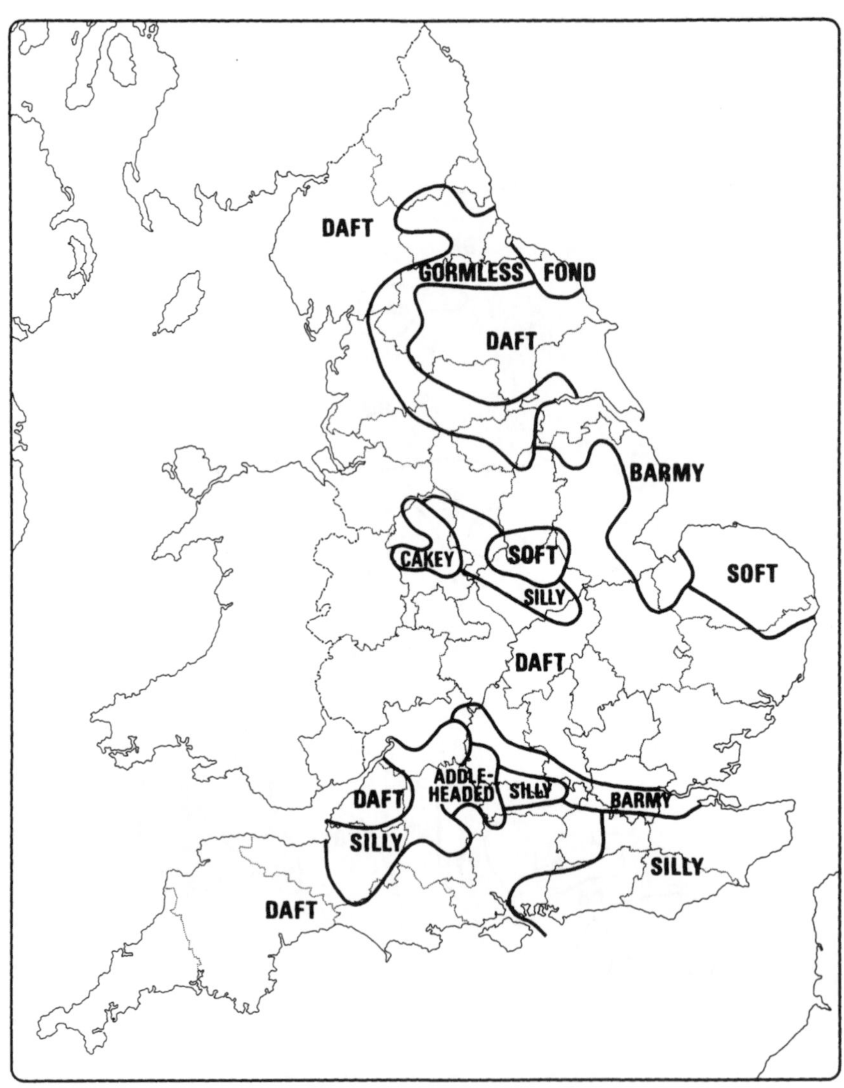

Map 145: SILLY (person)

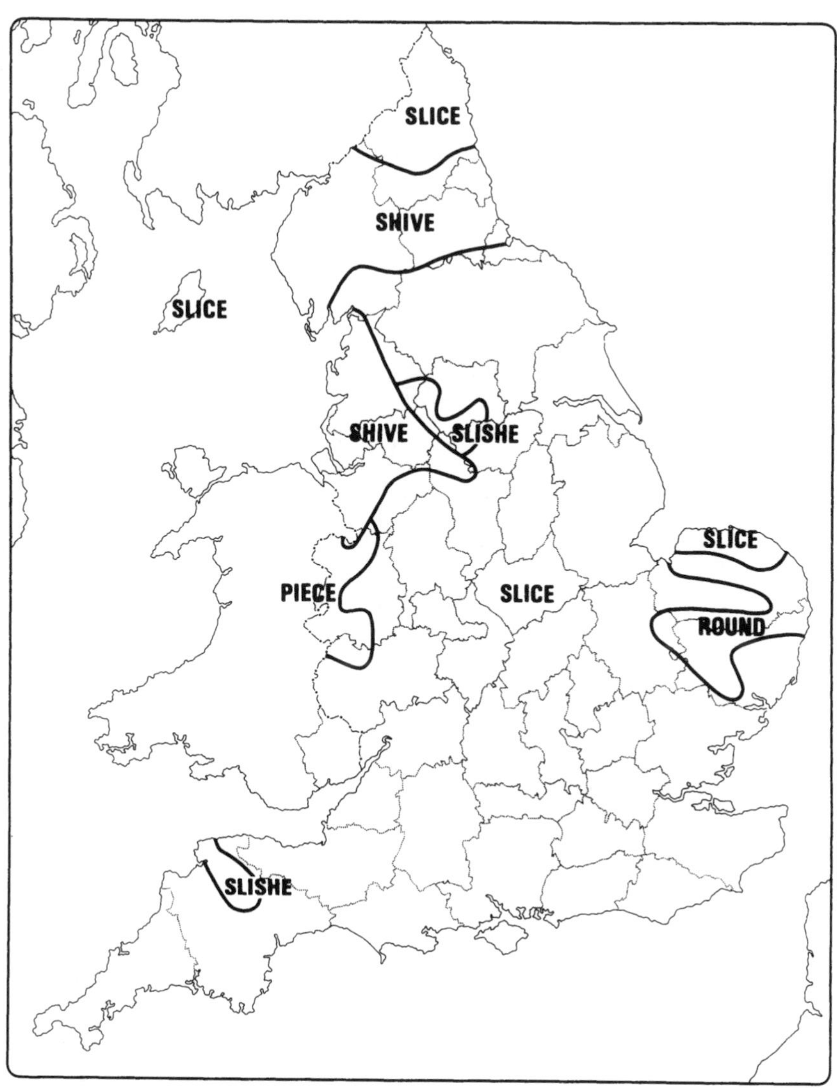

Map 146: SLICE (of bread)

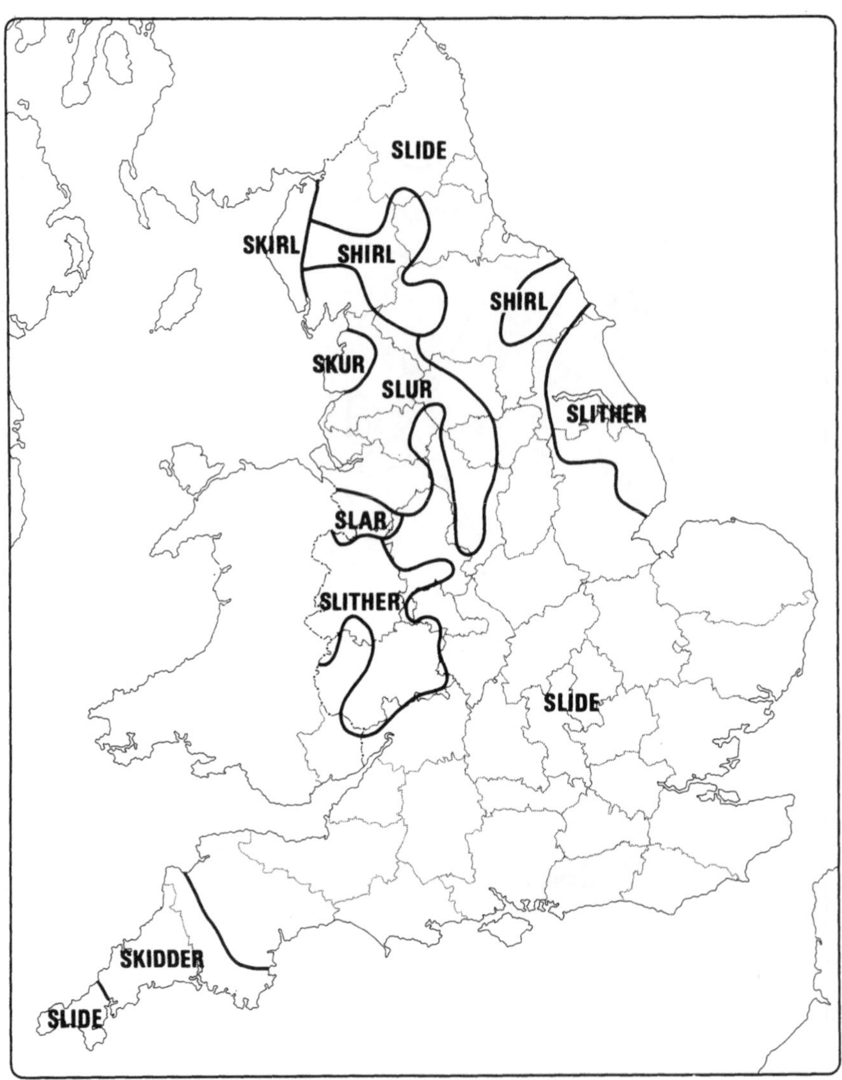

Map 147: SLIDE (to . . ., on ice)

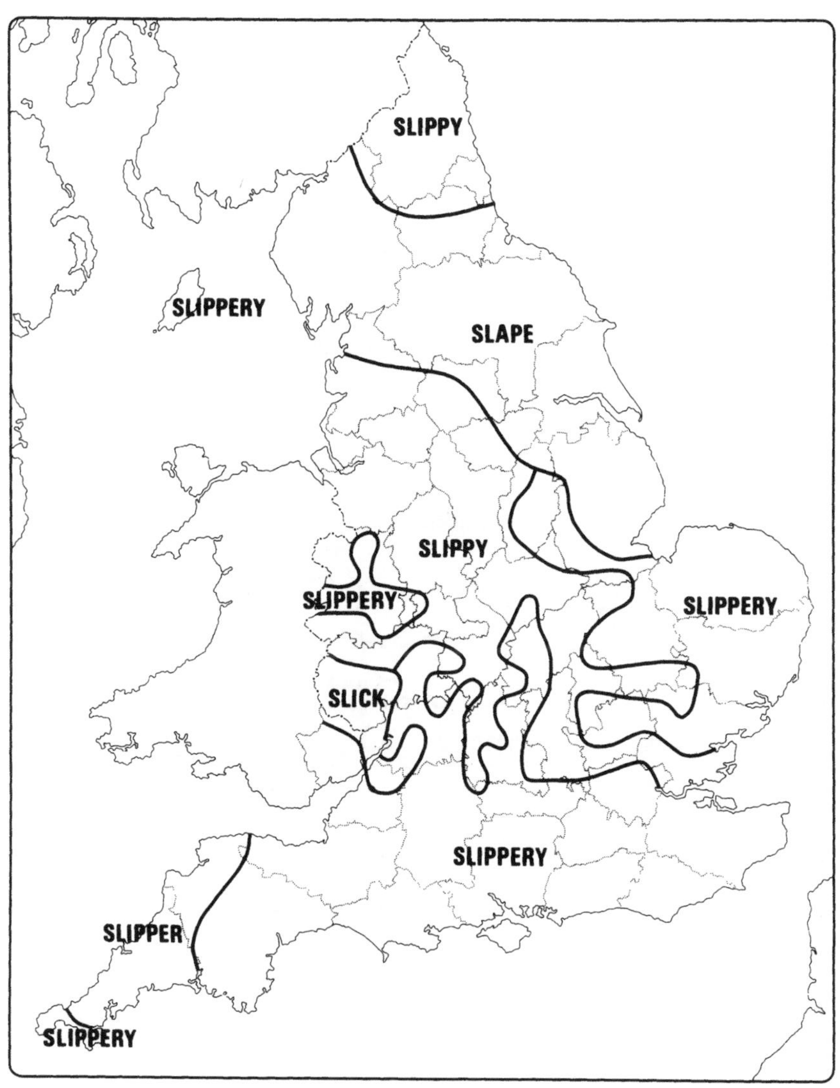

Map 148: SLIPPERY

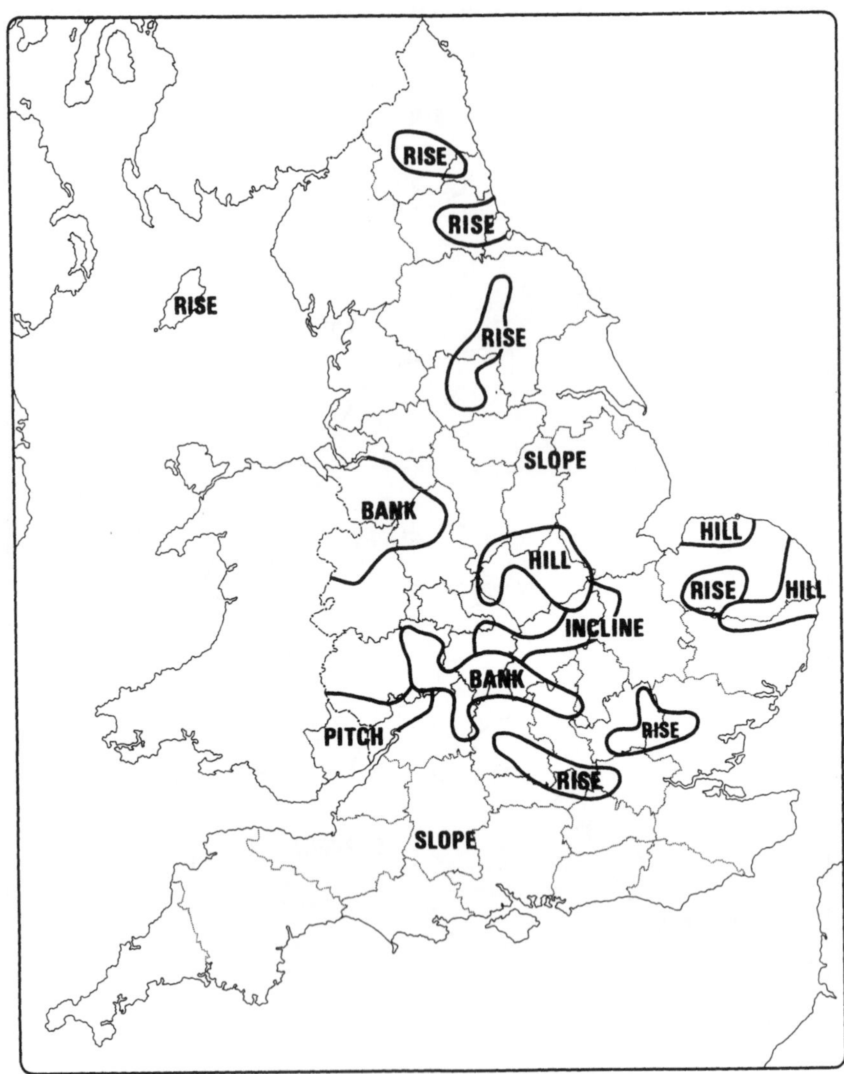

Map 149: SLOPE (an incline)

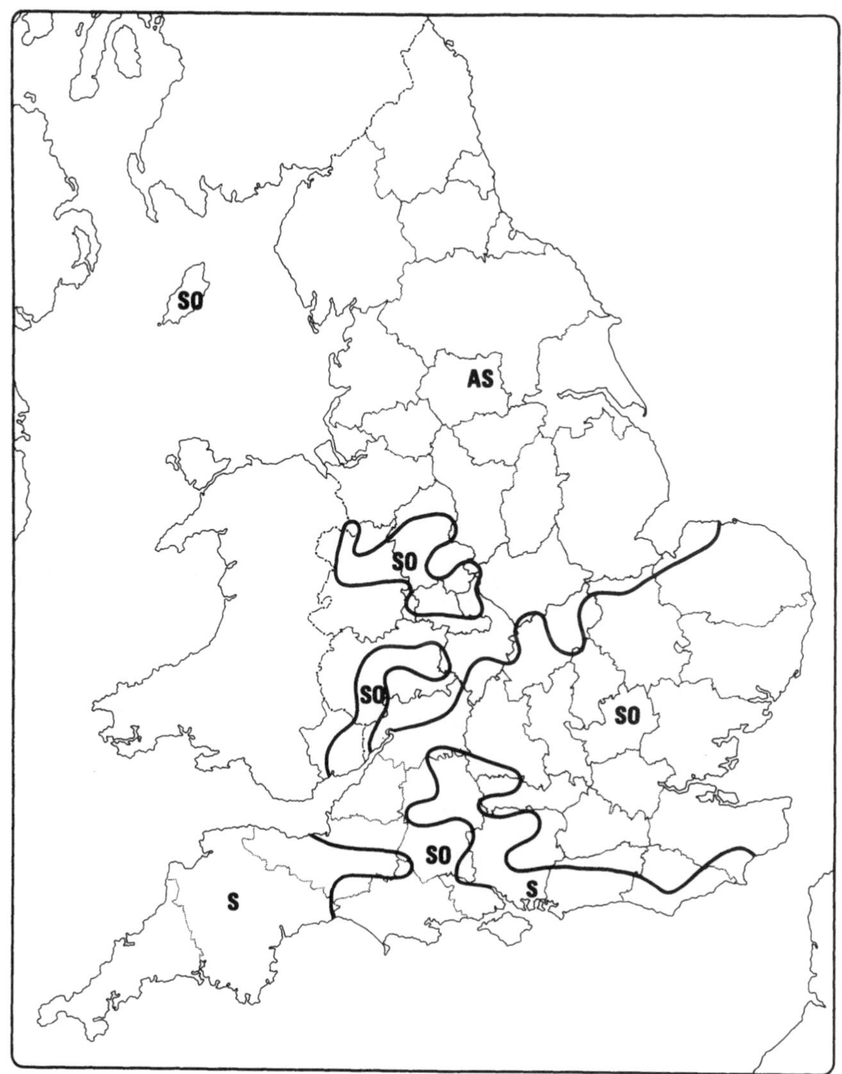

Map 150: SO (not … old as)
The S form represents, as it were, an intermediate pronunciation which could derive either from the first sound of SO (the more likely origin) or the final sound of AS.

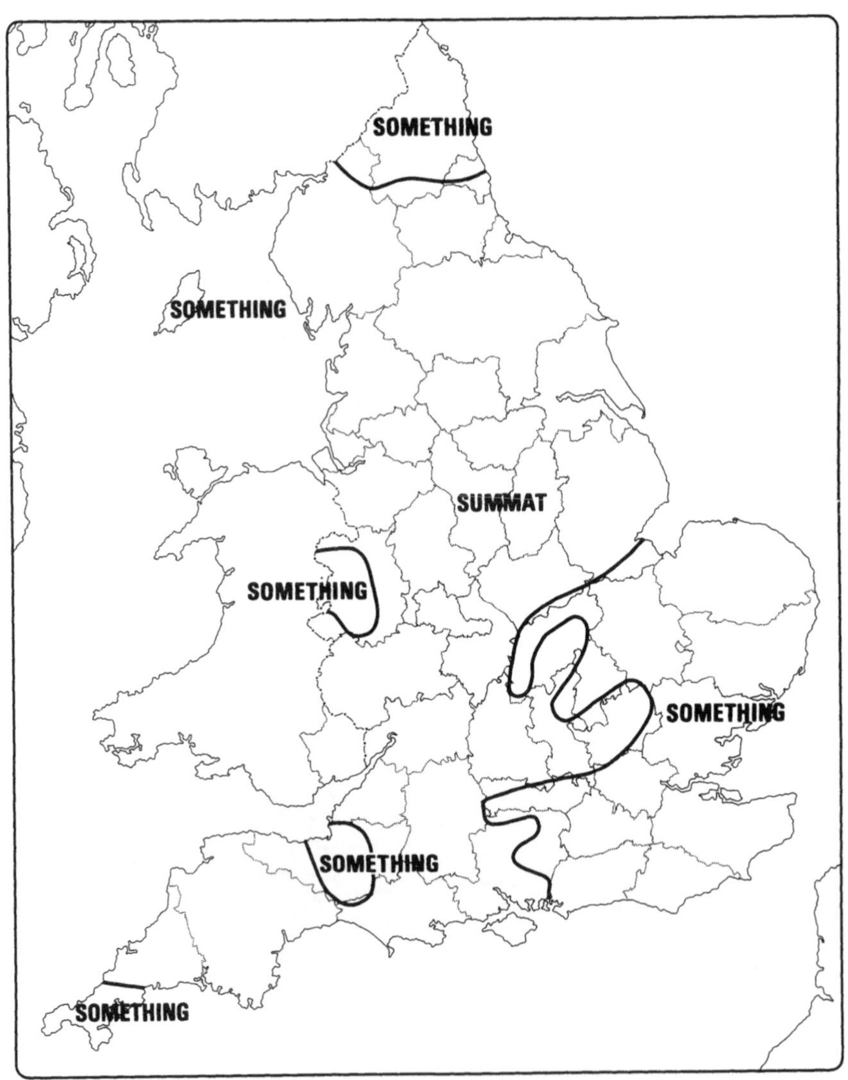

Map 151: SOMETHING

SOMETHING, the normal form in Standard English, is well established in East Anglia and the South East and is encroaching on **SUMMAT** ('somewhat') and its variant *summats* (found in parts of Nottinghamshire and Lincolnshire).

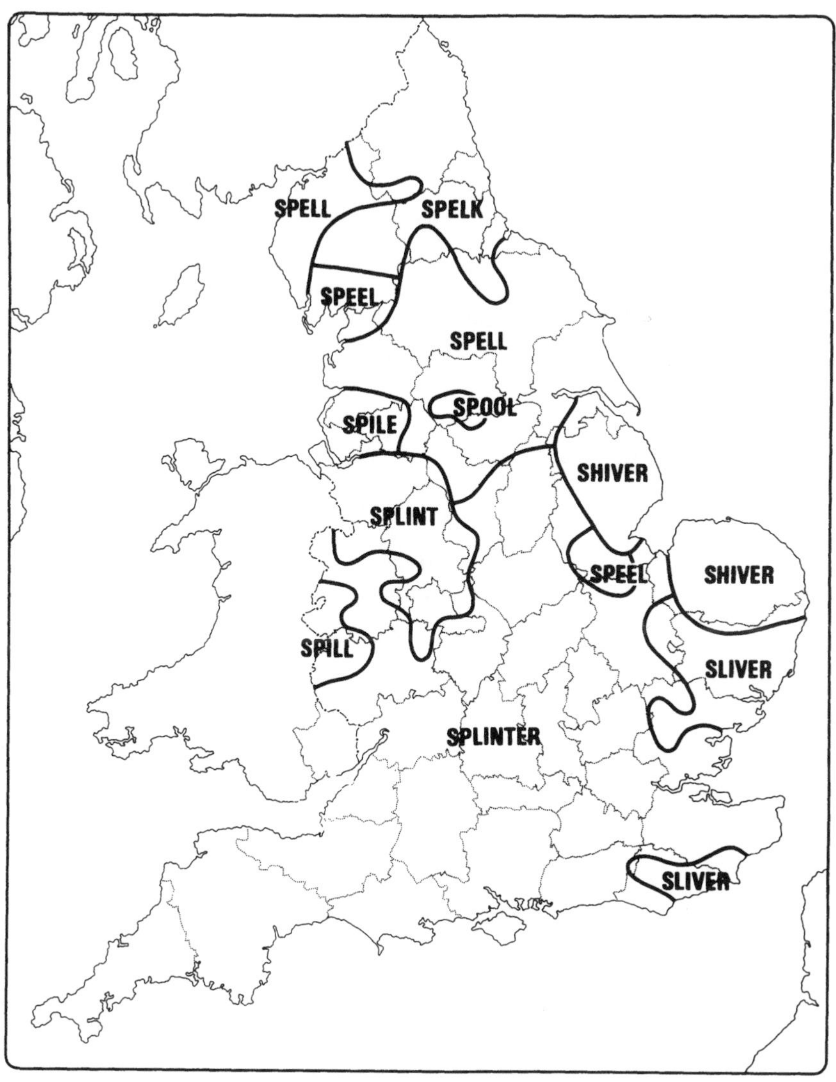

Map 152: SPLINTER (thin piece of wood)

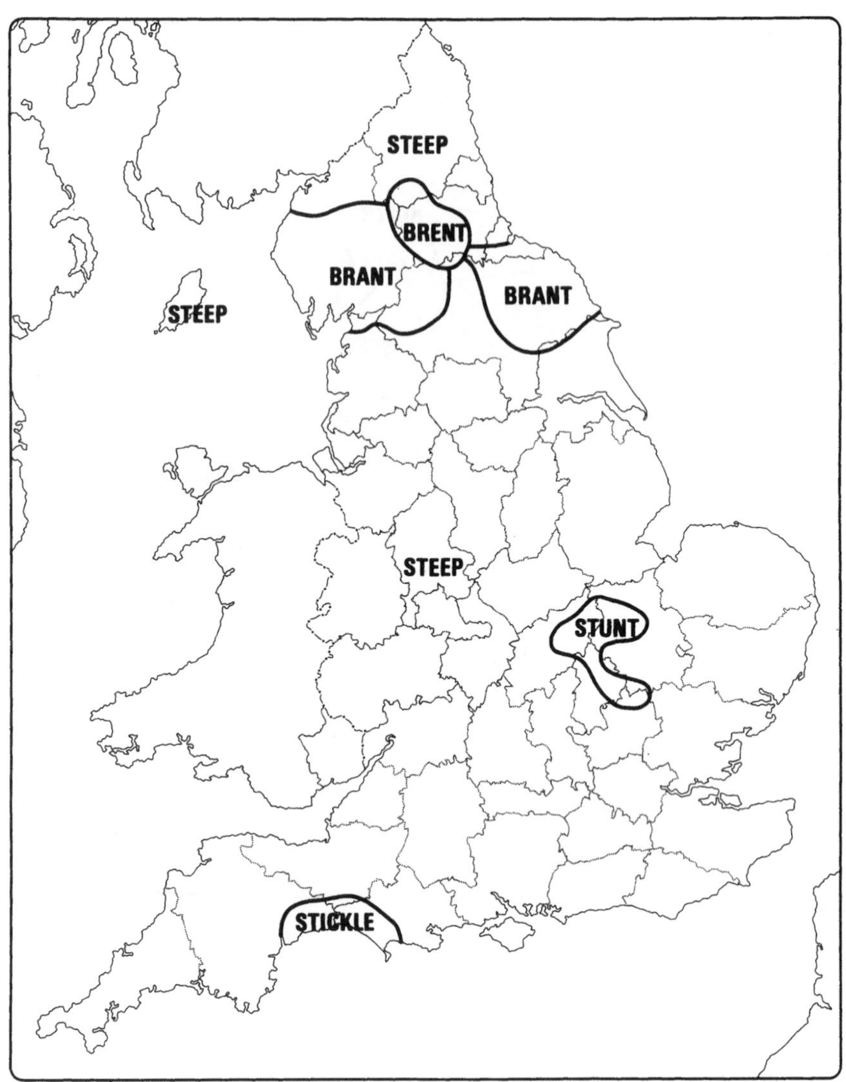

Map 153: STEEP (hill)

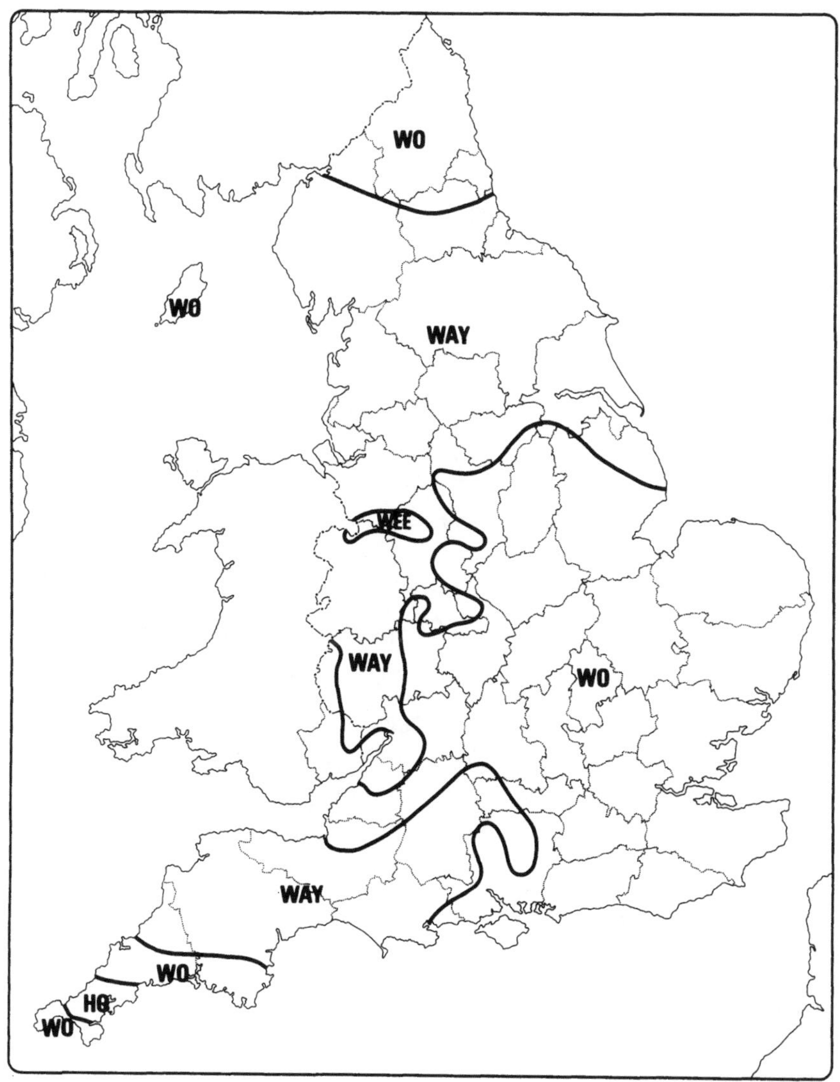

Map 154: STOP! (to horses)

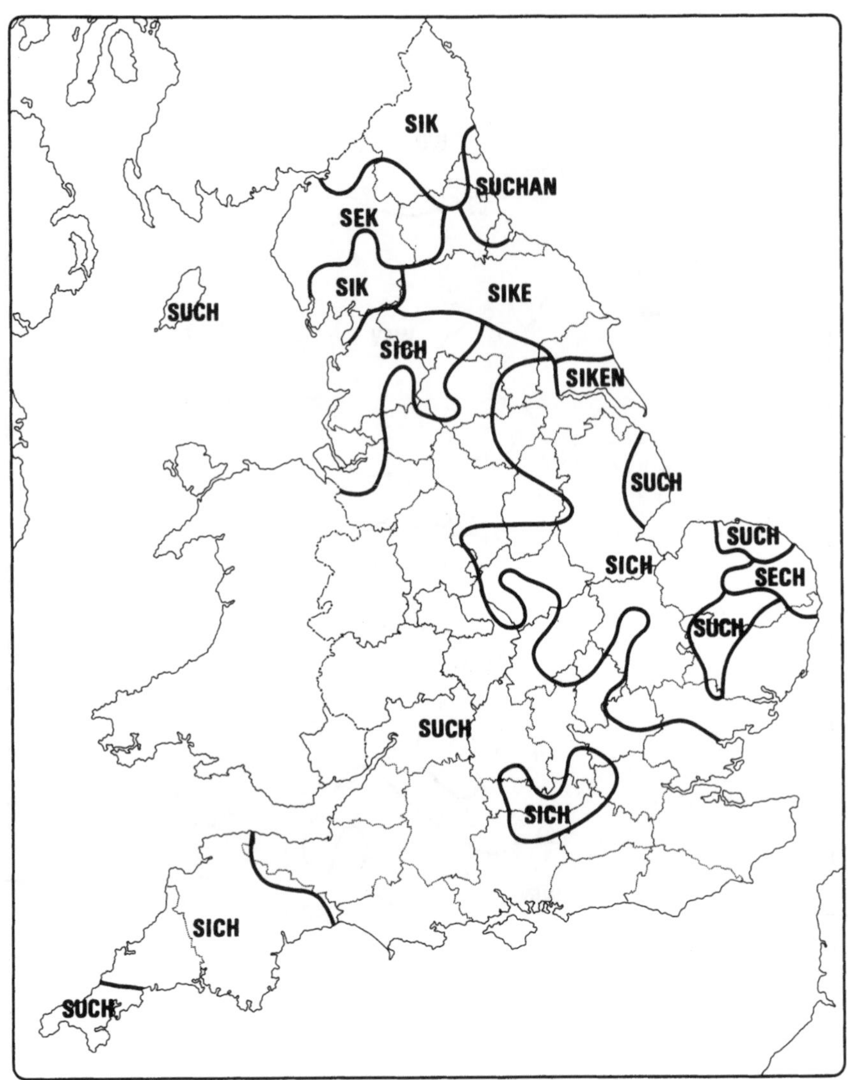

Map 155: SUCH (... a fool)

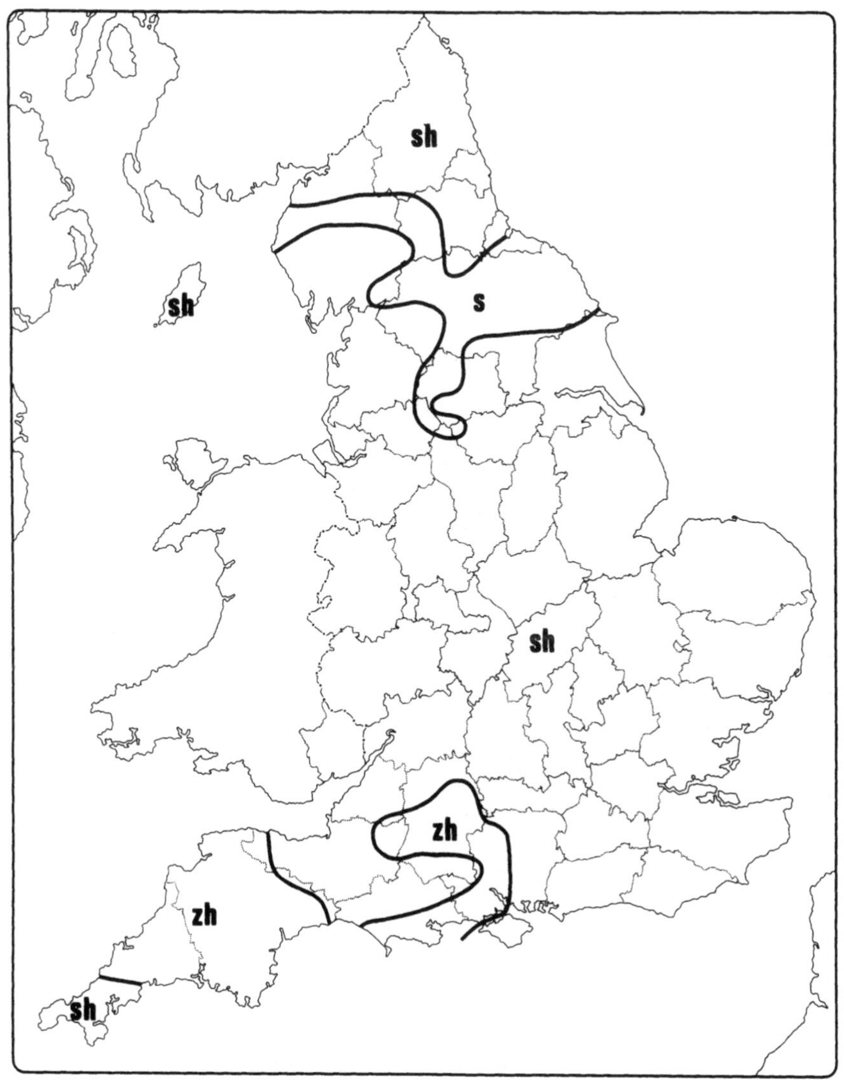

Map 156: S̲UGAR

s is an old feature rarely used today. **zh** is the same kind of 'voiced' sound found at the beginning of other words in the South West, see Map 55.

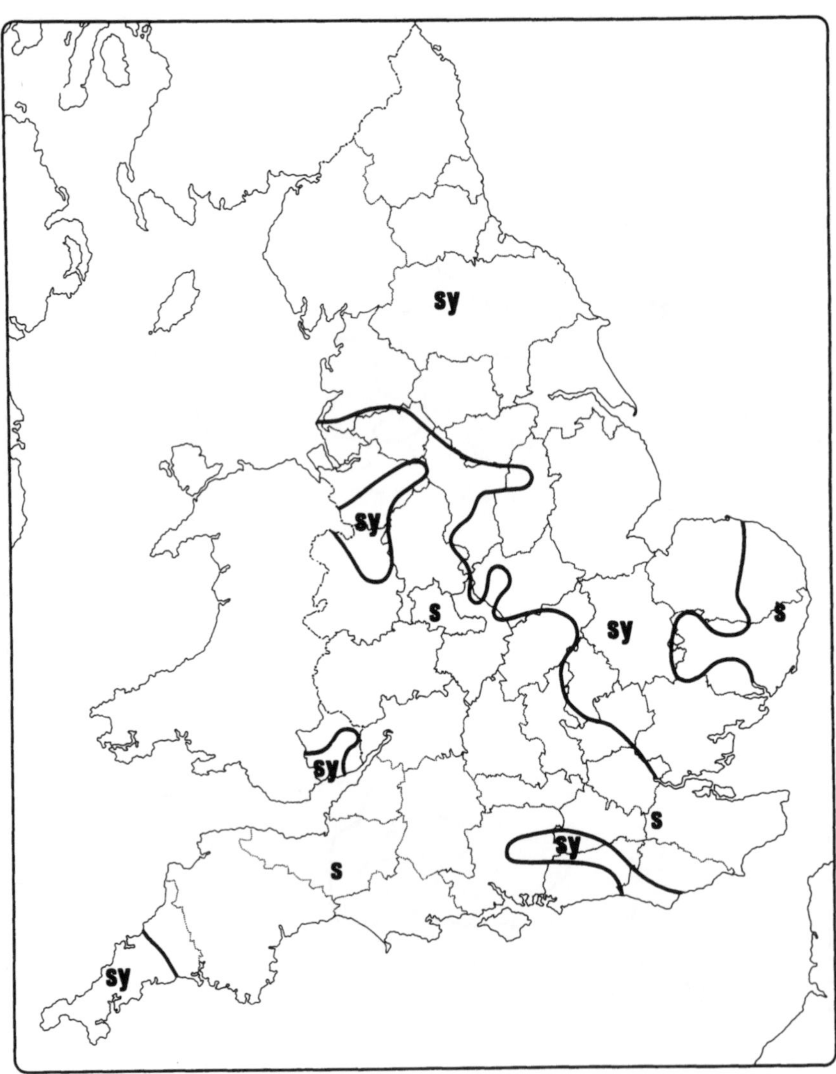

Map 157: <u>S</u>UIT

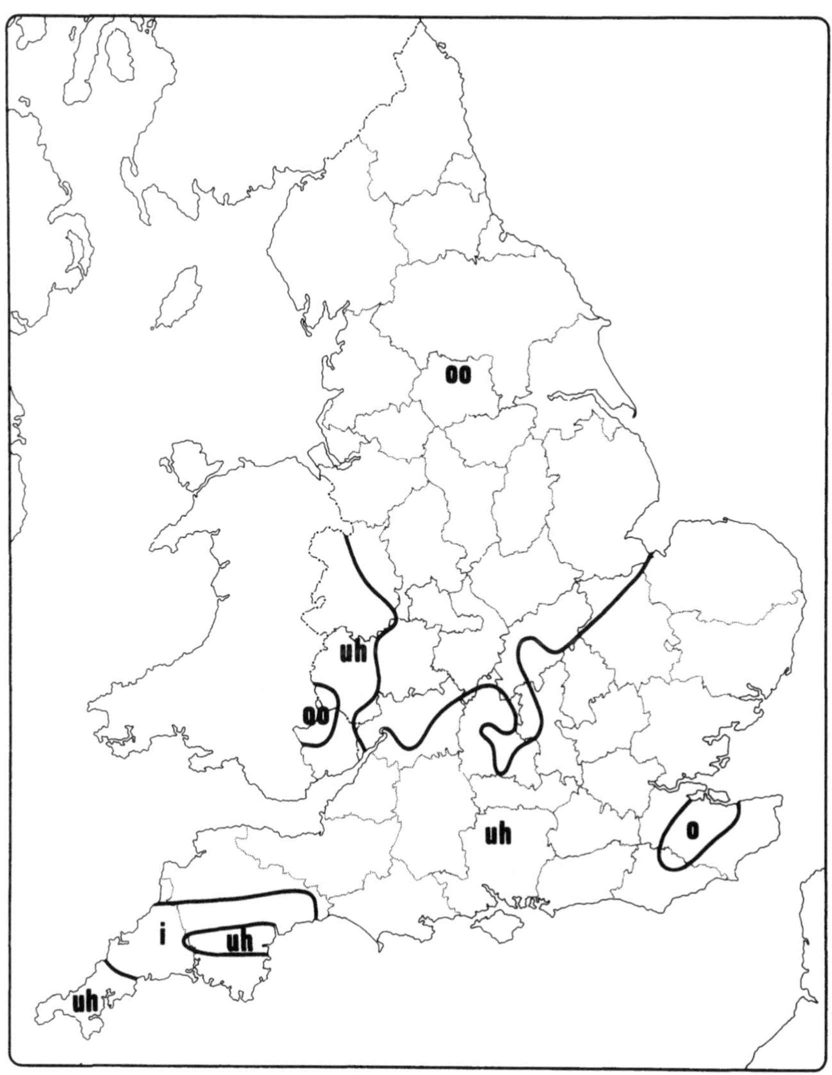

Map 158: S<u>U</u>N

oo, the oldest form, represents the short *u* sound as in *put*; the **uh** forms developed in the late sixteenth and early seventeenth centuries.

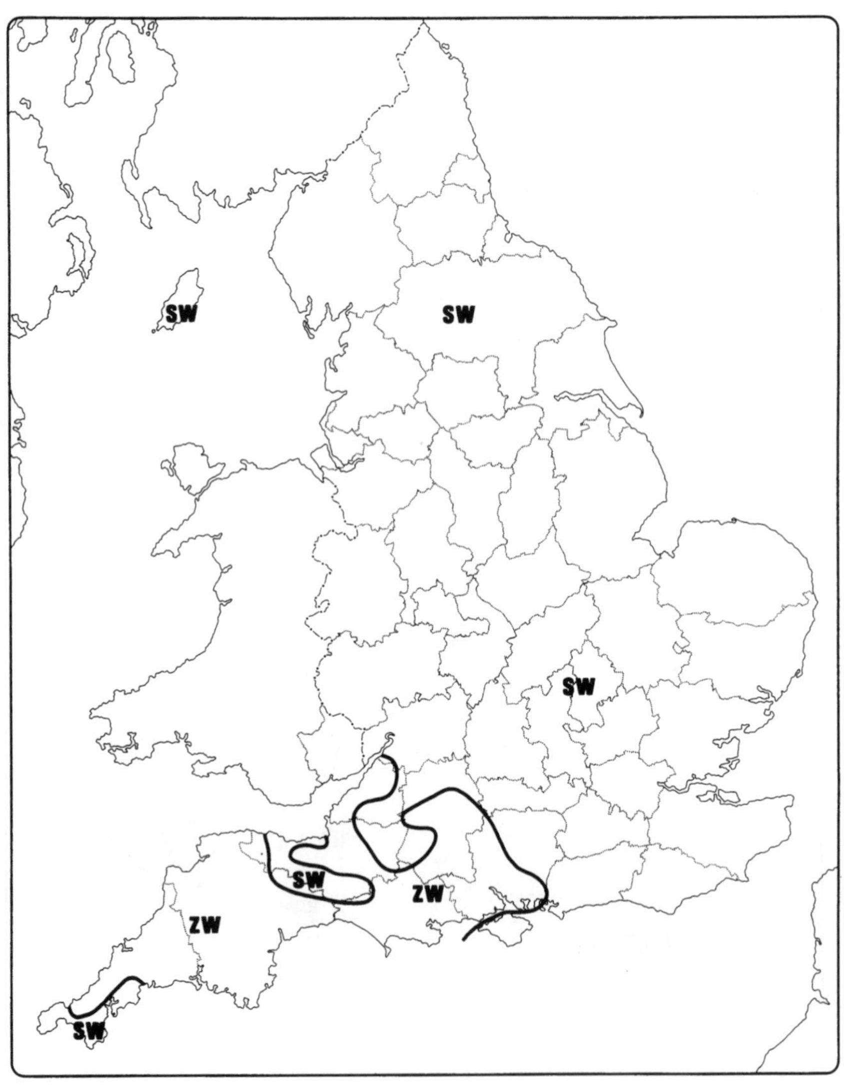

Map 159: <u>SW</u>EAT
For the 'voicing' of initial consonants see Map 55.

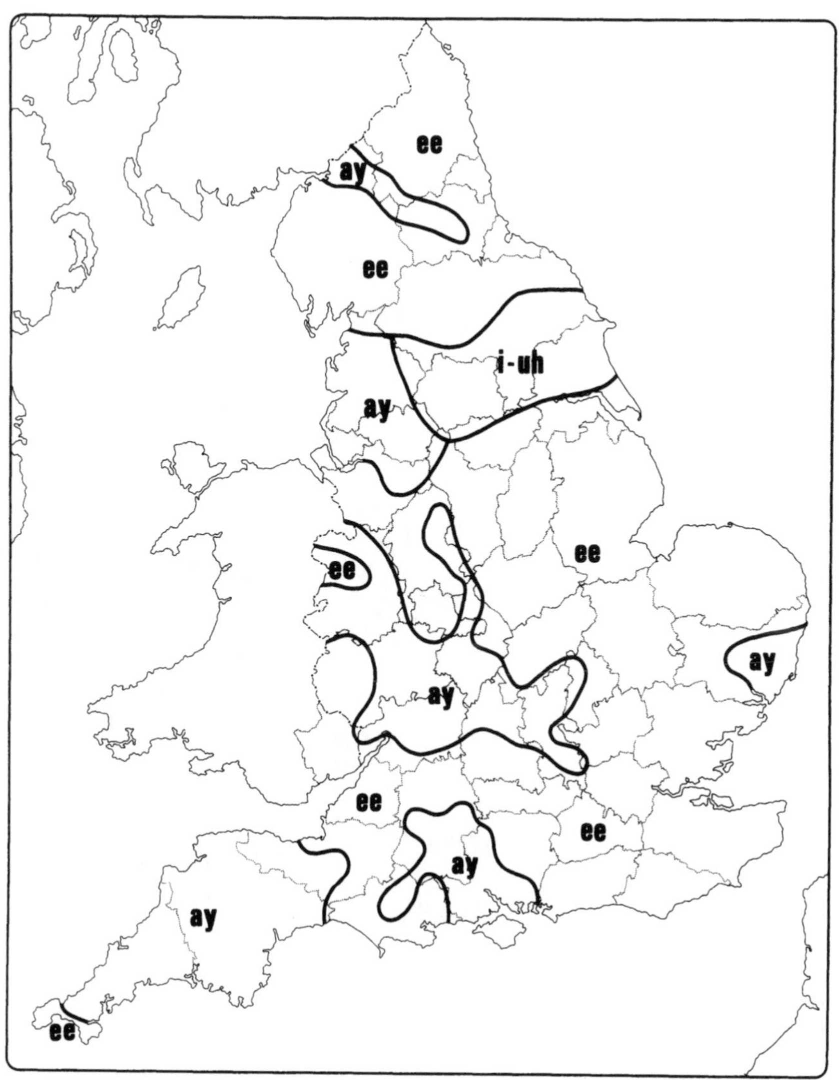

Map 160: TEA

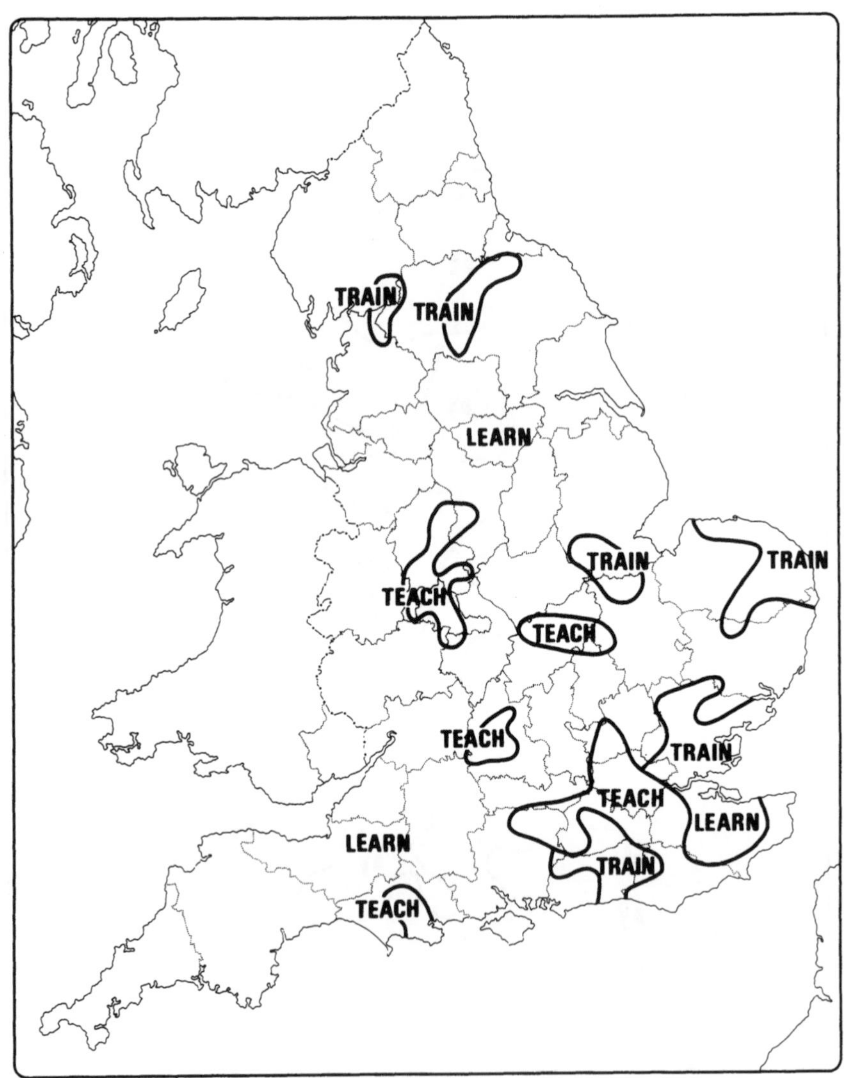

Map 161: TEACH (to . . . a dog)

The two forms **TEACH** and **LEARN** occupy clearly defined areas. It would be interesting to investigate whether *borrow* and *lend* also have distinct regional distributions.

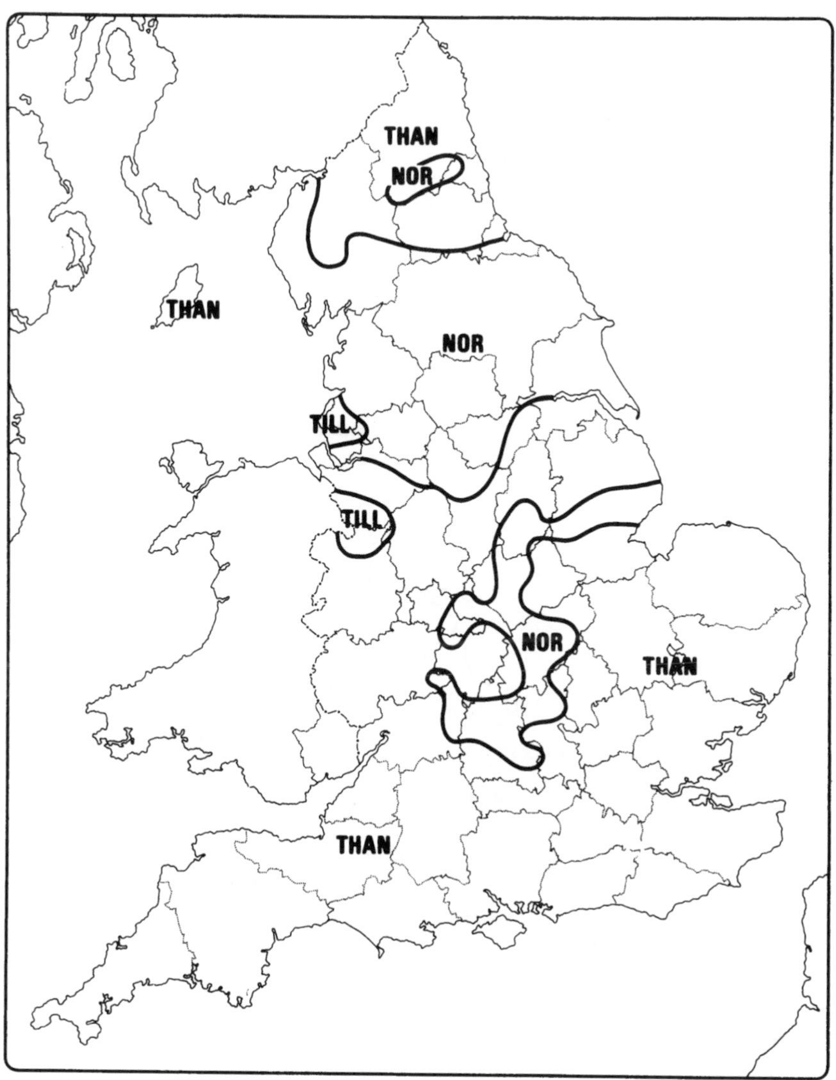

Map 162: THAN (worse . . ., older . . .)

THAN occurs widely in the areas dominated by **TILL** and **NOR**, suggesting that it is advancing at the expense of those words.

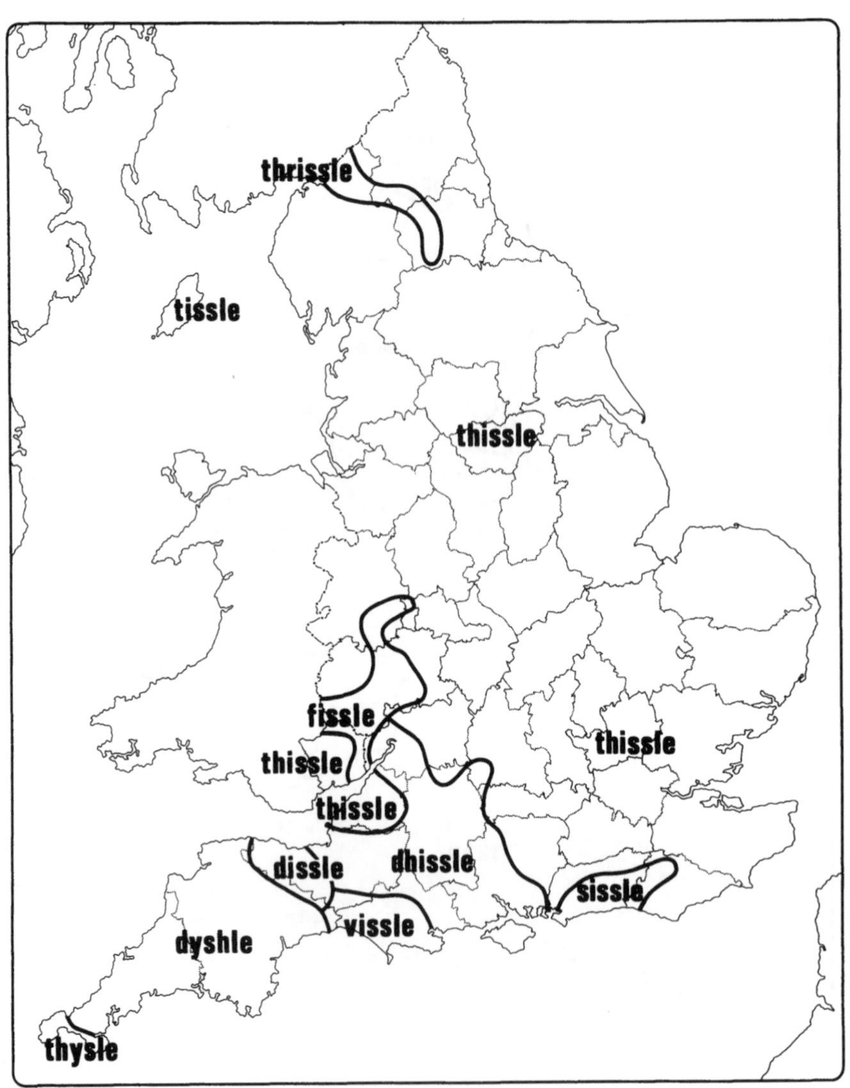

Map 163: <u>THISTLE</u>

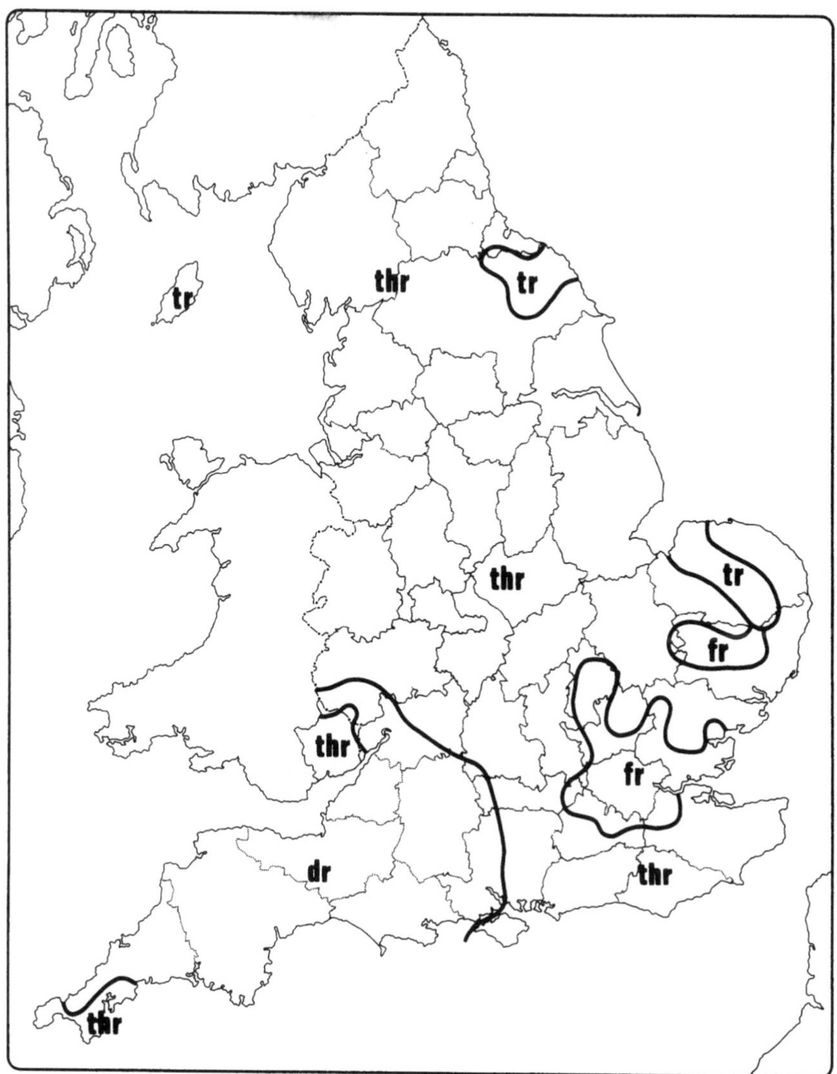

Map 164: THREE

dr is typical of the West Country, but note **thr** in the southwestern tip of Cornwall and in southeast Wales — English being learned comparatively late in both areas. **fr** is not only Cockney; it extends widely in the Home Counties and also occurs in Suffolk. For the 'voicing' of initial consonants see Map 55.

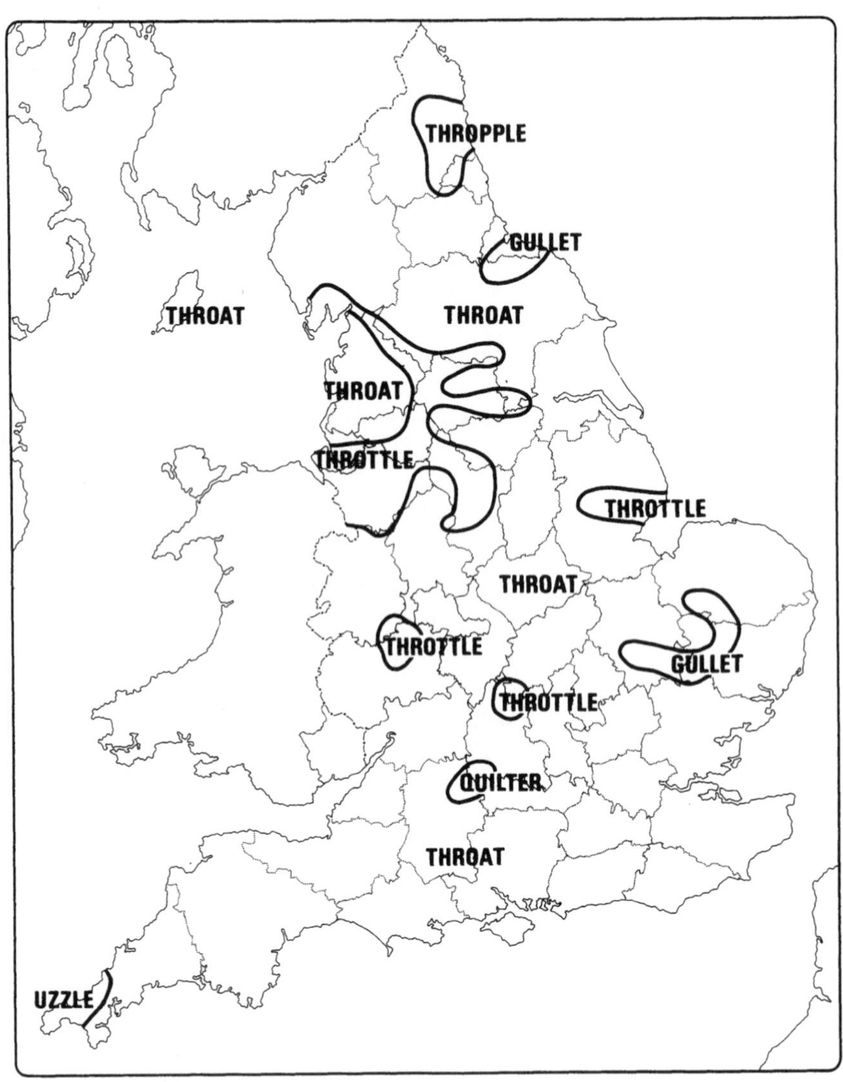

Map 165: THROAT

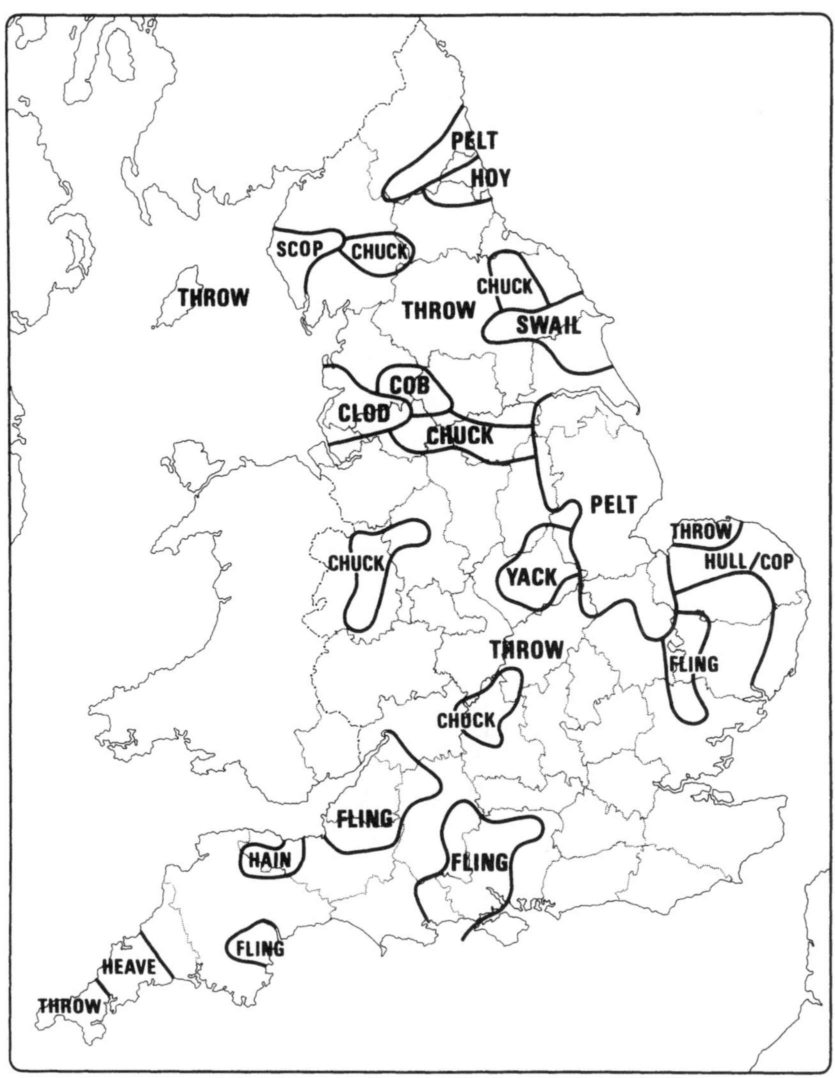

Map 166: THROW (to . . .)

THROW is found widely in the areas dominated by the other forms, suggesting it is establishing itself throughout the country.

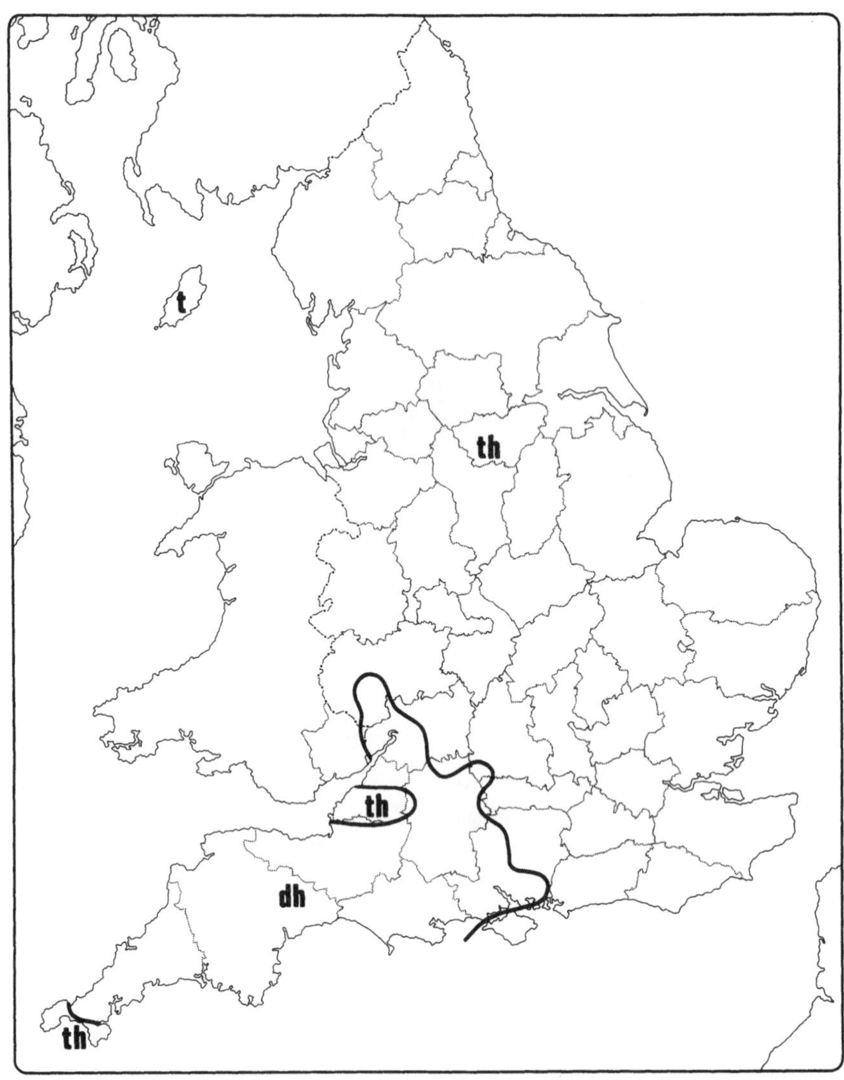

Map 167: THUMB
dh represents the 'voiced' *th* sound of words like *this*. For the 'voicing' of initial consonants see Map 55.

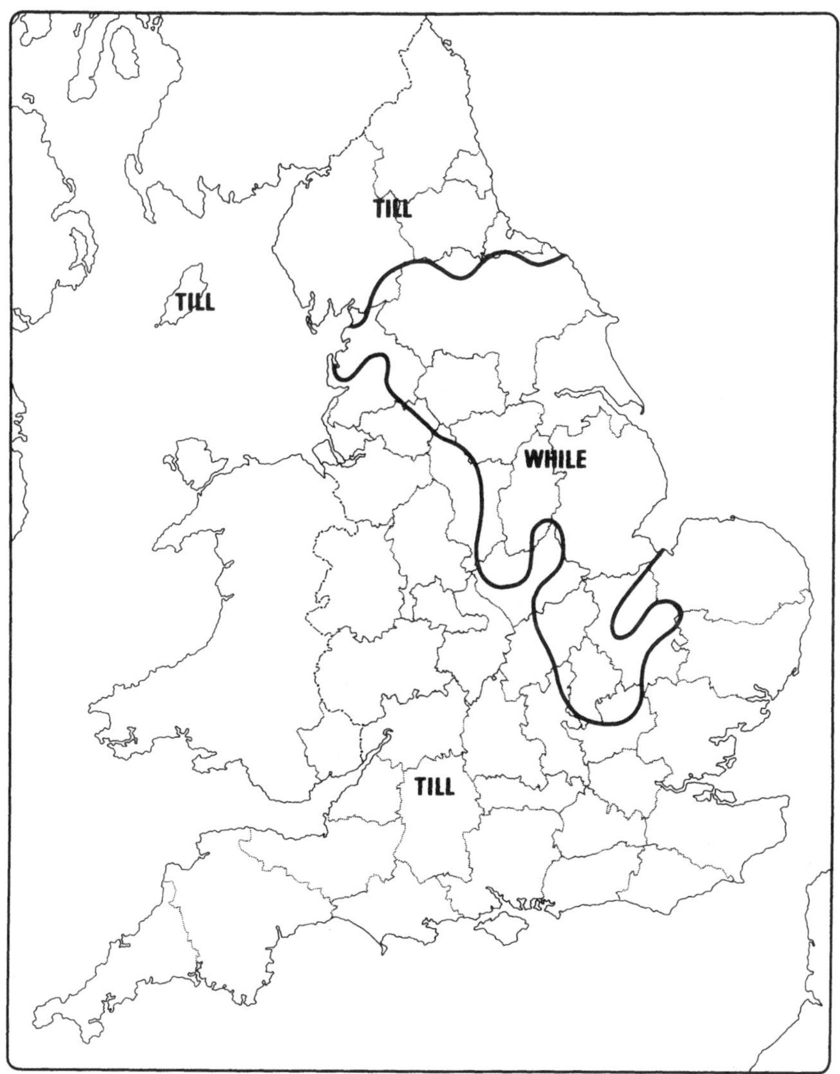

Map 168: TILL (wait ... Saturday)

TILL is widely known in the **WHILE** area. *until* is found occasionally but not widely in any dialect.

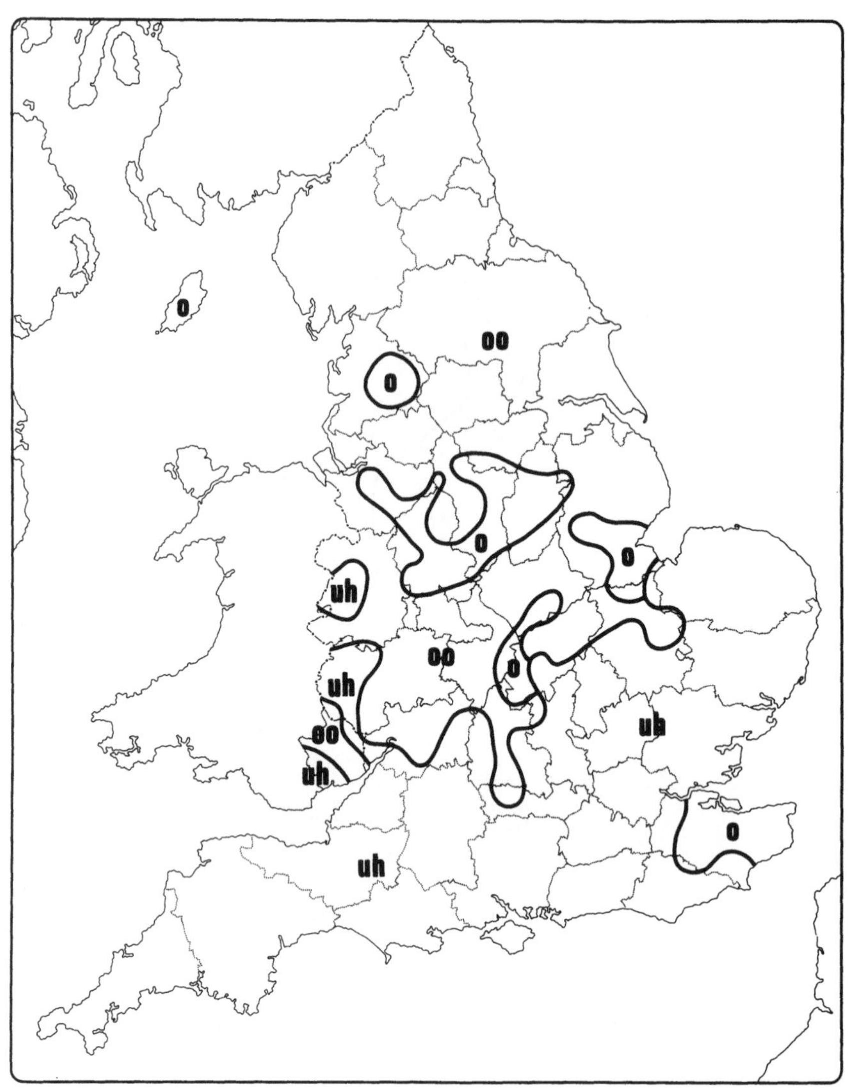

Map 169: TONGUE
oo is the short vowel, as in *put*.

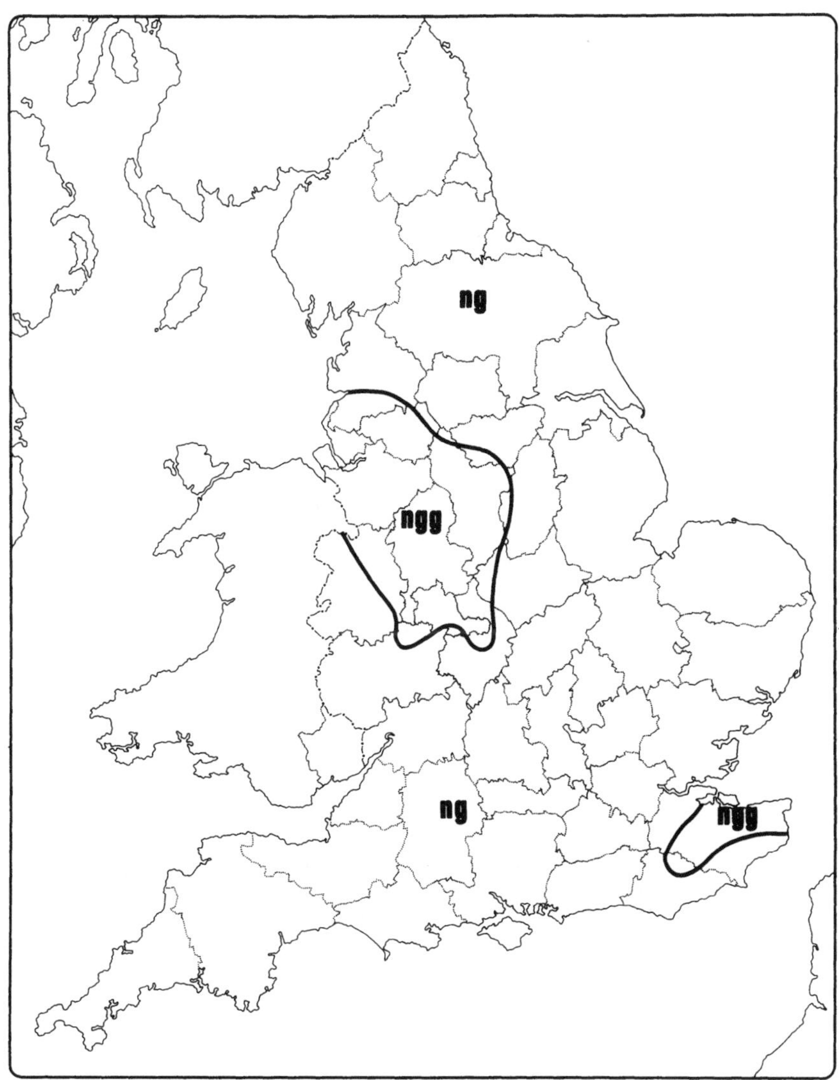

Map 170: TONGUE

The additional **-g** at the end of words which end in *-ng* is characteristic of the northwest Midlands, especially before a vowel, as in 'put your tongue out', 'singing'. It is interesting to note that **g** is also added in parts of Kent.

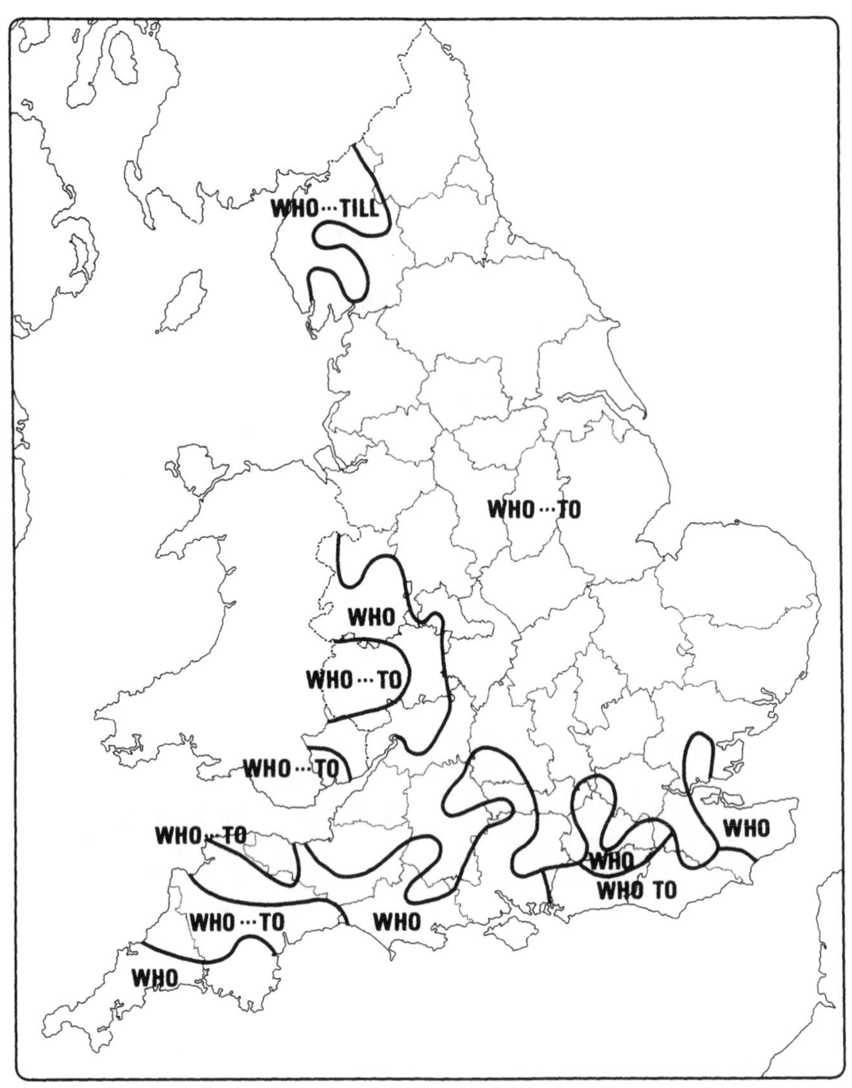

Map 171: TO WHOM (... I shall give it)

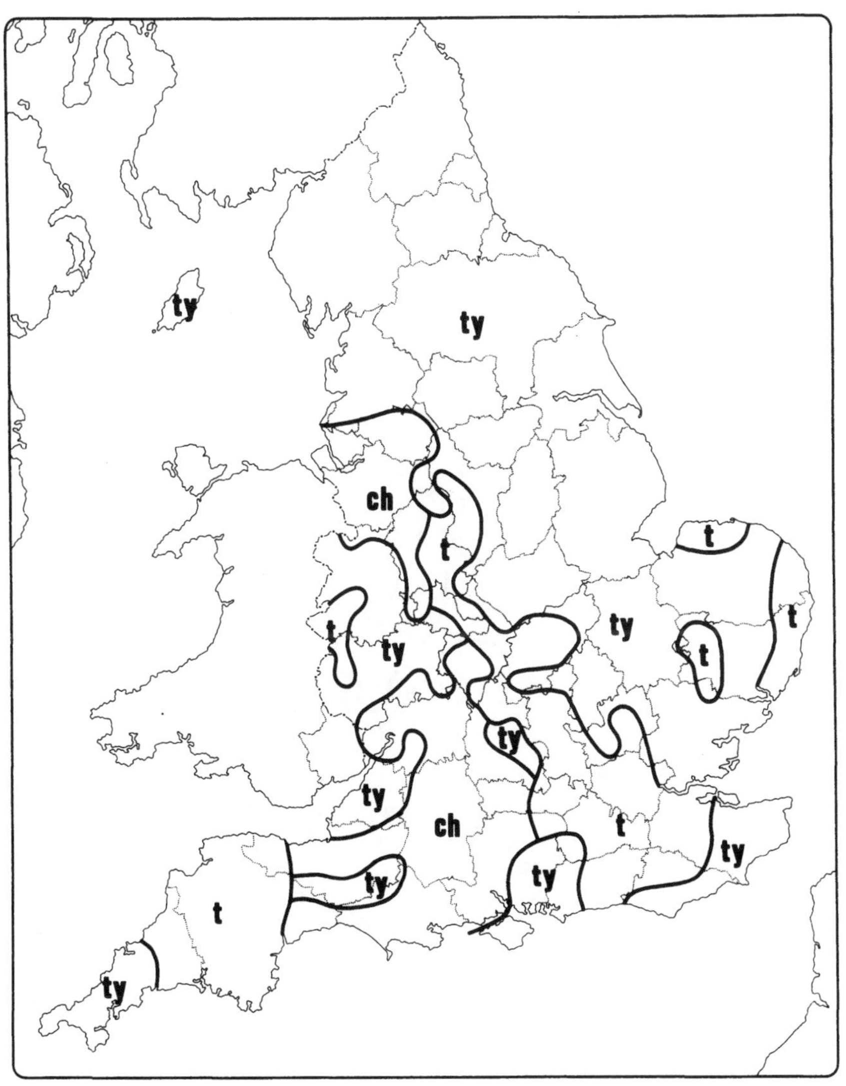

Map 172: TUESDAY

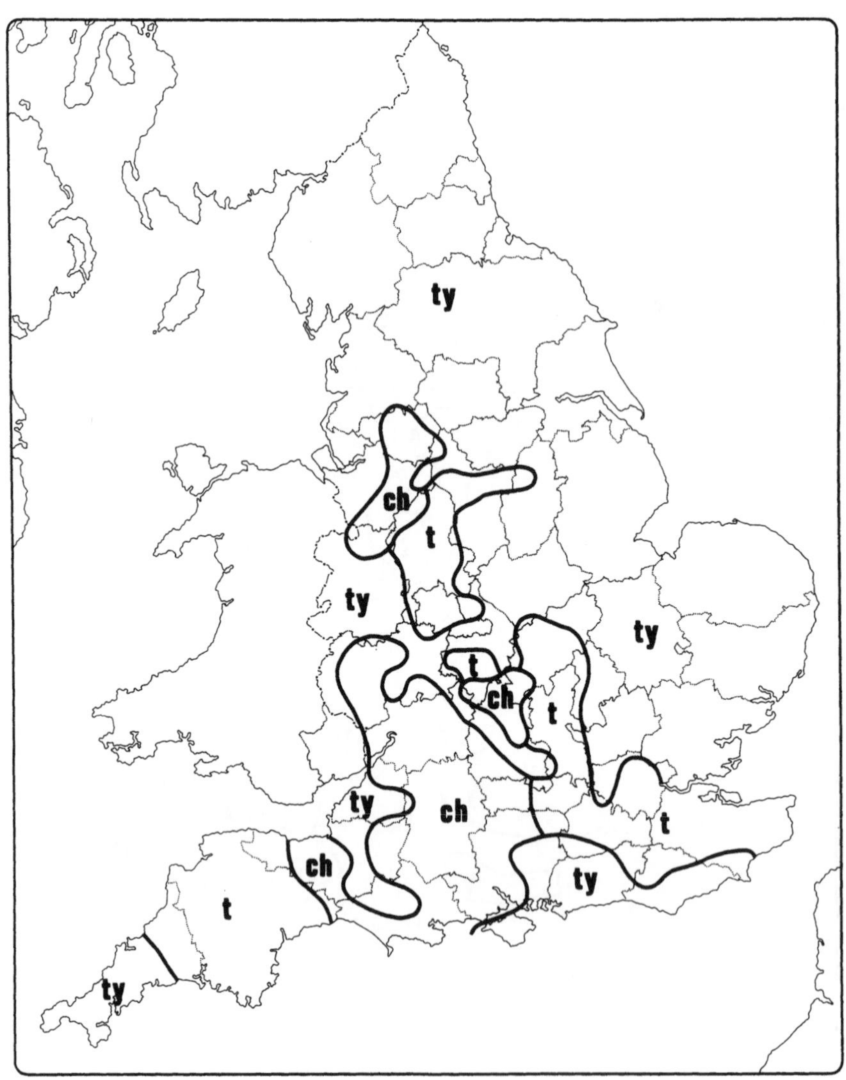

Map 173: T̲UNE

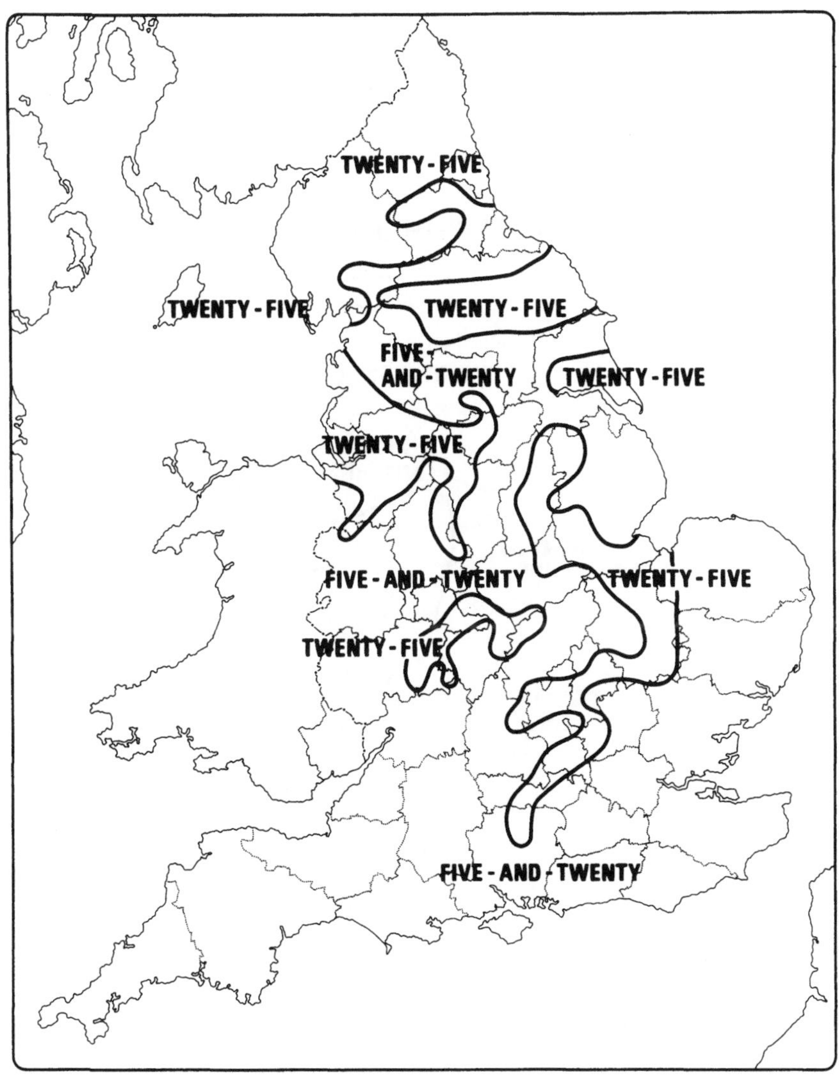

Map 174: TWENTY-FIVE (. . . to three, time)

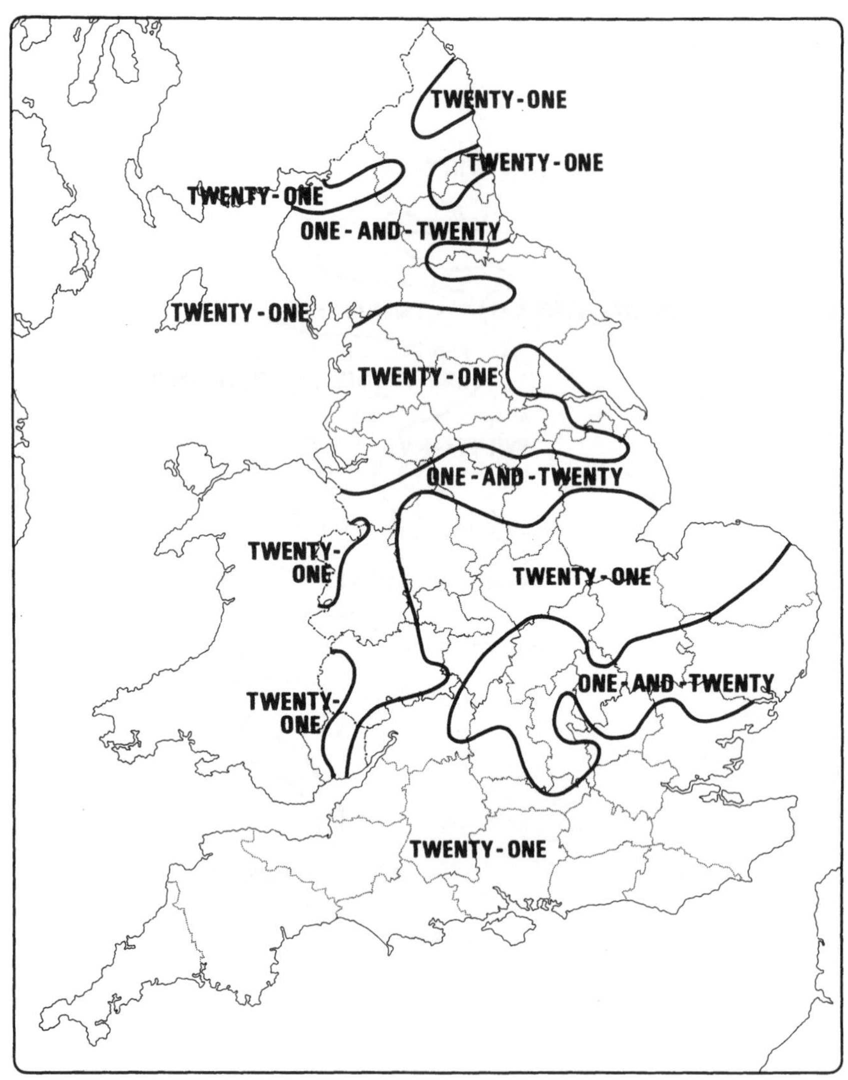

Map 175: TWENTY-ONE (age)

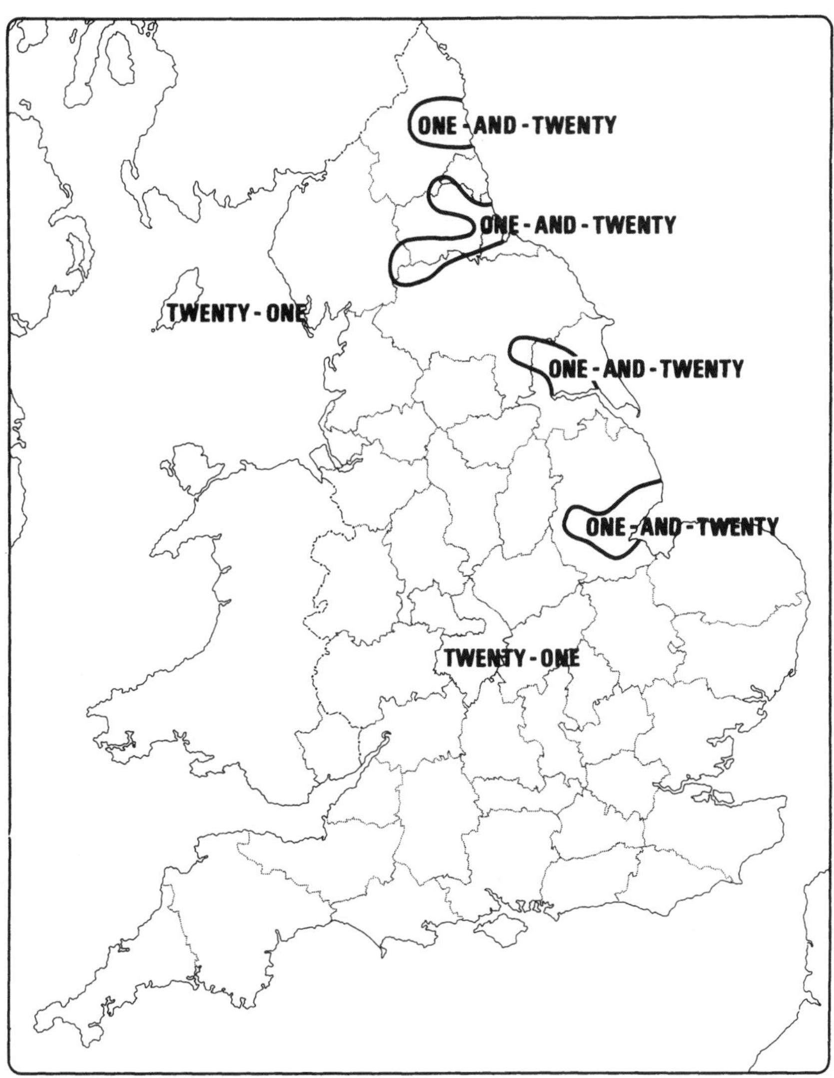

Map 176: TWENTY-ONE (number 21)

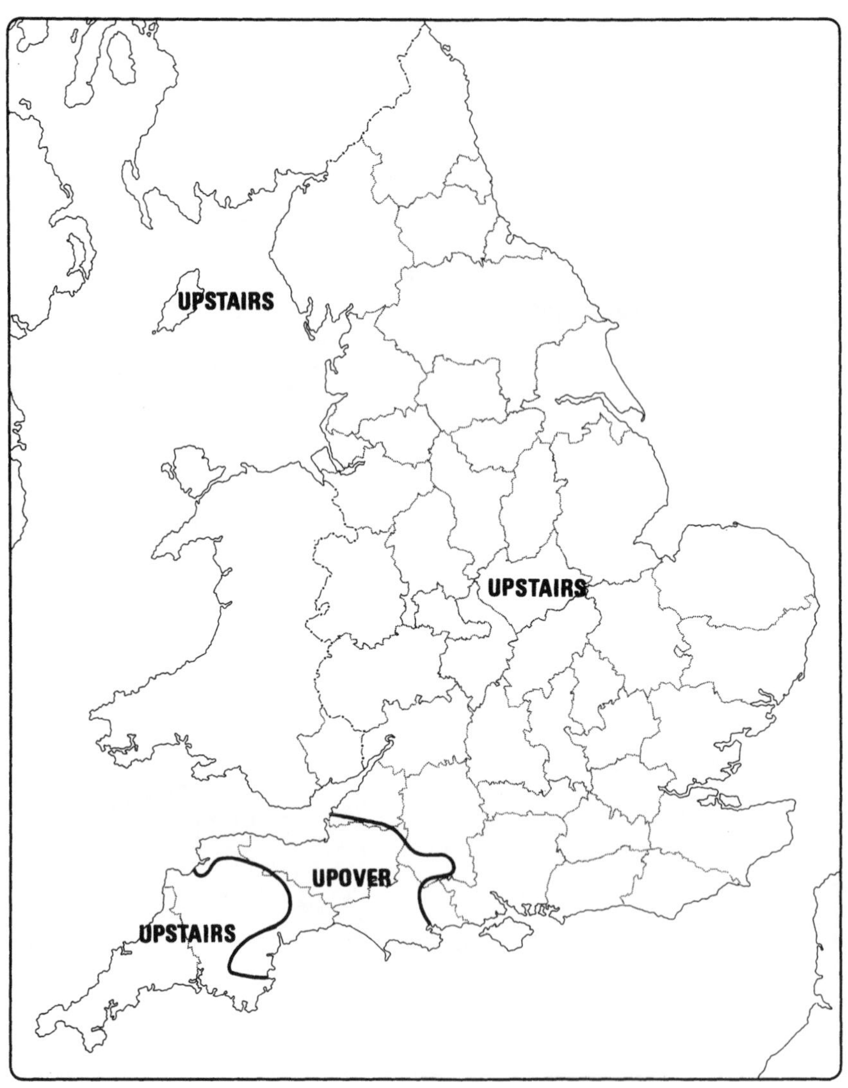

Map 177: UPSTAIRS

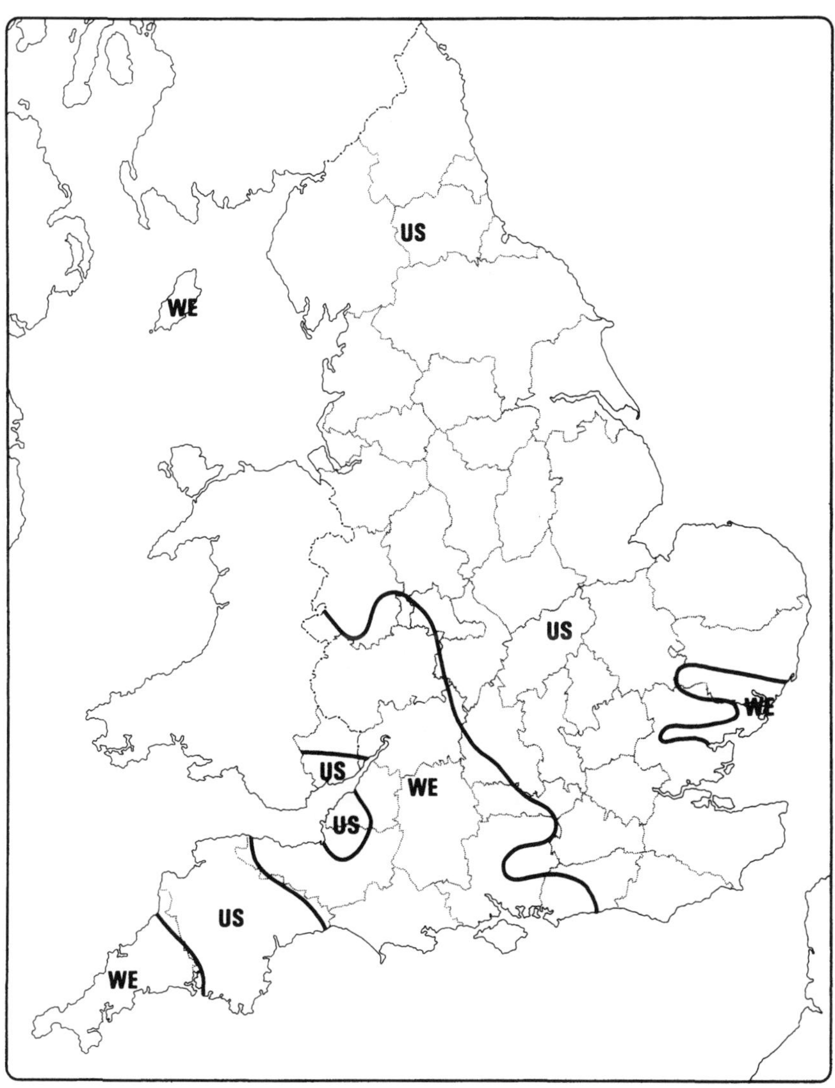

Map 178: US

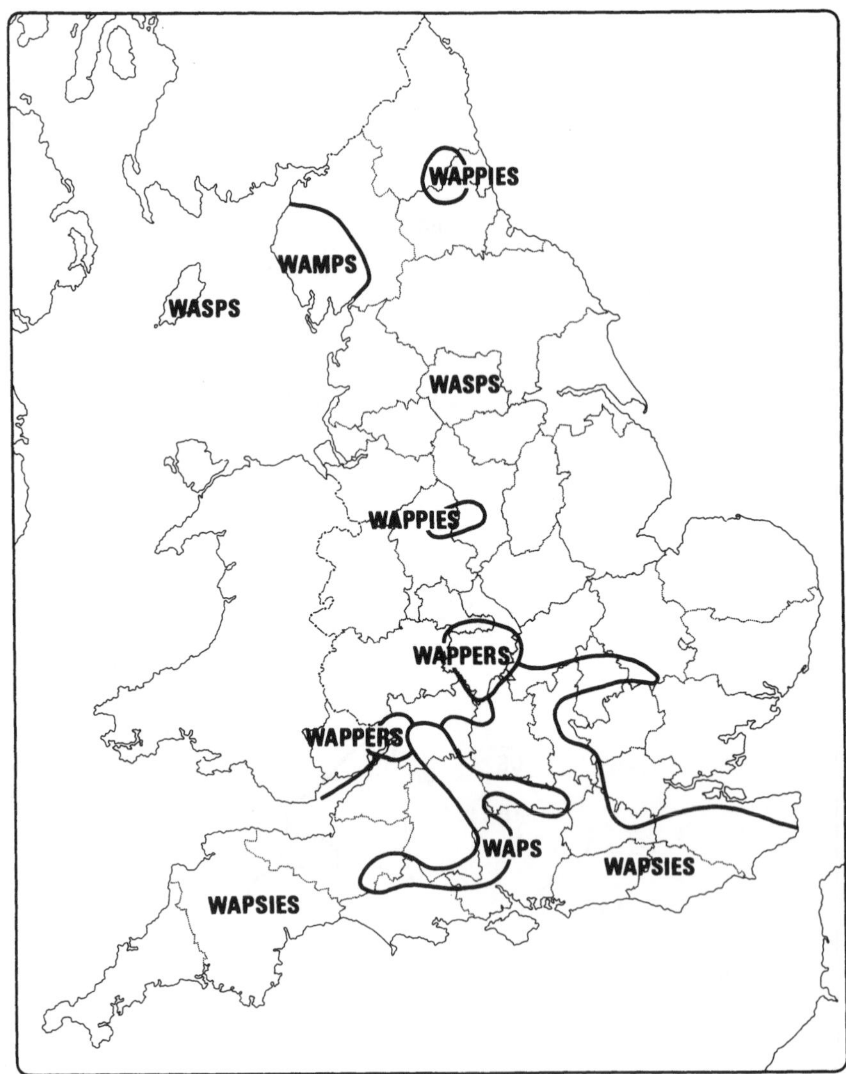

Map 179: WASPS

There are problems in the interpretation of these words as it is not always clear whether a given form is singular or plural. For example, **WAPS** sometimes appears to be the singular form of **WAPSIES**.

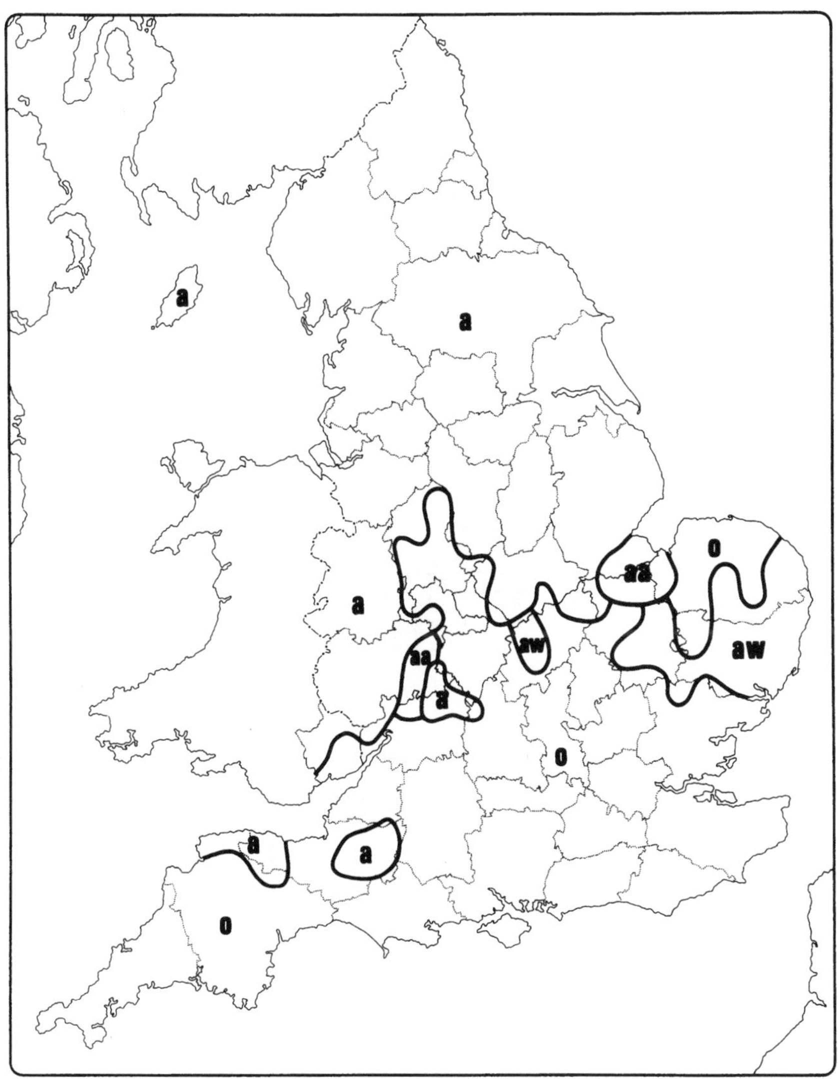

Map 180: W<u>A</u>SPS

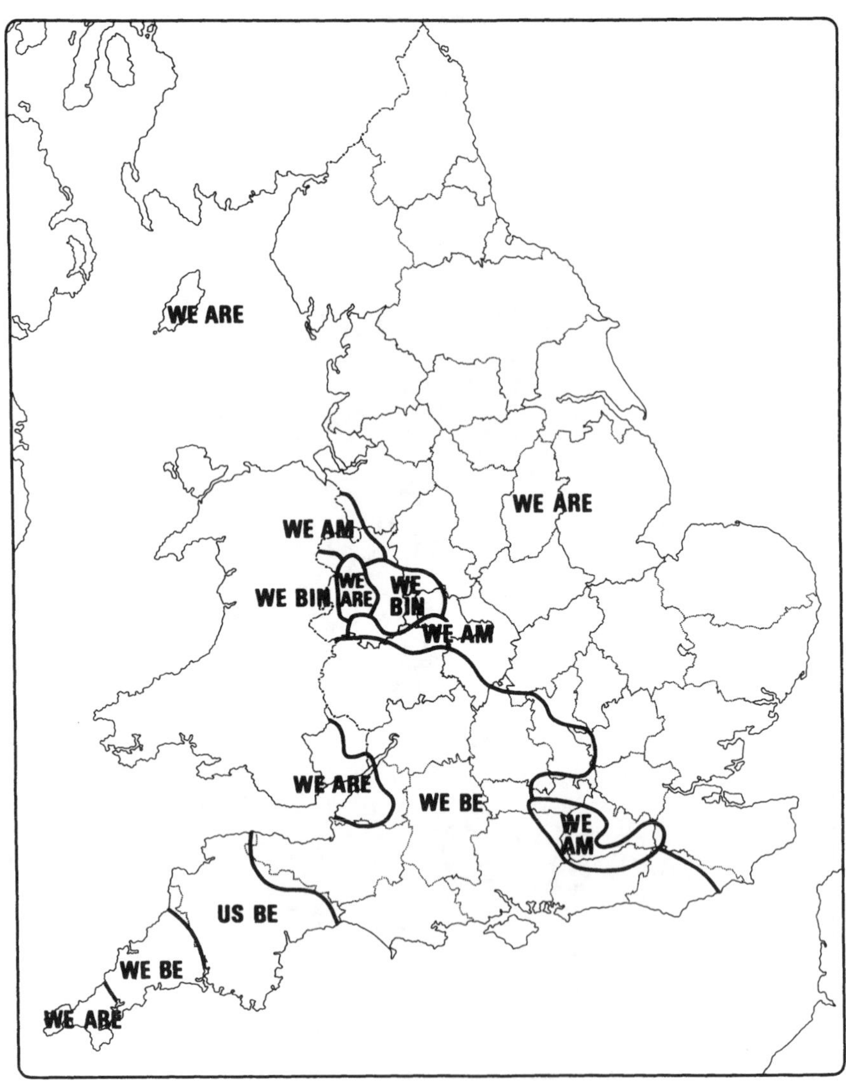

Map 181: WE ARE (oh yes . . .!)

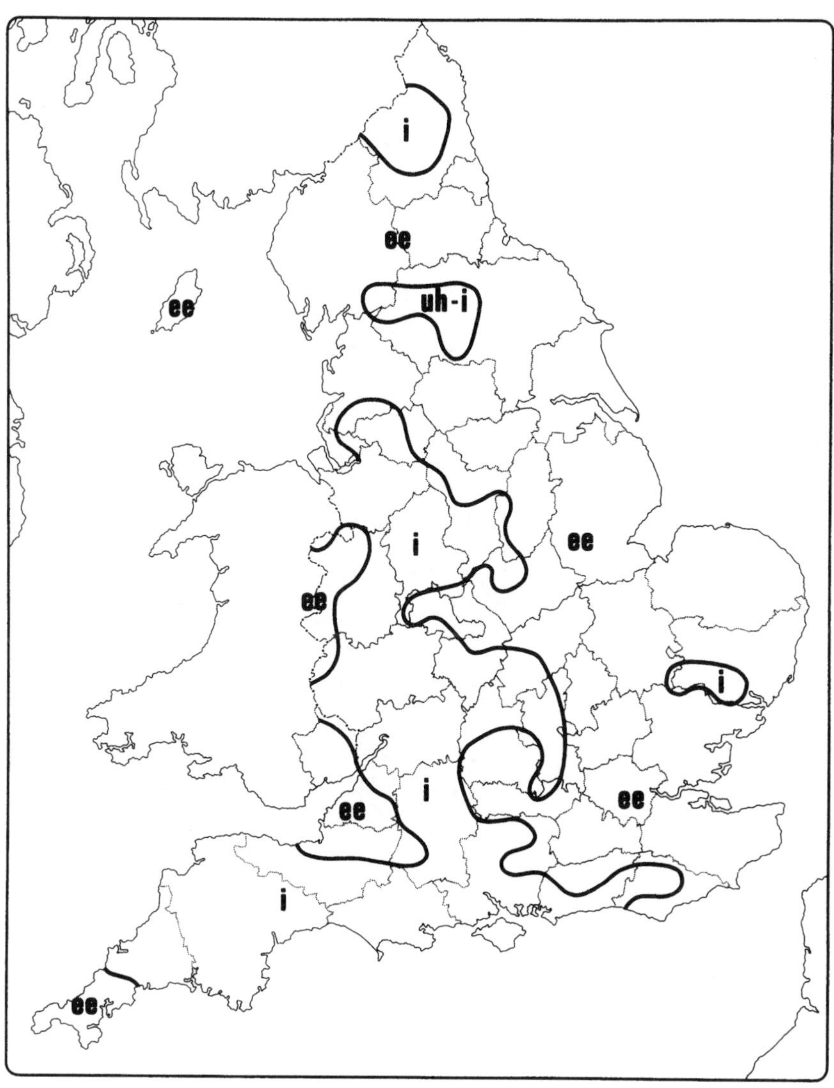

Map 182: WEEK

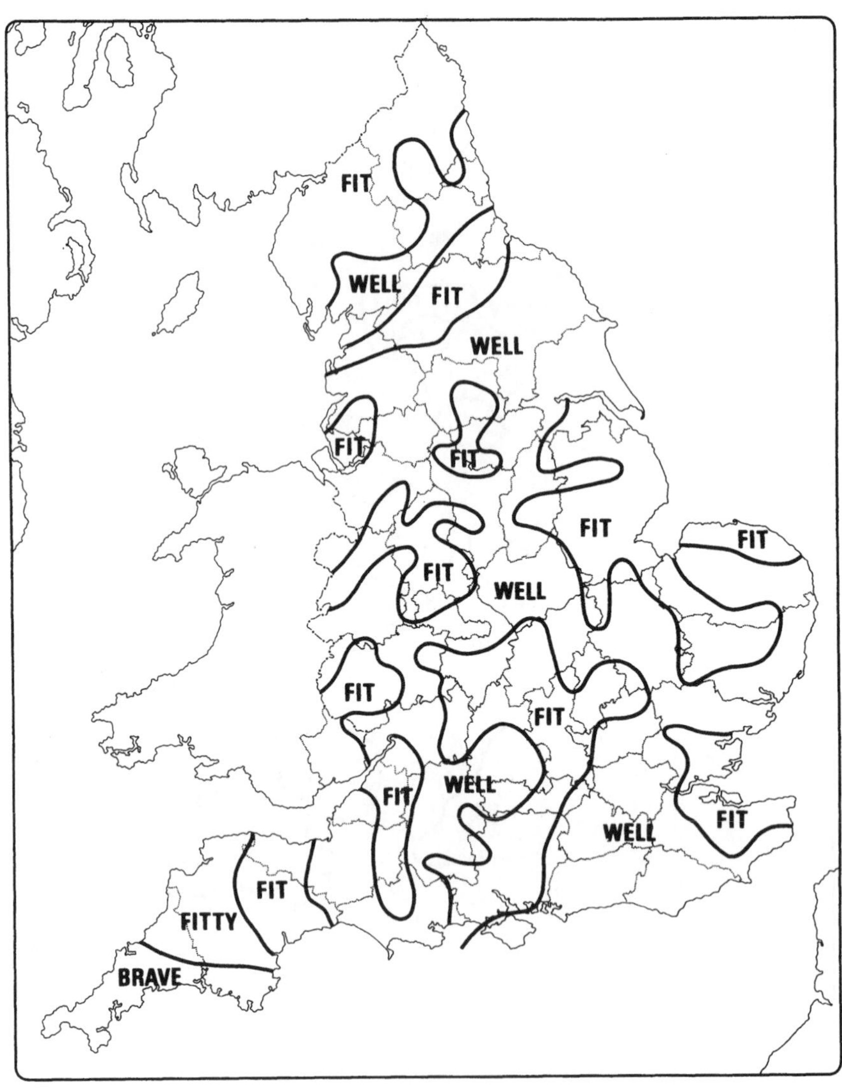

Map 183: WELL (health)

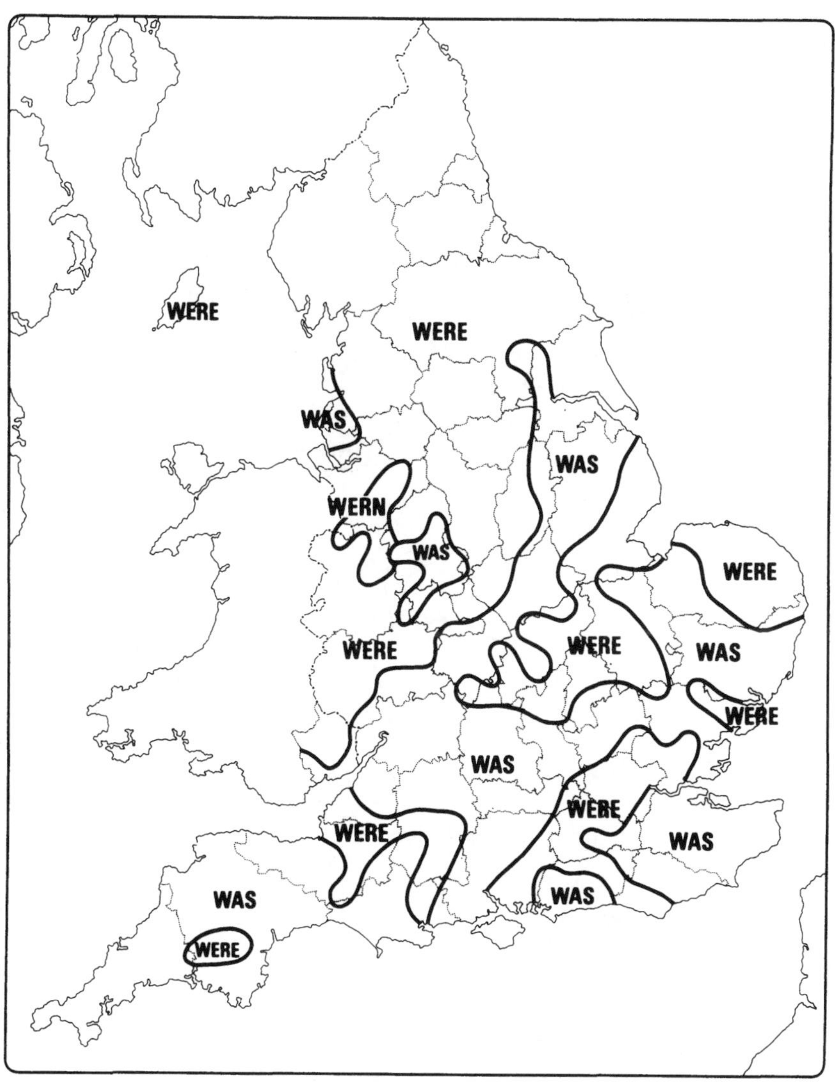

Map 184: WERE (we . . .)

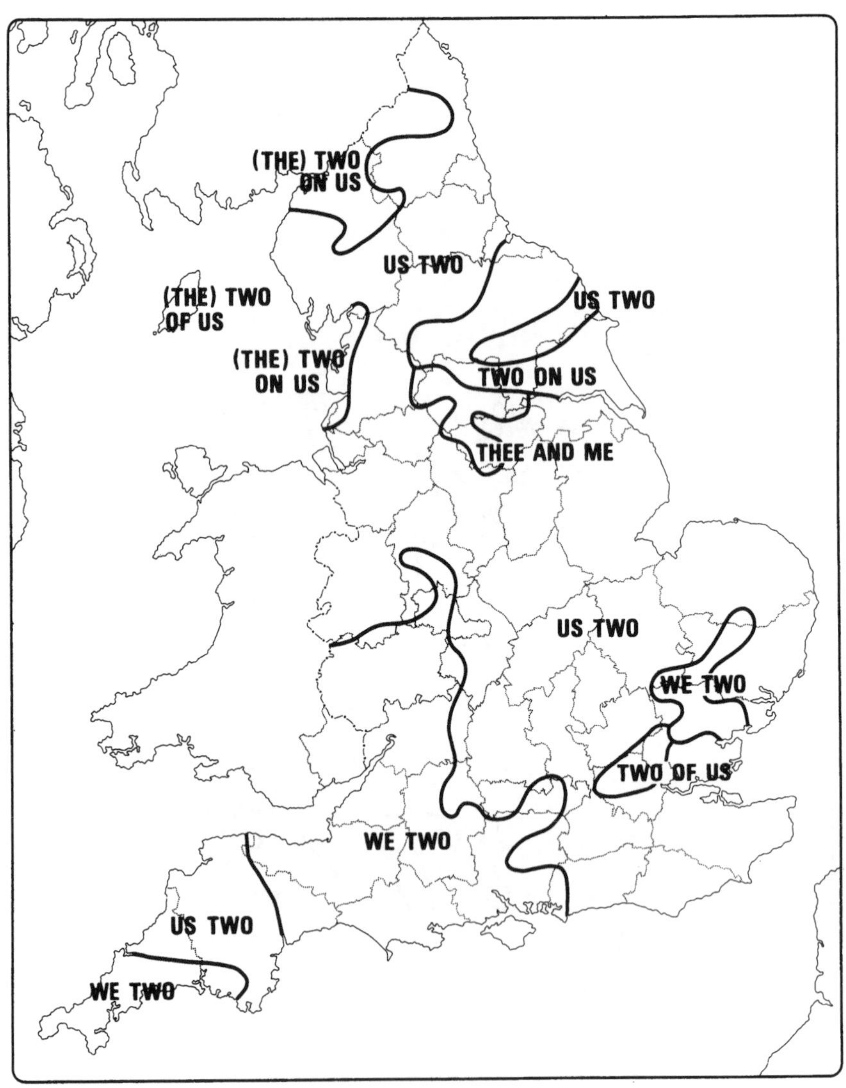

Map 185: WE TWO (just . . .)
US TWO is common in those parts of the North in which other forms dominate.

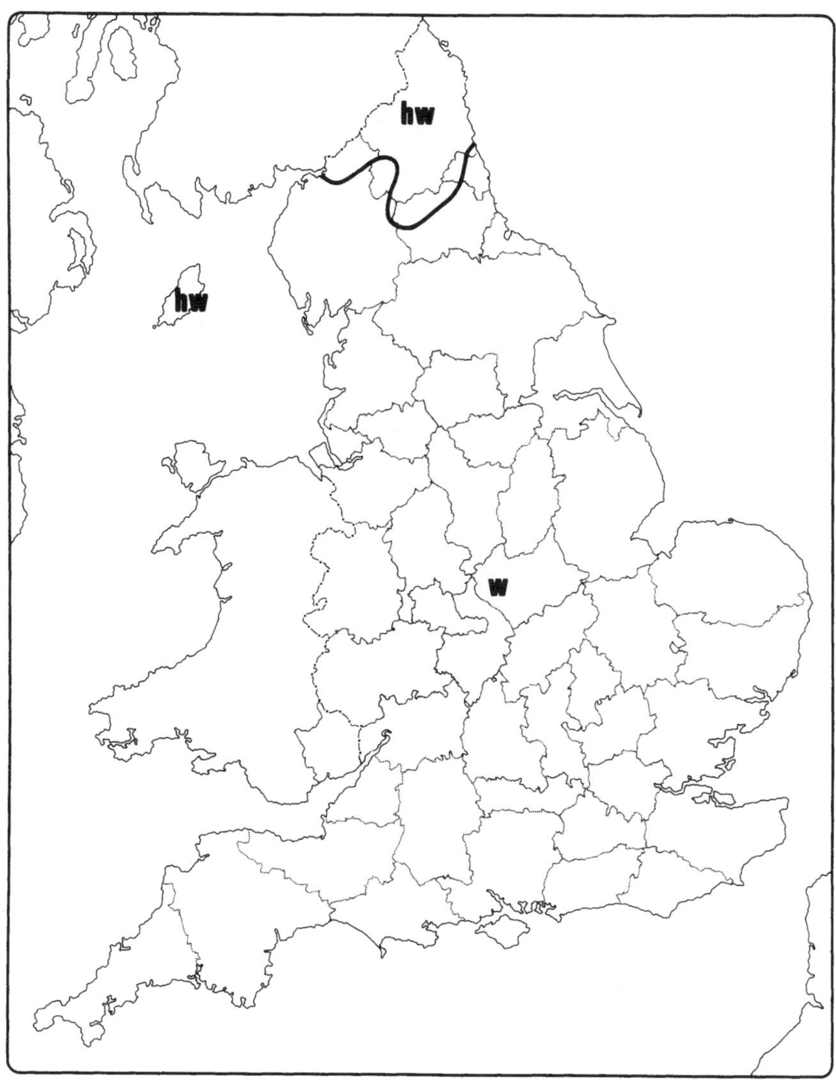

Map 186: <u>WH</u>EEL

In regional dialects **hw** is now confined to the extreme North East and Scotland, but is used by many speakers of Received Pronunciation throughout the country. Compare the forms of *quick* beginning with **hw-** and **w-** in Map 131.

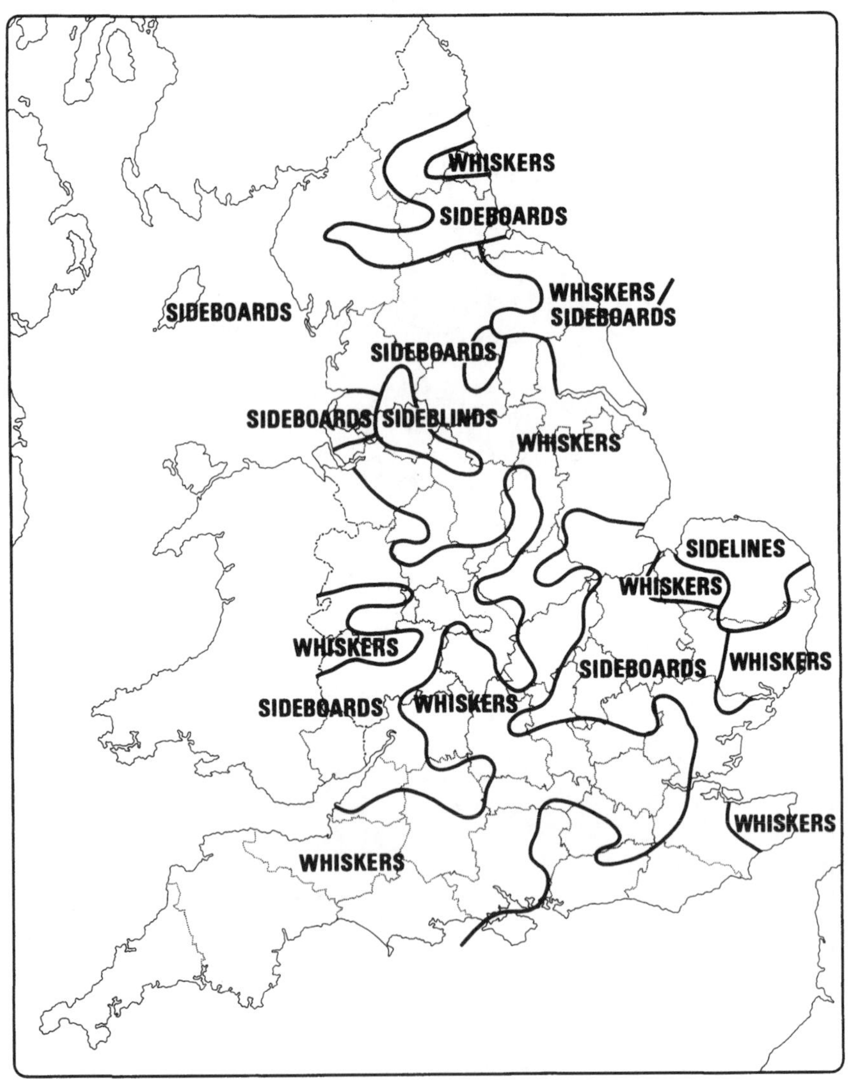

Map 187: WHISKERS

In those areas where **WHISKERS** is the usual word, some speakers use the term *side-whiskers*.

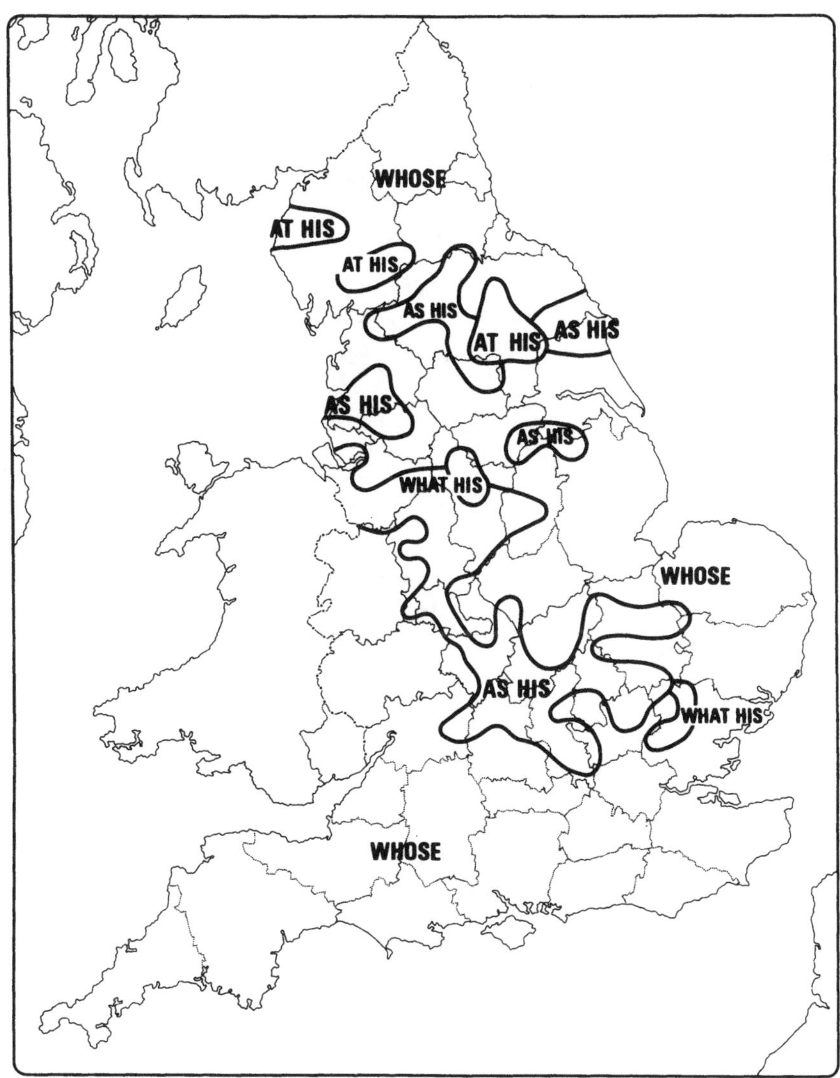

Map 188: WHOSE

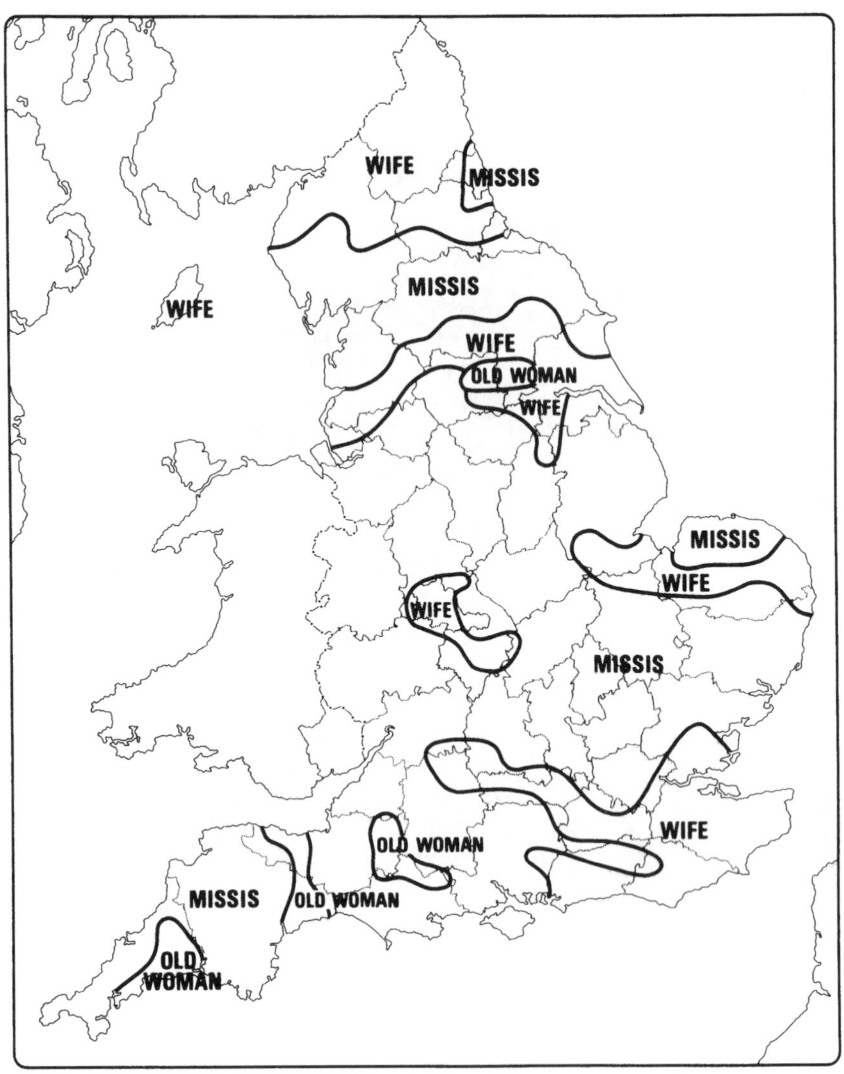

Map 189: WIFE (my ...)
The words shown are usually preceded by *the* or *my*.

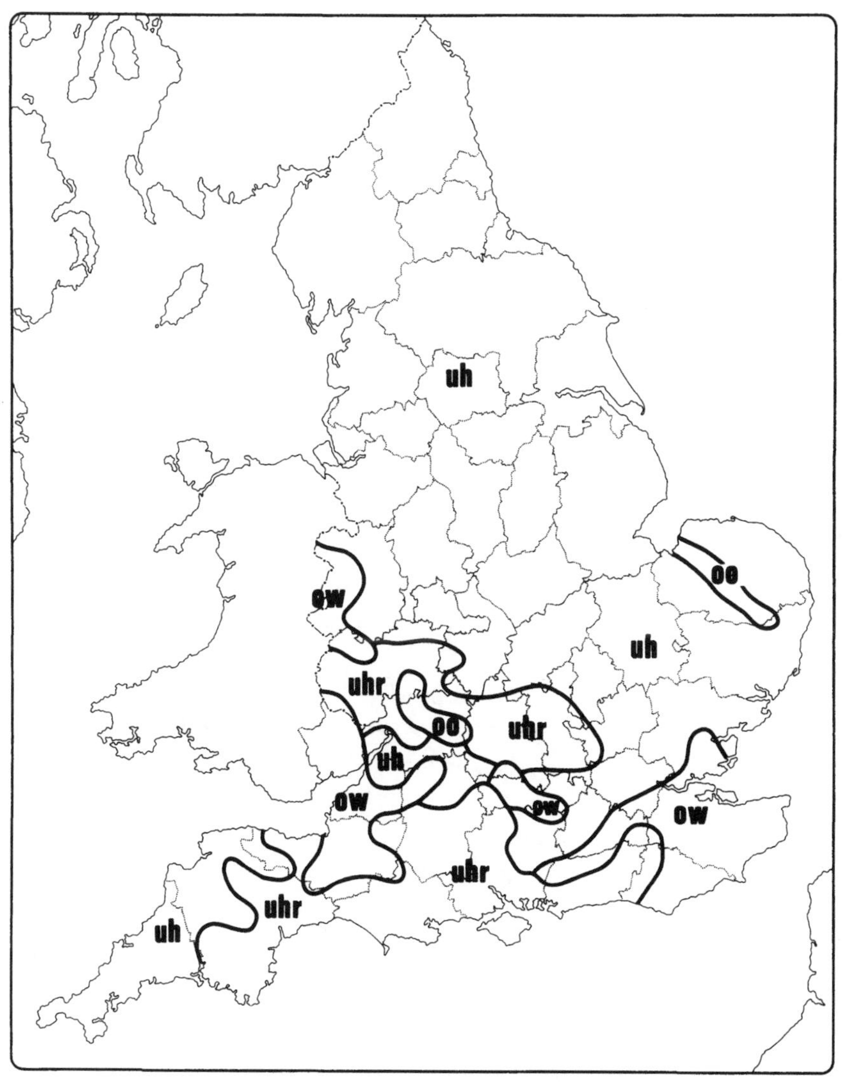

Map 190: <u>WINDOWS</u>
oo is pronounced short as in *put*.

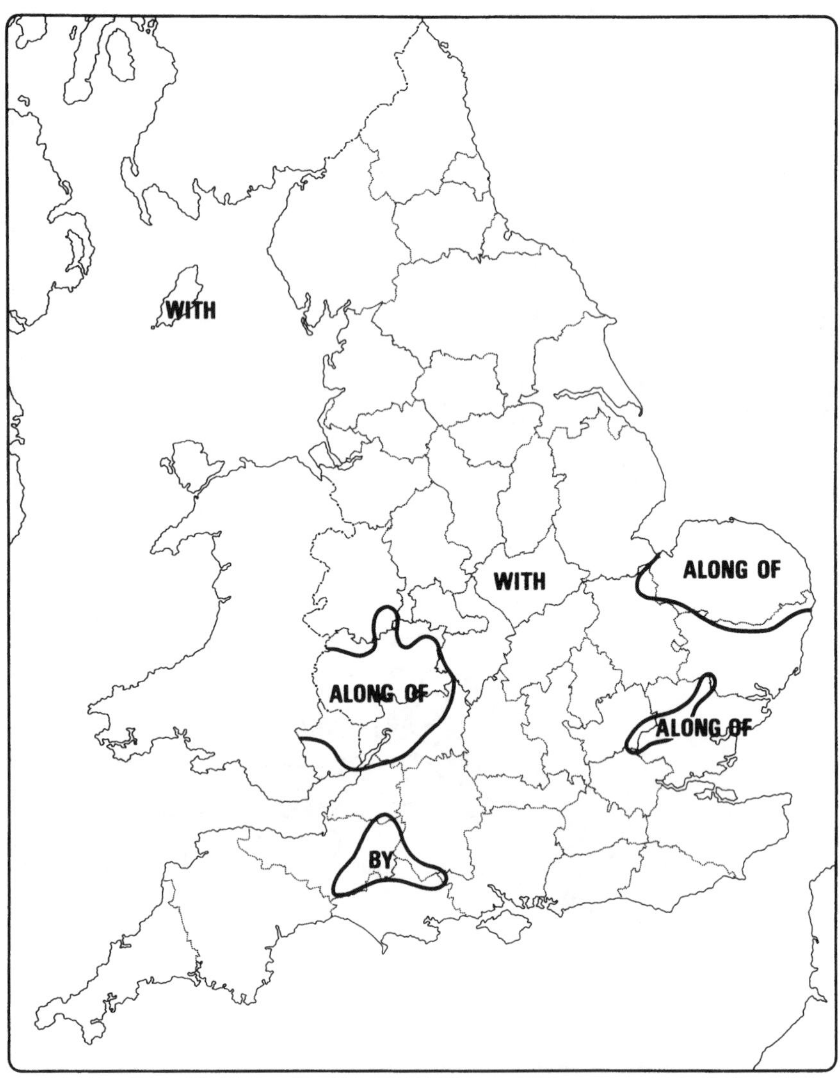

Map 191: WITH (come . . . me)
The **uh** (phonetic ə) forms in the Basic Material of the Survey of English Dialects have all been interpreted here as **OF**.

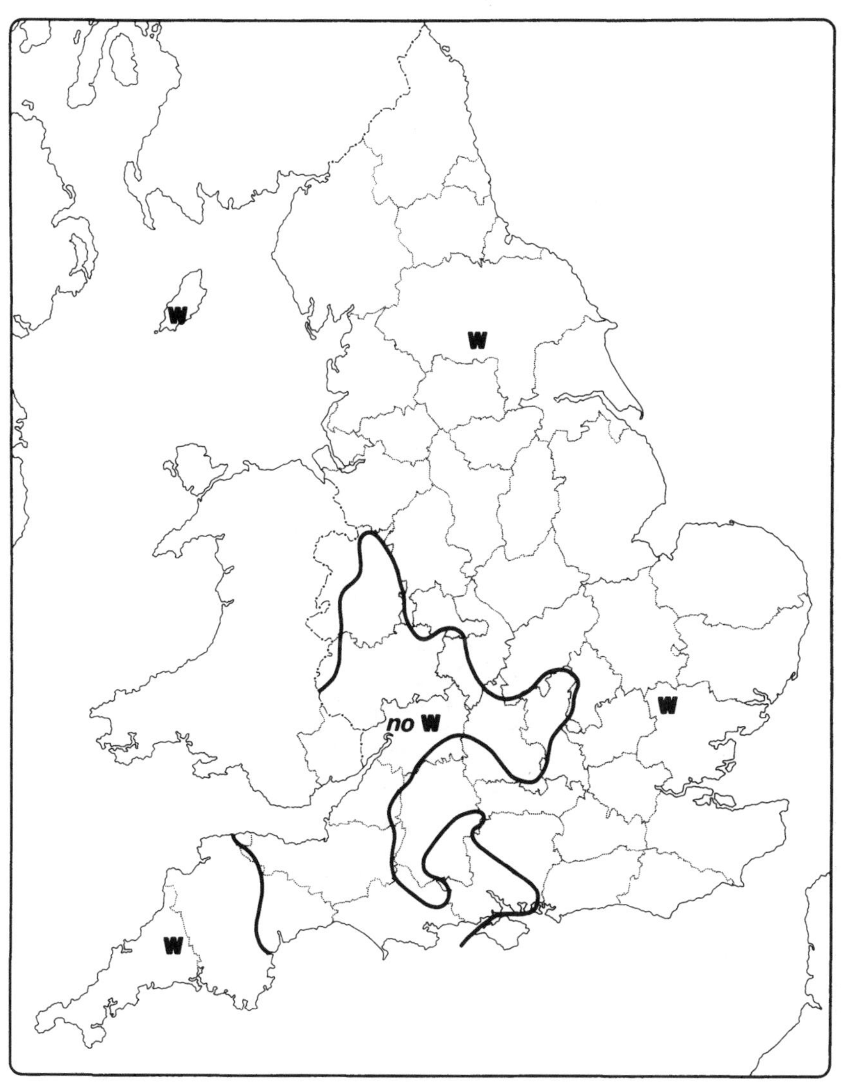

Map 192: WOMAN

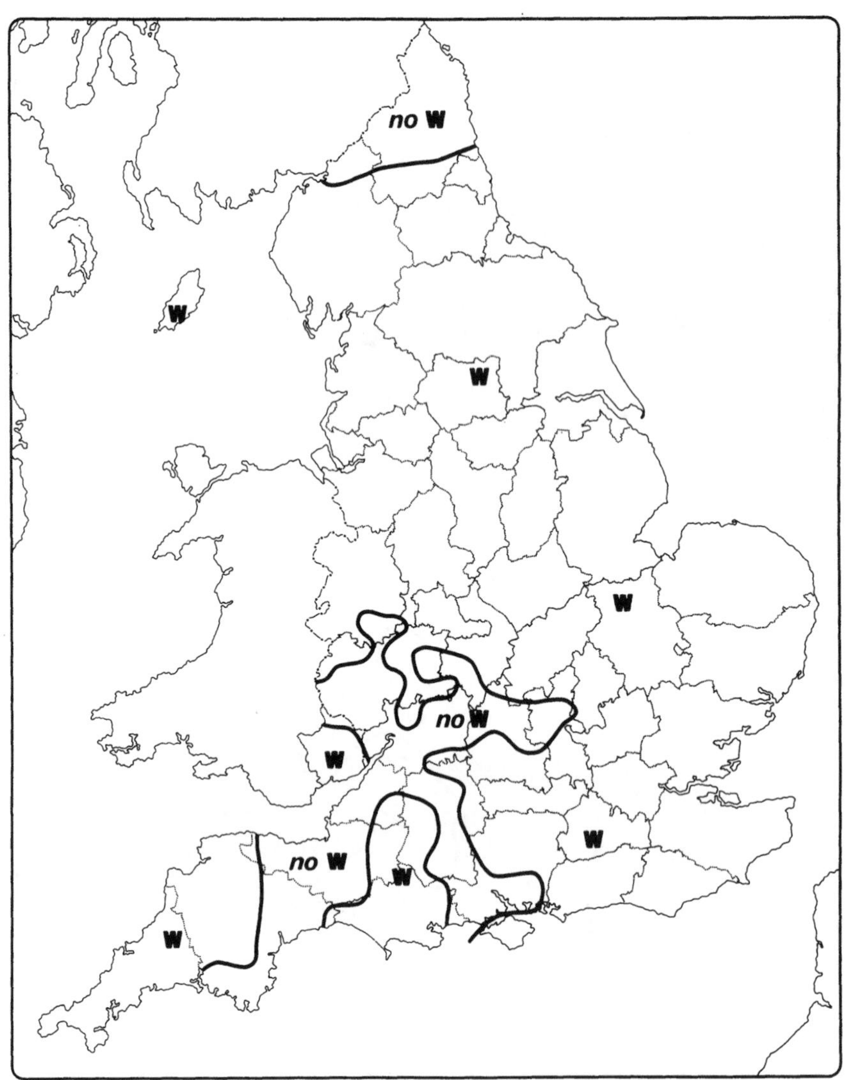

Map 193: W̲OOL

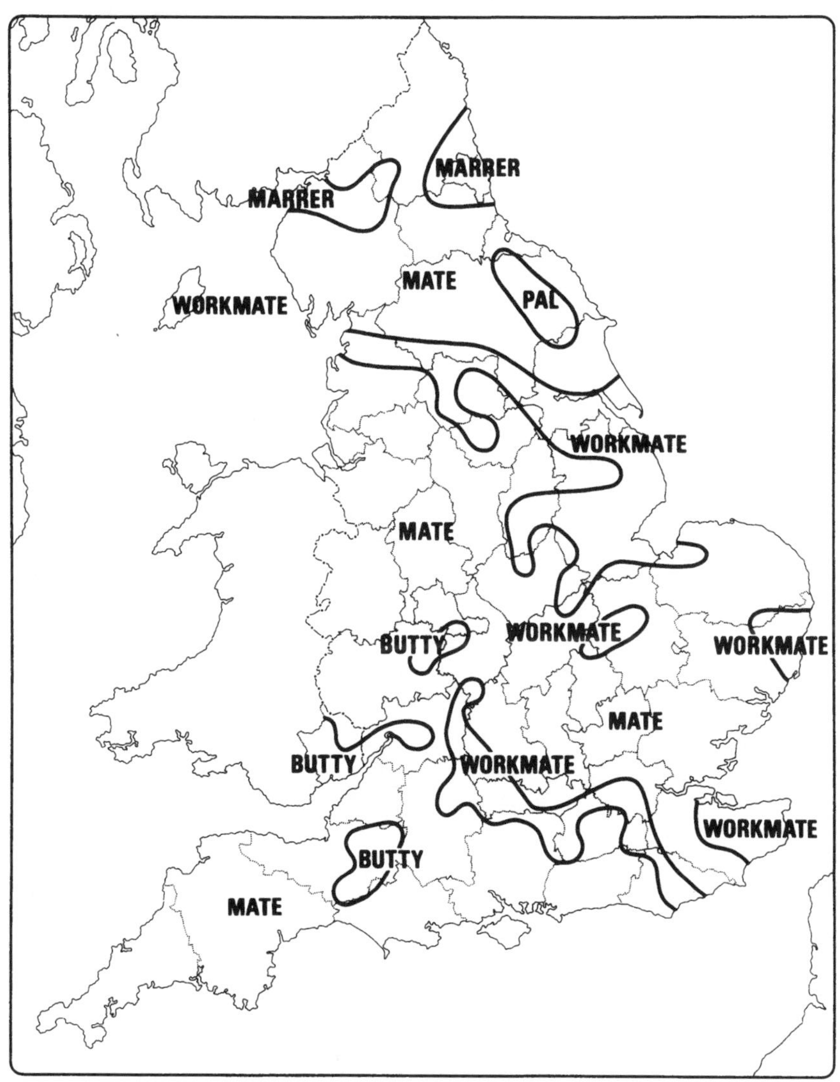

Map 194: WORKMATE

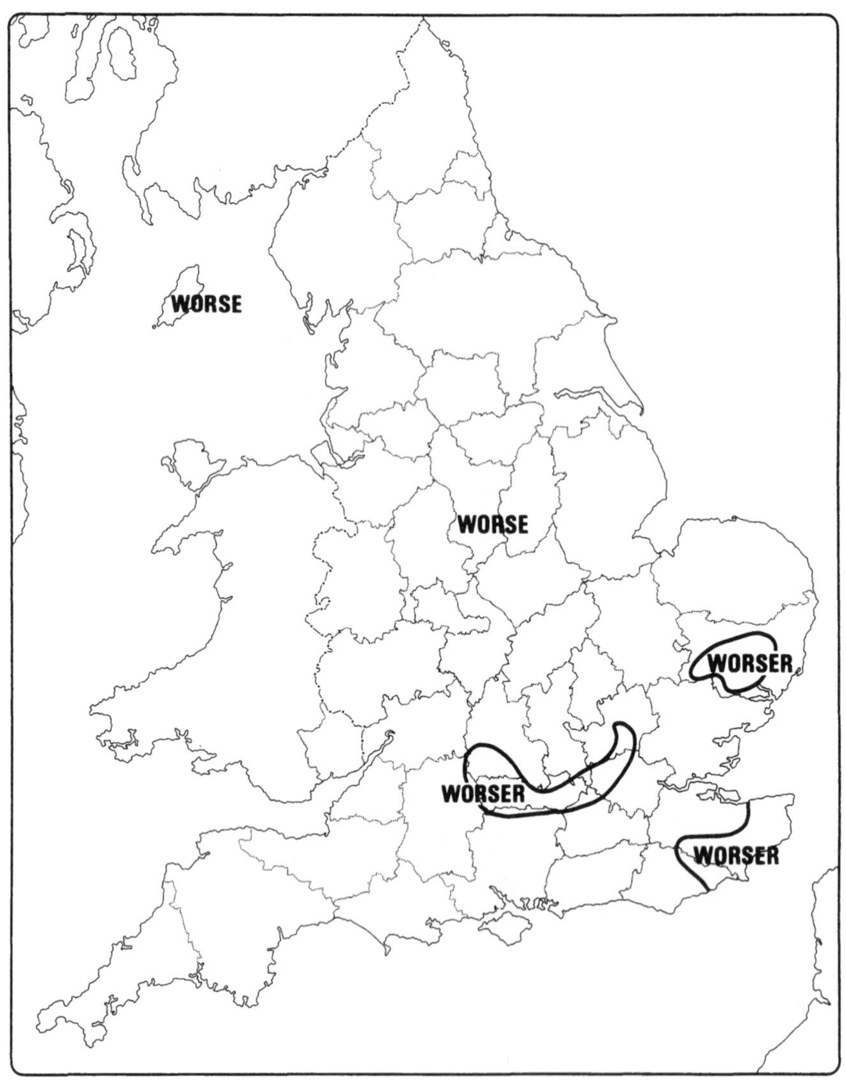

Map 195: WORSE (it is much ...)

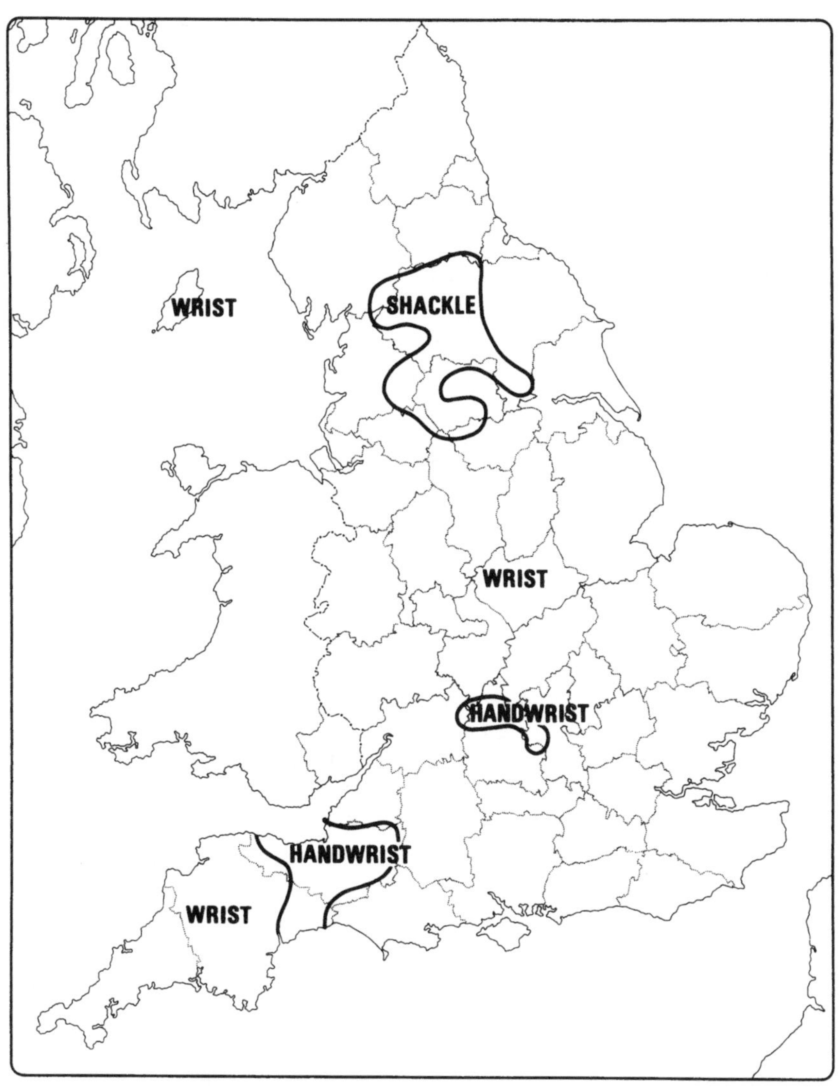

Map 196: WRIST

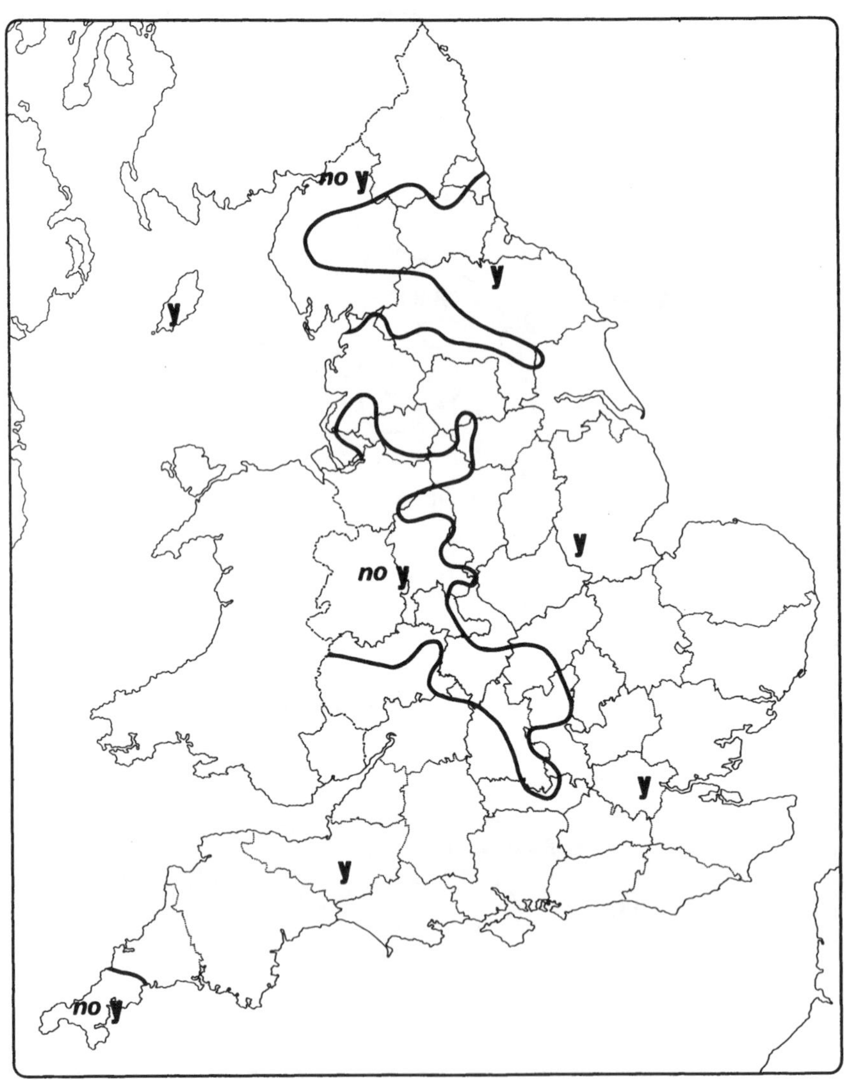

Map 197: <u>Y</u>EAR (this ...)

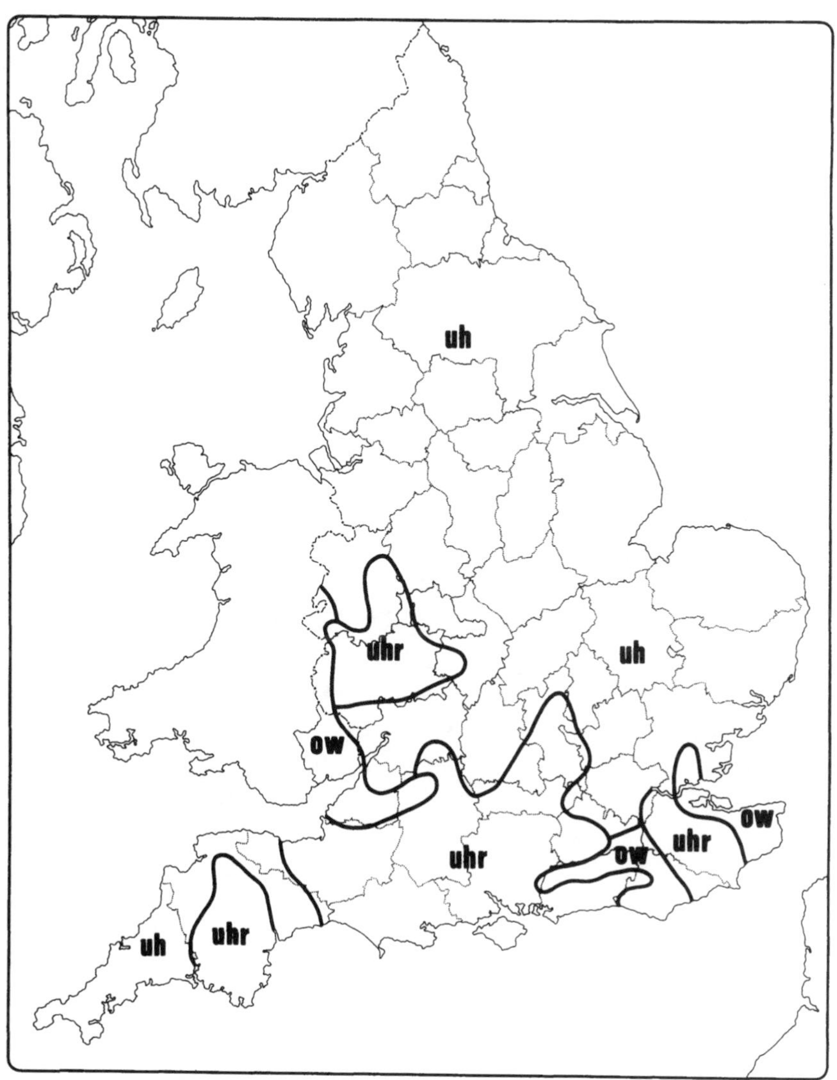

Map 198: YELLOW

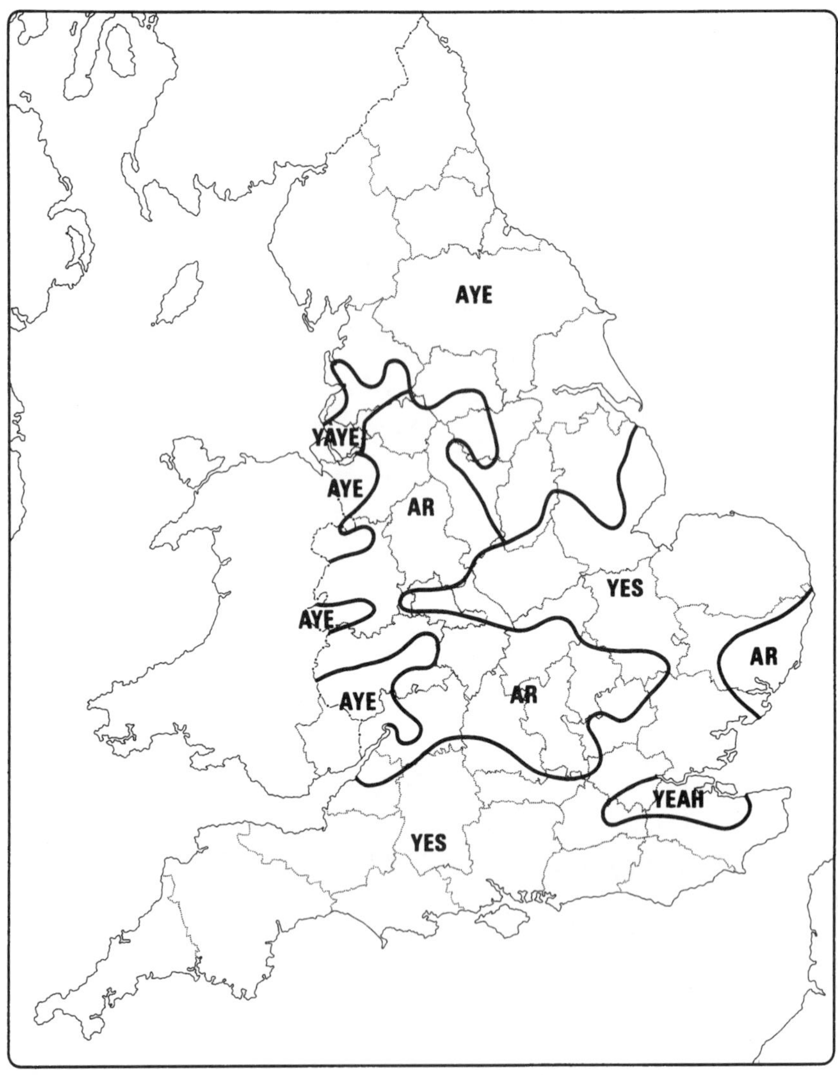

Map 199: YES (affirming)

Note that **AR** indicates that the vowel is long as in *far*; the *r* is not usually pronounced. For areas in which final **r** has been occasionally recorded in this word, see Map 11.

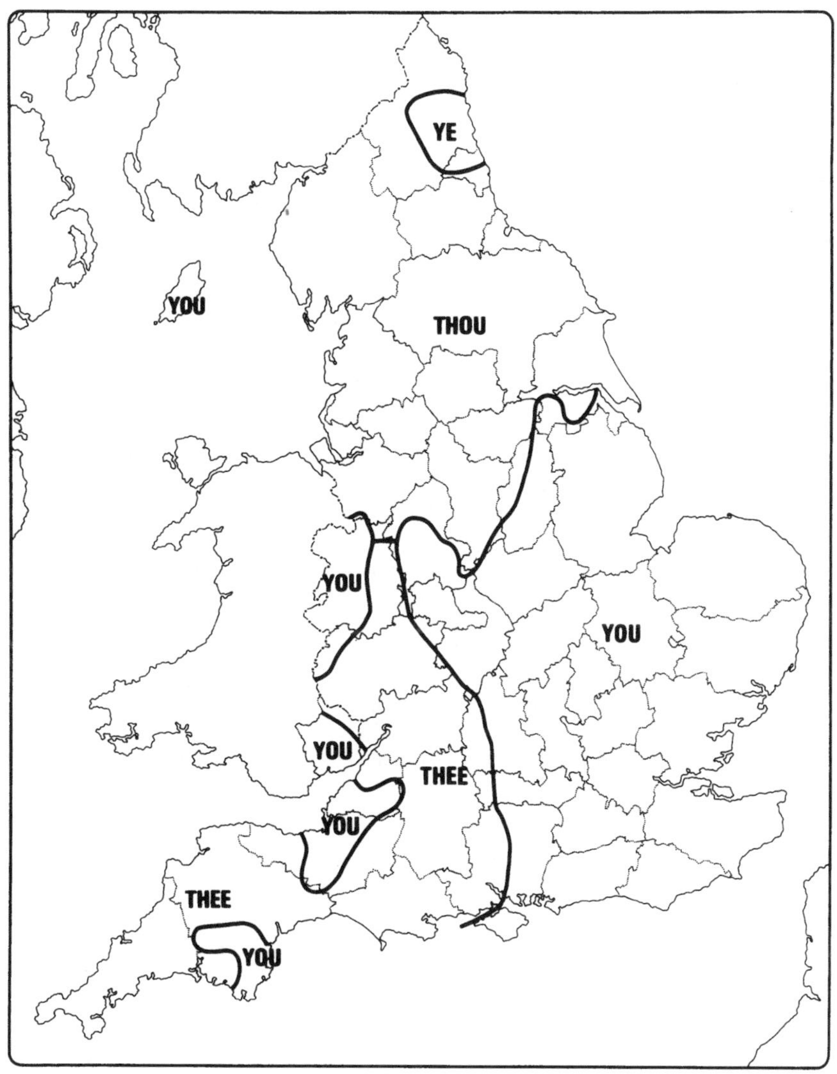

Map 200: YOU (. . . are)
In Standard English the pronoun *you* has supplanted all the other second person forms (THEE, THOU and YE), but they still linger in the dialects of the North and West.

Suggestions for Further Reading

Brook, G.L., *English Dialects*, London, André Deutsch, 1963

Hughes, A. and P. Trudgill, *English Accents and Dialects*, London, Edward Arnold, 1979

Kirk, John M., Stewart Sanderson and J.D.A. Widdowson, eds, *Studies in Linguistic Geography*, London, Croom Helm, 1985

Kolb, Eduard et al., *Atlas of English Sounds*, Bern, Francke Verlag, 1979

North, David J. and Adam Sharpe, *A Word-Geography of Cornwall*, Redruth, Institute of Cornish Studies, 1980

Orton, Harold, *et al.*, eds, *Survey of English Dialects*, Leeds, E.J. Arnold, 1962-71

Orton, Harold and Nathalia Wright, *A Word Geography of England*, London, Seminar Press, 1974

Orton, Harold, Stewart Sanderson and John Widdowson, eds, *The Linguistic Atlas of England*, London, Croom Helm, 1978

Petyt, K.M., *The Study of Dialect — An Introduction to Dialectology*, London, André Deutsch, 1980

Skeat, Walter W., *English Dialects*, Cambridge, Cambridge University Press, 1912

Trudgill, P. *On Dialect: Social and Geographical Perspectives*, Oxford, Blackwell, 1983

Wakelin, Martyn F., *English Dialects: An Introduction*, London, Athlone Press, 1972

Wakelin, Martyn F., *Patterns in the Folk Speech of the British Isles*, London, Athlone Press, 1972

Wakelin, Martyn, *Discovering English Dialects*, Princes Risborough, Shire Publications, 1978

Wells, J.C., *Accents of English*, 3 vols, Cambridge, Cambridge University Press, 1982

Wright, Joseph, ed., *The English Dialect Dictionary*, 6 vols, London, Oxford University Press, 1898-1905

Following up your Interest in Dialect

If you would like to follow up your interest in dialect further, a useful first step is to enquire at your library, archives or record office; some museums also have useful material. Universities, polytechnics, colleges of higher or further education, and perhaps local schools, may be able to offer advice.

The following academic institutions in England are among those which have specialised in dialect study:

Department of Applied Linguistics and Language Centre, Birkbeck College, University of London, Malet Street, London, WC1E 7HX.
Institute of Cornish Studies, Trevenson House, Redruth, Cornwall, PR15 3RE.
The School of English, The University, Leeds, LS2 9JT. (where, as already noted, the collected materials of the Survey of English Dialects are deposited).
Department of English Language, School of English, University of Newcastle upon Tyne, Newcastle upon Tyne, NE1 7RU.
Department of English Language, The University, Sheffield, S10 2TN.

Elsewhere in the British Isles and Ireland the major academic centres for the study of dialect include:

Department of Linguistics, University College of North Wales, Bangor, Gwynedd, LL57 2DG.
Department of English, The Queen's University of Belfast, Belfast, BT7 1NN.
The Welsh Folk Museum, St Fagans, Cardiff, CF5 6XB.
Department of Irish Folklore, University College, Belfield, Dublin 4, Republic of Ireland.
The Linguistic Survey of Scotland, University of Edinburgh, Edinburgh, EH8 9YL.
Department of English, University College of Swansea, Singleton Park, Swansea, SA2 8PP.

A number of societies exist for the study and conservation of regional dialects. These include:

The Devon Dialect Society, c/o Porch Cottage, East Budleigh, Budleigh Salterton, Devon, EX9 7DU.
The Lakeland Dialect Society, c/o Holly Cottage, Crosby Ravensworth, Penrith, Cumbria, CA10 3JP.
The Lancashire Dialect Society, c/o 6 Alfred Street, Farnworth, Bolton, BL4 7JT.
The Yorkshire Dialect Society, c/o School of English, The University, Leeds, LS2 9JT.

Other societies and publications which include dialect in their wider ranging interests are:

The Devonshire Association for the Advancement of Science, Literature and Art, 7 The Close, Exeter, EX5 4EY.

Northumbriana, c/o Westgate House, Dogger Bank, Morpeth, Northumberland, NE61 1RF.

Edwin Waugh Society, c/o 128 Market Street, Whitworth, Rochdale, Lancashire, OL12 8TG.

Wiltshire Folk Life Society, c/o Salisbury and South Wiltshire Museum, St. Ann Street, Salisbury, SP1 2DT.

Check to see if there are other societies, organisations or publications in your area. Your local information bureau may be able to help you. If you have difficulty in finding information, write to:

The Centre for English Cultural Tradition and Language, The University, Sheffield, S10 2TN.

which will act as a clearing-house for enquiries.

Index of Vocabulary Maps

(reference is to map numbers)

Index of Pronunciation Maps

(reference is to map numbers)

General Index

(reference is to map numbers)